THE HISTORY AND RECORDS OF QUEEN VICTORIA'S RIFLES 1792-1922

Volume 2

Monument erected on Hill 60 in memory of all Q.V.R. who gave their lives for King and Country in the Great War.

THE HISTORY & RECORDS OF
QUEEN VICTORIA'S RIFLES
1792–1922

COMPILED BY

MAJOR C. A. CUTHBERT KEESON V.D.

PRESIDENT QUEEN VICTORIA'S RIFLES
OLD COMRADES' ASSOCIATION

CONSTABLE & COMPANY LIMITED
LONDON : BOMBAY : SYDNEY
1923

REGIMENTAL BADGE.

PART III
THE AMALGAMATION OF THE FIRST AND SECOND BATTALIONS

CHAPTER I

THE AMALGAMATION OF THE 1ST AND 2ND BATTALIONS

THE AMALGAMATION

WHETHER by coincidence or design we know not, but certain it is that during the months of December, 1917, and January, 1918, both the 1st and 2nd Battalions were more or less engaged in " resting " though, as before said, there was very little real rest about it. The 1st were at Cambigneul from the 2nd to the 30th January. The 2nd were at Bridge Camp, in the neighbourhood of Elverdinghe, from January 2nd to 7th, when they went into billets at Houtkerque. On 8th, Lieut.-Col. E. G. H. Powell (Grenadier Guards) assumed command of the battalion in succession to Lieut.-Col. Parry. On January 12th there was an inspection and presentation of medal ribbons with a farewell speech by Lieut.-Gen. Sir Claud Jacob, 2nd Corps, as the battalion was leaving it. On 20th the battalion entrained at Proven and proceeded to Villers Brettonneux and thence by route march to La Neuville.

"Early in January," writes Capt. Collingwood Andrews (Brigade Staff), "it became known that all brigades were to be deprived of a battalion. This step was apparently necessitated by the low ebb to which our man power had sunk, with the constant difficulty of keeping battalions up to strength. Consternation and distress were great on all sides. It came as a heavy blow to the 1st Q.V.R. when it was announced that they were to be withdrawn from the 169th Brigade particularly when further details as to their fate were forthcoming. Eight officers and 200 O.R. only were to be transferred to the 2nd Battalion, the remainder being used to reinforce other units, if possible in the same division. The battalion which had fought continuously since 1914 was to be represented as a minority, both in officers and other ranks in the comparatively new second-line formation. But perhaps the bitterest pill of all was that the filling of the higher non-commissioned ranks was to be denied to them. First-line Battalion Regimental Sergeant Majors, Company Sergeant Majors and Company Quartermaster Sergeants were to be sent to the base and employed when and where required. Transports were to be retained in their present divisions. It was a mortal blow at the *esprit de battalion* of many units and it was in Territorial battalions that this esprit existed in its highest form. However, the situation was the same throughout the Army and had to be faced. The disintegration came by stages. First the surplus was posted to other units, some within the division and others outside. Then the spectacle of magnificent N.C.O.'s the backbone of the battalion, sent *en route* to the base ! It is no exaggeration to say they were broken-hearted. And lastly, on January 31st, the departure of the nucleus to join the 2nd Battalion."

As was only to be expected the men of the 1st Battalion were very sore on its being broken up as they were the senior and had seen over two years' service before the 2nd came out, but the feeling soon wore itself out and all hands settled down to make the best of things. As Rfn. Snoswell puts it, "There is only one 9th Battalion now and we are IT, and it is up to us to keep up the traditions that the two battalions have made. Our Colonel (Lieut.-Col. Powell) is out to make this THE Territorial Battalion, and I think the fellows will soon work together under the amalgamation. Nothing will suit him but the best, he is out to do the best for the men, and it is up to us to do our best. We have a big reputation to live up to, but I certainly don't think it will be spoilt now."

Composition of the Amalgamated Regiment.

Head-quarters.

Commanding Officer	Lieut.-Col. E. G. H. Powell.
Second in Command	Major R. H. Lindsey-Renton.
Adjutant	Capt. J. Nichols, M.C.
Assistant Adjutant	2nd Lieut. R. Johnson.
Intelligence Officer	2nd Lieut. E. F. Dickins.
Signalling Officer	2nd Lieut. G. R. Johnson.
Lewis Gun Officer	Lieut. H. G. Easterbrook.
Transport Officer	Capt. A. N. Philbrick.
Quartermaster	Major T. O'Shea, D.S.O.

"A" Company.

Company Commander	Capt. A. R. Hadden.
Second in Command	Capt. E. W. G. Hodgkinson, M.M.
	2nd. Lieut. F. J. Fletcher.
	,, ,, E. W. D. Astill.
	,, ,, D. Jarvis.
	,, ,, L. A. Leith.

"B" Company.

Company Commander	Capt. W. E. Bowler, M.C.
Second in Command	Lieut. L. Duncan.
	Lieut. C. A. G. C. Keeson.
	2nd Lieut. G. D. Mayer, M.C.
	,, ,, H. S. Hawkes.
	,, ,, A. Plummer.
	,, ,, H. V. Holloway.
	,, ,, S. C. Hall.

"C" Company.

Company Commander	Capt. G. E. Spenser-Pryse, M.C.
Second in Command	Capt. H. Samuelson.
	Lieut. T. C. Brandram.
	2nd Lieut. W. F. J. Prince.
	,, ,, F. N. Jenkins.
	,, ,, H. A. Harrison.

"D" Company.

Company Commander	Capt. H. S. Prince, M.C.
Second in Command	Capt. L. E. Calvert.
	2nd Lieut. A. L. Jones.
	,, ,, P. W. Powell, D.C.M.
	,, ,, H. Edwards.
	,, ,, W. H. E. Markham.
	,, ,, B. G. Wagstaff, M.C.

Officers on Strength but Employed away from Unit.

Attached 58th Division.	Major F. A. du Breul.
Attached M.L.O. Havre.	Capt. G. B. White.
Staff 58th Div. Depot Bn.	Lieut. W. A. McAdam.
Staff 58th Div. Depot Bn.	2nd Lieut. A. P. Cole.

Eight officers, viz. Lieuts. C. O. Tabberer and J. R. Plunkett and 2nd Lieuts. J. C. B. Prince, F. R. Wilson, E. W. G. Malcolm, V. G. Rayner, H. R. Smith, F. Fisher, C. H. Raven, L. W. Friend, R. C. Hurst and W. H. Graham and 207 O.R. were transferred to the 1/16th Battn. London Regiment, Queen's Westminster Rifles. Five officers and 150 O.R. were sent to the 13th London (Kensingtons), and 4 officers and 76 O.R. to the 4th London Regiment.

The following letters explanatory of the amalgamation were subsequently received :

War Office,
Whitehall, S.W. 1.,
11th February, 1918.

Dear Boyton,

With reference to your enquiry concerning the breaking up of the 1st Battalion, Queen Victoria's Rifles, I find on enquiry from France that it was not possible to maintain the 1st Line Territorial Force units complete, owing to the military exigencies of the moment, and it was decided to send the Head-quarters of the 1st Line battalions with a nucleus of not less than 12 officers and 200 O.R. to amalgamate with their 2nd Line units in England. Under this scheme, the 1st Line battalions therefore retain their names, records, funds and old soldiers, young soldiers only being drafted elsewhere. I think, therefore, that you will see that the Queen Victoria's Rifles will not lose either their name or old traditions, and I hope it will be satisfactory to those members who brought the matter to your notice.

I may add that Head-quarters at the present time do not necessarily mean the C.O.'s of the 1st Line battalions, as in some cases the O.C. 2nd Battalion is senior to the O.C. 1st Battalion as there is a different state of affairs now from what there was at the beginning of the war.

Yours sincerely,
Samuel Scott.
Major, P.S. to S. of S.

Sir J. Boyton, M.P.,
2 Park Square, West, N.W. 1.

THE FIRST AND SECOND BATTALIONS

War Office, Whitehall, S.W. 1.
23rd February, 1918.

DEAR BOYTON,

I find I made rather a bad error in my letter to you of the 11th instant, as when writing to you respecting Queen Victoria's Rifles I stated that "it was decided to send the Head-quarters of the 1st Line battalion with a nucleus of not less than 12 officers and 200 Other Ranks to amalgamate with their 2nd Line units in England." The last two words should have been left out, as the 2nd Line unit is not in England but in France. I must apologise most sincerely for such a slip.

Yours sincerely,
SAMUEL SCOTT.
Major, P.S. to S. of S.

Sir J. Boyton, M.P.,
2 Park Square, West, N.W. 1.

A/1231. Duke of York's Head-quarters,
Chelsea,
London, S.W. 3.
18th December, 1918.

O.C. Depot.
9th (County of London Battalion),
The London Regiment.

The attached copy of War Office letter number 35/Gen. No./1827 (A.G.2.a) dated 30th November, 1918, in which is recorded the war services of the 2nd Line battalion is forwarded for your information, and with a request that you will cause its contents to be made known to all concerned. Although marked "confidential," instructions have been since received that the letter need not now be so treated.

(Sgd.) H. MANSBRIDGE, Secretary,
Territorial Force Association of the County
of London.

Enc.

2 B

[Copy.]

Confidential.   War Office,
                                           London, S.W. 1.
35/Gen. No./1827 (A.G.2.a),   30*th November*, 1918.

MY LORD,

    I forward the following brief statement of the services rendered to the country during the present hostilities by the 2/9th (County of London) Battalion, The London Regiment (Queen Victoria's Rifles), feeling sure that it will be of great interest to you and to all those connected with the regiment.

    The recent reorganisation of Infantry in France involved the disbandment of certain battalions, amongst which is the 2/9th (County of London) Battalion, The London Regiment (Queen Victoria's Rifles).

    The battalion was formed on the 31st August, 1914, and after training in England proceeded overseas in February, 1917, landing at Havre on February 4th, and after receiving training in trench warfare with the 46th Division near Bienvillers took over part of the line on February 28th near Wailly.

    It was in line here when the German retreat to the Hindenburg Line began on March 18th; the battalion pushed forward and occupied the German positions near Blaireville, but was then taken out of the line and employed on road construction and other works and in training till the beginning of May. It then moved up to the front and was in the line of Lagnicourt and at Bullecourt in May and June and at Havrincourt in July. On July 22nd it carried out a small raid with success.

    After more training in August, the battalion moved north and was in line near St. Julien in September, taking part on September 26th in the successful general attack on the German positions north-east and east of Ypres. The battalion secured and consolidated its objectives, repulsed two counter-attacks and captured sixty prisoners.

    Subsequently it remained in the same area and when in trenches held the line near Poelcapelle from October to December.

In January, 1918, this battalion was disbanded and the personnel was distributed amongst other battalions of the regiment.

This battalion was affiliated to the King's Royal Rifle Corps which, by reason of the unique services rendered to the Empire, is well worthy of its regimental motto, *Celer et Audax*.

Although the 2/9th Battalion has been disbanded the officers, warrant officers, non-commissioned officers and the men have not been lost to the London Regiment; they have all been drafted into other battalions of The London Regiment and will continue to uphold the name and traditions of the regiment with the same spirit, loyalty and esprit de corps as they have done in the 2/9th (County of London) Battalion.

I have the honour to be,
Your most obedient and humble servant,
(Sgd.) G. M. C. MacDonagh, Lieut.-Gen.,
Adjutant-General to the Forces.

Colonel R. B. Viscount Esher, G.C.B., G.C.V.O., D.L.,
President, London Territorial Force Association.

A/1231.　　　　　　　　Duke of York's Head-quarters,
　　　　　　　　　　　　　　　Chelsea,
　　　　　　　　　　　　　　　London, S.W. 3.
　　　　　　　　　　　　　　　23rd January, 1919.
O.C. Depot.
9th (County of London) Battalion,
The London Regiment.

It is regretted that through an oversight your communication of the 21st ultimo regarding the 1/9th and 2/9th County of London Battalions has hitherto remained unanswered. The position is that the 1st Battalion of any unit in the London Regiment is regarded by the Military Authorities as the permanent one, the 2nd and 3rd lines raised during the war having been formed solely to meet the exigencies of the military situation, and are, therefore, regarded as temporary.

In the numerous cases in which amalgamations have taken place of the 1st and 2nd line battalions, they are invariably treated as the absorption of the 2nd line by the 1st line, leaving the one original battalion of the London Regiment. The point you raise would, therefore, seem to be immaterial, as all records affecting the two units in question will appear as the War History of the 9th County of London Battalion, The London Regiment, the prefixes of 1st and 2nd before the number of the battalions disappearing.

(Sgd.) H. MANSBRIDGE, Secretary,
Territorial Force Association of the County of London.

CHAPTER II

Preparing for the Great Attack

THE first week of February was spent in reorganising the new battalion now a unit of the Fifth Army, Gen. Sir H. Gough, and IIIrd Corps.

On 6th the battalion entrained at Corbie for Apilly and proceeded by route march to Marest, the first British troops to be so far south. The people here had hardly ever seen an English soldier as they had been in the hands of the Huns from the early days of the war. On the following day the march was continued, H.Q. and " A " and " B " Companies going to Rouez Camp and " C " and " D " to Liez Fort. This was one of a strong line of forts built by the French but had suffered considerably at the hands of the Germans before their withdrawal in 1917. On the 9th an officers' meeting was held in the fort and Col. Powell explained the position. Everyone anticipated an early attack by the Germans of which the fort was to be the very centre. "The position the battalion now occupied," explains Major Lindsey-Renton, "was known as the 'Battle Zone.' It had been decided that to resist the anticipated German offensive the line should be held in three zones, that is, three lines of defensive positions, the distance between the three zones varying according to the suitability of the ground for defence. These zones were known as the 'Outpost Zone,' the function of which was to keep observation on the enemy and to delay his advance while the troops in rear got into position. Behind this was ' the Battle Zone,' where the enemy was to be given battle and held up at all costs, and a third zone in rear. The area round Liez Fort was in an angle formed by the River Oise which east of Liez ran in a N. and S. direction but further south changed to an E. and W. direction."

Between February 10th and February 23rd the battalion

stayed in this area. There were little or no defences when the line was taken over and the men were kept hard at work all day digging posts " in full view of the Boches," comments an officer. " They must think we're fools and the kind of trenches we're supposed to dig are the damned silliest things we ever saw. Everybody here hopes we shall never have to man them. We dig the posts by day in view of the Hun until about 4 p.m. and then carefully camouflage them for the night. Why, no one has discovered yet." On 17th the Hun brought down the solitary British observation balloon in this area. The Germans had all this time taken but very little notice of the digging, but on 20th, when the posts were nearing completion they opened fire for a short time. There was no doubt they carefully registered the whole line for they refrained from further effort until the bombardment which preceded the great attack on March 21st when our men occupying these trenches were shot down in scores. On February 24th the Q.V.R. were relieved by the 7th Queen's (18th Division) and marched back to Rouez Camp. This, much to their regret, they left on the following day, and it was as well they did, for when the attack came the troops in Rouez and Fort Liez were wiped out to a man. Crossing the Oise at Chauny the battalion made its way to the Buttes de Rouy, two prominent hillocks with a narrow neck between them through which ran the main Chauny-St. Gobain road. Owing to their height they afforded an extensive view and their retention was of the utmost importance as should the enemy gain possession of them he would have a commanding view of the British and French back areas. On February 26th the Q.V.R. relieved the 7th London in the outpost line, " C " Company being on the left, " D " on the right with " A " and " B " in support. Battalion H.Q. were established in a farmhouse lying in a hollow on the outskirts of the village of Amigny-Rouy and the only building in an almost untouched state. The rest of the village had suffered the usual fate of places through which the Germans had retreated.

" As this was the area the Q.V.R. were in when the German attack opened," says Major Lindsey-Renton, " a general description of the ground is of interest. On the left flank of the battalion the River Oise ran E. and W. through what were

PREPARING FOR THE GREAT ATTACK

known as the Marshes of the Oise. The river and the marshes extending to a width of over 4,000 yards. In normal times these marshes were quite impassable to any troops except by one or two narrow tracks and on this account there existed no system of defence beyond two narrow belts of wire which extended from the left of the battalion to the river, a distance of over 1,500 yards. Owing to the unusually dry winter these marshes had dried up to a very large extent and had become easily passable for troops. In fact it was just possible, and was done by several people, to walk out for long distances over the marshes and reconnoitre the country without encountering troops either friendly or hostile. There was, therefore, this large gap on our left with the actual river running between us and the battalion on our left with whom we had no direct communication. The left of the battalion was on the edge of the marsh, where small posts were placed for purposes of observation and also to get sweeping Lewis Gun fire across the marshes. On the right of this a steep wooden slope ran through our line towards the enemy, who at this point were 1,500 to 2,000 yards away. The country between us and the enemy was much broken up by slight rises in the ground and small valleys in between, in which large bodies of men could collect without being seen from our lines. This necessitated keeping a post well forward in No Man's Land to overlook the area. In the centre of the battalion front was open country for about 500 yards with trenches in a bad state of repair and almost absolutely waterlogged. To the right of this the line entered a thick wood, the Faye de Servais, which was a portion of the Basse Forest de Couchy. This wood ran for a considerable distance both backward and to the right. In the wood small observation posts were maintained at its front edge while the main line of trenches ran some 200 or 300 yards further back in the wood. The whole of the latter was heavily wired, the trees being laced together in places for a depth of 50 to 100 yards.

"From the centre and right of the battalion front one looked straight into the St. Gobain Massif, the high thickly wooded ridge with the town of St. Gobain forming a clearing in the forest. Both the wooded slope on the left and the forest on the right of the line stretched back from the front line to the support line with the open country between them. This last always appeared to be a position of danger owing to the weakness of its defences. Some 1,500 to 2,000 yards behind the front line ran what was called the 'village line.' A system of trenches on the outskirts of the village of Amigny-Rouy. This was originally a kind of support or intermediate line but finally became the front line of the Battle zone. In the area betweeu Battn. H.Q. and the Buttes de Rouy the Oise crosses the marsh towards the south side and the river flows under a steep bank which overlooks the marshes.

"The battalion stayed in 'the Outpost Zone' between February 26th and March 10th, carrying out inter-company reliefs, 'A' and 'C' Companies alternating on the left and 'B' and 'D' on the right. While in the line every endeavour was made to strengthen the position. This portion of the line must have been a very quiet sector as the original French garrisons had lived not only in dug-outs but the majority of them in huts and shacks which would not have stopped a bullet. Moreover, the actual defences had been allowed to fall into a state of disrepair except the wire, which was good. New posts were dug by night and carefully camouflaged with grass and branches, and when once completed no one was allowed near them except in case of an attack being imminent.

" Owing to the great area of dead ground between us and the Germans on our left front it became necessary to have strong and continual patrolling to prevent the enemy collecting there and rushing our line by surprise. A permanent patrol party was formed and accommodated at Battn. H.Q. Two officers were in charge, Lieut. G. D. Mayer, M.C., and 2nd Lieut. Rampling, with Sergt. Coles (band sergeant), Cpl. Howell and others. These patrols went out nightly into the village of Servais which was in No Man's Land and lay in wait for German patrols, or for any sign of possible assembly on the enemy's part. They never met the enemy though they could hear considerable noise from the direction of his lines. Later on, when the patrolling was continued by the 2/10th Londons they got held up one night by wire and had some casualties."

As an incentive to be more than usually vigilant, Lieut. Mayer was promised a bar to the M.C. he had already received

PREPARING FOR THE GREAT ATTACK

if he captured a prisoner, and any man of his patrol fourteen days' leave.

The battalion was relieved by the 2/10th Londons on March 10th and returned to the neighbourhood of the Buttes de Rouy, Battn. H.Q., and one of the companies (" B ") going into huts and some large galleries which had been dug into one of the Buttes and the other three companies into the posts and trenches overlooking the Marshes. Work was feverishly pushed forward on the defences of the " Battle Zone," miles of wire being put out and a large number of additional posts and trenches dug and others strengthened, but it was not until March 19th, owing to continual changes being made, that the final dispositions were settled upon. On the previous day the Q.V.R. had gone into the outpost line taking over the whole brigade front with the four companies in the line in the following order from right to left : " B," " C," " D," " A," Battn. H.Q. being established in Amigny Keep, a strong point on the outskirts of the village. The next day these dispositions were again altered and the two right companies " B " and " C " were taken from the Outpost line and put in support " B " Company in the village line and " C " Company in what was called the left Buttes locality, being the left portion of the defence of the Buttes on top of the steep bank overlooking the Oise. Their place in the Outpost line was taken over by the Rangers.

Rumours had long been rife of an imminent great German attack and prisoners captured had disclosed the fact that the huge preparations for it were now nearing completion and that it might be expected any time from March 18th to 25th. More definite statements were to the effect that it would come off on the night of March 18th/19th or 19th/20th.

The following " Summary of Prisoner's Statement Regarding Offensive " was circulated for the information of the troops :

" (1) N.C.O. of 28th Foot Artillery Regiment, captured about ten miles N. of St. Quentin on March 18th, states his battery of 4 15 cm. hows. has received 1200 rounds including 300 gas shells. German attack expected to commence in two to three days from March 18th. It will be preceded by ten hours' intense bombardment, last two hours being gas shells. There will then be two hours' interval to allow air to clear and infantry and artillery will then advance simultaneously.

" (2) N.C.O. pilot of 44th Pursuit Flight, brought down near Ly Fontaine, March 18th, states certain that attack will be made on March 20th or 21st. Large air forces have been brought together opposite this front but have been used only sparingly so far and will not be fully disclosed till day of battle.

" (3) Prisoners of 227th R.I.R., 107th Division, taken S.W. of Villers Guislan, about fifteen miles N. of St. Quentin, March 18th/19th, state they are expecting relief by attacking troops any moment. They have been issued with additional nose-pieces to gas-masks on March 17th as increased protection. One prisoner mentions March 20th as date of attack, but his regiment is to be relieved first.

" (4) Two Alsatian deserters 414 Trench Mortar Company surrendered S. of St. Quentin (Pirealler) March 18th/19th. They state they do not know infantry in the line. Raid to be carried out March 19th/20th and large attacks March 20th/21st preceded by gas bombardment including T.M.'s in position on divisional front."

On March 22nd Brig.-Gen. H. C. Jackson, who had been appointed to command the 50th Division, bade farewell to the 175th Brigade in the following order :

> 9th London Regiment (Q.V.R.).
> 2/10th London Regiment.
> The Rangers, 12th London Regiment.
> 215th Machine-gun Company.
> 175th Trench Mortar Battery.

" It is with the deepest regret that I say good-bye to the Officers, W.O.'s, N.C.O.'s and Men of the 175th Infantry Brigade.

" I had the honour of commanding the brigade at home and when they first came to France. Since then they have never been in the line except under my command, and it is therefore an additional grief that I should have to leave them on the eve of their having to play their part in the great battle which is just starting. This part I know they will worthily fulfil. In the last fourteen months you have never failed to carry out any task I have asked you to perform. Your keenness, willingness and cheerfulness have been beyond all praise.

"One of your commanding officers, who luckily is still with us, once said that the 175th Brigade was a Happy Brigade. I hope that this is so, and that it may long remain so.

"Good-bye and good luck to you all.

"H. C. JACKSON,
"Brigadier General Commanding
175th Infantry Brigade.

"*March 22nd,* 1918."

Gen. Jackson was succeeded in the command of the 175th Brigade by Brig.-Gen. Richardson (Hussars). The regret at General Jackson's departure was shared by all ranks of the Q.V.R.

CHAPTER III

THE GREAT GERMAN OFFENSIVE, 1918

THE FIRST BLOW

IN his description of the Great Offensive of 1918 which was to be known to posterity as "The Michael Attack," Hindenburg says : "For the first time in the whole war the Germans would have the advantage of numbers on one of their fronts. Of course it could not be as great as that with which England and France had battered our Western Front for more than three years. In particular, even the advent of our forces from the East did not suffice to cancel out the immense superiority of our enemies in artillery and air-craft. But in any case we were now in a position to overwhelm the enemy's lines at some point of the Western Front without thereby taking too heavy risk on other points of that front. . . . From the start the ideal objective for my purposes was a complete break through the enemy lines, a break through to unlock the gates to open warfare. This gate was to be found in the line Arras-Cambrai-St. Quentin-La Fere." New principles had been laid down for the attack, the centre of gravity of which was to be found in thin lines of infantry, the effectiveness of which was to be intensified by the wholesale employment of field artillery and battle planes. Nothing, the Marshal says, was neglected to concentrate the entire fighting forces of Germany for the decision in the West. In the Orders issued by German Main Head-quarters it is stated : "The Michael attack will take place on the 21-3. The first attack on the enemy's lines is fixed for 9.40 a.m. (2) The first great tactical objective of the Crown Prince Rupprecht's Army Group is to cut off the English in the Cambrai Salient and reach the line Croisilles (south-east of Arras)-Bapaume-Peronne. If the attack of the right wing (17th Army) proceeds favourably this army is to press on beyond Croisilles."

A few days prior to the attack Lieut.-Col. Powell had gone away on leave and the command of the Q.V.R. devolved upon Major Lindsey-Renton, who gives the following account of the fighting : " At 4.45 a.m. on the morning of March 21st the air was rent with the noise of thousands of guns and trench mortars being fired and thousands of shells bursting. Everyone at H.Q. leapt up with a cry ' They're off.' On going into the open it was found that the mist was so thick that we could not see for as much as 100 yards. All the personnel of H.Q., batmen, pioneers, signallers, etc., were at once put into their prearranged fighting positions. The first thing that was noticed was that although Amigny-Rouy was being overwhelmed with a deluge of shells, both gas and high explosive, none were coming within 200 yards of Battn. H.Q. In fact, during the whole time the battalion was there no shell ever came really close.

" The first result of the mist was that an elaborate system of visual signalling established for passing down the S.O.S. quickly was of no use, and the ordinary telephone had to be relied on. Communication was got therefore by 'phone to the forward companies who reported no shelling on their front and no signs of the enemy. Throughout the whole of this period communication was maintained between Battn. H.Q. and the companies owing to the splendid work of the signalling section. Especial reference should be made to the work of Rfn. Newman and Rfn. Borrie, two linesmen on Battn. H.Q., who day and night in most dangerous circumstances were up and down the wires repairing them. Rfn. Newman was awarded the Military Medal for this ; Rfn. Borrie had already received it for work in 1917. At 8.50 a.m. the order was issued, ' Man Battle positions and report completion.' "

At 9.45 a.m. the following order was received at Battn. H.Q. : " Brigade instructs me to tell you that Beautor, T.30.d, is surrounded by enemy. You will keep special watch on marsh. Send your usual wire patrol with Lewis Gun out at frequent intervals. Report situation every half-hour. Use your power buzzer."

" The mist continued until about midday when it cleared and one was able to see for quite a long distance. On our own particular front there was no sign of an enemy attack, but to our left across the Oise it was clear both to the eyes and ears that very heavy fighting was going on. Rifle and machine-gun fire, bursting of thousands of shells, all pointed to an attack being in progress and it was also clear that the enemy were advancing. From the high wooded slope on the left of the battalion front line a good view could be got of the area north of the Oise, and when the mist had cleared away on the 21st and subsequent dates, masses of the enemy could be seen moving forward. On one occasion a battalion was seen on the march along a road which crossed the marshes from the enemy's lines to the point where the attack was progressing not far from La Fere. We were able to get the artillery on to them and the battalion scattered all over the place. On another occasion it was noticed that a number of tents had been pitched for some camp. Eventually about 200 9.2's were fired at the place. Generally, however, the targets offered were either too far off, or as the attack advanced our artillery withdrew too far back to fire and the few guns left were too busy. In the same way as the attack advanced the enemy got behind us, and on the morning of the 23rd we discovered a German observation balloon up which looked right into the back of H.Q. This necessitated restrictions on all movement round the farm."

At 4.12 p.m. Capt. Nichols, the adjutant, sent the following order to the O.C. " B " Company : " You may withdraw half your company at a time to living accommodation, but they must be ready to man battle position at ten minutes' notice. The full garrison on the bridge must remain in position."

" During the evening," continues Major Lindsey-Renton, " we received reports of the progress of the advance, and found that the enemy was pushing forward rapidly on our left flank, which now became a source of anxiety. Should the enemy throw a few small bridges across the Oise or even push down the marsh on our side of the river our left flank was turned. There was further a hard track across the marsh which left the marsh and became an ordinary road, passing by Battn. H.Q. making it possible that the first intimation of an attack would be the appearance of the enemy himself at H.Q. A post was therefore established at a small bridge which the track crossed and another platoon was brought up to defend the approach from the marshes. The belts of wire across the marsh were patrolled all night and as long as the mist lasted. The patrol party which had been established at H.Q. were used to patrol the marshes and the banks of the Oise to see whether the enemy was making any preparations to cross the Oise. The enemy patrolled the opposite bank as their voices could be heard in the mist. Seven or eight Germans were taken prisoners in the marshes having lost their way. Some of them belonged to the party who had been scattered by our artillery fire while marching on the road across the marsh. They provided us with a certain amount of amusement as they were complaining that they were a landsturm battalion and should not have been used as assault troops.

"As the enemy advanced French troops were rushed up to fill up gaps, and gradually the 58th Division got completely cut off from the rest of the English Army and came under the orders of the French. About half a mile or so behind the line of Battn. H.Q. and the village line was a raised road across the Marsh with a bridge over the Oise. This road was known as the Condren Causeway and led from the village of Condren on the N. side of the river to a spot known as the Old Wharf on the southern side. Previous to the attack the Engineers and Pioneers had been busy blocking up the arches where small streams ran under the road with the idea of flooding the marshes. They had been partially successful, and a large area of the marsh to the east of this road was under water.

" On 22nd and 23rd various conflicting reports were received as to the position at Condren where heavy fighting was in progress. The enemy gained possession of the town on 23rd or 24th, which gave him a road across the marsh by means of which he could cut off all the troops in the ' outpost ' and ' village ' lines. The bridge across the Oise was destroyed and machine and Lewis guns were placed in positions commanding the road. A platoon of the 4th Suffolks, the Divisional Pioneers, were attached to the Q.V.R. and formed a garrison for the ' Old Wharf,' while another company of (I think) the 10th London was also at our disposal for the defence of the left flank. The battalion was now responsible for the original front line, facing east, and also for the left flank, all the way from the front line to the Condren Causeway, a considerable frontage in view of the fact that the enemy were gradually getting further and further behind us, so that the left flank was a real source of danger.

"The enemy opposite our original front had also begun to get inquisitive ; patrols were out in the mist endeavouring to find out whether we were still in position, or owing to the situation on our left we had started retiring. On one occasion a small German patrol got into our Outpost line in the wood on our right flank, where they were met by the N.C.O. going round the posts. Some ineffectual firing took place and the patrol got away."

Rfn. H. V. Stone has something to say about these patrols : "I went, together with Rfn. Young," he says, "out on patrol on March 22nd, but when about 800 yards out in front of our wire we came across a large German raiding party coming over to attack 'A' Company's positions. We opened fire on them immediately, both having to lie flat as it was then 9.30 in the morning and broad daylight. We managed to keep them off for a little time, but Young got badly wounded, receiving five bullets in various parts of his body, and the last I saw of him was crawling towards our lines. Finally I was surrounded, and in the struggle lost my steel helmet and rifle and was captured. After this I had many adventures as a prisoner of war."

Continuing Major Lindsey-Renton says : "Repeated attempts of the kind were being made, and, supported by reports from higher authorities that 10 German Divisions were waiting to attack south of the Oise, were a source of anxiety. On 24th they captured a great portion of the town of Chauny where our Transport and Quartermaster's Stores had been, and these had to be got away somewhat hurriedly across the river to a place of greater security. The possession of Chauny gave the enemy another main route across the Oise even still further in our rear, so that gradually more and more troops, oddments collected from all over the place, had to be used to prolong and protect the left flank.

"On the afternoon of 24th the battalion received orders to withdraw 'A' and 'D' Companies from the Outpost line and to bring them back to the Village line, now the forward part of the battle zone. Battn. H.Q. were moved

Major R. H. Lindsey-Renton, D.S.O.

back to the Buttes de Rouy, the farm becoming ' B ' Company's H.Q. and the company itself which was commanded by Capt. W. E. Bowler, the left forward company."

A/R.Q.M.S. Taylor, who was with the Q.M.S. stores and transport in Chauny, kept a diary, from which we take the following extracts :

"March 21st. Rumble of guns terrific. Fritz had launched his offensive at last. The strain was terrible. We had to take rations out at night, so we were hoping that he was held. Limbers were out of the question so we used pack ponies. On striking across country one got away and after a lot of trouble on the part of the T.O. was recovered. How we did that journey I don't know ; we frequently had to put on our gas masks and the wonder to me is that any of us got back alive.

"March 22nd. We repeated the performance at night and on our return at 1 a.m. were informed that Fritz was expected to be in Chauny at three o'clock, and we were to withdraw to Manicamp. We were so beat that one or two of us fainted on the road from sheer exhaustion."

On the same date Lieut. Keeson who had been away on four days' leave, which he spent in Paris, arrived at Chauny on his way to rejoin the battalion and was told to remain there with the Transport. An entry in his diary for March 22nd runs : "About 9 p.m. the Transport lines were told to clear as Chauny was to be evacuated and bridges blown up next morning. Captain A. N. Philbrick, T.O., worked like a Trojan and got things away to Sinceny in record time. He also got the cookers out of the line where they had been in the Forêt de Servais, which was no easy task on account of the terrible state of all the roads and tracks due to the bombardment which the Boches kept putting down. It didn't worry Old Tim (Major O'Shea, Q.M.) at all. He was half undressed when the order came. He just redressed, put his kit and the Mess stuff in his buggy and drove off quite peacefully."

The next entry in R.Q.M.S. Taylor's diary reads :

"March 23rd. Extra troops were rushed up ; dismounted cavalry, British and French troops, and if I had only had a cinema I could have taken some of the finest pictures of the war. Our Transport had withdrawn to Besme, but we had the rations at Maricourt and had to await the Transport to take them up to the line. During the afternoon bridges were being blown up; Fritz was shelling repeatedly; our store hut was turned into a French dressing station; they, the French, were most efficient. The wounded, who were coming in very fast, were speedily attended to and hurried away on motor ambulances as fast as they arrived. Later on French armoured cars came along and I cannot speak too highly of the way those Frenchmen worked. About two o'clock while we were helping French wounded into the ambulances two motor lorries came along with a 60-pounder, officers in their shirt-sleeves on the front of the lorries, who seeing us leapt off and questioned us as to Jerry's whereabouts. I replied, ' According to reports he is about 1½ kilos away.' One of the officers said, ' Righto, we'll let the blighters have a few more,' and promptly had the gun wheeled round, a tree pulled down, and the gun blazing away in less than ten minutes. Things were by this time getting so warm and no limbers turning up we decided on our course of action for we had the whole battalion rations. We scrounged around for anything on wheels and eventually loaded up some 9 or 10 handbarrows and started off. About a mile up the road we spotted a large farm cart, on which we contrived to pile the lot and push it along, when up rides the T.O. and limbers. So we off-loaded, resorted and carried on up the line."

Col. Powell rejoined the battalion after the withdrawal from the Outpost line had been carried out. Resuming his narrative Major Lindsey-Renton proceeds :

"On the evening of March 25th the enemy had entered Noyon, many miles away in our rear, and had started turning a battery or two about, firing at us from behind. One particular battery was a source of considerable annoyance as it fired into the back of the Buttes de Rouy where the entrances to the galleries and chambers were, making ingress and egress quite exciting at times. During the next few days a number of orders and counter orders were received as to holding our position. First the French authorities considered our line of the utmost importance and to be held at all costs, then came an order that the battalion would withdraw some miles back, leaving a rearguard to cover the movement. Arrangements were all made and the companies started destroying stores and damaging everything of value, and rendering bombs, etc., unserviceable, when the order to withdraw was cancelled by another that the line was to be held at all costs.

"On March 27th the following readjustment took place : Six platoons of the Rangers who were holding the front line on our immediate right came under the orders of the Q.V.R. These platoons were under the command of Capt. Spencer. The remainder of the Rangers under Col. Bayliffe were joined by six platoons of Q.V.R. under Capt. Samuelson. These platoons had been in support and they now helped to prolong the left flank in the neighbourhood of Chauny. This left the battalion holding the whole of the brigade front plus a large left flank in a thin line with no support for a considerable distance in rear."

The new line taken up extended from the Amigny-Rouy-St. Gobain Road (inclusive) right to the Oise Marshes on the left, a distance of nearly two miles. This front was held by the four platoons of "B" Company, two platoons of "A" and two of "D," all in line, Capt. Bowler being responsible for the sector. This officer says : "The situation on the left was as follows : The enemy during his advance was using the Oise as his left flank and at the time of the withdrawal to Amigny-Rouy, Tergnier, Fargnier and Chauny had all been occupied by his troops so that except for the protection afforded by the Oise our left flank was entirely exposed for a considerable distance. The task of watching this exposed position was given to two platoons of 'C' Company who were responsible for the line from Condren Causeway to Amigny-Rouy railway station."

The enemy patrols had shown great activity, especially opposite "B" Company's position, and had made a number of attempts to find out the weak spots in the line and to filter through. "B" Company, however, under Capt. Bowler displayed equal alertness and energy, giving them a good reception every time they approached, and no doubt impressed them with the idea that the line was thickly held, which was not the case. In describing these attacks, Capt. Bowler says : "Two patrols each composed of 1 sergeant and 15 men had been left to cover the withdrawal during the night March 24th/25th and at dawn one of them, 'D' Company, rejoined its company after an encounter with the enemy. The patrol of 'A' Company was captured. A gap in the wire had been left for the return of this patrol and the first indication that anything had gone amiss was the appearance of a strong body of the enemy, who attempted to rush that part of the position held by No. 7 Platoon (Sergt. Wyatt). They were beaten off successfully. About noon an attack was made by a party of the enemy, 100 strong, on the front held by No. 5 Platoon. This also was unsuccessful. A long well-wooded spur or ridge ran through the centre of the position, so that it was possible for the enemy to get to close quarters in this particular sector unobserved. A further attack developed along the ridge about 1 p.m., the enemy making use of petrol bombs which set the grass and furze alight. This attempt also failed though at one time the enemy nearly managed to reach the position. 2nd Lieut. Rampling (No. 6 Platoon) was entirely responsible for the repulse of the attack. On the following night two more efforts were made to penetrate our positions on No. 5 Platoon's front. A fighting patrol, consisting of about 20 men under Cpl. H. Barnes, dispersed the enemy on each occasion. Beyond these and similar encounters no further attack was made on the sector up till the time the battalion was relieved by the 2nd Londons on the night of Friday, March 29th/30th."

"The astounding features of the defence of this locality," concludes Capt. Bowler, "were first, the entire absence of artillery support, two 3-in. trench mortars being the only guns on that front ; second, the absence of even infantry support. The whole of the troops available were spread out over the large area of close country, and they were completely successful in maintaining themselves with nothing but their own arms for five days and nights against all attacks. The casualties in 'B' Company during this period were 1 killed and 15 wounded."

Referring to these moving events Rfn. Snoswell, who as a stretcher bearer was, in comparison with the fighting men, in the comfortable dug-out at head-quarters, has something to say as a looker-on : "We are in the doings this time," he says, on March 28th, "but luckily not in the worst of it. It has come as a surprise to us all. Fritz has done something ; how much we don't know. Rumours fly about, but of one thing there is little doubt, there has been plenty of scrapping, and it has not all gone in our favour. Still we have hopes all will yet be well. The weather has been gorgeous, but the nights are cold. On top of that there has been very little sleep for the fellows in the platoons. I have not been so badly off as my job is intermittent, and I live in a dug-out all the time, while they are out in the trenches and have to be on the qui vive the whole time with their nerves almost at breaking-point. It has been a rough time altogether. You ought to see me now. Water is scarce, and I have not had a wash or shave for about a week. I have a most respectable beard. Oh, to have a night's kip without the worry of shells and possibility of attack ! It is now ten days since I took my boots and puttees off, except once to change my socks." On Easter Sunday, March 31st, he continues : " So far we have not been in the actual fighting. Our particular job seems to be holding the line, and they keep on dodging us about from one part to another. We are feeling a bit tired, not having a full night's rest for a fortnight. We were very nearly in a big scrap this morning. As it was we stood by for five or six hours owing to it, but our good fortune won the day and we kept out, but it was a near squeak."

" The battalion remained in the Amigny-Rouy-St. Gobain-road position," continues Major Lindsey-Renton, " until the night of 30th March, having been the front line of the brigade since the night of 18th with everyone undergoing great strain and anxiety, knowing day by day that the enemy were getting further and still further in their rear while waiting to attack them in front as well as from the rear and flank. On the night of 29th/30th the battalion was relieved and marched back to Pierremande and Bichancourt, where they were employed in preparing a new line of resistance which was being made.

" While the battalion was here the enemy made a strong effort to seize the crossings over the Oise at Chauny, some of which were still in our hands. He succeeded in driving out some of the troops that were there and isolating another body. A counter-attack in the afternoon by the 18th Entrenching Battalion, which was attached to the 58th Division, restored the position and took a good batch of prisoners. These prisoners were annoyed at being captured in the flush of victory, but were quite resigned as they said it would only be for a fortnight, as the Germans would have won the war by then."

During the retreat a terrible catastrophe overtook the Q.V.R. Towards the end of 1917 the 2nd Battalion officers started the formation of a brass band. Sufficient money was subscribed among them and their friends to provide a splendid set of instruments, and Sergt. Coles, a clever musician, was entrusted with the difficult task of forming a band. With only one or two trained players at his disposal he did remarkably well and their performances when the battalion was out of the line were much enjoyed by the men and played no small part in keeping up their spirits and discipline. The instruments had been stored for safety in a house in Chauny and during the bombardment a 5·9 shell scored a direct hit upon it wiping out at one fell swoop the band of which the Vics had been so proud. One instrument only was saved.

On March 30th the following general order was communicated to the battalion :

IIIrd Corps, No. G. O.8687

" The following general order received from Gen. Humbert Commanding Third French Army is forwarded for communication to all ranks :—

" 'The Army Commander desires to express his profound admiration of the efforts of the French troops and of their comrades of the British Army. For the last two days they have offered a resistance which has barred the progress of the enemy, but the task is not yet finished. It is still of the greatest importance to gain time to carry out an operation the results of which may be decisive.

" ' It is therefore essential to hold on to our positions at all costs.

" ' The enemy too is greatly fatigued. We have powerful artillery support. The troops of the Vth Army Corps, of the IIIrd Cavalry Corps and of the IIIrd and XVIIIth British Army Corps are defending the heart of France. A realisation of the grandeur of this task will show all ranks their duty.'

"C. G. FIELD,
"B.G.G.S.,
IIIrd. Corps.

" 29th March, 1918.
" Officer Commanding,
   9th London Regiment (Q.V.R.).
   2/10th London Regiment.
   16th Entrenching Battalion.
   175th L.T.M.B.
" Major Worthington's Composite Battalion.
   " For information.

"Captain J. W. G. WYLD.
"Brigade Major,
" 30th March, 1918."   " 175th Infantry Brigade.

C.S.M. Wheaton, of the Q.V.R., but transferred to the Civil Service Rifles, and captured on March 23rd, tells the following tale of his sufferings as a prisoner of war : " We were eventually fighting back to back and as the last resource charged the machine-guns, only to be brushed aside like so much grass. I was trying to get the remnant of the company together and get them away one by one, when I was told by the men that they were all surrendering, so was obliged to do so too or be shot. I decided quickly to surrender as I could serve no useful purpose dead. We were then marched from 4 p.m., 23rd March, to 2.30 a.m. on 24th without food, to a wire cage. The cold was intense and everything was as miserable as it was possible to be. At nine o'clock we received a small slice of black bread, and some lucky ones got a teaspoonful of marmalade. We then marched to Caudry, where we were sorted out by the Huns into our divisions. From there we were sent by rail to Le Quesnoy, sixty men in a truck, no room to sit down and no food. We reached Le Quesnoy by 27th and were placed in another cage and again sorted out. I was selected to go to Munster ; all the rest of my company were left behind. The reason being that I was a C.S.M. I arrived on 28th and was given some sour liquid and a bath, and told off to huts which were in a filthy state. Our daily routine was to parade at 6.30 p.m. to be counted ; ' coffee water ' at

eight o'clock ; stewed swede soup, very thin, at twelve ; roll
call at 3 p.m. and 7 ; followed by more stewed swedes. Bread
(black) used to be issued daily after last roll call, each man's
portion being about 5 inches long, 1½ inches thick and 3 inches
broad. This was intended to serve as the next day's ration, but
it was never safe to try and keep it till next day as it was sure
to disappear. So everyone ate it as soon as it was issued. We
were only allowed to write two letters and four post cards each
month, and I have reason to believe that all of these did not
reach their intended destination. Our meals were sometimes
supplemented by an issue of some foul-smelling fish which I
could never summon up courage to tackle ; also mussels which
usually ran to six to a man. We were all treated alike, N.C.O.'s
and O.R., with the exception that those above the rank of
corporal were not compelled to work. We were all inoculated
three times in as many days. Our only exercise was to wander
round and round the inside of the lager until tired and then—
with the permission of the insects—to sleep. All that we
could see was the sky. After enduring this life for three months
and very nearly slipping through my clothes, I received my
first food parcel through the British Red Cross and then my
life became better. These parcels and smokes were a heaven-
sent blessing, and when we got them we could live without the
aid of Jerry's food. I was more fortunate in getting my
parcels than some of the other boys because I was stationary
and at a base camp. When the Armistice was signed the
senior W.O. in our lager, who was President of the British Help
Committee, formed by the prisoners of war under the Red
Cross, got permission to go to Holland to arrange the transport
of the 6,000 odd prisoners attached to this camp. I took charge
in his absence. He wired to me to get the first 1,000 off on the
morning of November 16th, and after working all night with a
small staff of about 20 O.R. we had them on parade next
morning, much to the astonishment of the Germans, who owned
that they could not have worked things so successfully. This
was on 16th November and by 30th we were the last to
leave."

CHAPTER IV

"With Our Backs to the Wall"—Hangard Wood

ON April 3rd the Q.V.R. were relieved by a battalion of the 363rd French Infantry Regiment and marched to Praast, where it was billeted for the night. "This march," states Major Lindsey-Renton, "was the first stage of a long round-about journey necessitating crossing the Aisne and going as far as Villers Cotterets to entrain there for Amiens, in front of which the British Armies were settling down in a state of greater stability than had existed since the opening of the offensive. We were interested to read a little later of the lucky escape the whole brigade had had including the Q.V.R. Some few days after our relief by the French the Germans attacked our old positions, captured the Buttes, and got as far as, and captured, the position we had left, taking 3,000 prisoners."

The Q.V.R. were now part of the Fourth Army under Gen. Sir H. Rawlinson.

The journey by train from Villers Cotterets was not entirely an uneventful one. "During the night," says Major Lindsey-Renton, "we heard strange noises which we could only ascribe to fog signals. After a while the noises got more pronounced, one which seemed to come from somewhere quite close at hand reproducing all the several noises of a shell. We then discovered that the said noises were not fog signals but French guns in action. The train was running along in front of the French batteries and the Germans were shelling the railway. It was not many seconds before all lights were out and hardly a voice could be heard along the whole length of the train. Shortly afterwards the train entered Longeau Station in front of Amiens and the Q.V.R. started once more for the front."

According to the Regimental War Diary the battalion in the

course of this round-about journey was at Villers Cotterets on April 5th and 6th; at dusk on 7th it moved up to the line running in front of Villers-Bretonneux relieving the 18th Australian Infantry, " A," " B " and " D " Companies being in the line with " C " Company in support.

"The trenches at Villers-Bretonneux," according to Lieut. Keeson, " were only slits in the ground, very wet and miserable. Plenty of dead Huns about. The Australians evidently enjoyed this sector. They brought a Hun plane down by M.G. fire and it fell just in front of the trench I'm in. I went out to look at it. They killed one pilot and took the other prisoner. We got a light gun off it. Battn. H.Q. sent up plenty of wine to the troops from Villers-Bretonneux. One noticed that the runners seemed to do very well in that line."

The Germans attached enormous importance to Villers-Bretonneux and made a number of desperate onslaughts upon it. It was the key to Amiens and in his autobiography Hindenburg says : " We ought to have shouted into the ear of every single man 'Press on to Amiens. Put in your last ounce. Perhaps Amiens means decisive victory. Capture Villers-Bretonneux whatever happens, so that from its heights we can command Amiens with masses of artillery.' " He further tells us that the Allies fully realised what the loss of Villers-Bretonneux would mean to them. " They threw against our advancing columns all the troops they could lay hands on, the French appeared and with their massed attacks and skilful artillery saved the situation."

On Tuesday, April 9th, the Q.V.R. were relieved by the 2/10th London Regiment and went into billets at Boves, which was reached after a very hard and exhausting march. The next day it was heavily shelled and some of the men had to clear out of the town into the fields. While the battalion was here it was rumoured that it was in for a " show." Orders were issued and everything was cut and dried, even to officers having to wear privates' tunics, but the " show " had to be postponed owing to the Intelligence Branch saying that the Boches themselves were going to attack.

Rfn. Penberthy recounts a little incident that happened at Boves : " 'A' Company were billeted in a very comfortable schoolroom, where we were fed like fighting cocks, porridge, bacon and jam for breakfast, roast meat and vegetables for dinner, hot bully rissoles for tea and a good tot of rum to finish up the day. We had a very easy time, only the inspection of rifles, after which we were allowed to amuse ourselves as we liked. Although we were within reach of the Huns' long-range guns there were a few civilians who persisted in remaining in the village. Taking advantage of this Rfn. Pritchard borrowed a pair of black and white check trousers, an old frock coat and a silk hat, while two other fellows procured some ladies' dresses. Pritchard making advances to the two young ladies *à la* Charlie Chaplin kept us all in roars of laughter." This incident, trifling in itself, seems to have aroused extraordinary notice, for mention is made of it by quite half a dozen of the contributors to our history. One officer adds : " Rfn. Pritchard, while dressed up, stopped a car containing a French staff officer in the real Chaplin manner, thoroughly annoying the occupant who wanted him arrested as an insolent civilian. When the car drove off Pritchard ran alongside the car in the approved Chaplin style and was greeted with roars of applause." His two companions were accosted by two real French ladies who were very inquisitive concerning their underclothing, and admired it so much that their wearers, having finished the play, made them a present of it.

On April 11th was issued the famous " Special Order of the Day " by Field Marshal Sir Douglas Haig :

To all Ranks of the British Army in France and Flanders.

Three weeks ago to-day the enemy began his terrific attacks against us on a fifty-mile front. His objects are to separate us from the French, to take the Channel Ports and destroy the British Army.

In spite of throwing already 106 divisions into the battle and enduring the most reckless sacrifice of human life, he has as yet made little progress towards his goals.

We owe this to the determined fighting and self-sacrifice of our troops. Words fail me to express the admiration which I feel for the splendid resistance offered by all ranks of our Army under the most trying circumstances.

Many amongst us now are tired. To those I would say that

victory will belong to the side which holds out the longest.
The French Army is moving rapidly and in great force to
our support.

There is no other course open to us but to fight it out.
Every position must be held to the last man; there must be
no retirement. With our backs to the wall and believing
in the justice of our cause each one of us must fight to the end.
The safety of our homes and the freedom of mankind alike
depend upon the conduct of each one of us at this critical
moment.

       D. HAIG, F.M.,
         Commander-in-Chief,
           British Armies in France.

General Head-quarters,
 Thursday, April 11*th,* 1918.

On April 13th the battalion moved to the reserve line near the Bois de Gentelles. Two days later it was relieved by the 35th Australians and went into billets at Blangy, where the men spent a very cheery three days—" Plenty to eat, drink and smoke. Men did not work very hard. Cleaned themselves up and got rest," says one of them. Just before relief on 15th, H.Q. Company had a very nasty spell of shelling, one man being blown to pieces. On 18th the battalion once more took over the reserve line in Gentelles Wood, relieving the 3rd London Regiment. On the following day the Field Marshal's Special Order of April 11th was re-published by Gen. Sir H. S. Rawlinson, G.C.V.O., K.C.B., K.C.M.G., General Commanding the Fourth Army, who added, "In re-publishing this Order of the Day I desire to lay special stress on the importance of Amiens, the defence of which has been entrusted to the Fourth Army. I rely upon every officer, non-commissioned officer and man to hold the line which the Army now occupies to the very last. This Order is to be communicated to every officer, non-commissioned officer and man in the Fourth Army, and it will be read out to his men by every platoon commander in the Infantry, and by every section commander in the Artillery."

During the succeeding five days the companies were warned that it was probable the Germans were likely to attack at any moment, and many things pointed to this. Villers-Bretonneux was very heavily bombarded with gas and H.E. shells, as were also the villages of Cachy, Domart, and Gentelles. The Q.V.R. Battn H.Q. especially suffered from both kinds of fire. During this period the battalion was reinforced by drafts from England consisting mostly of under-age boys. The companies at this time were under the command of the following :

" A " Company . . Capt. A. Hadden.
" B " ,, . . Lieut. C. A. G. C. Keeson.
" C " ,, . . Lieut. G. D. Mayer, M.C.
" D " ,, . . Capt. H. Samuelson.

On the evening of 23rd Lieut. Easterbrook took over command of " C " Company, owing to Lieut. Mayer becoming, a casualty through sickness.

On the night of April 23/24th, the battalion was holding the Southern Reserve Sector astride the Longeau-Domart Road, with three companies in the front line and one in reserve. Orders had been received on 23rd to the effect that the Q.V.R. would relieve the 3rd Londons on the night April 23rd/24th in the front line on the right of Hangard Wood, and accordingly the company commanders on the evening of 23rd made a reconnaissance of that position, returning about midnight.

" About 3.45 a.m. on the morning of 24th," relates Lieut. Keeson, " the enemy put down a heavy bombardment covering a very large area with gas and H.E. shells. Almost at its commencement a large gas shell hit ' C ' Company's H.Q. and killed 2nd Lieut. Plummer, Cpl. Gallop and Rfn. Russell. Lieut. Easterbrook [1] was badly hit and died a few hours after in a C.C.S. 2nd Lieut. E. Bell was evacuated from ' C ' Company with shell shock. ' D ' Company also came in for a good share of gassing, and Capt. Samuelson was evacuated suffering from gas poisoning. ' A ' and ' B ' Companies were more lucky and only suffered a few casualties, most of them slight. Meanwhile things were rather obscure, and it was noticed that no S.O.S.'s were going up on our front. It was subsequently

[1] Died of wounds 25/4/18.

ascertained that they were damp and would not work. With
dawn came a thick mist, which made things more difficult still.
Battn H.Q. kept ringing up the companies for news but failed
to get much. By good fortune most of the wires to companies
held and useful information was received throughout the
morning from ' D ' Company who were in touch with a French
Artillery observation post. During the morning a gunner
suffering from shell shock dashed into ' B ' Company with a
rambling story about Cachy being attacked by enemy with
tanks, which immediately put the wind up ' B ' Company as
Cachy was on their left flank and not very far away. The mist
rose a little and a good deal of movement was observed near
the front line though no definite news was received until a
mounted patrol of Yeomanry (Northumberland Hussars),
who had ridden well up to the front, appeared and gave information that Villers-Bretonneux and the front line were
occupied by the Germans. About 11 a.m. the battalion was
reinforced by the 8th London Regiment (Post Office Rifles).

" About midday the battalion was ordered to move forward
and take the place of the 2/10th London as counter-attack
battalion. The 2/10th had counter-attacked and was holding
with the elements of the 3rd Londons a position near the
support line. The 2/10th in this charge were led by Lieut.-Col.
Symonds, D.S.O., who fell, mortally wounded, at the head of
his men. This move of the Q.V.R. was carried out in artillery
formation and was complete by 4.30 p.m. without casualties,
except one which occurred in Battn H.Q. personnel. The H.Q.
of both the 9th and 2/10th were in a small quarry on the reverse
slope of a hill. The place of the Q.V.R. in the Gentelles line
was taken by the 11th Royal Fusiliers.

" The Q.V.R. were in small holes in the ground dotted on
the hillside in the neighbourhood of Battn. H.Q. The Germans
kept this area under very heavy shell-fire, mostly 8-inch.
There were many casualties. ' B ' Company had all its
stretcher bearers knocked out. Battn. H.Q. in the quarry
suffered especially. The actual H.Q. was a small tin hut
which most miraculously was not touched. In the quarry
there was an R.A.P. round which the wounded were lying,
the 8-inch shells bursting among them causing many death
casualties to them and the stretcher bearers. Very good work

was done by Capt. Gourlay, R.A.M.C., Sergt. F. Lloyd and Sergt. Coles, the former bandmaster, who was mortally wounded while attending to the injured. About 9 p.m. orders were received for the battalion to take part in a general counter-attack on the old front line. The Australians on the left were told off to recapture Villers-Bretonneux, which they eventually did ; the Q.V.R. on the right to retake the old front line running through Hangard Wood. A brigade from the 18th Division linked up the Q.V.R. and the Australians. Company commanders were sent for and reached Battn. H.Q. about 9.10 p.m. and were dismissed a quarter of an hour later after the scheme had been explained to them.

"The attack was to start at ten o'clock, so there was very little time left to instruct the platoon commanders, assemble the men and form up on the tapes. As a matter of fact some of the men left the tapes hardly aware that they were attacking ; some even had rifles slung and carrying spades or picks. In consequence platoon and section commanders had to run along the line explaining as the troops advanced. In the meantime the C.O. and the Adjutant accompanied by four runners had marked out a line and assembled the battalion. The order o. attack was four companies in line, with three platoons each in the front and one platoon each in support. Order of companies from right to left ' A,' ' B,' ' C,' ' D.' ' A,' ' B ' and ' C ' were got on to the jumping-off line in their proper formation. There was, however, not sufficient time to get ' D ' into position and it was therefore held in reserve. But there was also no time to warn ' A,' ' B,' and ' C ' that ' D ' Company was not attacking.

"At 10 p.m. ' A,' ' B ' and ' C ' Companies started off in line, the right of ' A ' Company meeting with practically no resistance skirted the wood and struck their objective. Finding no one there and being unable to get into touch with the remainder of ' A ' on their left, they withdrew slightly in order not to expose their left flank while collecting stragglers from other companies. In the wood itself some resistance was encountered, mostly from machine-guns hidden in the under-growth and Capt. Hadden told his Sergt.-Major (C.S.M. McKenna) that he was going to see how things were on the left. He was never seen again.

"When the line of machine-guns was reached the Hun gunners left their guns and tried the usual 'Kamerad' dodge, but the men, especially the newly arrived draft—it was their first time in the line—would have none of it and killed most of them. Three machine-guns and about 50 prisoners were taken here. Two amusing incidents occurred here also. A big German stretcher bearer who had been taken prisoner was being escorted down by a wounded Vic. when one of the new draft suddenly broke from the line and began to go back. When asked where he was going he said with a laugh, " Just to bayonet that big ——." The other incident was the capture of a very indignant young Hun officer. He began to argue that the escort did not know his way down, and produced a compass to verify it.

" 'A,' 'B' and 'C' Companies, or what remained of them, reached a ride running through the wood parallel with the front line. There the battalion was reorganised and it was discovered that Capt. Hadden was missing. Lieut. Keeson, commanding 'B' Company, then took command of 'A' and 'B' Companies. The other officers present were Lieut. Calvert and 2nd Lieut. Holloway of 'B' Company, and 2nd Lieuts. Fletcher and Jarvis of 'A' Company. The battalion lined the ride and measures were taken to protect the flanks. Lieut. Keeson, with Sergt.-Major McKenna and four men, made a reconnaissance and discovered a movement on the right front. This was found by scouts to be some of the 3rd Londons and some of the 2/10th Londons. Among them was an officer of the 3rd who knew the posts to be recaptured and acted as a guide. The Q.V.R. then pushed forward and occupied the posts of the southern edge of the wood; while doing so an interesting incident occurred. Three men appeared out of the darkness and asked "Who are you." Our reply was "Q.V.R. Are you 'D' Company." The reply to that was "Hands up." The men turned out to be Germans. They were accounted for, but not until after the officer of the 3rd Londons had been shot in the neck.

"A platoon of 'C' Company which had lost direction now joined up, coming from the southern edge of the wood. This platoon had killed many of the enemy and had made some prisoners. With the platoon were 2nd Lieut. D. Lavington and Sergt.-Major Munnings, M.M. Then as many posts as the number of men would allow were occupied while 2nd Lieut. Jarvis went out with a patrol endeavouring to get touch with the troops on the left. This proved to be impossible; strong resistance was met with and it was afterwards found out that there was a gap of about a mile. A runner was sent back to Battn. H.Q. immediately the posts were occupied, giving the dispositions. About midnight the right platoon of 'A' Company under 2nd Lieut. S. C. Hall joined up with about 50 men, including Sergt.-Major Lott and 'B' Company H.Q. personnel of 'B' Company who had lost touch in the dark. Great difficulty was experienced in evacuating the wounded, there being no stretcher bearers left and few men could be spared to take their place. As the attack was made so suddenly rations could not be drawn, and their want was felt, especially that of water.

"About midnight 'D' Company were ordered to get into touch with the left of the line by skirting the northern edge of the wood and to connect up between the right of the 54th Brigade and the left of the battalion. The northern portion of the wood was found to be occupied by the enemy, and the distance from the right of the 54th Brigade being too great, the company was withdrawn at dawn to support position where touch was got with the Rangers (12th Londons) on the left and the 2/10th Londons on the right. During the night the left of 'B' Company while in the wood was attacked by machine-gun and rifle fire and had to face in both directions to deal with it. During the remaining hours of darkness the positions were consolidated. In the early morning of the 25th considerable damage was inflicted on the enemy by our snipers. Cpl. Champ of 'B' Company also did very good work with his Lewis gun. The enemy's artillery fire on this day was very heavy and a number of casualties was suffered. German aeroplanes were flying low over our positions all day long.

"On the evening of 25th orders were given for 'B,' 'A' and 'C' Companies to withdraw and dig a line of posts joining up the right of the front line with the support line on the left so as to enable our gunners to form a satisfactory barrage line for a French attack which was arranged for the morning of 26th. This work was in progress when the order for relief came through. On relief the battalion withdrew to a small wood near Glisy. Four enemy machine-guns and 72 prisoners were sent back, and all companies claimed to have killed a considerable number of the enemy with rifle fire and bayonet."

CHAPTER V

THE FIGHT IN THE WOOD

AN interesting account of the actual fighting is given by Lce.-Cpl. S. O. Stroud, D.C.M., M.M., " B " Company, who says : " The battalion was holding the reserve position on the right of Gentelles Wood (near Villers-Bretonneux) and had completed about four days in the line when on 23rd of April orders were received that the battalion would relieve the front line the following night. I was detailed as guide for 5th Platoon to go up to the front positions to find out the route, together with the company commanders and other platoon guides, an N.C.O. being taken from each platoon. We paraded about dusk (eight o'clock) and proceeded up to the front B.H.Q. When we arrived there we had to wait some time for the guides, but eventually moved off over a hill. We had gone nearly 200 yards when a German aeroplane came over and dropped some bombs on a road which at the time was crowded with ration limbers and caused a large number of casualties. We reached the front positions, and after looking round them we returned to the reserves, where I found the fellows still at work on the trenches. It was about 12.30 a.m. when we got back so I assisted another corporal in sorting out the rations and post. This occupied about an hour, when we went in our bivouac for a rest, but I felt too restless to get to sleep and about three o'clock the German guns opened out. I rushed along the trench and gave the order to ' Stand to,' and then anticipating a move proceeded to pack my kit. By seven o'clock things were a little more quiet and we were able to have breakfast. Great credit was due to the cooks in having a hot breakfast ready under such conditions and with gas shells dropping around. We remained 'standing to' all the morning and a patrol was sent up to the front line to ascertain

the position under Cpl. Caddy (who went over with me that
night and I regret was killed a few days later). In the afternoon we had orders to move up to the front and proceed in
small parties under cover of the woods. On reaching the front
positions we commenced to dig in as the Germans were shelling
rather heavily. I had just completed digging a shelter for
myself when 'A' Company were moved and I took over one
of their shelters along with my platoon sergeant and another
corporal. Feeling rather tired, as I had no sleep the previous
night, I was soon lost in slumberland and the next I knew was
being awakened by the sergeant-major to turn out in battle
order. We were not long in getting out and moved up to the
'kicking-off' point. A few words from my platoon officer and
we were away. We went some distance before a shot was fired,
for I doubt whether the Germans knew we were attacking, as
it had been ordered so suddenly and in the dark they did not
discover us until we were close to them. On getting near to the
edge of Hangard Wood a machine-gun opened a heavy fire
which was telling heavily on us ; but it was soon put out of
action and we were able to advance into the wood. I concerned
myself in keeping the line straight, but had not gone far into the
wood when we came upon a nest of posts which we soon cleared.
We carried on until a post on our left held us up, but when the
M.G. fire slackened we were able to go on and got into the
open again. Then another machine-gun opened a terrific fire
and we were obliged to get down and open fire with our rifles.
I was expecting the left to advance while we kept the gun
engaged, with the idea of surrounding it, but after waiting
some time to see what was developing I decided to get back
into the wood and take up position, and I then went along with
a sergeant and two other men to try and get in touch, as we
seemed to be disconnected. I advanced along the far edge of
the wood, where there was a large number of dead Germans—
apparently there had been some heavy fighting here—when
the machine-gun that had held us up opened fire in my
direction and I decided to get further into the wood, but had
not gone far when I came on a German machine-gun post.
I put my rifle up to fire but it jammed, so I called out to the
men who I thought were following me to fire, but they were
nowhere to be seen. I was too much engaged in seeing that

THE FIGHT IN THE WOOD

none of the Germans were alive to notice that the men were not there when one of them, realising how I was placed, fired, wounding me in the leg. I then rushed at him and settled his business, but while I was dealing with him the other rushed off. After this, as I did not know the nature of my wound, I thought I had better get back. While doing so I came upon a party of men of the battalion who had taken up a position and told an N.C.O. where the Germans were and then carried on back. I was nearly out of the wood on our side when I saw three men rush round a tree, and thinking they were our men I challenged to let them know I was there, but hearing them talking in German I rushed up, killed one and was just thinking about taking the other two prisoners when five more came up out of a hole in the ground. I covered them as they came out with my bayonet as my rifle was useless. After making sure they were not for fighting I searched them and then marched them back. On the way down I came across one of our fellows wounded and made the Germans take him up. When I thought we were practically safe from rifle fire a machine-gun opened all round and wounded one of the prisoners in the back, but with a run we quickly got out of range and then came through the German barrage. I could not stop the Germans going through owing to them not being able to speak English and I could not make them understand my French, but we reached B.H.Q. without further trouble and I left the wounded man they were carrying at the Regimental Aid Post and handed the prisoners over. As I did not like the situation, thinking the flank was exposed and the wood not thoroughly cleared, I went in to see Col. Powell and Capt. (now Major) Nichols and explained the position, and after detailing what I thought was the state of affairs I went into the R.A.P. for treatment and was soon away down the line."

For this exploit Lce.-Cpl. Sidney Oscar Stroud was recommended for a bar to his Military Medal but instead was granted the D.C.M.

C.S.M. G. H. Lott (" B " Company) has also something to say of interest : " That evening sudden orders were received to go over at 10 p.m. There was no time for much explanation. We just dumped our spare kit (never to see them again as it proved) and marched off in the darkness. As quickly as possible we shook ourselves out into two waves with 'D' Company in support. A barrage opened on the wood in front and we all started off. It had all happened so quickly that few of us had realised that there was a stunt on. Jerry must have been even more surprised than we were, for a large number surrendered; those we captured were fine-looking chaps. Their rifle pits were dug all along the edge of the wood, each man's kit being neatly laid on the parados and rifles, etc., all ready on the parapet. They left everything and gave themselves up, but those inside the wood put up a good fight and we had many casualties, but Jerry had more." In describing the events of the second day of the battle C.S.M. Lott goes on to say: "We were crowded in like sardines in an old shallow trench, not knowing the situation and being out of touch with B.H.Q. We were heavily shelled all day and also bombed by an aeroplane which flew over very low. No one had any rations as B.H.Q. had been unable to get them forward to us the night before, but it was hardly a time when one wanted much to eat. A good deal of sniping was going on all day. Cpl. Bunting, a wonderful chap at observation and intelligence work, spotted some Germans on the move and Lce.-Cpl. Joyce did good work with his Lewis gun and bagged a number of the enemy. At dusk we all thought we were 'for it,' for heavy artillery work was being done by both sides. Jerry was firing lights of all colours and we were prepared for a visit. Later on during the evening we retired by platoons to a prepared position just behind the wood. I shall never forget what happened when I was left behind with Lieut. Calvert in charge of the last platoon. We were being fired at by M.G.'s from our rear and Cpl. Brown and Rfn. Bowes had both been shot through the back, so imagine our feelings when through the darkness we could see a line of men advancing on us very stealthily from behind with fixed swords. I thought it was all up, but challenged, and the reply came, 'Who are you, old thing?' It was the relief and we were soon off to more comfortable quarters."

It will be seen from the foregoing accounts that although Hindenburg is silent on the subject that the Germans were in possession of Villers-Bretonneux for a few hours. This is confirmed by the dispatch (para. 66) from Sir Douglas Haig,

C.I.C., who thus describes the action : " On 23rd April a more serious attack, in which four German divisions were employed against the British forces alone, and German and British tanks came into conflict for the first time, took place on the Allied front between the Somme and the Avre Valleys. At about 6.30 a.m., after a heavy bombardment lasting about three hours, the enemy advanced to the assault on the whole British front south of the Somme, under cover of fog. In the ensuing struggle German tanks broke through our line south-east of Villers-Bretonneux and, turning to north and south, opened the way for their infantry. After heavy fighting, in which great losses were inflicted on his troops both by our infantry fire and by our light tanks, the enemy gained possession of Villers-Bretonneux ; but was held up on the edge of the wood just west of that place by a counter-attack by the 8th Division. South of Villers-Bretonneux, some of our heavy tanks came into action and drove back the German tanks, with the result that the enemy's infantry were stopped some distance to the east of Cachy Village which formed their objective. North of Villiers-Bretonneux all attacks were repulsed.

" At 10 p.m. on the night of 23rd/24th April, a counter-attack was launched by a brigade of the 18th Division and the 13th and 15th Brigades of the 4th and 5th of the Australian Divisions, Major-Gen. Sir J. J. T. Hobbs, K.C.B., commanding the latter division, and met with remarkable success. A night operation of this character, undertaken at such short notice, was an enterprise of great daring. The instant decision to seize the opportunity offered, and the rapid and thorough working out of the general plan and details of the attack on the part of the IIIrd Corps Commander and divisional and subordinate commanders concerned are most worthy of commendation, while the unusual nature of the operation called for the highest qualities on the part of the troops employed. It was carried out in the most spirited and gallant manner by all ranks. The 13th Australian Brigade, in particular, showed great skill and resolution in their attack, making their way through belts of wire running diagonally to the line of their advance, across very difficult country which they had no opportunity to reconnoitre beforehand.

" At daybreak Villers-Bretonneux was practically surrounded by our troops. During the morning two battalions of the 8th Division worked their way through the streets and houses, overcoming the resistance of such parties of the enemy as were still holding out. That afternoon Villers-Bretonneux was again completely in our possession. In this well-conceived and brilliantly executed operation, nearly 1,000 prisoners were captured by our troops. A German tank was left derelict in our lines and was salved subsequently."

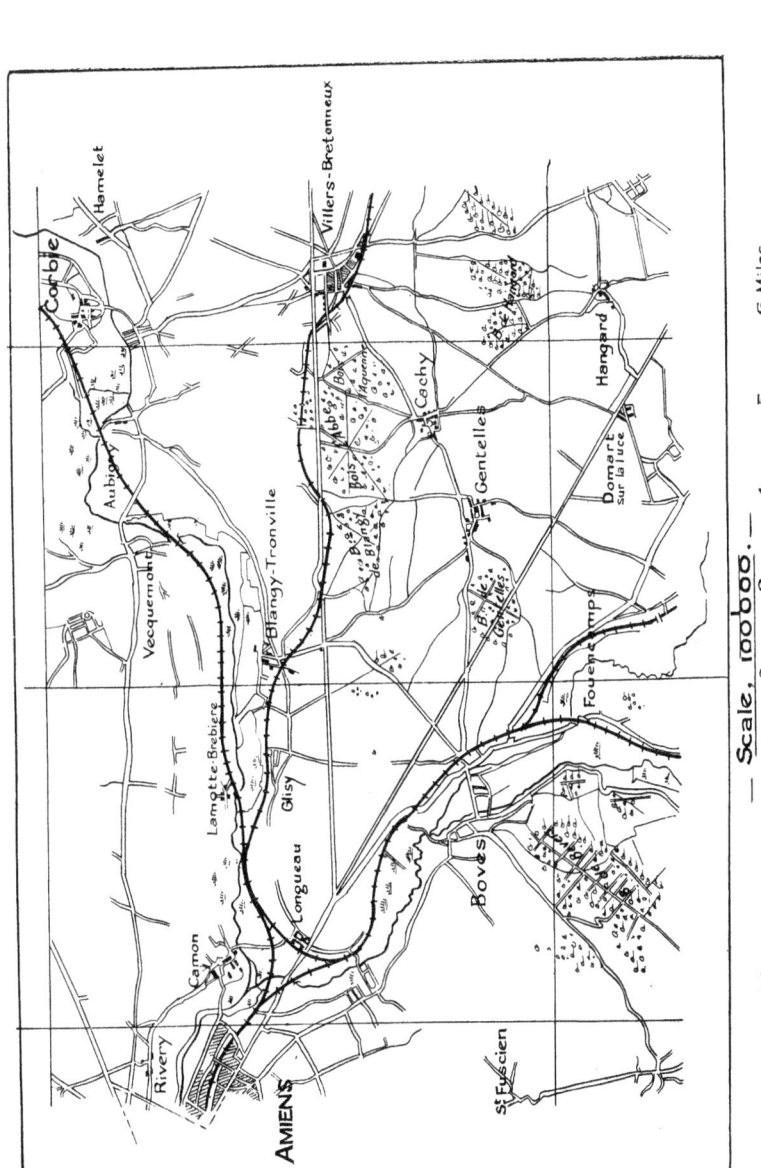

CHAPTER VI

OFFICIAL DISPATCHES AND COMPLIMENTS

IN connection with these operations the following Divisional Order was issued :

G.S. 1524/1.

With the exception of the few hours which it took to bring up the Division from the Oise to the Somme, the Division has been in the battle from its commencement till to-day. Notwithstanding this long period of strain and fighting, the Division has more than upheld its fine fighting reputation. On each occasion that it has been fighting alongside the French their Commanders have congratulated me on the fine fighting qualities they have observed in the Division.

The G.O.C. Fourth Army bade me convey his thanks and congratulations to all ranks for their share of the stout defence of Amiens.

During the five weeks' fighting, the Division has engaged no less than eleven different German Divisions, and it is with the greatest pride in the Division that I now take this opportunity of thanking and congratulating all ranks for all they have done for the Empire.

I fully realise the hardships, intense fatigue, discomforts and dangers the Division has been through, and it is splendid to think that, in spite of all, the stout hearts of the 58th have overcome all and fought with gallantry deserving of the highest praise. On no occasion has the enemy attacked this Division without suffering colossal losses, and it is these losses that are going to be his undoing.

It is now a question of how long he can stand going on losing men at the present rate. Our duty to our country is to go on giving him blow for blow. Already the Americans are coming in to swell our ranks, and the time will soon come when we shall crush our enemy.

During our period of rest I want to have no training in the afternoon ; but I wish every man to remember that he must do his utmost to train well in the morning. Training is practising to beat the enemy, and as such it is of the utmost importance ; so I know that all ranks of this Division will do their best.

The counter-attack at night on the front Villers-Bretonneux-Hangard Wood taught us the value of delivering a counter-attack at night before the enemy has had time to organise his defence ; so I intend to practise this after the men are rested. With this exception training will be confined to the morning only.

Once again I congratulate all ranks of the 58th for what they have done in this great battle.

A. CATOR,
Major-General,
Commanding 58th (London) Division.

28th April, 1918.

The following complimentary messages were also received :

G.S. 1324.

173rd Infantry Brigade (4).
174th Infantry Brigade (4).
175th Infantry Brigade (4).
C.R.A. (4).
C.R.E. (4).
58th Division. M.G.C. (1).
1/4th Suffolk Regiment (1).
A.D. . . .3 (1).
Signals (1).
" Q " (1).

Forwarded. The following message has also been received from the Army Commander :

" Please convey to the 2nd Battalion and 3rd Battalion London Regiment my warm thanks for the gallant way in which they held their portion of the front during a very difficult period, and to the 9th Battalion London Regiment for their determination and gallantry in the counter-attack of the 25th."

      (Sgd.) D. F ANDERSON,
       Major,
    General Staff, 58th (London) Division.

29th April, 1918.

          April 29th.

MY DEAR RICHARDSON,

  I must send you a line to thank you for the valuable aid given by the 9th and 10th Battalions of your Brigade to the 173rd during the recent fighting.

  The 10th Battalion were splendidly handled by Col. Symonds, whose loss we all greatly deplore, and after he became a casualty by Capt. Gould, who showed great skill and courage and materially helped to stem the enemy's advance.

  The 9th Battalion, called upon at very short notice to counter-attack, were also extremely well handled, and the success they gained on the south reflects the highest praise in their grit and determination to succeed against a particularly difficult objective. I am afraid their losses are heavy and all in the Brigade will regret this.

  Would you very kindly convey to both battalions the thanks of myself and my Brigade for the gallant aid and support, and also to the 12th Battalion who came up in support of my left flank and made it secure.

       Yours sincerely,

       (Sgd.) RIVERS WORGAN.

Officer Commanding,
  9th London Regiment (Q.V.R.).
  2/10th London Regiment (Q.V.R.).
  The Rangers, 12th London Regiment.

  The above letter from Brig.-Gen. Rivers Worgan, Commanding 173rd Infantry Brigade, is forwarded for information.

      (Sgd.) ?
        Captain,

1st May, 1918. Brigade Major, 175th Infantry Brigade.

Officer Commanding,
 9th (Res.) Battalion, the London Regiment.

The Brigadier-General Commanding, in sending out the following extract from a letter from the G.O.C., 58th Division in France, wishes me to convey his congratulations to all ranks of the 9th Battalion, and he hopes that the extract may be given all the publicity in the battalion that it so justly deserves.

" We had a good show on the 24th of April when the Hun got badly mauled and did no good. What delighted me that night was that the 9th Londons, who were full up of 18 and 19 year old lads, did a fine counter-attack through Hangard Wood, killed a great number of Huns and captured 4 officers and 80 O.R. They are most anxious to have another go."

(Sgd.) R. L. Pearson,
Major,
Brigade Major, 1st London Reserve Brigade.

Blackdown, 15th *May*, 1918.

The following honours were gained by the battalion in this battle of Hangard Wood :

Military Cross

Lieut. C. A. G. C. Keeson. For most conspicuous gallantry in Hangard Wood on April 24th. This officer led his company to their final objective with the greatest courage and dash. Although his left flank was exposed and the Germans were behind him he quickly grasped the situation, and taking command of all the troops in the area he consolidated and held his position. By reorganising the other companies which had been scattered in the wood, and by the decisive manner in which he handled his men, he was responsible for the capture of 50 Germans and some machine-guns. Throughout the operations he rendered clear and accurate reports of the situation which were of the greatest value.

French Croix de Guerre

2nd Lieut. H. V. Holloway. Under the most intense artillery fire he held and consolidated his position. By his personal courage and utter disregard of danger he successfully handled the many difficult situations with which he was confronted. Inspired by the fine offensive spirit of their officer his men inflicted many casualties on the Germans. Throughout the operations 2nd Lieut. Holloway showed himself to be a highly capable and imperturbable leader of men.

Distinguished Conduct Medal

Lce.-Cpl. Sydney Oscar Stroud, M.M. (This non-commissioned officer's fine exploit is fully recounted in the account of the battle.)

Military Medal

Sergt. George Lyons. Throughout the attack and subsequent consolidation he was indefatigable, and although exposed continuously to heavy artillery and machine-gun fire he was to be seen everywhere encouraging and leading his men. Under his fine leadership his men inflicted severe casualties on the enemy.

Rfn. Frank Finch. On the night of 24th/25th Rfn. Finch discovered a French horse ambulance without a driver in Domart. He drove three loads of English and French wounded to the Advanced Dressing Station, and also many more to the motor ambulances on the Domart-Longeau Road. During the whole time he was driving the Domart-Longeau Road was being heavily shelled. The evacuation of large numbers of French and English was due entirely to the very fine courage of Rfn. Finch. Rfn. Finch was instructed to carry out this work of evacuation by Battalion H.Q.

Cpl. Albert Irons. For great gallantry on April 24th, east of Gentelles Wood, and subsequently on April 25th in Hangard Wood. This N.C.O. connected up the line between Battn. H.Q. and the companies early in the morning of April 24th under very heavy artillery fire, and was largely responsible for the maintenance of communication between Battn. H.Q. and the companies. In view of the obscure situation this forward communication was of the greatest value. On the evening of April 24th in the attack on Hangard Wood he rushed an enemy machine-gun post and succeeded in capturing both the garrison and the gun. Later, on April 25th, when the situation was not clear, he succeeded in bringing reliable information to Battalion H.Q. although under heavy artillery and machine-gun fire.

Lce.-Cpl. Thomas Audrey Barnes. This N.C.O. displayed the greatest courage and fearlessness in leading his men in the attack on Hangard Wood. When the troops became scattered in the wood he rallied them and led them on. Throughout the operations his cheerfulness, combined with his offensive spirit, were a fine example to all around him.

Lce.-Cpl. Frederick Sherlock. After three successive platoon commanders had become casualties he took over command of his platoon. During the attack on Hangard Wood and the subsequent consolidation he handled his men with great courage and skill. By his personal disregard of the fire to which he was constantly exposed he encouraged all ranks near him.

Concerning the end of Capt. Hadden very little is known. Rfn. G. N. H. Stranger says: "We were in small groups as we came close to the edge of the wood, and for some reason we wavered for a moment before entering. The then commander of 'A' Company (Capt. Hadden) seeing the halt dashed forward and into the wood waving his stick, followed shortly by us. I certainly think he rallied us at a windy moment. I happened to be right behind him when he dashed forward, and he was never seen again from that time."

Capt. Archibald Robert Hadden was the elder and only surviving son of the late Rev. R. H. Hadden, Vicar of St. Mark's, North Audley Street, W. 1, Chaplain-in-Ordinary to Queen Victoria and Hon. Chaplain to King Edward, and of Mrs. Hadden, of Hazel Hatch, Addlestone, Surrey. He was born on October 22nd, 1889, and was educated at Westminster and Christ Church, Oxford. While an undergraduate he was gazetted to the Q.V.R. in February, 1909, and promoted Captain in September, 1914. He served on the staff of the 3rd London Infantry Brigade, under General Monck, from August, 1914, to January, 1917, when he went overseas to rejoin the Q.V.R. His death was officially assumed as having occurred on April 25th. He married, in 1915, Evelyn Forster, only daughter of the late Dr. Tunnicliffe, of North

Finchley, and of Mrs. Tunnicliffe, and left a son born in August, 1916.

Many a gallant man fell during the two days' fighting. " B " Company alone had 8 killed, 2 missing, 28 wounded and 1 gassed. Among them was our old friend, Rfn. Ernest Edgar Snoswell, from whose cheery letters we have made so many extracts. Prior to the war he was in the employ of Messrs. Hicks, Atkinson and Co., of London and Melbourne, and was an earnest Christian worker, first taking a class in the Trinity Congregational Church, then with the Webber Street Mission, Blackfriars, and afterwards at the Hope Mission in the same locality when the two were combined. Following this he took up the Superintendence of Cornwall Road Baptist Church Sunday School. Within a month of the outbreak of the war he had offered himself, but was turned down on account of an injury received in a bicycle accident. Feeling he must do something he joined the City of London Red Cross detachment and continued with it until March, 1915, when he determined to undergo an operation so as to fit himself for service and entered Guy's Hospital. On April 29th he joined the R.A.M.C. at Chelsea, and went to Roehampton Camp, where he was trained. While here a further operation was deemed necessary. On his recovery he applied to rejoin his old battalion, the Q.V.R., in which he had served five years before the war, leaving it in 1913, and in which his younger brother, Arthur, was already enrolled. Writing to the widow, 2nd Lieut. Norman C. Lockley, says : " On the afternoon of the 24th inst. our company was ordered to counter-attack the enemy, and while getting into position we came under heavy fire. With several casualties among us your husband was most gallantly performing his duty as stretcher bearer. He had just rushed from his shelter to attend to a wounded comrade when he was killed by a further shell. He had acted as my stretcher bearer through all the recent hard fighting and no one had worked harder, more bravely, or more cheerfully, and his death came as a sad shock to all of us." Cheery to the end he concludes his last letter home, written the day before he was killed : " I was feeling quite clean this morning, having had a wash and shave for the first time since last Thursday (five days) ! Two of us washed, shaved and cleaned our teeth in a quart of water! Not so bad that. We might do it every day, but water is precious, and if we wash in it, well, we can't drink it, can we ? We prefer to drink it, but seeing we may not be going out yet awhile we thought we had better get this coating of dirt off at least, and you can't realise how nice and clean it makes one feel. I might add we used a mess tin for washing in, the same one which I use for all my meals."

Rfn. F. A. Penberthy, one of the stretcher bearers on this occasion, says, " Lce.-Cpl. McTagart, ' A ' Company, 3 Platoon, was going over the top when, half-way to his objective he was hit by a bullet in the arm. I offered to bandage it up but he politely refused saying he was all right and telling me to go on. An hour or so previous we were in a sunken road and ' A ' Company were digging funk holes, when Jerry opened out a heavy barrage with 5·9's. Rfn. Langston, 3 Platoon, was wounded in the heel by a splinter. I helped him on the stretcher after bandaging his foot. He took out a fag and smoked, keeping a cheerful countenance. About the same time Rfn. Clark, No. 1 Platoon, was hit in the chest by a piece of shell and bled profusely. I held his hand and cheered him as best I could while a stretcher was being fetched, and then helped to carry him to the First Aid Post. He was delirious at intervals and died within a few hours. A stretcher bearer, well-known to us as ' Jumbo,' though I believe his proper name was Green, was hit while stooping down to attend to a wounded man. He was a most courageous fellow and was always on the spot when anyone was hit, putting hope into them and bucking them up by his smiles, tenderness and sympathy."

"Amongst the missing," writes C.S.M. Lott, " was Rfn. Halls, the most wonderful runner I have ever known. He seemed to be able to see in the dark and to find short cuts by instinct. He knew no fear, and the more work he had to do the better he seemed to like it." Lieut. Keeson, referring to his loss, states " He was a jolly good man."

CHAPTER VII

A LULL IN THE FIGHTING

THE relieving battalion was the 8th Queen's and the "more comfortable quarters"[1] proved to be a camp in a wood near Glisy. But here "Old Tim" had tea ready awaiting the men, and as the march had been a very tiring one it was more than welcome. On the morning of 26th Gen. Jackson paid the Q.V.R. a visit, and in the afternoon the battalion proceeded by route march to Pont de Metz. On the road they were met by Gen. Sir H. Rawlinson, Commanding Fourth Army, who shook hands with each Company Commander as he passed and called out to the men "You did well at Hangard. I expect you are glad to be out of it. You all look fit. Good-bye and good luck to you." It is hardly necessary to say that the men were delighted.

On this day Capt. F. H. Ralls, M.C., joined the battalion and took command of "D" Company. On 27th the march was continued to Riencourt, and on 28th to Ailly-le-Haut-Clocher for a welcome six days' rest. Of course there was the usual training to be done, but the men had plenty of time for rest and recreation. During this time Capt. Bowler rejoined and took over the command of "B" Company. On May 4th the officers indulged in a full mess dinner, the first of the kind for a very long time. Two days later the 58th Division moved into IIIrd Corps Reserve, the battalion leaving Ailly-le-Haut-Clocher in buses at 10 a.m. and "debussed" at Contay, marching thence to Bois Robert and remaining there in bivouacs for the night. Next morning the battalion was moved forward to the Baizieux defence system, "A" Company relieving a company of the Royal West Kents, "C" one of the 19th Londons and "B" and "D" going into hitherto unoccupied trenches. About a month was spent in the system, the battalion taking

[1] See p. 392

its turn in the front and support lines. C.Q.M.S. Taylor, writing on 18th, says, "I had just arrived at the support line when Fritz put up one of his 'windy' barrages just as a working party of fifty men had gone out and they got fairly caught in it with the result that we had nineteen casualties. Lce.-Cpl. Hull and Rfn. Ellis were killed and Sergt. Lyons and sixteen others wounded. I was fairly busy that night, but Sergt. Thomas, since awarded the D.C.M., worked like a Trojan. All these poor wounded chaps passed me in the trench and Sergt. Lyons said 'Hullo, Quartermaster, the blighters have got me again.' We had to send him away on a stretcher." For the next day the whole of the area held by the battalion was heavily shelled. On 20th 2nd Lieut. Dickins was wounded. The battalion remained in the system occupying various trenches until the last day of May when it was relieved by the 7th Queen's. Then followed four peaceful days under canvas in a little wood east of Bichancourt, the training including the digging of a cable trench to Warloy. On June 5th the brigade moved to another wood south-east of Molliens-au-Bois, and again went under canvas in the wood which was packed with troops owing to the Hun bombing. Three days were spent in company and specialist training including an inter-platoon firing competition, which was won by No. 11 Platoon, "C" Company, with 357 points. On Sunday 8th, there was a Church Parade followed by an armoured car demonstration. During the night a "Warning Order" was received for a move at 2.30 a.m. and for the 58th Division to be transferred from the IIIrd to the XXIInd Corps (Lieut.-Gen. Sir A. Godley). Accordingly the whole brigade marched to Villers-Bocage, where it "embussed" for Briquemesnil, marching thence to Bourgainville, where the men went into fairly comfortable rest billets vacated by the 37th Division. Here, says one of our friends, "the battalion had a very happy spell as they were able to get wine and champagne, the first time for weeks!" During the training which lasted up to 18th the battalion won the brigade Lewis gun competition.

On June 18th, the 58th Division rejoined the Third Army, moving by buses, via Amiens, to the old wood S.E. of Molliens and took over the camp from the 2nd Londons. Here a very peaceful time was spent in Divisional Reserve varied by the usual in and out of the line business, each battalion of the 175th Brigade taking its turn in the Lavieville line. On Monday, June 24th, the Q.V.R. relieved the 6th Londons in the front line, remaining in for five days. " This," says Lieut. Keeson, " was a fairly quiet sector except for ' D ' Company who were rather troubled by a Trench Mortar and sustained several casualties, some being killed. This part of ' D's ' sector was in a hollow and ran through an old casualty clearing station. From this Capt. P. Selwyn Clarke, R.A.M.C., rescued a lot of surgical equipment. There were rumours that there were the bodies of a number of the wounded who had been unable to get away when the Boches shelled it and even of nurses who shared their fate, but we did not see them. The place certainly did not smell very sweet."

Relieved on 28th by the Rangers (12th Londons), the Q.V.R. moved into close support behind Diamond trench, Darwin Reserve and Darling Reserve, where another quiet four days' spell was passed, the men being chiefly employed in improving the reserve trench system. The first portion of July proved equally quiet and was spent in the same sector and in much the same fashion as was the previous month. Lieut. Keeson, under date of July 4th, writes : " The Australian Battalion on our right raided the enemy position on their front at 3 a.m. We had a ' Chinese attack ' on our front, i.e. we bombarded the enemy position on our front with shells and gas projectors in order to distract the Boches' attention from the Anzacs. The Boches retaliated with a very stiff and prolonged bombardment causing 14 casualties, 4 killed and 10 wounded, of whom two at least afterwards died. ' B ' Company was the worst sufferer, Sergt. Wyatt being fatally hit. Also little Rfn. Petherick, one of the general favourites of the company. He was a typical little Cockney, always cheery ; one of No. 7 Platoon's Lewis gunners. He was in charge of a gun team at the time and was getting his gun ready, and cheering up the rest of the section when he was hit. He had both arms and legs broken. He was cheery up to the last and died the same evening in the Advanced Dressing Station at Montigny. Major Nichols (Adjutant) and I went down to the cemetery at Montigny, on Sunday 7th, where he was buried. The Pioneers had put up a beautiful cross."

On July 8th while in the support line on the Lavieville-Baizieux sector an order was received at 8.30 p.m. to "Man Battle Positions." All companies were reported in position by 11.25 p.m. This proved to be a "Test Order" and was carried out by the whole of the Fourth Army. No other notable incident occurred until July 17th, though the shelling during the whole period 12th–20th was reported to be above the normal. On 17th a company of Americans was attached to the Q.V.R. for instruction, one platoon to each company. Among them was an American dentist and many of the "Queen Vics" availed themselves of the opportunity to get their teeth set right. During one heavy bombardment one American who was asked to give his views on the subject said, "Guess I wish President Wilson was still writing notes."

On the day following the arrival of the Americans the battalion was again heavily shelled especially in the neighbourhood of H.Q. and a few casualties caused. Lce.-Cpl. Stiles and 2 O.R. were killed and one officer and one O.R. wounded. An American "litter bearer," as they call the stretcher bearers, was killed just outside the H.Q. dug-out. One shell burst right over the roof of this dug-out cutting the telephone wire, and Lce.-Cpl. Newman and Rfn. Borrie, both H.Q. linesmen, dashed up and after a while joined the two ends together again, only to find that they had joined one end to a coil of wire lying on the dug-out roof! On the next day a couple of bombs were dropped from an enemy aircraft and burst close to Battn. H.Q. The remainder of the month passed without anything worthy of comment occurring.

CHAPTER VIII

COMMENCEMENT OF THE ALLIED OFFENSIVE

WITH the coming of August, things began to liven up. There was a feeling in the air that something out of the ordinary course of events was about to happen. On 2nd there was great excitement, for the news came through that the Boches had retired. This to some extent proved to be correct. Patrols from the Rangers had penetrated into their old front line which was found vacant and in a disgusting state. Nevertheless it was at once occupied by the British. The Q.V.R. went on August 3rd to Vignacourt by bus, arriving at 7 a.m. on 4th. The same evening they were inspected by the Brigadier-General. It was understood that the battalion was now in for a long rest, but during their journey along the Amiens road en route to the "embussing" point, lorry after lorry, full of shells, and guns of all calibres, were observed moving to the front and doubts about the rest began to spread. When, on reaching the buses, it became known that the 2/10th had suddenly been ordered off somewhere the men knew the worst. On 4th they were told that there was to be a "push," but no one then realised that it was the beginning of the great Allied offensive which led to the final overthrow of the Hun. On August 6th the battalion moved by motor bus to Francvillers and marched to Bois Escardonneuse. The whole of 7th was spent in the wood, no one being allowed to show himself outside. Everybody was prepared for a scrap and all equipment overhauled and made good. In the evening the Germans put down a heavy barrage which led some to fear that the plan of attack had been discovered; they also made a raid on the battalion in front of the Q.V.R., but were counter-attacked and nothing further happened. At this time the battalion was in Corps Reserve.

On 8th the British attack at Amiens started. "On the strength of what I have heard," writes Q.M.S. Taylor, "I got up at 4 a.m. and at 4.30 to the tick witnessed the kick-off. It was wonderful to see the barrage that our guns put up and the host of observation balloons and aeroplanes in the early morning mist, a weird and wonderful morning." Lieut. Keeson in his account of the battle says: "We were just beginning to congratulate ourselves that we should not be wanted, when, together with the Rangers, we were ordered up to the Ballarat-Roma line, our old reserve line. We passed many German prisoners on the way up including a regimental commander. Our wounded told us things were going on well. We arrived at the line about 3.30 p.m., and we had not been there more than a few minutes before we were ordered up to Malard Wood and placed at the disposal of the 18th Division. We were told that Malard Wood was a good way behind our advancing troops. Hall and I and a couple of runners (Rowan and Seamen) were sent off in advance to find a position in the wood where the battalion could halt. When we got there we found the Boches were holding the east edge of the wood and that the 173rd Brigade were held up. We met the battalion, which was halted in a ravine just outside the wood. Gen. Cochran of the 173rd Brigade, under whose command we were now placed, then arrived and consulted with Col. Powell. The battalion was then ordered up to Malard Wood to support the 2/2nd London who were attacking. It was now seven o'clock. This attack failed and the C.O. appreciating the situation moved up 'B,' 'C,' and 'D' Companies to the east edge of the wood at the same time collecting remnants of other battalions. The order was 'B' on the left, 'C' centre, 'D' on the right, 'A' in reserve and forming a defensive flank. Battalion H.Q. was in a poky little Hun dug-out. Patrols were sent out and forward posts established. A battery of six German field guns which had been deserted, one officer and a few O.R. were captured during this operation.

"The morning of 9th was quiet and the posts were visited by the C.O. During the afternoon heavy shelling took place. At three o'clock orders were received to withdraw to the ravine west of the wood and to act as reserve to the Rangers, who were taking part in a general advance at 5.30.

Americans were on the right of the Rangers. I went on ahead with the C.O. and we had to run the gauntlet as the Huns were shelling the place like blazes. We got back safely, however, and while waiting for the battalion to come along the C.O. tried to snatch a few minutes' sleep as he had been on the go for hours. No sooner had he settled down than a message came along that he was to report at Brigade H.Q. to take command of 175th Brigade as the B.G.C. had been taken ill. I woke him up, gave him the order and we found the spot on the map. He was just starting along a path when a heavy shell dropped right in the middle of it. I suggested he should take an alternative path when ' plonk ' came another heavy into the middle of that. We could not help laughing and he walked off midway between the paths and arrived safely at Brigade H.Q. The battalion then came along and Capt. F. H. Ralls, M.C., assumed command, Major Lindsey-Renton, second in command, being on battle surplus. The attack proved successful, but owing to heavy casualties sustained by the Rangers and the Americans we were ordered to move forward at 8 p.m. ' C ' Company reinforced the Rangers on their objective, ' A ' formed a defensive flank facing S.E. and ' B ' and ' D ' were in support. Battalion H.Q. was in a ravine where the men soon got some shelters rigged up. We found all the Yanks' packs thrown down near us with no guard over them. I am afraid they lost a lot of their Gillette ration razors and macintoshes that night."

The Americans, who had been rushed up in motor buses, went straight into the attack without any preparation.

Early the next morning Lieut. Keeson was wounded by a machine-gun bullet passing through his side and back and was invalided home. Captain Bowler, M.C., however, takes up the story : " On the night of 9th/10th the Q.V.R. relieved the sadly reduced battalion of Rangers who, with a few Americans, were holding a line of posts which followed roughly the line Morlancourt-Etinhem Road, one mile S.E. of Morlancourt. The dispositions after relief were : ' C ' and ' D ' Companies in the front line, ' A ' in support and ' B ' in reserve. The battalion was ordered to attack the following morning, August 10th, the objective being the old Amiens Defence Line and representing an advance of 2,000 yards. ' C ' Company (Capt.

Samuelson) led the attack and got into the Bois de Tailes, but was held up by the hostile resistance encountered. The eastern face of the wood was commanded by the enemy and every effort to get forward was stopped immediately by concentrated machine-gun and trench mortar fire. 'B' Company (Capt. Bowler) was ordered to reinforce 'C' Company and push on with the advance. It accordingly deployed from the Bray-Corbie Road and advancing in extended order was soon through the wood. The hostile artillery fire was particularly heavy at this time and a number of casualties was sustained. Having absorbed 'C' Company, 'B' was reorganised under cover of the wood, objectives were allotted to each platoon and the attack was recommenced. The platoons went away in fine style and within an hour had captured the whole of the Amiens Defence System on a frontage of 1500 yards. A battery of field guns, a number of machine-guns and much artillery equipment and ammunition were included in the booty taken in the attack, which was carried out without a barrage or the assistance of tanks and in broad daylight. Our casualties were 3 officers and about 60 O.R."

It was found that a gap of approximately 800 yards existed between the Q.V.R. and the next battalion on their left and during the night this was filled by the Royal Berks (12th Division). August 11th proved fairly quiet though there was some indiscriminate shelling and machine-gun fire. Snipers, too, were active and towards the evening the area was bombarded with gas shells. During the night the Q.V.R. right post was taken over by the 12th Battalion, who came in between it and the Americans. Standing patrols were maintained throughout the night with the battalions on either flank. On 12th the 58th Division was relieved by the 47th (London) Division, the 22nd London Regiment taking over the positions held by the Q.V.R. who moved to the Bois Escardonneuse. The following four days were spent in cleaning up, and on 17th Field-Marshal Sir Douglas Haig, Commander-in-Chief, came over and inspected the 175th Brigade. The Q.V.R. were instructed to carry out a practice attack for him to watch. The Field-Marshal expressed his satisfaction at what he saw and especially with the handling by subordinate commanders of the units under their control. He laid great stress on the

MAP No. 17.

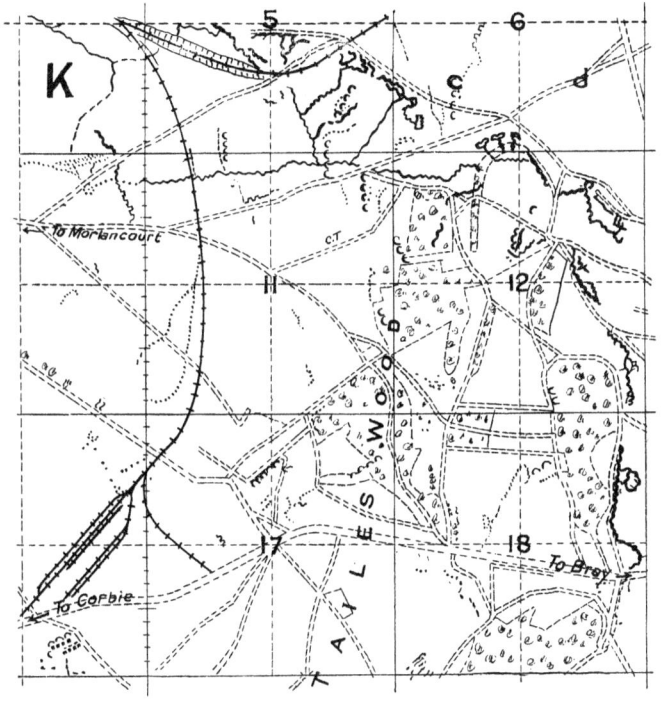

TAILES WOOD. AUG^T 10TH 1918.

importance of platoon commanders, saying : " I always said before the war that it was most important to keep good platoon commanders. It is platoon commanders who are winning this war." In the course of conversation, says Major Lindsey-Renton, then in command of the Q.V.R., " he laid special stress on the following principles : Always throw reinforcements and reserves into places where progress is being made and not into places where you are held up. The further you progress where you are successful the more difficult it will be for the enemy to hold out in other places."

In the course of a general order issued on August 16th Gen. Sir H. Rawlinson, Commanding Fourth Army, says : " The assault was launched on the morning of 8th with commendable vigour, and, after heavy fighting, the first objective and portions of the second objective were won. During 9th and 10th fighting continued until, in spite of vigorous opposition, the front was finally established on the line of the old Amiens defences. The 12th, 18th and 58th Divisions, which were all heavily engaged, succeeded in winning the several objectives allotted to them, and I desire to convey to them my warm thanks for their gallantry and determination during a period of no little difficulty. The progress made on the flanks by the 58th and 12th Divisions in face of determined opposition reflects high credit on the leadership and drive of these two divisions, for the enemy met them with vigorous counter-attacks on several occasions, and, in the case of the 58th Division, succeeded in temporarily regaining possession of the Chipilly spur."

CHAPTER IX

THE HAPPY VALLEY—AUGUST 22ND/31ST

DURING a period of ten days spent in the Bois Escardonneuse a platoon of " D " Company, under Lieut. Powell, gave a musketry demonstration with tracer bullets with special reference to the fire power of a platoon where fire control and fire discipline is good. The demonstration went off very well and was highly interesting. While the battalion was resting the 58th Division had carried out an attack on the Happy Valley which was successful at first, but a counter-attack drove the assaulting troops back to a line west of the Meaulte-Bray Road. It was on August 22nd that the battalion quitted Escardonneuse Wood. The day previous a warning order was received that it would move at one hour's notice from " 19 hours " (seven o'clock). At 4.45 the brigade marched via Bonnay, Mericourt and Treux into the old front line trenches. Shortly after occupying them a message arrived announcing that a strong enemy counter-attack was being made on the 47th Division and that the 175th Brigade was to stand to. At 10 p.m. it was ordered to proceed at once to the old Amiens Defence Line, east of Tailes Wood. At 2.30 on the morning of August 23rd the movement was completed, " D " being the left forward company and " B " right forward company, with " A " in support and " C " in reserve. The company commanders were : " A," Capt. Mayer ; " B," Capt. Bowler ; " C," Lieut. Hodgson, and " D," Lieut. McAdam.

It is interesting to note that at this period the three battalions forming the 175th Infantry Brigade were all commanded by officers of the Q.V.R., the 10th being under Major J. Nichols, M.C., in the absence of Lieut.-Col. Cawston, himself an old " Queen Vic.," the 12th under Major S. J. M. Sampson, M.C., and the 9th under Major R. H. Lindsey-Renton.

At 10.30 a.m. all battalion commanders were summoned to attend a conference at Brigade H.Q., when orders were given for the attack to be resumed at 1 a.m. on 24th. The brigade objective was approximately a line 200 yards east of the Bray-Fricourt Road. The attack was to be carried out by the Q.V.R. on the left and the Rangers on the right with the 10th in reserve. Troops of the 47th Division were attacking on the left, and the attack would bring the line up to that held by the Australians, whose left flank was in the neighbourhood of a chalk quarry (in L.3.d.). " The main difficulty of the attack," says Major Lindsey-Renton, " was Happy Valley—a deep valley about 100 to 300 yards wide with steep banks on the west and east sides. This valley was known to be full of dugouts where the enemy could take refuge from our barrage. The success of the enemy's counter-attack at the previous attempt was reported to have been due to a number of the enemy emerging from these dug-outs and so getting the attacking troops from behind. To deal with this one company of the 2/10th was ordered to be attached to each of the assaulting battalions for ' mopping-up ' purposes. In addition the Civil Service Rifles (15th London) of the 47th Division were detailed to follow in rear of the brigade to mop up the valley from north to south. During the afternoon of 23rd officers went out to reconnoitre the area for assembly which was to be just behind the front line as then held ; the reconnaissance, however, showed that the line was from 100 to 200 yards further west. About 11.30 p.m. the battalion moved up to the assembly area. Owing to the brightness of the moon I feared that the enemy would see the troops assembling for the attack and cause considerable trouble and many casualties. As a matter of fact the enemy's machine-guns were very active, especially on the left in front of ' A ' Company, who had some difficulty in getting into position, and it is probable that he did see movement even if he did not put it down to an impending attack.

"At 1 a.m. on 24th the barrage came down and the attack started. The Q.V.R. attacked in the following formation : ' A ' Company (left) and ' D ' Company (right) in the first wave to take the actual objective laid down for the battalion ; ' B ' Company (left) and ' C ' Company (right) in the second wave, having as their task the digging of a support line on the reverse side of the high ground running through F.27 central. One platoon from each of these companies was attached to the leading wave to deal with any immediate mopping up required until the arrival of the companies from the 10th when they were to rejoin their companies. The companies from the 10th attached to the battalion followed in rear of the second wave. Considerable opposition was met with in the Happy Valley and some stiff fighting took place. ' A ' Company in trying, apparently, to keep touch with the 47th Division who had edged off to the left a considerable distance, left a gap between their right and the left of ' D ' Company and when ' B ' Company came up in the second wave several machine-guns were giving trouble. These were rushed and their crews killed. Capt. Bowler did considerable execution in the fighting, as did Sergts. Ridgeley, Keats and Dunn. On the right ' D ' Company had a similar experience, and 2nd Lieut. Powell caused the enemy many casualties. After the Valley had been captured the mopping-up was carried on under difficulties owing to the night being much darker and the dug-outs difficult to find. I did hear later that 100 prisoners were captured here more than twenty-four hours afterwards, though there were a large number of troops moving through the Valley throughout the 24th.

"The situation when the battalion started consolidating was as follows : ' A ' Company, as mentioned, had gone off to the left ; ' B ' Company, being unable to find either ' A ' Company or the 47th Division, who were still some distance to the left of ' A ' Company, had two platoons in an old trench (which ran through F.27.a. and b.) forming a defensive flank facing north. The remainder of this company dug in (in F.27.a.) in touch with ' C ' Company on their right ; a large gap existed between ' C ' and the 12th. ' D ' Company had reached the road running N. and S. through F.27.b. and d. and were not in touch on either flank. The enemy still had some men in the trench, and 2nd Lieut. Powell captured a machine-gun and its crew of six.

"At dawn Battn. H.Q. as well as those of the 10th and 12th moved forward to the Forked Tree (L.2.b.05.95) in accordance with Brigade Orders. In the early hours of the morning difficulty was experienced in organising the position satisfactorily, as on both flanks troops began to move back, finding themselves isolated and close to enemy machine-guns and snipers who were very active throughout the day, and who, owing to the open nature of the country and the close range, made all movement dangerous and caused some casualties. This movement fortunately was soon stopped and later in the morning the situation became as follows : The battalion of the 47th Division on the left in response to Capt. Mayer's request moved down to the right ; 'A' Company was thus enabled to move to the right also though it was still mostly in the 47th Divisional area. Posts were pushed out between 'A' and 'B' Companies to connect up. One company from the 10th came forward to the road and filled up the gap between 'D' Company—who were in the position where 'A' should have been—and the 12th. This line was held for the rest of the 24th and would—but for subsequent events—have been adjusted in accordance with the orignal plan under cover of darkness.

"During the early hours of the morning Battn. H.Q. was subjected to a heavy and sustained fire from 5.9 and 8-in. howitzers. The position being near the junction of three sunken roads and a railway was an obvious mark and was in addition under observation from the high ground in the direction of Trigger Wood and Ceylon Wood to the east. It would have been impossible, there being little or no cover, to remain there without incurring heavy casualties, and Battn. H.Q. together with those of the 10th and 12th moved forward to the east bank of the Happy Valley. This place was also under continual shell-fire throughout the day, but some protection was afforded by the bank. At about 1.40 p.m. on 24th orders were received that the attack would be resumed at 4 p.m. the same day. These orders had been considerably delayed in reaching Battn. H.Q. A conference was held with company commanders at 'B' Company's H.Q., and orders were hurriedly issued. In view of the fact that the assembly had to take place in the open and under continual sniping and machine-gun fire it was impossible to form up in a really suitable formation. Great difficulty was in fact experienced in assembling.

"As no barrage came down at 4 p.m., as arranged, I inquired of Major Sampson, commanding the 12th, whether he knew what was the matter, and was informed that the attack had been postponed. The official order for the postponement only reached Battn. H.Q. at 5.15 p.m.

"On August 24th Capt. Ralls was acting as Second-in-Command to me. He should normally have gone on 'Battle Surplus,' but orders had been received that he should stay with the battalion. When the order for resuming the attack was received I asked Capt. Ralls to come up with me to assist me in getting ready for the attack. We left Battn. H.Q. in the Happy Valley and proceeded towards the front line, talking over plans for the attack as we went. Just as we were approaching the road on which the front line was I heard the report of a rifle. Capt. Ralls gave a sigh and sank to the ground. He did not die at once though unconscious. I got hold of two stretcher bearers to look after him as I had still to issue the orders for the expected attack. He died shortly afterwards. Thus died one of the most gallant officers in the battalion, one who had been with us from the start and had risen from being a rifleman to commanding tha battalion in action. Ralls commanded the battalion on August 10th and got a bar to his M.C. for his splendid work on that occasion.

"The postponed attack was ordered for 2.30 a.m. on the morning of 25th. The objective of the attack was to pass over the Gulley east of Happy Valley and capture Bronfay Farm and the trenches east of it. The assault was made by all three battalions of the 175th Brigade, the Q.V.R. on the left, 10th in the centre and Rangers on the right. The Civil Service Rifles (15th London) of the 47th Division were attacking on the left and the Australians on the right. The objective allotted to the Q.V.R. was the line between Billon Copse and Bronfay Wood. The battalion assembled for the attack on both sides of the road running N. and S. through F.27.7. and d. The assembly was carried out undisturbed and at 2.30 the barrage came down and the attack commenced. The battalion attacked in the following formation : 'B' left, 'C' right in the front line, 'D' and 'A,' the latter under the command of 2nd Lieut. Powell, in succession to Capt. Mayer who had been wounded on the morning of 24th, in support.

"Very little opposition was met with from the enemy, but some difficulty was encountered at the outset in getting to the objective owing the the Gulley east of Happy Valley having very high and steep banks with several turns in it which tended to throw the troops off their direction, and also to a thick mist that made it impossible to see more than a few yards. At first units got mixed up and were ignorant as to where they were and as to the position of the troops on their flanks. In a short time, however, they were organised and pushed forward to the objective, which was occupied along the whole brigade front. The 173rd Brigade which had been following up closely now pushed through and carried on with the attack. In the afternoon orders were received that the battalion would be relieved that night by the Post Office Rifles of the 174th Brigade and would go into bivouacs. The night was extremely dark and rain fell heavily throughout the night so that the battalion did not get back until well into the early hours of 26th. The casualties in this attack amounted to 3 officers and 70 O.R.

"The battalion rested until the afternoon of 27th when orders were received for it to go forward and occupy the trenches between Billon Wood and Contour Wood. Here they remained until the evening."

The last days of the month were passed in continual movements from one position to another. On 28th the Q.V.R. relieved the 2/3rd Londons in newly captured positions in Support Copse. On 29th it was apparent that the enemy had gone back, and patrols sent out failed to locate him at all. Another move was thereupon made in the direction of Maurepas. On 30th orders were received for the battalion to hold itself in readiness for an advance guard action in conjunction with the 1/4th Suffolks, 2/10th Londons and the Rangers. The two first named succeeded in establishing themselves on their objectives, but the 9th and 10th, who were to pass through them and mop up Marrieres Wood, found it impossible to do so on account of machine-gun fire from the west end of the wood. Careful reconnaissance was made and the enemy appeared to be holding the wood in some strength. On 31st the 174th Brigade passed through the 175th, capturing Marrieres Wood and the high ground beyond, and the Q.V.R. proceeded to the S.E. corner of Maricourt, where guides conducted them to bivouacs in a valley near Fargny Wood (A.28.b.A.29.a.).

On August 25th the following congratulatory messages were published for circulation among the units of the 175th Brigade :

24/8/18.

(a) From Gen. Rawlinson, Commanding Fourth Army :

Last night's operations appear to have been wholly successful on the right where the 47th Division gained all objectives. Please convey to that Division my best thanks and hearty congratulations on their success. I hope they will hold on firmly to the positions they have won so gallantly.

(b) From Gen. Godley, Commanding IIIrd Corps :

The Corps Commander has much pleasure in forwarding the above message, and wishes to congratulate you and all ranks of your Division on their successful night attack and good bag of prisoners.

175th Infantry Brigade.

The Divisional Commander particularly wishes to thank all ranks of your Brigade for the invaluable assistance given by them in to-day's operations.

(Sgd.) G. T. TURNER, Captain,
For Lieut.-Col. G.S., 47th London Division.

24/8/18.

9th London Regiment (Q.V.R.).
2/10th London Regiment.
The Rangers, 12th London Regiment.
175th L.T.M.B.
" C " Company, 58th Battalion M.G.C.

The Brigade Commander has great pleasure in forwarding the foregoing appreciations of the work of the Brigade during the present operations. He wishes them communicated to all ranks.

Captain,
A/Brigade Major, 175th Infantry Brigade.

25/8/18.

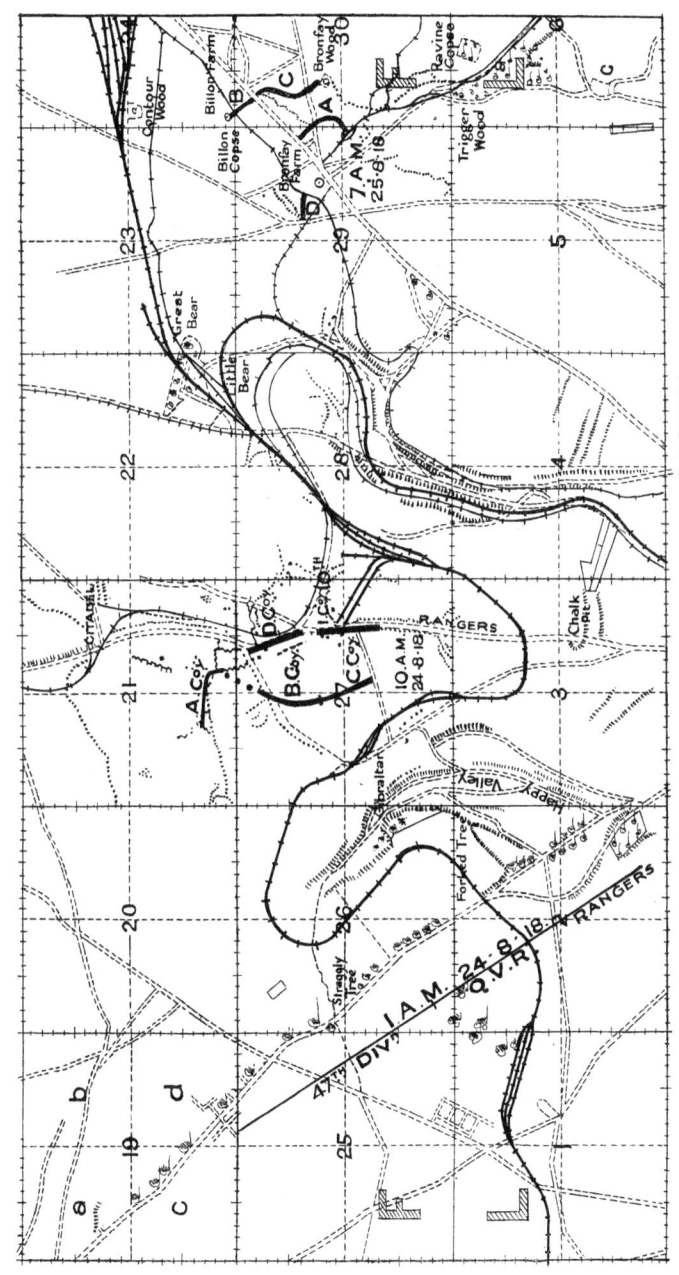

HAPPY VALLEY AUG: 24-25 1918.

In connection with these operations the following honours were awarded :

MILITARY CROSS

Lieut. A. E. Mills. When it was believed that the enemy were retiring he went forward in charge of patrols, and, in spite of strong resistance, overcame all opposition. During the advance he kept Battalion Head-quarters informed, and it was largely through his courage that the enemy rearguards were driven in.

Lieut. (A/Capt.) W. E. Bowler, 17th Battalion, attached 9th Battalion London Regiment. In two successive attacks this officer led his company across very difficult ground to the final objective on both occasions. He was indefatigable, accounting for 23 of the enemy, helping to restore the line, and consolidating after both attacks. After being wounded in the hand the morning of the second attack, he carried on, setting a fine example of endurance.

Capt. P. S. Clarke, R.A.M.C. After an unsuccessful attack he went out into No Man's Land and attended to many wounded, being exposed to heavy shell and machine-gun fire the whole time. His courage and coolness were a fine example to the stretcher bearers working under him and encouraged them in their difficult and dangerous task.

2nd Lieut. P. W. Powell, D.C.M. In two successive attacks this officer led his platoon across very difficult ground, gained his objectives and consolidated. The first morning he killed 2 of a machine-gun crew and compelled 6 more to surrender. Later he went out and wounded two snipers while a third ran away. The next morning, going ahead of his platoon, he met 6 of the enemy and accounted for 4 with his revolver. His personal courage had a wonderful effect on his men.

CHAPTER X

Epehy and Kildare Post

September 1-25

ON August 30th Lieut-Col. Powell had arrived and once more took over the command of the battalion, which remained at Fargny resting and training until September 6th. During this period Lieut. Gen. Godley, Commanding IIIrd Corps, paid a visit to the H.Q. of the 175th Brigade and congratulated Battalion Commanders on the splendid work done by their officers and men. On September 5th Col. Powell met with an accident owing to a bridge over a branch of the Somme giving way under his horse, and had to go to hospital. During his absence the command of the battalion again devolved upon Major Lindsey-Renton.

B.Q.M. Sergt. Mark Brawn, one of the most popular non-commissioned officers that ever served in the Queen Victorias, was killed September 1st, 1918. He was serving at the time as lieutenant and quartermaster of the 4th Battalion of the Bedfordshire Regiment which was attached to the 63rd Royal Naval Division. Lieut. F. Hawkings, an old Victoria himself, but then holding a commission in the "Ansons," happened to be present at the time. He says: "It was about two miles north of the village of Henin, behind the Queant-Drocourt Switch line. At about 10.0 p.m. a few low-flying Boche planes came over dropping groups of half a dozen spring bombs. One of these caught the Bedfords' transport lines, killing or maiming sixty horses, and also killing a N.C.O., 4 men and poor old Mark. His old comrades who always remember him as one of the best, will be glad to know that his death was instantaneous. It was rather a coincidence that I should have been the only old Q.V.R. present. I halted by the transport lines and there met him. I had just left him when the bombs fell."

On September 6th the 175th Brigade received orders to take over the line from the 140th Brigade (47th Division). Officers were sent forward to reconnoitre the new area and about 5 p.m. the Q.V.R. " embussed " and proceeded via Bouchavesnes and Moislains to the Nurlu-Peronne Road. This was unusually far for buses to go. The battalion relieved four companies of the 15th and one of the 21st Londons in the line, relief complete being announced at 1 a.m. The 2/10th London Regiment was on the left and the 74th Division (dismounted yeomanry) on the right. They had recently come from Palestine. "On arrival at Brigade H.Q.," says Major Lindsey-Renton, " I learned that the brigade was to carry out an attack on the following morning by the 10th on the left and the Q.V.R. on the right, with the 12th in support. The objective for the battalion was the high ground just east of St. Emilie, an advance of 7,000 yards. A section of 18-pounders, a machine-gun section and two Stokes' trench mortars were attached to the battalion. The attack, which was carried out without an artillery barrage, started at 8 a.m. on 7th, the Q.V.R. advancing a quarter of an hour earlier in order to get level with the general line of troops on either flank. The formation of attack was as follows : ' A ' Company (Lieut. Crosbie) on the left, ' B ' Company (Lieut. Hodgson) centre, ' C ' Company (Capt. Samuelson) on the right and ' D ' Company (Lieut. Lockley) in reserve. Each of the front-line companies had two platoons in the first wave and two platoons in the second. ' D ' Company attacked with its four platoons in line."

Little opposition was met with until the leading lines approached Saulcourt Wood (E.15), where they were held up for some time by heavy M.G. fire from the direction of the wood and also from Grebaucourt Wood (E.21). The right of " C " Company, with the 74th Division on their right, soon cleared the last-named wood, but their left as well as " A " Company and the 10th Battalion on the left were still held up by the fire from Saulcourt Wood. At the same time the enemy's artillery, which up to this had been quiet, became very active and shelled all round the area where the battalion was, special attention being paid to the line of the wood and Grebaucourt Wood as soon as " C " Company had entered it. A couple of

18-pounders were turned on to the suspected M.G. area and were shortly assisted by further guns from Brigade H.Q. " A " Company then attacked the southern portion of Saulcourt Wood and began to push through it and " B " Company to push down the valley between the two woods the right flank maintaining touch with " C " Company and the 74th Division who were pushing forward towards Villers Faucon (E.22 and 23). Two platoons of " D " Company were instructed to clear the southern portion of the wood and to mop-up behind " A " Company. Seven prisoners were captured here. The advance continued without serious opposition until Jean Copse (E.16) was reached, when more machine-gun fire came from the direction of the spur running S. from Capron Copse (E.17. a. and b.). The spur was attacked and the enemy withdrew, but as soon as the line reached the crest of the spur it came once more under heavy M.G. fire from the direction of Epehy (F.1) and also heavy artillery fire. The three leading companies then advanced rapidly down the slope under heavy enfilade fire until they reached the railway embankment (E.18.c.), where they were under cover.

The situation about noon was as follows : On the left the 12th Division had been held up for some distance west of Epehy and in rear of the 10th Londons. As Epehy was still held by the enemy the 10th were unable, despite several attempts, to advance further than Capron Copse, from 800 to 1,000 yards in rear of the Q.V.R., while the latter in their advance towards the railway embankment had closed considerably to the right, leaving a large part of the battalion front uncovered. On the right " C " Company were in touch with the 74th Division, who were pushing patrols through St. Emilie. A patrol from the Q.V.R. had established itself at the station (E.18.d.). " D " Company were therefore sent forward to the Capron Copse line to act as a defensive flank. " A " Company were ordered to send out posts to link up with " D " across the valley, while " A " and " B " were ordered to feel to their left. No further advance could be made to the objective during the day owing to the situation on the left.

Late in the afternoon verbal instructions were received that the 58th Division were very anxious that the battalion should push forward during the night and occupy the trench system

N. and E. of St. Emilie. "A," "B" and "C" Companies, under Capt. Samuelson, pushed forward at dusk by a series of strong patrols and after overcoming opposition occupied the line of trench running S.E. from the railway (E.18.b. to road F.19.b.). By dawn on 8th all companies were in position, though very scattered owing to their numbers and the distance to be occupied. The right of "C" Company were in touch with the 74th Division, who were, however, some distance behind. It subsequently transpired that on the morning of 8th the Q.V.R. were the most easterly of all British troops in France. The total advance for the day was 7,400 yards; casualties: 3 officers, 116 O.R. During the night orders were received from the brigade that the 74th Division were taking over a bigger front and would be pushing through the Q.V.R., who would be withdrawn from the line and go back to Guyencourt (E.2.d.).

In the morning a battalion of the 74th Division started to attack through the Q.V.R., but were held up before reaching them. The Q.V.R. were therefore unable to withdraw, but in the course of the day the relieving battalion gradually closed up and took over that position of the line not held by the Q.V.R. In the afternoon the order came through to withdraw to trenches and huts on the outskirts of Guyencourt. All companies reported in by 1 a.m. After a rest lasting three days the battalion was back in the line again, but the tour of duty in the sector was fairly quiet on the battalion front and proved quite a rest for the men after their recent experience of fighting and advancing. On the morning of September 12th the enemy put down a heavy barrage on the brigade front, especially on the portion held by the 12th Londons and shortly afterwards raided Tottenham Post and killed or captured most of the garrison. Immediately following the raid about fifty of the enemy were seen in Wood Farm, just S. of Tottenham Post, and the artillery was put on to them. One hundred rounds rapid fire from a battery was put on to the spot and no more was seen of the Hun. Lieut. Adamson and four O.R. were killed on this day by a shell. Nothing more of interest occurred until Sunday, September 15th, when the 174th Brigade relieved the 175th, the position held by the Q.V.R. being taken over by the Post Office Rifles.

On September 12th the following general order was circulated :

"To all ranks of the IIIrd Corps.

"On leaving the IIIrd Corps, which I have had the honour to command temporarily, I wish to place on record my deep appreciation and admiration of the valour and endurance displayed by the troops during their recent victorious advance.

"Since 11th August, when I took over command, the divisions of the Corps have advanced some twenty-two miles on a frontage of four and a half miles, taken some 28 towns and villages, captured 7,300 prisoners (including 146 officers) and secured some 42 guns, besides innumerable machine-guns, trench mortars and stores of all description.

"During this time eighteen German divisions have been encountered, seventeen of which have had to be withdrawn broken from the line. All arms have contributed to this success. While the Infantry have pushed on with unflagging vigour, allowing the enemy neither rest nor respite from attack, their repeated assaults have been ably covered by the machine-gun corps and by the field and heavy artillery, whose sustained fire has played no small part in overcoming the hostile resistance.

"The mounted troops and cyclists of the IIIrd Corps and XXIInd Corps have rendered conspicuous service in patrolling, reconnaissance and liaison work.

"The 12th, 18th, 47th and 58th Divisions have been engaged in hard fighting continuously for over a month, nevertheless their dash is undiminished, and their zeal in attack and skill in manœuvre have forced the enemy to retire hurriedly, abandoning in succession a series of strong positions, many of which were protected by formidable wire entanglements.

"The 74th Division, which has recently joined the Corps, has already given proof of its prowess in several hard fights.

"For the results achieved, my warmest thanks are due to the commanders and all ranks of the Divisions, heavy artillery and all Corps troops. I also wish to thank the signal service, engineers and tunnellers, medical and all administrative services for their continuous labours, which have rendered an

STE. EMILIE AND EPEHY SEPT 7TH, 8TH 1918.

advance of this nature and speed possible, and contributed so materially to the successful result.

(Sgd.) ALEX J. GODLEY,
Lieutenant-General,
Commanding IIIrd Corps.

September 12th, 1918."

Writing on September 18th, Lieut. A. N. Philbrick (transport officer) says : " Yes, the battalion has had a pretty sticky time, and there are many good fellows gone, though, all considered, our luck as regards officers' casualties holds good. The battalion has gone up this morning, having been out only two days. They are in reserve for a stunt once more which means they'll drop into it once again, I suppose. I wish to God we could get out for a decent spell. The men are wonderful, but they're very, very tired. Personally I have had a comparatively slack time this last week, but previous to that I was working more or less at top pressure. I had 14 horses and 3 mules put out by an instantaneous fuse 5·9 when my lines were in the wood on August 10th. Another donkey lost a chunk of himself the other night, but he's doing well."

Two days later the 175th Brigade relieved the 173rd in the line in Poplar Trench (X.26) and Fir Support. On the same night orders were issued that the 10th and 12th Londons were to attack Kildare Post and trenches. In order to enable them to pass quickly over their trenches the Q.V.R. received orders to bridge them, and this was done by raising duck-boards from the floor of the trench which had been the British front line at some time before the German advance. At 5 a.m. on 21st the 2/10th and 12th advanced under an artillery barrage, passing through the Q.V.R., but owing to heavy casualties from machine-gun fire from both Kildare Post (X.28.b.) and Limerick Post (X.21.d.) they were forced back almost to the original line and ended up in Kildare Avenue.

The Q.V.R. passed the night of 21st in Poplar Trench. About 7.30 next morning orders were received that the battalion must prepare to renew the attack on the order to move. A little later the Brigadier-General Commanding 175th Brigade called at Battn. H.Q. and said that the Division wanted the attack to be carried out that day as soon as an attack which was taking place on Limerick Post had succeeded, but should that not come off the battalion would have to attack at night. Major Lindsey-Renton, O.C., pointed out that it was known that there were machine-guns in Kildare Post and that the enemy were still in possession of the high ground to the north and that an attack by daylight would be in grave danger of failing, and asked that it might be carried out by night. The General agreed, but said that orders from higher authorities were urgent. Major Lindsey-Renton, however, pressed his point and eventually, after a conference at Brigade H.Q., he was informed that permission had been obtained to carry out the attack in the night. The Division on the left of the Q.V.R. were to attack Limerick Post from W. to N., and at the same time the Q.V.R. were to attack Kildare Post from the W., while a company of the 1/4th Suffolk (pioneers), who were to be attached to the battalion, would assemble in the neighbourhood of Catelet Copse (X.28.d.), which was in British hands, and attack from the S. A lifting barrage of twenty to thirty minutes was also arranged for. During the afternoon information was received that a company of the Division on the left had attacked Limerick Post and had been driven back, and also that the head of the battalion in Kildare Avenue had withdrawn some distance down that trench. It was further reported that the Germans had placed machine-guns in front of Limerick Post and, it was believed, also in front of Kildare Post. Accordingly the barrage arrangements were altered to suit the new conditions. The battalion attacked at 9.30 p.m. on a front of 700 yards, and by keeping well up to the barrage succeeded in taking all its objectives after some stiff fighting in the trenches. Several machine-guns and a Lewis gun were found in the Post. Some of the enemy in their flight fell in with the Suffolks who took seven prisoners, including one officer. The casualties among the commissioned ranks were particularly severe. Lieut. Sedgeley and 2nd Lieuts. Hunt and Sanctuary were killed, 2nd Lieut. Lacey died of wounds, and 2nd Lieut. Redman was wounded.

Rfn. C. Smith gives the following account of the adventures of his company (" A "). " We filed out from Poplar Trench just after nine o'clock on Sunday night, wet and cold and laden with bombs and Lewis gun panniers, Lieut. Crosbie in command.

We took up our position amid a good deal of grousing, and then patiently waited for 9.30, at which time the barrage opened and we were off, making for Kildare Post, 'A' and 'B' Companies taking the first wave. By this time German shells were dropping unpleasantly near and things began to get very lively. We had gone some distance, obviously a little too quick, for we ran into our own barrage and unfortunately had several casualties. The order was then given to lie down, which we did, taking advantage of any cover we could find, for the air was simply singing with shrapnel, and every now and then came a burst of machine-gun fire. As we got nearer the German position there was a good deal of shouting, and it was evident that the Huns were aware that something more than an ordinary barrage or the usual strafe was afloat. Very lights were being sent up continually, and with such a brilliant light any moving object could be seen. But thanks to our artillery, whose fire was so accurate, the German gunners were unable to bring their guns into action. We so surprised them that when we entered the trench the Germans had fled, leaving their machine-guns, mail, packs and rations behind. The Tommies were soon busy among the last named. The first thing we did after occupying the trench was to post sentries and establish machine-gun posts in case of a counter-attack. This completed we soon settled down, hoping our rations would reach us. Everything went off very quietly. We passed the night keeping a good look out, and when daylight broke the sentries worked in reliefs, the usual one hour on and two off. About twelve o'clock the alarm was given to stand to ; everyone on the firesteps. The Germans had contrived by the aid of tall thistles, which were abundant in the neighbourhood, to approach within about fifty yards of our trench without being seen. Using bombs and machine-guns a number of them managed to reach our lines, but were immediately driven out or disposed of with our own bombs. Sergt. Hart and Cpl. Lowe, with several bombers, followed on their heels and the position was soon restored."

In another letter descriptive of the same action, Rfn. S. Gray states : " We met with a little resistance in the form of machine-gun fire, but I think on the whole Jerry was taken by surprise. We got to one of his trenches where we found a machine-gunner at work, and he was promptly put out of action by Sergt. Hart, but, unfortunately, not before he had laid low one of our officers, Lieut. Hunt. After passing through this trench and bombing all dug-outs we came to the sunken road which led to our objective, and which owing to the rain and the constant shelling was in a horrible condition. We finally got to our objective and found that Jerry had got wind of us coming and had made off. It was on the following day while holding this position that Sergt. Hart and Rfn. Rossi won their Military Medals. During the morning a party of about thirty Huns made a bombing raid on our trench, but kept out of range of our hand grenades. Rfn. Rossi went forward by himself and drove them back with hand grenades, leaving about five or six dead behind them. After that Sergt. Hart went forward with a small party of men and again drove them off."

Concerning this raid by the Germans, Major Lindsey-Renton says the enemy, about fifty strong, came down the sunken road unperceived under cover of the bank and forced an entry into Dados Lane and Dados Loop and started bombing outwards. "The situation at one time became serious as the supply of bombs began to run short, but Capt. Peabody of the 12th Londons in Kildare Avenue organised carrying parties and sent up bombs and Lewis gun ammunition. At the same time bombs were sent up by Battalion H.Q. and after considerable fighting, particularly on 'B' Company's front, the enemy were driven back, leaving two killed and two wounded prisoners in our hands, and the position was re-established. During the fighting Lieut. Hodgson had some hard work as the enemy nearly reached his Company H.Q. 2nd Lieut. Lacey, who afterwards died of his wounds, also did stout work in driving out the enemy." The prisoners belonged to the 2nd Guards Division.

During the night of 23rd/24th the Q.V.R. were relieved by the 9th Royal Fusiliers, belonging to the 12th Division, who were taking over the line in accordance with the plan of the attack fixed for 18th. The Q.V.R. marched to Villers-Faucon, where they found the battalion cookers awaiting them with tea and porridge, and embussed at 6 a.m. for Trones Wood on the old Somme battlefield. They arrived at 8.30 a.m. and spent the day resting in old dug-outs. In the afternoon,

Major-Gen. Ramsey, commanding the 58th Division, and Brig.-Gen. Cobham, commanding 175th Brigade, called and congratulated the battalion on the fine work it had done. The Divisional Commander reported that Gen. Rawlinson, commanding the Fourth Army, had rung up to congratulate the battalion on the success of its attack on the evening of September 22nd.

During the advance the transport section had hard work to keep up with and supply the front line, as the following incident described by Rfn. Fauset will show : " We were at a place called Lieramont, where our divisional baths were situated. There were five limbers, each with teams of four mules. Going up to the trenches with the rations we had to call at the baths for clean clothing for the boys. To get to the baths we had to go along a track diagonally across a twenty-acre meadow. When we arrived at the beginning of this track we found that Jerry was shelling its whole length with shrapnel and 5·9's. Lce.-Cpl. C. B. Sellick, in charge of the convoy, gave the order to halt while he counted how many shells burst in a batch, and timed the pauses between the batches in order to ascertain if he could get the convoy across the open during an interval. He counted eight in each batch and reckoned there was just the chance of getting through, so he gave the order to trot, which we did, and just as the last limber got clear the next shell fell. It was one of the hottest two minutes' ride we ever had."

Events were now moving very swiftly. At ten o'clock on the night of September 26th there commenced the bombardment heralding the combined attack on the Hindenburg line—"The Decisive Battle of the War," as it has been called. No less than 1044 field and 593 heavy guns took part in it ; tanks, armoured cars, and even a brigade of cavalry, were held in readiness to join in the attack, which was launched at 5.55 a.m. on 29th under the veil of the morning mist. The attack was delivered on a front of 25 miles from the River Sensee to north of St. Quentin, while the French and Americans on the one side and the Belgians and the British troops in Flanders on the other were to co-operate. The main attack was entrusted to the Fourth Army on the right of the British line combined with subsidiary operations by the Third and First Armies.

The 46th, North Midland (Territorial) Division, IXth Corps, particularly distinguished itself in this attack, crossing the canal, storming Bellenglise and all the fortifications beyond it; by 3 p.m. they had fixed themselves solidly in the positions assigned for capture. The 32nd Division following passed beyond them and also reached their objectives on the greater part of their front. At a cost of 800 casualties the 46th Division claimed 4200 prisoners and 70 guns out of the total booty of 5000 prisoners and 90 guns which fell to the IXth Corps. In the course of the three succeeding days the remainder of the Hindenburg and the Hindenburg Reserve Lines were captured. By October 6th the enemy's position was becoming desperate. On 1st St. Quentin was taken. On 9th Cambrai was regained. On 10th the British took Le Cateau; Bulgaria had already surrendered and Damascus had fallen.

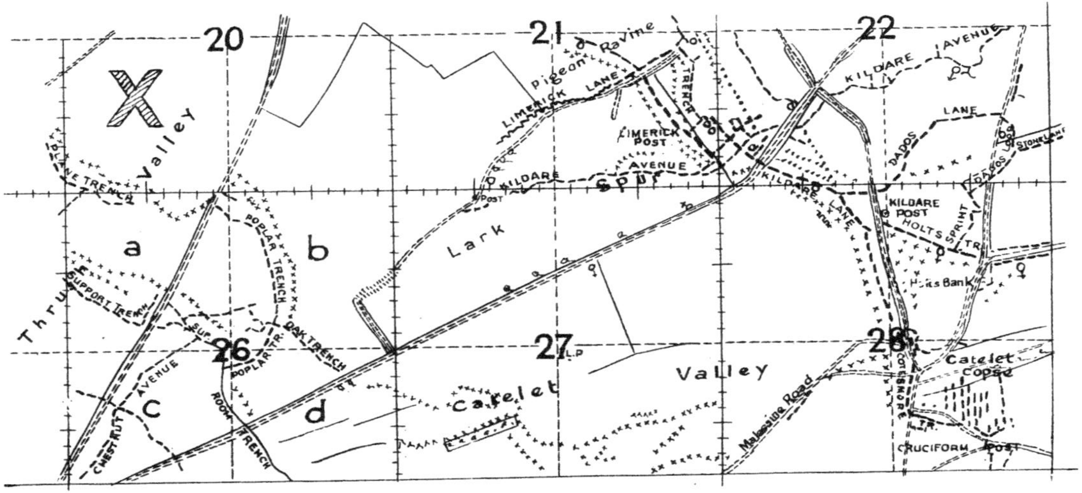

MAP No. 20.

KILDARE POST. SEPT. 22ND-23RD 1918.

CHAPTER XI

OPEN WARFARE AT LAST

THE battalion stayed near Bernafay Wood until the 26th September, on which day the 58th Division was transferred to the VIIIth Corps. On this connection the following Corps Order was issued :

"58th Division,
"G.S. 14/5.
" 58th Division.

" It is with the greatest regret that I bid au revoir to the 58th Division.

" Throughout all the operations of the IIIrd Corps since March, 1918, the Division has not only fought with gallantry and determination, but also with that spirit of mutual co-operation and comradeship which ensures success.

" I wish also to convey my personal thanks to Gen. Ramsey, the staff and all ranks of the 58th Division for their loyal support and for the manner in which they have always ' played up.' I trust it may be my good fortune, at no distant date, to have the Division in my Command again in further victorious operations.

(Sgd.) R. BUTLER,
Lieut.-Gen.,
Commanding IIIrd Corps.

IIIrd. Corps H.Q.
26th September, 1916."

Writing on the same day to the President of the Q.V.R. Old Comrades Association, returning thanks for a gift of writing paper, envelopes, etc., Major Lindsey-Renton says, "It will, I am sure, be of interest to the O.C.A. to learn that the battalion has recently been doing very fine work indeed and has earned high praise in many quarters. I am not exaggerating in saying that their work is at present a subject of conversation well behind the lines. In the last six weeks the battalion has carried out no less than five full-dress attacks, and in every case gained the objective and held it. On two occasions they succeeded after other troops had failed. It has been my fortune to be in command of the battalion during the last four attacks, so that I speak from first-hand knowledge when I say that the battalion has been congratulated by various commanders up to, and including, the Army Commander, who only the day before yesterday sent a message by our Divisional Commander to congratulate and thank the battalion for having done a very important bit of work which they had been called upon to do. The battalion had taken its objective, which a previous attack had failed to reach, and held it against a counter-attack."

For the good work of the battalion during these operations Major Lindsey-Renton was awarded the D.S.O.

On the morning of 28th September, the battalion left Bernafay Wood and marched to Dernancourt, via Montauban, Mametz, Fricourt and Meaulte, part of the road traversed by the old 1st Battalion when on its way from the Somme to Picquigny in 1916. At Dernancourt Col. Powell who had recovered from his accident rejoined the battalion and took over command. At the railway station the men were entrained for Aubigny, from whence they marched to Canblain l'Abbe, where they were stationed in the Upper Camp. Three days later found them in the line again west of Lens, having relieved the 9th Royal Sussex (24th Division).

On October 3rd " A " and " B " Companies pushed forward through Lens and established a line of Posts. The 173rd Brigade, however, which was on the right of the Q.V.R., managed to cross the front of the latter and joined up with the 20th Division on the right in front of Lens, completely cutting out the 175th Brigade, which was then withdrawn.

Signaller W. Wells gives a rather exciting account of an incident which occurred at the Green Grassier on this night: "I was detailed to take an officer of 'D' Company to an outpost which at that time was held by No. 8 Platoon. Our way lay along a railway embankment which was well under cover until we had to cross the railway by climbing the embankment, which was a huge slack heap. On our way up I met a signaller who had just come from the outpost, and he warned me that Jerry was busy sniping along the particular piece of railway we had to cross. When we arrived at the bottom of the slack heap I was leading, and no sooner had I shown myself than ' ping,' and a bullet whizzed past my face. I bent low and bolted for it. From the time I started to the time I got under cover I had no less than four shots fired at me, none of which, luckily, found its target. When I had an opportunity to look around I found that the officer had very wisely dropped into the nearest shell-hole. I shouted to him to try and reach me by way of a beaten track which ran direct to the trench I was in. He followed my example, bending low and running, but he had hardly got half-way when ' ping ' went another shot and he ' clicked.' He dropped to the ground and lay there moaning. I went on and brought a stretcher bearer back with me. When I returned to him I found that an officer of the R.F.A. was with him in a shell-hole. I saw a corporal on his way back to Company H.Q. and asked him to send up a stretcher and bearers. The R.F.A. officer suggested we should get the wounded officer away, and as it was getting dusk we decided to try. The wounded man managed to crawl to the railway and we got him under it by means of a convenient shell-hole and so into the trench. By this time the bearers from Company H.Q. had arrived and he was got away in safety. The officer was, I believe, Lieut. Quick of ' D ' Company. He had been hit in the back, the bullet narrowly missing his spine. I considered myself a very fortunate person and thanked my lucky star that I came through O.K."

On October 6th the Q.V.R. moved into hutments on Marqueffles Farm and spent a couple of days in cleaning up and firing on the range. The 175th Brigade relieved the 174th in the line on October 9th, the Q.V.R., less one company, which was attached to the Rangers in the line, being in Reserve. The 10th, 11th and 12th are all classed as " quiet days," with slight shelling at night. On 13th the battalion moved forward to Harnes, east of Lens, the first British troops seen there since 1914.

The Q.V.R. relieved the 6th London Regiment in the front line on October 15th, and on the morning following advanced by platoons, crossing the canal, de la Haute Deule, by improvised bridges. " D " Company pushed forward through Bois d'Harpondieu and cleared the wood, " C " Company maintaining touch on their right. " A " sent out patrols, obtaining liaison with the Royal Berks on their right while " B " moved forward in support along the canal bank. In conjunction with the brigades on their flanks the advance was continued next day due east, meeting with little opposition. At night the battalion was relieved by the 12th (Rangers) and returned to billets at Roncheaux, where, says R.Q.M.S. Taylor, "The people made a wonderful fuss of us. The boys had the time of their lives." The same kind of reception met them at Auchy and Rumegies, which was reached on 21st, no fighting or anything of particular interest having occurred during the four days' advance. On this day the enemy's resistance stiffened a little, and there was a good deal of shelling at night, the entrances to Rongy, close outside which village the Q.V.R. were billeted, being systematically bombarded.

In a general description of the last few weeks Capt. H. Samuelson writes : " October, 1918, found the Queen Victoria's moving, as were the rest of the Army, in an easterly direction. It was open warfare at last—the kind of warfare preached at courses and always laughed at. The day of those who had known open warfare in South Africa had come. The normal formation of advance was one battalion of the brigade as Advanced Guard, with two 18-pounders attached to them, the remainder marching in column of route. The daily trek was about seven to ten miles, according to the amount of opposition encountered, which at first was not great. On crossing the Belgian frontier near Howardries, on our way to the river L'Escaut, the battalion was spotted by the enemy from Fort Maulde and was forced to make a hurried move to the village of Rongy, where it was shelled intermittently with gas throughout the night to the terror of the inhabitants. Dr. Selwyn Clarke was ceaseless in his efforts to get them to some place of safety."

" On the afternoon of 22nd October," writes Rfn. J. S. Garrett, " we were all packed up and ready to move, having

received orders to that effect the same morning and marched
by platoons to Rongy, a place just a couple of kilometres or
so the other side of the border line of France and Belgium, the
whole distance being a matter of six miles. All went well until
about half of our journey had been covered and we were in
sight of Rongy when Jerry started to throw those funny little
things commonly known as high velocity shells at us and at an
artillery position which had been taken up during the morning
in a field on the right of the road behind some very thick
shrubbery. We were told that Jerry had already knocked out
one gun that morning, an 18-pounder, and his shells were getting rather too near to be pleasant. The order came from
the front to halt and to spread out a bit. There were several
G.S. wagons on the road, some halted and others coming from
the direction of Rongy. We were not long halted as Jerry
abated his shelling somewhat and we carried on and had
reached the outskirts of Rongy itself when he started again,
distributing his shells over a wider area. On our left stood a
large château and running parallel to it was a very broad road
lined with tall trees, as is usually the case in most French and
Belgian roads. We were ordered to scatter and my platoon,
No. 9 of 'C' Company, hurried down this road and spread
ourselves out in a field on the right of the road. The cooker,
which was following in the rear of the company, came down
the road at a gallop, and what with the speed it was travelling
and the red-hot cinders from the fire and the steam rising from
the water jolted out of the dixies, it made a very good imitation of a fire engine dashing to the rescue. But the real reason
for its hurry was to get out of range of Jerry's shells. After a
quarter of an hour's strafe we eventually made our way into
Rongy and took cover in a barn in which were a few artillerymen. Two platoons managed to get in and remained for about
twenty minutes listening to the dropping shells and ducking
our heads every time one whizzed over the barn. We finally
all got settled down in billets, where we felt more or less safe.
Somehow it seems to be a natural instinct with soldiers that
if they have a cover of any description for their heads, a waterproof sheet even, they are quite safe and no shell will harm
them. After a meal and the necessary sentries had been
posted we all made ourselves as comfortable as we could.

2 G

About half-past ten p.m. we were all rudely awakened by a loud crash and a shower of tiles and plaster from the roof. There was a scramble for a few seconds and all with one accord put on their gas masks, for the crash turned out to be a gas shell falling through the roof. The room was thick with fumes of mustard gas, so we all retired into the street where we found the air clearer, but still tainted. Several more shells were dropped in a close area and many other troops were in the same plight as ourselves. Captain Samuelson advised us not to return to the barn as the gas still hung about, so we made for a big house further up the road and settled down again. If I remember rightly Major Gould's (2/10th) batman was killed, also Major Lindsey-Renton's horse, which Capt. Samuelson was using at the time."

According to the War Diary the casualties arising from this incident amounted altogether to 20

Somewhere about this time the following message was officially issued to the Division : " The following appreciation of the 58th (London) Division is quoted from a German document captured at Lenin Lietard. 'The 58th Division were identified on this front by 7 prisoners of the 2/2nd London Regiment on 4th October. They were put into the line just north of Lens, and it is not certain whether they were put in to strengthen the line or to relieve the 24th Division, whose right boundary is south of Avion. The 58th Division is considered an excellent Storm Division. They were engaged twice in the heavy fighting between the Somme and the Scarpe last month, during which period they had exceedingly heavy casualties. Between 23rd September and 4th October the Division was out in rest.' "

CHAPTER XII

Triumphant Progress—Armistice Day

"ON reaching the banks of the River L'Escaut," relates Capt. Samuelson, " a delay of some days followed, the Q.V.R. being mostly engaged in doing outpost duty in farms and isolated buildings. During this period it was made manifest to us that the characteristics of the Hun had not altered much, as a woman was shot while crossing from their lines to ours in company with a child, although a German sentry group had allowed them to pass. Indeed, the plight of the inhabitants was pitiful at this time ; they were flocking back to their old homes mostly to find them in ruins ; on one day they were driven in front of the Boches to a place ten miles off and the next suffered to return, forming an endless procession between the retreating and the advancing armies along roads already congested with our transport. They brought with them all their earthly belongings, tied in bundles, in many cases carried by children, and the heavier articles packed in barrows on top of which was frequently seated a disconsolate-looking invalid or aged person.

" The Boches were holding Fort Maulde, an old French fort standing in marshy ground on the west bank of the river. They had strengthened the position with wire and it was apparent that to take it by storm would prove an expensive operation. At this time the whole length of the line was held up. Plans were discussed for crossing the river by means of rafts and light boats, and these operations were actually rehearsed in the moat of the château at Rongy, but amid general feelings of relief the orders were cancelled. One or two Lewis guns had already found a watery grave at the bottom of the moat and their teams saw a very good prospect of their joining them there. The Boches, however, announced their departure one night by setting fire to the fort and once more the order was ' en avant.'

"On through the village of Flines les Montagnes in France and thence crossing into Belgium again near Wiers. Here the inhabitants gave us a great welcome ; everyone carried bunches of flowers which they freely distributed as they danced around the men, cheering all the time accompanied by the local band which played the 'Marseillaise' and 'La Brabanconne' alternately. In spite of the enthusiasm of the moment we had to be eternally on our guard as the Hun had prepared and left for the benefit of the unwary quite a number of ' booby traps ' in the shape of doors whose handles when turned started bombs, and other eccentricities.

"If the welcome we received from the small villages was enthusiastic a greater surprise was in store for us when we reached the town of Peruwelz, the entire population of which, some 9,000, flung itself upon the battalion as we entered. It became quite impossible to move, and as the first arrivals we naturally were in the thick of it. As one of the first mounted officers to enter, with every available space on my horse bedecked with flowers, I must say that the Square presented a most wonderful sight. The noise was too great for anyone to hear what anyone else was saying ; the Maire was addressing us, or so we understood, in terms of welcome ; the band was playing, everyone was shouting, while mounted officers were pulled off their horses and carried shoulder high round the Place. The Q.V.R. spent the evening in the suburbs of the town on the banks of the Mons-Tournai Canal. Thence the march was resumed via Va Voiterie, Basacles, Quevaucamps and Stambruges to Ecacheries. At Neuf Maison at 9.20 on the morning of November 11th runners came from Battn. H.Q. to say that ' hostilities would cease at 11.00 hours.' Very forcible intimations were given to them by some of the O.C. companies that they had heard that tale before. But this time it was true ! We gazed at each other in unbelief, like the followers of Cortez ' silent upon a peak in Darien '—in our case Belgium.

"The 'Cease Fire' was sounded at eleven o'clock by our buglers in the town square, just as they had done on many an occasion after an Aldershot field-day. The next morning a

Battalion Thanksgiving Service was held. It is peculiar to note that probably the only night when rations did not arrive was on Armistice night, owing to the fact that we had been advancing so rapidly that railhead had been outrun. With this one exception an unbroken record stands, I believe, to the everlasting credit of our dear old quartermaster, Tim O'Shea and the Transport."

Attempts by the officers to properly celebrate the occasion seem to have been only partially successful. Capt. Samuelson tells us that the Mess cart scoured the country for leagues around in search of viands and victuals, but all efforts only produced a certain amount of local poison. Nevertheless, a cheery night was spent by those at Battalion H.Q.

R.Q.M.S. Taylor describing the unexpected end, says: "We (transport) advanced as far as Beloiel, where we stayed the night and were to move forward the next morning. But at 10 a.m. I was standing outside the billet with a couple of sergeants, when Brig.-Gen. Cobham came along, stopped, and said, 'No doubt you will be pleased to hear that the Armistice is signed and hostilities will cease at 11 a.m.' The troops went mad, cheered, and behaved generally like schoolboys. At 11 o'clock, our buglers sounded the 'cease fire.' The reaction put the troops in a high state of nervous tension, but after a few weeks they were their old selves once again. All of us who had seen it through did 'thank God' that the end had come!"

On November 17th the following order was issued to the 175th Brigade and the other units of the Division:

58th (London) Division.

I wish to express to all officers, N.C.O.'s and men serving under my command my warm appreciation for the very valuable and gallant services rendered, and for the indomitable and cheerful spirit shown by them during the recent operations.

From 8th August to 29th September the Division delivered twenty-two attacks, each carried out with the greatest gallantry and success. From the commencement of the enemy's withdrawal in October, the division continued to press back his rearguards with the same spirit and determination as was shown on the battlefield of the Somme.

The co-operation of all units of the division and the untiring efforts of the various staffs are points on which I wish to express my special admiration. F. RAMSEY, Major-General,
17/11/18. Commanding 58th Division.

In the transition period immediately following the Armistice the greatest difficulty that confronted the higher ranks was the solution of the problem, how to kill time without killing discipline, and to direct the spirit of the men into the right path. There was the usual training each morning generally followed in the afternoon by a football match and band performances in the evening. On November 25th Elementary Educational Classes were started. The Padre, as a rule, was appointed Educational Director with one officer per company as lecturer. These classes subsequently became a regular feature of Company Training and were held daily. Inspections, too, were of frequent occurrence.

The Q.V.R. had quitted Ecacheries two days after the cessation of hostilities and had moved to Stambruges, which was destined to be their stopping-place until December 19th. Here on December 2nd, the 58th Division was reviewed by Sir Henry Horne, Commander of the First Army. His appreciation was conveyed to all ranks in the following Special Order of the Day :

" Gen. Sir H. S. Horne, K.C.B., K.C.M.G., Commanding the First Army, at his inspection of the division yesterday expressed to the Divisional Commander entire satisfaction with the appearance and bearing of all ranks.

He considered that the general turn out and condition of arms and equipment, as well as the steadiness on parade and the march past, were worthy of the highest praise.

The Army Commander desired that his congratulations should be conveyed to every individual on this evident determination to maintain the high standard of esprit de corps traditional to the British Army in France.

He further signified the pleasure it gave him to have a chance of seeing almost in its entirety a unit that during long and heavy fighting has made so great a name for itself as has the 58th (London) Division."

3/12/18.

On December 5th, H.M. the King, accompanied by the Prince of Wales and Prince Albert and the Army Commander, visited Stambruges. There was no formal inspection, but the troops collected at the cross-roads, open places in the village and other points of vantage. The Royal party drove up in cars, and then alighting continued the journey on foot walking through the village and speaking to the men who lined the roads. The King spoke occasionally to some of them and had a great reception, as also did the Prince of Wales. The throng was so great that they could hardly regain their cars.

Nothing of any particular interest happened in the succeeding days. A cinema opened in the village on December 8th and proved a welcome change of amusement. On 10th, Brigade Ceremonial Guard Mounting was started. A battalion dancing class was inaugurated on 12th with Cpl. Spicer as M.C. On 18th a *Bal Masque* was given, held under the auspices of the Rangers, and on 20th the battalion left Stambruges for fresh billets at Leuze. On 24th Christmas festivities started, mutual hospitalities were extended by all regiments of the brigade and a very happy Christmas Day was spent. "Everyone from the C.O. downwards," so it is recorded, "let themselves go."

On New Year's Eve a Torchlight Tattoo was held in the Grande Place by contingents from the Q.V.R., Rangers and 2/10th under the management of Col. Powell, who was responsible for the training and evolutions of the men. It was a very fine piece of work. The parade took place at 9.30 p.m. with massed bands and 40 men from each battalion. At the conclusion of the drill "Exit 1918" was marked by the "Last Post" and "Hail 1919" by the "Reveille."

CHAPTER XIII

Transport Difficulties

"It is a pretty general saying," writes Cpl. Sellick, "that the men in the trenches won the war. Certainly he had the actual fighting to do, but there are others to whom a share of the credit is due, those others who made it possible for them to carry on." Amongst the foremost of these were the regimental transports, and no war story of Queen Victoria's Rifles would be complete without some appreciation of their work. The difficulties encountered by the Transport Section of the 1st Battalion and the manner in which they were always surmounted have been told in the early chapters of this history. The section, it will be remembered, at the time of embarking for France was under the command of Lieut. Shepherd ("Dick") who was invalided home in the spring of 1915 and who was succeeded by Lieut. (later Captain) K. L. MacKenzie, "Mack," as he was known to all from General to Rifleman. Before the war, Lieut. MacKenzie had had many and varied adventures in different parts of the world and his experience proved of great value when faced by the ever-changing situation as Transport Officer. "His method of commanding men," says Major Lindsey-Renton, "was not always orthodox but his personality enabled him to get the best out of his men who developed a high sense of 'esprit de section.'" Lieut. MacKenzie would be the first to admit the invaluable support he received from Sergt. J. Reeves, who was awarded the D.C.M. for his splendid work with the transport. Sergt. Reeves, or 'Jimmy,' as he is affectionately known, joined the Bloomsbury Rifles in 1900 and came over with them on the amalgamation. In 1911 he was appointed Transport Sergeant and formed the section. He served in that capacity with the 1st Battalion until the amalgamation of 1st and 2nd in January, 1918, when he and the whole transport section were, to the great regret of all, sent down to transport duties at the base. On the reformation of the Territorial Army in 1920, Sergt. Reeves rejoined the Q.V.R. with many of his old section. In 1921, thinking the time had come for a younger N.C.O. to have his chance, he resigned.

Officers and men in the line have always regarded the transport as a "soft job." They certainly did not experience all the discomfort and dangers that the troops in the trenches went through and casualties among them were very few, but the mental strain of going up night after night from a position of comparative or even absolute security into the zone of actual danger is considerably greater than that of continually living in that zone.

When the battalion was at rest the transport was not, their work was never finished. When on the march the transport would be the last to get settled in their billets and then their horses had to be looked after, for with them, as with all good mounted troops, it was "horses first, men afterwards." At times the strain on men and horses was exceptionally severe. In the operations in the Ypres Salient in 1915 and 1917 the nightly journey with rations was more than usually trying. Traffic on these occasions had almost always to go through Ypres, or in very close proximity to that unhealthy town, which with all the roads to and from it were continually strafed by heavy shell-fire from guns of every calibre.

Probably the battles of the Somme were the worst experiences the transport had to undergo; men and horses were tried to the limit. The wastage among the latter was very heavy, and many months of careful treatment and feeding were required before the horses that had survived were restored to good condition. The ground to be traversed was a slough of mud broken up by innumerable shell-holes and quite impassable to wheeled traffic. As a result all rations and stores had to be carried by pack animals necessitating an increase in the number of men and animals employed each night. The approach to the trenches was continually subjected to heavy shell-fire, the enemy's artillery searching for any column moving up. In addition it was no easy matter to find the position of the battalion which frequently depended upon the success or failure of some operation, the result of which was not known until the transport was on its way. Despite these difficulties night after night Capt. MacKenzie's figure would appear at the entrance of a dug-out, edge of a trench, or lip of a shell-hole, wherever in fact, H.Q. chanced to be, with the cheering news, "Good evening, Sir. The rations are up."

It is a well-worn saying that "an army marches on its stomach" and it is impossible to overestimate the value of the transport contribution, by the never failing regularity in bringing up stores and rations, to the final success of the British Armies.

In more peaceful occupations the 1st Battalion transport maintained its high standard; at horse shows and transport inspections it came out with flying colours. During the summer of 1917 a Brigade Horse Show and Athletic Meeting was held in the Château grounds at Grand Bullecourt amid most delightful surroundings. On this occasion the Q.V.R. Transport section excelled itself. For weeks the men had been working on horses, wagons and harness, with an utter disregard of overtime, until on the day of the show the condition of the exhibits was beyond belief. The competition between the various units was very keen, each being equally determined to be second to none. The Q.V.R. came out on top winning first prize for field kitchen, limber with light draught horses and pack pony. The competition for the cookers, as the field kitchen was called, was especially keen, being looked upon as *the* event. In addition, second prizes were gained with the Officers' Mess cart, single heavy draught horse and single mule, and a third for a limber with pair of horses. Finally a special prize for the best vehicle in the show was won by the Q.V.R. field kitchen. This was one of the several shows held from time to time in which the fortunes of the Q.V.R. transport varied.

The 2/9th London Transport, which subsequently became the 9th Londons (Q.V.R.) Transport, is also worthy of a word of recognition. This section was first formed in September, 1914, and left London with the 2nd Battalion in October with the noble aggregate of three animals. At Crowborough the section was at first under the command of Lieut. Strong and, according to Cpl. Sellick, "its material was strengthened by the addition of some old crocks requisitioned from the R.E. stationed nearby together with some old harness and wagons. The latter were so full of defects that it was only through sheer cussedness that the parts held together. The harness, likewise full of defects, was not blessed with the same cussedness and had to be held together with bootlaces and bits of string. The next contribution consisted of some horses which we had to fetch at 4 a.m. on Boxing Day, and a fine old picnic we had in getting them to the camp. They were strung out all along the road, not being led but leading the men who were supposed to be in charge of them, with one or two loose animals fetching up the rear ; these every now and again would dash into an adjacent field and help themselves to the best of what was there and then with a few bucks chase after the main column. We also had four Studebaker wagons, which gave us infinite trouble in negotiating the narrow country lanes. The section was ultimately completed by a pack of mules, which were sent to Woodbridge in August, 1915, under the charge of Lce.-Cpl. Kent. At this time the section was under the command of Lieut. Elliott, who did some really excellent work in putting it on a working basis and training it for the work which it was later called upon to do. Thereafter we had a quick succession of officers, Lieut. Bull, Lieut. Reed, Lieut. McAdam and then the one to whom the 2nd Battalion owed so much after their arrival in France, Lieut. (later Captain) Philbrick. It was notoriously bad weather on the day we landed and we were compelled to pitch our horse line out in the snow from which next day we extricated the harness with difficulty besides having to shoot one of our animals that had been kicked during the night. This might have been considered a bad omen, but we had too much work on our hands to think about omens, and subsequent events happily proved it to be otherwise.

" We received our baptism of fire at Birles where the battalion first went into the line. We looked upon the experience more as a novelty than anything else, and luckily there were no casualties. Thereon the dangers seemed to grow worse, especially when we got to Bullecourt, but when we reached Belgium in August, 1917, we really thought we had got to the wrong side of the River Styx. Here we had two memorable stunts. The first happened on the night of September 22nd/23rd and the other on the following night. On the first occasion we were under orders to take up forty-eight hours' rations to the battalion who were ' going over ' in the morning. We arrived at the appointed time only to find that Jerry had a barrage up on the place (St. Julien) where we were supposed to dump. This prevented the ration party from coming to meet us, and it also looked as if it would prevent us from reaching our objective. It was decided not to wait for the ration party but to follow on at intervals of five minutes and dump the rations. The first driver got rather too close to a gas shell and was slightly gassed, but he kept on and succeeded in dumping his load. Then the Hun took it into his head to move his barrage a little further over and the shells began dropping between the limbers. It was perfectly marvellous that anyone of us escaped. Three times we made a move to dodge the barrage, and finally succeeded in accomplishing our errand, all the loads being dumped without our having incurred a single casualty. The battalion ' went over ' on the following morning and in the evening we were ordered to take up water for the men. Owing to the continual shelling the roads were in a dreadful state and reconnaissances had to be made to ascertain if we could get the limbers up to the appointed places. On this occasion it was decided to make the attempt with half-limbers. The shelling, as on the previous night, was heavy and we advanced at intervals. The 2/12th Londons were going up at the time to reinforce the 2/9th and a number of the first-named were wounded in passing through the limbers. The first half-limber went up and dumped its load, but before the second half-limber could reach the spot part of the first load had been blown up. However, the remaining loads were dumped without mishap, although one of the pairs was frightened into starting off at a canter across the shell-holes towards the front line. Fortunately the driver managed to pull up in time.

"During our own great push in August, 1918, the battalion ' went over ' one morning about midday. Direct communication was broken and we were faced at night with the problem of getting the rations up without knowing exactly where the battalion was to be found. It is a great tribute to the work of

Capt. Philbrick on that night (and subsequently on the Somme) that the rations were delivered to the battalion within one hour of the time that they gained their new position in front of Malard Wood. For two years we were entrusted with the rationing of the battalion and supplying them with ammunition and material without its once being disappointed."

CHAPTER XIV

Concert Parties

FROM the earliest days concert parties proved to be one of the chief assets in entertaining the troops and even before the departure of the Q.V.R. for France and in the 2nd and 3rd Battalions at home " smoking " and " bohemian concerts " were of frequent occurrence. The first concert organised abroad was one held at Bailleul some time during the winter of 1914–1915, the wettest winter on record. An amusing account of it appeared in the *Evening News* of February 3rd, 1915. The great " turn " was Sergt. Fisher with a dozen men of " D " Company in what is now called a " Jazz Band Stunt." Dressed in their fur trench coats and sleeping caps they looked, we are told, " half-way between a Cossack and a pantomime monkey." Sergt. Fisher sported a second fur coat worn upside down as breeches and resembled our old friend Robinson Crusoe. They had biscuit tins for drums, combs covered with tissue paper and penny trumpets purchased locally, and—" So it goes on for three hours on end. It's amazing ; everybody serious ; everybody enjoying himself, and music, actual music, got from combs and biscuit boxes ! " From another source we learn that Ernest Thesiger recited an old friend, " Paula and Her Pearls." Much interest was centred during his item on the faces of some padres who chanced to be present.

Members of the Q.V.R. contributed very largely to the " Whizz-Bangs," the celebrated 5th Divisional Concert Party, formed in the autumn of 1915. " Early in 1916 the management of the troupe was taken over by Lieut. Forsyth, Q.V.R., under whose able guidance it remained until 1918, and attained a high standard of performance " (*The 5th Division in the Great War*, Brig.-Gen. Hussey and Major Inman).

About one-half of the equally famed " Bow Bells," formed in 1916, belonged to the Queen Vics.

THE QUAVERS

A history of the Q.V.R. in France and Belgium would hardly be complete without a reference to the QuaVeRs. It is true they had no existence prior to November 11th, but this fact is claimed by them as a distinction rather than otherwise. On the conclusion of the Armistice, when the battalion was moved to Stambruges and leisure hours were longer than had ever been believed possible, it became obvious that regular amusements had to be found. A concert at Rumegies, just before the conclusion of hostilities, had shown that the musical talent among the Q.V.R. was above the average, and a couple of concerts given at Stambruges on December 1st and 4th confirmed the fact, so that it only remained to choose the most suitable performers for the formation of a successful concert party.

2nd Lieut. R. Johnson, Lce.-Cpl. Powell (" D " Company), Rfn. H. Boulden (" C " Company), and Rfn. L. Webb (" D " Company) were obvious choices as singers. Sergt. A. S. Palmer (H.Q. Company), Cpl. Lowe (" A " Company), and Cpl. Shute (" C " Company) were to provide a lighter form of entertainment, and the party was completed with Rfn. T. Gorrell (H.Q. Company), as a magician, Rfn. J. Riach (" D " Company), as comedian, and Lieut. N. C. Lockley, to whom we are indebted for these details of their career, as pianist. The last-named had also to undertake the responsibilities of producer, Lieut. Johnson those of stage and business manager, with Sergt. Palmer as aide-de-camp to both. With real singers, comedians, a magician and an accompanist, all seemed complete, but the crying necessity arose—" What about a girl ? " A pathetic appeal in battalion orders produced two volunteers, and one of these, Rfn. Elliott (H.Q. Company), was chosen. Afterwards popularly known as " Cissie," Elliott worked hard, having had no previous experience in that line and blossomed out as " Our Girl." Later a second girl joined the party in the person of 2nd Lieut. W. E. Smith. He had played girl's parts before though his voice was hardly suitable for them—alas, he sang baritone !—but his make-up was so good and his dancing and acting so splendid that even the Divisional General lost his heart, and in a speech after one of the concerts said, " And as for Flossie, she's the prettiest girl I've seen."

Thus far all went smoothly, but the real work had yet to start. Costumes, music, shoes, properties are all problems which can be solved in a few minutes in England, but in Belgium, where nothing could be got from London under a fortnight, each of these was a serious proposition. It soon became apparent, however, that for the QuaVeRs there were to be no insurmountable difficulties, and with everyone in the battalion, from Col. Powell and Major Lindsey-Renton down to the regimental tailors, not only willing but anxious to help, mountains became molehills and all that was needed was to continue rehearsals and choose a date for the first performance. At Stambruges there was a first-rate theatre, the best in the division, and the first concert was all but ready when the move to Leuze took place on December 20th. Here was taken a new theatre, subsequently known to fame as " The Victoria Palace," but by no means on the palatial scale of that at Stambruges, though comparing favourably with some of the B.E.F. theatres.

The Quavers made their first bow to the public on Christmas Eve, when the dress rehearsal took place before the members of the 155th Labour Company, who had been invited to attend and who remained to the end blissfully ignorant that it was but a rehearsal. With the cheers of this audience ringing in their ears it was with confidence that on Boxing Day the Quavers awaited the rising of the curtain. No confidence, however, could have anticipated the reception they actually got. " I'm sure that you'll agree with me that we're proud of the Quavers," was the C.O.'s comment, and from the cheers that followed it was plain that the battalion did agree.

The programme of the first performance (done on a clay in green and red ink by Lce.-Cpl. C. Goldie) was as follows :

26th Dec. Xmas, 1918. Leuze.

FIRST APPEARANCE OF THE QUAVERS.

Programme

1. The Quavers . . . Fall In.
2. Cpl. Shute . . . In Logic.
3. Lce.-Cpl. Powell . . Will Sing.
4. The Quavers . . . Will Concert.
5. Sergt. Palmer . . . In Cuthbert.
6. Lieut. R. Johnson . . Will sing " Pals."
7. Cpl. Shute & Rfn. Riach . Will Talk.
8. The Quaver's Xmas Number—
    Rfn. Boulden in the . "Happiest Xmas of All."
9. Sergt. Palmer, Cpl. Lowe &
    the Quavers . . In The Indian Rag.
10. Rfn. Gorrell . . . Prestidigitateur.
11. Lce.-Cpl. Powell and Rfn.
    Boulden . . . Will sing again.
12. Rfn. Elliott . . . "Our Girl" in "I'm in Love with a Soldier and a Sailor."
13. The Quavers . . . In "A Russian Quartette."
14. Rfn. Riach . . . Will be Thoroughly Miserable.
15. The Quavers . . . In a Coster Burlesque.
16. Finale.

At the Piano. Lieut. N. C. Lockley.

The programme was repeated for the benefit of the battalion a day or two later, for its civilian friends and for the Rangers and the 2/10th Londons. Meanwhile rehearsals proceeded for a new programme which was to be something entirely fresh. This took place on January 4th, when, if possible, it met with an even better reception. Numbers which immediately became popular were : "Isn't She a Busy Little Bee ? " "Hong Kong " and " A Cosy Corner." By this time the fame of the " Quavers " had spread to other parts of the division and they were asked to tour. On Monday, January 13th, with much éclat, and the help of a lorry (Mascot attached) the tour commenced, and the following places and units visited :

January 13. Queveaucamps . A.S.C. Divisional Train.
,, 14. Beloiel . . F.R.A. 291st Brigade.
,, 15. Stambruges . 4th Battalion Suffolk Regt.
,, 16. Grandeglise . R.F.A. Ammunition Column.

A return was made to Leuze for the week-end and the round of visits again began on Monday, January 20th. On that evening the 58th Battalion M.G.C. at Roucourt were visited. On the two succeeding days the Quavers fairly put their heads into the lion's mouth by appearing at the Cinema Hall, Peruwelz, the home of "The Goods," the far better known Divisional Concert Party. Two crowded houses cheered them long and lustily and the lion did not bite. On the Wednesday afternoon a wire arrived from the battalion bidding the Quavers to return at once for a "command" performance before Gen. Sir Arthur Holland (Corps Commander), at the Victoria Palace. With Sir Arthur were the Divisional General, Major-Gen. Ramsey and Brig.-Gen. Cobham. At the conclusion of the programme Sir Arthur Holland, in thanking the Quavers, pointed out that during the war they had been soldiers and were artists afterwards. May the Quavers be forgiven if, when they continued their tour the next day, they found their tin hats uncomfortably small.

Two other visits were paid to units at Blaton and Grandsmesnil and the Quavers then returned to Leuze to put the finishing touches to their third programme. On January 28th Gen. Ramsey paid them the compliment of commanding another performance, motoring over from Peruwelz with a number of friends whom he had specially invited to enjoy the concert.

The new programme was submitted for the delectation of their fellow " Vics " on Sunday and Monday, February 1st and 2nd. The mother battalion's enthusiasm evinced no sign of diminishing though the entertainment appeared to lack some of the swing and go of previous shows. Lieut. " Caruso " Johnson certainly scored a personal triumph with " Mandalay " and " A Winder Courtship " while the " Crocodile Crawl " and " The Old Bran Pie " served to swell the list of favourites.

About this time the party had the misfortune to lose some of its principal members who were placed on the sick list. But this was not the worst calamity that befell it. The sword of Damocles, in the form of demobilisation was suspended over it and carried off two of the most prominent of the party. Lieut. Johnson, who with his admirable singing and stage personality, not to mention his indefatigable work off the stage, returned to his scholastic duties and the London concert platform, while Sergt. Palmer, another tower of strength both on and off the stage, was also "demobbed," and a like fate befell Rfn. Elliott ("Cissie"), Jones ("A" Company) and Cohen ("C" Company). The last-named had proved himself a most ready and efficient property master. Rfn. Gorrell, whose wizardry had always so completely bewildered his audience, also left for England on leave. It was consequently a sad and woefully depleted party which gathered to discuss the fourth and final programme, but all expressed themselves confident of still being able to produce a show quite up to the accustomed standard. This was given on Sunday and Monday, February 16th and 17th, when two crowded houses showed by their enthusiasm that the Quavers' last effort at least equalled any of the previous shows. It went with a swing from start to finish. Lce.-Cpl. Powell and Rfn. Boulden, in their duet, "The Rivals," "When I get my Civies on Again" and "The Pride of the Pier," were the most popular numbers in the programme. Cpl. Shute had succeeded to the stage-managership, and under his supervision the Quavers made their last bow in Belgium. By hard work, a happy camaraderie in the party, the loyal support of the whole battalion and perhaps the absence of the cares of military life all combined to make the Quavers Concert Party a success.

On 14th June, 1919, the Quavers assembled together once more and gave a performance exactly as it was presented in Belgium, before a crowded and delighted audience in the Queen Victoria's Drill Hall, 56 Davies Street, London, W. 1. No attempt was made to bring the programme up to date nor was any effort to introduce effects which were impossible in an out-of-the-way Belgian village. All the old favourites were present, and all helped to prove the boast that "the musical talent among the Q.V.R. was above the average."

Here is an extract from the *Cologne Post*—the newspaper of the British Forces in Germany—of 24th May, 1919 : " The Q-Vics. the concert party of the 9th London Regiment, make their debut on Whit-Monday evening, June 2nd, at Niederaussem. 2nd Lieut. Smith has organised the party and Rfn. Ling and Howes will be responsible for the production. ' Jock Ling ' was formerly with the 58th Division Concert Party. Bobby Howes is well known in the vaudeville world as one of the originals in the Gotham Quartette." Again on June 6th the *Post* says : " After a most successful first night show on Monday last the Q-Vics made their second appearance before an enthusiastic audience on Wednesday evening. For the combination and general excellence of their performance the Q-Vics are to be commended. Notwithstanding the Lilliputian dimensions of the stage, and the inconveniences common to a rural concert hall, the whole thing went with a swing."

Marching Song of the Queen Victoria's Rifles
(9th London Regiment)
The Q.V.R. Song

The regiment has a song of which the men never tire and raise it upon the slightest provocation, both in peace time and in war. Who was its author and composer, when and where it originated endless questions have failed to solve.

I'll give you one, Sir. Way ! way ! for the Black Brigade.
   What is your one, Sir ? One for the Queen Victoria's, the best of the whole Brigade, Sir.

I'll give you two, Sir. Way ! way ! for the Black Brigade.
   What are your two, Sir ? Two, two for myself and you, and here's a jolly good Health, Oh ! One for the Queen Victoria's, the best of the whole Brigade, Sir.

I'll give you three, Sir. Way ! way ! for the Black Brigade.
   What are your three, Sir ? Three, three for the Colonel, two, two for myself and you, etc.

I'll give you four, Sir. Way ! way ! for the Black Brigade.
   What are your four, Sir ? Four for the Sergeant-Major, three three, etc.

I'll give you five, Sir. Way ! way ! for the Black Brigade.
   What are your five, Sir ? Five for the rest of the Black Brigade and four for the Sergeant-Major. Three, three, etc.

I'll give you six, Sir. Way! way! for the Black Brigade.
What are your six, Sir? Six for the Cook-house Door, Boys, five for the rest, etc.

I'll give you seven, Sir. Way! way! for the Black Brigade.
What are your seven, Sir? Seven for the seven pals in my tent, and six for the Cook-house Door, etc.

I'll give you eight, Sir. Way! way! for the Black Brigade.
What are your eight, Sir? Eight for the eight bold Captains, Seven for the seven, etc.

I'll give you nine, Sir. Way! way! for the Black Brigade.
What are your nine, Sir? Nine for the Cooks of the Army Shield, and eight for the eight, etc.

(*Last verse very slow.*)
I'll give you ten, Sir. Way! way! for the Black Brigade.
What are your ten, Sir? Ten for the Ten Commandments, Nine for the Cooks of the Army Shield, and Eight for the eight bold Captains; Seven for the seven pals in my tent, and Six for the Cook-house Door, Boys; Five for the rest of the Black Brigade, and Four for the Sergeant-Major; Three, three for the Colonel; Two, two for Myself and You, and Here's a jolly good Health, Oh! One for the Queen Victoria's, the best of the whole Brigade, Sir. Amen.

Mr. Frank Kidson, of Leeds, the eminent authority upon folk-lore songs in a note to the editor, says: "This song is an adaptation of a popular Folk Song, known in every district. It is sometimes called 'The Dilly Song,' and copies are in *English County Songs* collected by Miss Broadwood and Fuller Maitland (page 156), and in Baring-Gould's *Songs of the West* and elsewhere. All these songs vary in detail and in tune. Miss Broadwood's version begins:

I'll sing you one oh. Green grow the rushes.
What is your one oh?
One and one is all alone and evermore shall be oh.

I'll sing you two oh. Green grow the rushes.
What is your two oh?
Two and two for the lily white boys clothed all in green oh.
One and one is all alone and ever more shall be ho.

I'll sing you three oh. Green grow the rushes.
What is your three oh?
Three three for the rivals. Two and two for the lily white boys, etc. etc.

CHAPTER XV

WITH THE ARMY OF THE RHINE

EARLY in February, 1919, it became known that the Queen Victoria's Rifles were to join the Army of Occupation, concerning which the following Special Order had been issued on Armistice Day:

"TO ALL RANKS OF THE FOURTH ARMY

"The Fourth Army has been ordered to form part of the Army of Occupation on the Rhine in accordance with the terms of the Armistice. The march to the Rhine will shortly commence, and, although carried out with the usual military precautions, will be undertaken generally as a peace march.

"The British Army through over four years of almost continuous and bitter fighting has proved that it has lost none of that fighting spirit and dogged determination which has characterised British armies in the past, and has won a place in history of which every soldier of the British Empire has just reason to be proud. It has maintained the highest standard of discipline, both in advance and retreat. It has proved that British discipline, based on mutual confidence between officers and men, can stand the hard test of war far better than Prussian discipline based on fear of punishment.

"This is not all. The British Army has, during the last four years on foreign soil, by its behaviour in billets, by its courtesy to women, by its ever ready help to the old and weak, and by its kindness to children, earned a reputation in France that no army serving in a foreign land torn by the horrors of war has ever gained before. Till you reach the frontier of Germany you will be marching through a country that has suffered grievously from the depredations and exactions of a brutal enemy. Do all that lies in your power by courtesy and consideration to mitigate the hardships of these poor people, who will welcome you as deliverers and friends. I would further ask you when you cross the German frontier to show the world that British soldiers, unlike those of Germany, do not wage war against women and children and against the old and weak. The Allied Governments have guaranteed that private property will be respected by the Army of Occupation, and I rely on you to see that this engagement is carried out in the spirit as well as in the letter.

"In conclusion, I ask you one and all, men from all parts of the British Empire to ensure that the fair name of the British Army, enhanced by your exertions in long years of trial and hardship, shall be fully maintained during the less exacting months that lie before you. I ask you to show the world that as in war, so in peace, British discipline is the highest form of discipline, based on loyalty to our King, respect for authority, care for the well-being of subordinates, courtesy and consideration for non-combatants, and a true soldierly bearing in carrying out whatever duty we may be called upon to perform.

"(Sgd.) H. RAWLINSON, General,
"H.Q. Fourth Army, November, 11th, 1918."

Demobilisation commenced as early as January 14th when a draft of 1 officer and 35 O.R. were sent off. This was followed eleven days later by another big draft. "You ought to see the send-off they get," writes an eye-witness. "I hate it personally. I never did like good-byes, especially when bands play 'Auld lang syne,' etc., and you see the lorries fade out of sight with the faces of fellows you've lived with, played with, fought with, and loved for all these long weary years. And even they going home, at the last moment nearly broke down. Strong bronzed men blubbing is quite a common sight." Gradually the battalion began to dwindle down in numbers, but to the last a lot of good men remained, some of them having signed on to serve with the Army of Occupation for a year, under their own officers and with Col. Powell as O.C.

On Feb. 17th a grand "Farewell Concert" was held for all those whose names were down for home. The men gave Col. Powell a great reception.

On February 20th the battalion, now reduced to little more than the strength of a single company, was reinforced by drafts from the 2/24th, 2/2nd, 2/10th and 12th Battalions London Regiment, men ineligible for demobilisation and volunteer officers. It was reorganised into four companies with a total strength of 800 men. It entrained at Leuze at "14 hours" on Friday, February 28th, to join the Light Division of the Army of Occupation at Duren, where it arrived on March 2nd having "passed through most glorious country," as one rifleman describes it. Detraining at the station the men were marched to billets in the town. Duren is a town of considerable manufactures, in the Prussian Rhine province on the right bank of the Roer. Here the Q.V.R. remained until April 6th, during which period nothing of particular interest happened. Occasionally the battalion was called upon to "stand-to" in billets when trouble was expected with strikers in the district, but it always fizzled out. Training went on the same as usual, while the establishment of the battalion varied from day to day, drafts constantly being received from different battalions and others being dispatched home. Once about 10 officers and 300 O.R. arrived from the 2nd K.R.R.C. This gave the battalion a paper strength of approximately 90 officers and 1100 Other Ranks. At this time the Light Division consisted of :

    1st Brigade. 3 Battalions Rifle Brigade.
    2nd Brigade. 9th London Regiment,
                        6th London Regiment,
                        1st Battalion Royal Irish Rifles.

At first it was under the command of Major-Gen. Sir R. D. Whigham, K.C.B., D.S.O., and subsequently Major-Gen. G. D. Jeffreys, now G.O.C. London District.

On April 7th the Division moved from Duren area to an area between that town and Cologne, the 9th going to Niederaussem and Oberaussem, two very small villages in an agricultural district. Here a period of eight weeks was spent in peaceful training. On 12th Col. E. G. H. Powell quitted the battalion and was succeeded by Col. E. Powell, D.S.O. (Rifle Brigade). Capt. Duncan, M.C. and several more officers of the Q.V.R. were also demobilised at the same time. Col. E. Powell only remained with the battalion about three weeks and was then succeeded by Lieut.-Col. F. R. Day, D.S.O. (Norfolk Regiment).

About the middle of May when uncertainty prevailed about Germany signing the peace, several divisions of the British Army of the Rhine, as it was then designated, were concentrated on the outpost line of the Cologne bridgehead ready to move forward into the interior in conjunction with the Belgian Army on the left and the French and Americans on the right. The Light Division moved up and garrisoned Cologne. The Q.V.R. were split up into companies and groups guarding docks and dumps with their H.Q. in some old German barracks in Riehl, a suburb of Cologne. These barracks were capable of accommodating two divisions and were very comfortable. Each battalion had a huge house apart from the main buildings for the officers, with a spacious mess room with a musician's gallery, lifts from the kitchen and the very latest appliances for the use of the servants. There were further both flower and kitchen gardens, and what was even more appreciated, a hard tennis court. These comfortable quarters were evacuated, with many regrets, on July 1st and the battalion returned to its old billets at Niederaussem. A week later the Light Division relieved the Lowland Division in the outpost line, the Q.V.R. taking over from the 6th K.O.S.B. Two companies were disposed in the outpost line while two remained with H.Q. in Wald, a town of some 6000 inhabitants about two miles in rear. These companies worked in reliefs of fourteen days. The duties of the outposts consisted in guarding all roads leading from the occupied area into the "Neutral Zone" with patrols between such posts to prevent the passage of civilians without the necessary permits or engaged in smuggling unauthorised commodities out of the occupied area. The troops were billeted in estaminets or houses and were quite comfortable, in fact it was quite an easy job they were on and infinitely preferable to the training in Wald. A good deal of smuggling went on, especially in cigarettes, as the Germans in the unoccupied area would pay five or six marks for a packet of English cigarettes which could be purchased in the occupied area for one mark or thereabouts, but as the troops were allowed a big proportion of all the confiscated articles they were naturally very keen. If caught the Germans had to pay a fine in addition to having their goods confiscated. One smart rifleman was offered a bribe of 100 marks to let the offender go. The bribe was accepted, but unfortunately for the Hun another Tommy had spotted the game and he was promptly run in. Another time quite a number of civilians were caught coming from the unoccupied area and presenting forged passes bearing very good imitations of the British stamps. They were brought before the Military Court where their *modus operandi* was exposed. It appeared that a Dutchman representing himself to be a British officer arrived at a town adjacent to the outpost line and set up a permit office; the normal channel for obtaining these permits was for the civil authorities to apply through the German Army H.Q. to the British H.Q. and the pass was sent back in the same way, the process naturally taking several days. The Dutchman said he was authorised to grant passes at a moment's notice for "special" reasons which must be very urgent, the fee charged for the same varying according to the haste with which the pass was required. All the offenders were fined and sent back, but by the time they arrived home the Dutchman had thought it wise to quit his office for the benefit of his health. His little game lasted about a fortnight and was said to have proved very profitable.

At Niederaussem, life for the Q.V.R. was none too strenuous an affair and much time was devoted to sport. The battalion cricket team was the best in the brigade and supplied two members to the divisional eleven. A few football matches were played although it was getting late in the season. At rifle shooting the Q.V.R. did well and at the Light Divisional Athletic Sports they carried off the cup given for the highest number of points obtained per regiment. They also ran their own concert party.

Towards the end of August demobilisation commenced anew and the battalion gradually weakened in strength, as, in fact, did the whole of the Army of the Rhine. By the middle of October only the Cadre remained. It was under the command of Capt. Corbett, M.C. and Sergt.-Major Porter, who accompanied it on its return to Davies Street on November 11th, 1919.

" My own impression of the Germans during our occupation,"

says Lieut. Sidney C. Hall (Assistant Adjutant), from whose diary this account has been compiled, "was as a man with all the wind knocked out of him; he was most servile and took every advantage of the troops to make money. The prices of articles required by soldiers were constantly going up. Although we were billeted for several months in private houses we had very little trouble with the civilians, much less than we should have had if we had been in England. We heard of isolated cases of soldiers getting knocked about by civilians but we did not experience anything of the kind. It was quite an interesting and educational six months, also very comfortable."

PART IV
THE THIRD BATTALION

THE THIRD BATTALION

ORIGINALLY an "Excess Company" of the 2nd Q.V.R. the 3rd Battalion increased in strength until, on 5th of November, 1914, it numbered 54 N.C.O.'s and 390 men with some half-dozen officers, of whom Major R. M. P. Willoughby (T.F. Reserve), was the senior. Until the 2nd Battalion left for Crowborough on November 23rd the H.Q. in Davies Street sheltered both contingents, and in the circumstances there was at times considerable overcrowding. Those concerned will not readily forget the early days in that wet and foggy November, during which Cock Yard opposite was utilised for drilling the newly joined recruits. Fortunately, experienced instructors were to be found among the rejoined members of the Q.V.R., not the least invaluable among them being Clr.-Sergt. Bower, who was installed *pro tem.* as Sergeant Major. A word of gratitude is due to the Y.M.C.A. who lent their excellent Physical Training Instructors from their gymnasium in Tottenham Court Road to put the men through varied and original exercises. Messrs. Naylor and Clarke, the instructors in question, ingeniously improvised apparatus in which the park railings and chairs played a part, or arranged the men in pairs so as to provide each other with gymnastic apparatus of a live sort. The portion of Hyde Park in which the exercises were carried on lay between the Marble Arch and the Tea House and daily large crowds gathered to witness the performance. The able-bodied men among them were promptly tackled by recruiting parties detailed for the purpose and to their credit they generally yielded readily enough and were forthwith hastened off to H.Q. to be "sworn in," and in an hour or two to reappear as Riflemen. For Platoon Drill and Musketry Instruction the number of rifles to be found at Head-quarters was just, and only just, sufficient to permit the training of half a platoon at a time. This was done under the supervision of Capt. H. J. Page, formerly of the Bloomsbury Rifles, who for this purpose had gone on a "refresher course" and had obtained a certificate as First-class Musketry Instructor. The miniature range in the basement of H.Q. and a Solano Target in the Drill Hall were constantly in full use.

The afternoons were spent as a rule in route marching which proved most invaluable for recruiting purposes, the battalion being preceded by the band under Regimental Bandmaster W. A. Farley and the buglers under Bugle-Major W. E. Broome. On these occasions Mrs. Page would head the column in her car, its sides placarded with stimulating patriotic posters, and distributing with ingratiating smiles leaflets urging the eligible forthwith to join Queen Victoria's Rifles. This gave a great fillip to the recruiting of the regiment, and pictures of the car were shown on the film at the Palladium and other theatres and also appeared in the daily and weekly illustrated papers.

As was the case with both the 1st and 2nd Battalions an "Equipment Fund" was started and generous response made thereto by friends of the regiment, the inhabitants of the Parish of St. George's, Hanover Square, and the surrounding district. Other buildings adjacent to H.Q. were placed at its disposal, a hut was erected in the square garden to provide accommodation for recreation and refreshments. Here "Recruiting Concerts" were held, notable among them was the entertainment arranged by Lady Lloyd, at which Gen. Sir Francis Lloyd, Commanding London District, was present, also one by Lord and Lady Farquhar when the regiment was honoured by the presence of the Princess Royal and Princess Maud; among others present on this occasion were the Marchioness of Ripon, the Marquis de Soveral, Lady Strathcona and Lord Edward Grosvenor. Among those who contributed musical items during the evening were Lady Maud Warrender and Miss Margaret Cooper. At the conclusion of the programme a stirring recruiting speech was delivered by Col. Shipley of the 1st Q.V.R. who was back from the front on short leave. Other memorable concerts were given by the Duke and Duchess of Somerset and by Lord and Lady Hollenden. The

THE THIRD BATTALION 481

last named also entertained the battalion, one thousand strong, to luncheon at the old Star and Garter after manœuvres at Richmond Park. It would be impossible to overstate the debt of gratitude the Q.V.R. owed to Lady Strathcona, whose son, the Hon. A. J. B. Howard, then held a commission in the regiment. He subsequently transferred to the Scots Guards.

Besides the deficiency of rifles another difficulty the 3rd Battalion had to contend with was that of billeting. Accommodation at Davies Street was limited, although every hole and corner were utilised, including even the two billiard tables, both on top and underneath, to the utmost extent of what may be called the available blanket-power. It was accordingly decided to follow the practice adopted by the 1st and 2nd Battalions while in London and allow all men, who had homes to go to, to spend the nights there, returning in the morning in time for drill. The result fully justified this course, for there was no case of desertion or trouble of any kind arising in consequence ; indeed the men probably did much useful recruiting work in their own neighbourhoods among eligible relatives and friends.

Speaking generally in regard to the recruiting campaign in London during the early days of the war, the experiences of the 9th Battalion belied the charge advanced against the Territorial Force that it possessed insufficient reserves. This was far from the fact, at any rate in the case of this, and probably the majority of the other London Battalions which supplied so large a proportion of the Territorial troops. Trained men who had served before the war and had retired and who immediately rejoined, formed the main source of the material which had so promptly filled up the 1st and 2nd Battalions and also provided a substantial nucleus to form the backbone of the 3rd Battalion, especially as regards the all-important element of experienced instructors and non-commissioned officers. At no time was there an insufficiency of men in the 3rd, or Reserve Battalion as it became, to fill up losses caused in the ranks of the two battalions on active service. On the other hand drafts of men enlisted specially for the Q.V.R. were sent to other regiments. By Easter, 1915, the Q.V.R. had not double, but counting second and third lines together, between three and four times their original establishment. In the summer of 1915 the 3/9th stood nearly

1000 strong after complying with the demands for drafts, dispatched in every case as soon as asked for. At a later period, January, 1916, it was 1540 strong of which some 1200 were under training for drafts.

On 26th January, 1915, Col. J. A. Bradney, C.B., T.D., was appointed to the command of the 3rd Battalion Q.V.R. He had formerly commanded the 2nd Monmouthshire and had been chairman of the Monmouthshire Territorial Association. The battalion was at once reorganised and officers posted to companies as follows, to date from February 8th :—

"*A*" *Company*
Capt. R. M. P. Willoughby.
Lieut. R. G. Oram.
2nd Lieut. A. J. B. Howard.
2nd Lieut. W. Goodinge.
2nd Lieut. W. S. Stranack.

"*B*" *Company*
Capt. H. J. Page.
Lieut. H. P. Rashleigh
(Signalling Officer).
Lieut. G. M. Critchett.
Lieut. A. S. Buchanan.
2nd Lieut. R. H. Sampson.
2nd Lieut. G. P. Fildes.

"*C*" *Company*
Capt. R. W. Henderson.
Lieut. G. G. Nathan.
2nd Lieut. H. S. Blackwood.
2nd Lieut. C. A. G. C. Keeson.

"*D*" *Company*
Capt. S. S. C. Probyn.
Lieut. G. Inglis.
Lieut. E. Wright
(Machine-gun Officer).
Lieut. L. D. Flemming
(Transport Officer).
2nd Lieut. W. McBride.

Captain J. E. A. Hunter (Acting Adjutant).

Closely following upon this reorganisation the battalion was called upon to supply its first draft of men to fill up vacancies in the senior battalions. In this case some 200 partially trained men were dispatched to the 2nd Battalion to complete their training and to fill the places of reinforcements sent from that battalion to the 1st Battalion in the trenches. This draft was soon followed by another, of 94 men.

Early in April news came that the battalion was to go into camp, and on the 21st of the month the officers gave a farewell

THE THIRD BATTALION

tea in the Grosvenor Square hut to their many kind supporters. Princess Arthur of Connaught honoured the entertainment with her presence and on a brilliantly fine spring afternoon it developed into a regular garden party.

In view of the pending move Col. Bradney placed the recruiting in the hands of Company Sergt.-Major H. W. Arnold (afterwards Capt. K.R.R.C.) and a staff of 50 O.R., all recently returned home from the front. These promptly set to work to organise a strenuous campaign. Districts were allotted to specially detailed squads and the principal thoroughfares were thenceforth systematically patrolled by the N.C.O.'s or men working in pairs. At night the local places of amusement, including cinemas, were regularly visited and at the latter films of the 3rd Battalion engaged in strenuous training were often exhibited. One of the returned Riflemen then addressed the audience, the personal appeal from one who had actually seen service at the front, proving a valuable factor in obtaining the many hundreds of recruits resulting from these efforts.

One of the last events to vary the daily routine is not likely to be forgotten by those present. The Palladium Theatre had invited the battalion to their performance and Col. Bradney seized the opportunity to make a recruiting speech from the stage. Almost immediately following upon his last words the glorious but tragic news came through of the holding of Hill 60 by Lieut. Woolley and his handful of Q.V.R., the story of which is told on an earlier page. The news was communicated to the regiment and the audience from the stage.

On the following day, April 24th, the battalion was inspected on the Horse Guards' Parade by Sir R. Pole-Carew, K.C.B., C.V.O., and on May 4th left Head-quarters for its last march through the streets of London on its way to Tadworth. Here a strenuous, if uneventful, time was passed in training ; the men being exercised in everything that the military mind deemed necessary and in every kind of athletic sport. Officers were sent in regular rotation on various " courses." This continued until 25th of June when the order came through that only 459 riflemen, with H.Q. and 14 officers were to remain at Tadworth and the remainder were to return to London under the Second-in-Command. There these resumed the former routine of drilling in the public parks and route marching ;

the more advanced men were retained at Tadworth for selection to complete drafts as and when required.

On 7th July Gen. Lloyd inspected the camp at Tadworth and expressed his special approbation of the regularity and good order obtaining. On 30th the whole brigade proceeded to Richmond, to be joined there by the London contingent of the Q.V.R., excepting a small detachment left behind to carry on the recruiting campaign. Here the troops took possession of that eastern strip of the Park entered from the Kingston Road by " Chohole Gate," not open to the public and known as King George's Farm. Here they were quite uninterfered with by the public and found admirable training-ground.

On the first anniversary of the sailing of the 1st Battalion for France, November 4th, a memorial service for fallen members of the Q.V.R. was held in St. George's Church, Hanover Square, and was very largely attended. The Rev. R. H. Sinclair, Chaplain of the Regiment, gave a highly interesting address and Chopin's " Marche Funèbre " was played on the organ. The service was concluded by the singing of the National Anthem, and the sounding of the "Last Post" by the battalion buglers. On the following evening, and in celebration of the same event, the 3rd Battalion gave a very successful concert at Chohole Gate Camp. Sergt. Arnold Feore acted as stage-manager and musical director, and Lieut. W. S. Stranack as president.

The 3rd Battalion prolonged its stay at Chohole Gate Camp until 11th January, 1916, when it left for an even longer sojourn in the Hutment Camp at Fovant, south of Salisbury Plain, between Salisbury and Shaftesbury. A week later a draft of 100 men was dispatched overseas direct to the 1st Battalion. On 24th Field-Marshal Lord French came over and inspected the battalion. Drawn up in four companies of fully trained men and two companies of men partially trained, all in "their best boots" as per battalion orders, the parade met with gratifying approval from the Field-Marshal, who subsequently promulgated the fact in a special order of the day.

Work was now becoming increasingly specialized, the division of the various classes being so arranged as to give good variety together with opportunity for combined drill and training, a somewhat complicated time table being required.

The battalion was now getting the benefit of officers and non-commissioned officers returned from actual war service overseas and the practical teaching of up-to-date warfare was thoroughly instilled into all ranks. Trench fighting, bombing, digging were leading items, while specialist classes were formed for the training of signallers, scouts and snipers, stretcher bearers, runners and Lewis gun manipulators. Every man, officers and riflemen alike, had to go through a bayonet fighting course in which great havoc was committed upon a row of suspended sacks, usually decorated with ferocious representations of Hun physiognomy or facetious legends. As each man completed the various courses he was transferred to the draft-finding companies, which were trained together as far as possible until the call came for them to go abroad. These companies were staffed for the most part with officers and N.C.O.'s with war experience. The men, now exempt from physical training and bayonet fighting practice, next went through a course of special training under Major S. V. Shea, musketry instructor, who went out with the 1st Q.V.R. It was reckoned that under this system a civilian could be turned in the course of three months into an infantry soldier ready in all respects to take his place in the firing line.

A fourth division of the battalion consisted of "unfit platoons," made up for the most part of war-scarred soldiers who, after a short period of recuperation, were expected to be fit to rejoin the battalion at the front.

Training for athletic sports was pursued with equal vigour and in various fields the 3rd Q.V.R. more than upheld the name of the many famous sportsmen who have preceded them. At Richmond the battalion had succeeded in carrying off but one event at the Army Sports held on October 7th, the somewhat unexpected one, for riflemen, of "Mounted Wrestling," thanks to the strenuous coaching of Sergt. Toop, the transport sergeant, and some good horsemen among the officers, including Lieut. W. F. Russell-Jones and 2nd Lieuts. Stranack, Fife-Cookson and Fielding, the transport officer, and, though last not least, Lieut. R. P. Pollard, appointed medical officer in May, 1915, full of equine guile from his native Ireland and a universal favourite under his soubriquet of "the Doc." In the final heat the Queen Vics triumphed over the A.S.C.

Under the auspices of Capt. Oram and Sergt.-Major Porter, himself a fine long-distance runner, every encouragement was given to the men to make themselves proficient in various sports. The Southern Counties Cross-Country Association Military Race Committee promoted a cross-country race over a course of 4½ miles at Fovant on 28th June, 1916. A field of 42 teams turned out, each of the four companies of the Q.V.R. being represented. After some very close racing the winners were found in "A" Company of the Q.V.R. who finished in 28 minutes 45 seconds, beating the next team ("C" Company, L.R.B.) by just on a minute and a half, their time being 30 minutes 15 seconds. In addition to a handsome silver cup for this performance the Q.V.R. also won a silver bowl for the unit prize, the times of the three first in regimental teams to count. The record of the Q.V.R. ran :—

"A" Company	28 minutes	46 seconds.
"D" „	31 „	34 „
"B" „	33 „	13 „
Total	93	33

"C" Company's time was 33 minutes 37 seconds.
The times of other competitors were :—

L.R.B.	93 minutes	56 seconds.
Post Office	94 „	29 „
7th London	97 „	8 „
1st „	97 „	40 „
6th „	97 „	50 „
10th „	100 „	38 „

At the general athletic meeting of the 3/1st Division held on 12th August the Q.V.R. won the Inter-Battalion Athletic Championship of the Division, together with the Divisional Inter-Company Championship which was taken by "A" Company (Capt. Oram).

In the cricket field the Q.V.R. were very much to the front. Led by Major Shea (or Shea-Simonds, as he now is known) and the Padre, W. V. Jephson, they were successful upon many occasions. The eleven and their supporters were hospitably entertained at Compton Chamberlayne by Mr. Charles Penruddocke and by Lord Wilton at Wilton Park and elsewhere in the neighbourhood. Matches were also played with the L.R.B., the 4th, 7th and 11th London.

It may also be mentioned as a further laurel earned among the brigade courses at this period that the 3rd Q.V.R. Vickers' gun team emerged top of all the units with 607 marks out of a possible 680, and the battalion's Lewis gun section obtained a good second—385 out of 430, the top team making 390—in the special courses through which all the sections of these arms in camp were put in July, 1916.

"Poison Gas"—the unofficial organ of the 3rd Battalion Queen Victoria's Rifles—ran to two issues, No. 1, 12 pages, in February, 1916, and No. 2 in April, 16 pages. It was essentially an officers' mess production with a circulation of about thirty copies. The editors were believed to be Capt. Hamilton and Lieut. Deakes, and in regard to No. 2 Lieut. Lane.

With the approach of autumn preparations began for instituting a new regime at Fovant. The system of the supply of drafts and the training of reserves had for some time been causing the authorities great searching of heart. The recruiting sources of many units were proving inadequate, and to meet the situation a practice had been growing up of transferring men from their own regiments to make good losses in others, a practice which was extremely distasteful, to put it mildly, to the men concerned, destructive alike to regimental feeling and the benefit of training in close comradeship. Men eager to be sent out to their own first line units at the earliest moment had been known to "go sick" when detailed for a draft destined by rumour for some other regiment, and a reform was clearly overdue. This took the form of general training reserves from which men required could be dispatched to any regiment of the same arm while the regiments which had not entirely depleted their reserves were permitted to continue training in regimental reserve units. Among these were the London Territorial Infantry, and for them grouped regimental training reserve battalions were arranged. Men desiring to do so could accordingly join one of these battalions direct and be trained to that extent regimentally, eventually being dispatched overseas to the regiment of their own selection. In the case of the Q.V.R. such a grouped reserve unit was arranged in conjunction with the 11th (Finsbury) Rifles and the 12th (Central London Rangers), the new unit being constituted on 1st September, 1916, and called the 9th (Reserve) Battalion London Regiment. The command was given to Lieut.-Col. E. J. M. Gore, T.D., of the 11th and the epitaph of the 3rd Q.V.R. was pronounced by Col. Bradney in his last order, dated 31st August :

" As this is the last day on which this unit is to continue as a separate battalion the Commanding Officer takes this opportunity of thanking the officers, non-commissioned officers and men for the support they have continually given him. During the seventeen months he has had the honour of commanding the battalion the work done by the officers and non-commissioned officers in training the men for drafts, and by the men who have been trained, has been eminently satisfactory and worthy of the traditions of Queen Victoria's Rifles. During this period no less than 2,036 men have been trained and dispatched either abroad, or to the 2nd Battalion, and on no occasion has any complaint been received in regard to them."

PART V
APPENDICES

APPENDIX I

I

THE FIRST VOLUNTEER RIFLE CORPS
THE DUKE OF CUMBERLAND'S SHARPSHOOTERS

WHEN the Territorial Force supplanted the Old Volunteers on the 1st April, 1908, the names of many famous regiments disappeared from the Army List; some were lost sight of altogether, while others blossomed forth under new titles. Among the former was the St. Giles's and St. George's (Bloomsbury) Rifle Volunteers, officially known as the 19th Middlesex R.V., while among the latter was the Victoria and St. George's Rifles, known for fifty years as the 1st Middlesex. The two regiments were amalgamated under the name of Queen Victoria's Rifles, the 9th County of London Regiment. The Victoria and St. George's Regiment was in itself a combination made up of the Victoria Rifles and the St. George's Rifles, respectively the 1st and 6th Middlesex, which were amalgamated on the 1st June, 1892. Each of the three regiments had a history of which its members were justly proud.

THE VICTORIA RIFLES

This celebrated corps claims a direct and unbroken connection with the old Volunteers of the Napoleonic era. Authentic records are lacking, but according to tradition the Victoria's were the descendants of the Duke of Cumberland's Sharpshooters, a regiment whose services were accepted by His Majesty King George III on 5th September, 1803. About the middle of August of that year a Committee, under the patronage of His Royal Highness Ernest Augustus, Duke of Cumberland, met at the Vestry Room of St. Paul's, Covent Garden, where they resolved—" That it being the opinion of high military authority that Corps of Sharpshooters would be eminently useful in and about the Metropolis, they determined to offer their services to the Government as a Corps of Riflemen to be called the Duke of Cumberland's Sharpshooters."

The inauguration of the regiment is thus described in a Journal of the time (10th September, 1803) :—

" On Saturday last there was a General Meeting of the Gentlemen of the Duke of Cumberland's Corps of Sharpshooters, at the Shakespeare Tavern. The business of the meeting was opened with the reading of a Letter from the Marquis of Titchfield, Lord-Lieutenant of the County of Middlesex, signifying His Majesty's most gracious approbation and acceptance of the offer of the Corps. A very condescending and flattering Letter was then read from his Royal Highness the Duke of Cumberland—in which, after paying several deserved encomiums to the zeal and exertions of J. T. Barber, Esq., of Southampton Street, Strand (a gentleman well known in the circles of literature and the arts), in forming this Corps, His Royal Highness nominated him ' as a very fit and proper person to have the honour of commanding the Duke of Cumberland's Corps of Sharpshooters.' His Royal Highness concluded by trusting that this recommendation would meet with every Gentleman's concurrence. The letter was received with great applause, and the nomination followed by the unanimous suffrage of the Corps. Mr. Barber then rose, and assured the Gentlemen that the partiality which they had shown him by so warmly supporting the distinguished nomination with which he had been honoured, should be ever engraven on his heart. Whatever the abilities might be for which they had been pleased to give him credit, he declared, exertion at least should not be wanting on his part to maintain the respectability and spirit which the Corps so eminently possessed, and advance the rapid progress which they had already made in military manœuvres to an effectiveness, which would render them conspicuous in the eyes of their countrymen, and which alone could render them worthy of the Royal auspices under which they had been raised. At the same time he wished it to be understood, that the greatest attention would be paid in appointing meetings so as to fall as much as possible in the usual intervals from professional avocations, and to render those meetings in every respect agreeable and even amusing, although subservient to the necessary strictness of discipline. Mr. Barber then nominated Palmer Stone, Esq., late of the 38th Regiment, an officer of considerable experience and ability, and Richard Houghton, Esq., to be First and Second-Lieutenants of the First Company. Both Gentlemen were unanimously elected."

The services of the regiment were accepted by the Government on the 5th September, 1803, the authorised establishment being as follows :—

                Companies 3
                Establishment per Company . . . 70
                Total 210
                Field Officers 1
                Captains 3
                Subalterns 6
                Sergeants 6
                Corporals 9
                Drummers 3
                Effective Rank and File 210

His Royal Highness

Ernest Augustus

Duke of Cumberland,

Born June 6: 1771.

APPENDIX I

TERMS OF SERVICE
Under the Defence Acts, 43 Geo. III, Caps 55 and 96.

ALLOWANCES REQUIRED AND GRANTED
Pay . . . . . . None
Clothing . . . . . . None
Contingencies . . . . . None

Mr. John Thomas Barber, subsequently known as Barber Beaumont, was born on the 21st December, 1774, in Marylebone. He manifested an early taste for art, and in 1791 entered the Schools of the Royal Academy, where he gained several medals, and from 1794 to 1806 was an exhibitor. He took up miniature art and was appointed miniature painter to the Duke of Kent and Duke of York. In after-life he became known as the Founder of the first Savings Bank, the Provident, and also of the County Fire Office and Provident Life Office. He was also a Magistrate for Middlesex and Westminster.

The uniform of the newly raised Regiment was of rifle green with a short cavalry jacket and tight trousers; brass buttons, with the letters " D.C.S.S."; tall shako with long feather plume, black gaiters. For undress white tights were worn. The Officers wore a hanging hussar jacket trimmed with fur. That of the Commandant, Major Barber Beaumont, and a couple of plumes hang on the wall of the Officers' Room at Regimental Headquarters, 56 Davies Street, W. 1. They were presented to the Victoria Rifles by his grandson, Capt. Spencer Beaumont, in January, 1889.

Following the meeting at the Shakespeare Tavern above quoted the following advertisement appeared in the daily papers :—

" DUKE OF CUMBERLAND'S CORPS OF SHARPSHOOTERS.

Gentlemen desirous of becoming members of the Duke of Cumberland's Sharpshooters are requested to observe that no person is eligible as a candidate whose height exceeds six feet or is less than five feet three inches, or who does not possess personal activity. A reference to two respectable householders, resident in the Metropolis, will be deemed sufficient introduction for such Gentlemen as may be unacquainted with the Members of the Corps.

A Committee will sit every day this week from 12 to 2 o'clock at the Shakespeare Tavern, Covent Garden.

By order of the Committee,

RICHARD HOUGHTON, Sec."

Apparently no time was lost in obtaining their uniforms or in acquiring proficiency. The *Sunday Review* of October 23rd, 1803, just seven weeks after the acceptance of the Corps says :—

"DUKE OF CUMBERLAND'S SHARPSHOOTERS.

Yesterday this highly respectable and useful Corps, commanded by Capt. Barber, were inspected in the Toxopholite Ground, behind Gower Street. At eleven o'clock Lord Harrington, Lord Petersham, General Burrard and Colonels Jenkinson and Leslie arrived, when the Corps began its evolutions. After passing twice before the General and his suite, in ordinary and in quick time, they went through their skirmishing manœuvres to the satisfaction and surprise of every person present, military or otherwise. They formed into an extended line, the front rank discharging their rifles, and giving way for the rear to advance, who, having fired, remained firm at their post, the front rank again advancing in the same order, keeping up an alternate discharge and advance of the most rapid kind. All was silent, not a word could be heard from the Corps, the command being given by a whistle, so that an enemy must be unconscious of their approach in everything but the effect of their guns. Having advanced in this way to a considerable distance, they retreated in the same order, at the sound of the bugle, firing and falling back. Another mode of annoyance was then practised, as singular in its appearance as expertly performed ; the Corps advanced to certain positions, laid themselves on their bellies, took aim, and discharged their rifles, rolling again upon their backs, at full length, to load, and by this means keeping up an incessant and well-directed annoyance. After some time spent in this way, the whole Corps, at the sound of the whistle, leaped up and fled with the utmost precipitancy. Then rallied, took a fresh position and repeated their former movements."

The *Morning Chronicle* had a similar report of the inspection, and adds, " Lord Harrington complimented the Corps on the rapidity and dexterity with which they acquitted themselves."

Captain Barber's solicitude for his men and the philanthropic ideas which he developed later on are shown by the following advertisement which appeared in the London papers on November 16th, 1803 :—

"Duke of Cumberland's Sharpshooters.—At a Meeting of the Officers, Non-Commissioned Officers and Privates of the Duke of Cumberland's Sharpshooters, held yesterday at the Garrick's Head, Bow Street, Covent Garden, Captain Barber in the Chair.

Resolved unanimously, That at a time so momentous as the present, when Britons actuated by one sentiment, have so nobly come forward to enrol themselves in defence of our most gracious Sovereign, those Laws and Liberties so well secured to us by our

APPENDIX I 495

glorious Constitution, it must be obvious to the Members of every Volunteer Corps, that in the training and disciplining such an immense body of men, accidents of the most fatal kind may frequently happen ; by which a family, depending exclusively upon the exertions of its father, may in addition to its irreparable loss, be in one instant involved in the greatest misery and distress.

It is therefore incumbent on the Commandant of each Volunteer Corps to adopt some plan, by which the sorrows of the widow or relative depending on that Volunteer who shall meet with any fatal accident, may be soothed by the alleviation of distress, whenever such relief may be requisite.

Resolved unanimously, That the above Resolution be forwarded to the General Committee for their consideration, on Friday evening next, November 18, who will devise the most eligible means for carrying a plan proposed by one of its members into immediate effect.

Resolved unanimously, That the Thanks of this Meeting be given to the Chairman for his zeal and attention on this important occasion."

In 1804 Capt. Barber compiled and published a little duodecimo volume, *Instructions for the Formation and Exercise of Volunteer Sharpshooters*. It was published by the well-known military library of T. Egerton, and printed by C. Roworth, Bell Yard, Fleet Street, the price being 2s. 6d. The author states that these instructions were originally composed only for the use of the corps which he commands, but that he was solicited to print them by many volunteer officers engaged in similar service. They are confined to the operations of a single company, and are divided into two parts, treating : (1) Of the rifle and the practice of firing ; (2) Of the exercise and manœuvring of the company. Twelve " Bugle-horn Calls of Sharpshooters " are added in score ; and also ten signals for the whistle, which, says Capt. Barber, " being very dissimilar, though confined to one note, have been found sufficiently distinct, and would often render the whistle a valuable substitute for the bugle-horn in actual service." Interspersed throughout the 126 pages are many little passages throwing light upon the Cumberland Sharpshooters. For instance, we are told " the guns in the Duke of Cumberland's Sharpshooters have of late (and since then in other corps) been fitted up with the back sights within two inches of the breech, and have in consequence been found to afford a more ready aim and fire more correctly than when they were placed in the ordinary way " (i.e. near the middle of the piece). He recommends " a notch squared at bottom like a saw mark, as affording a much clearer sight than a triangular one," and to get a clear view of the foresight and to obviate any light shining upon it he bends " a piece of tin (afterwards blackened) about an inch and a half wide, round the sight to the barrel so as to enclose it in a sort of archway."

The modern sharpshooter adopts the same gadgets when regulations permit. Capt. Barber also quotes the "Regulations for Firing, established in the D.C.S.S." from which we learn that the men were divided into three classes; no man who is not classed as a marksman shall be permitted to fire at a greater distance than 100 yards; a man that puts five shots out of six in the target, two days out of three, firing from the shoulder at the distance of 100 yards, will be placed in the third class; the third class will fire at the distance of 150 yards, six shots each day—three from a rest and three from the shoulder; when equally successful in this class he will be placed in the second class; the second class will fire, from a rest, at 200 yards, six shots each day; upon similar success in this class he will be placed in the first class; the first class will fire, from a rest, at 300 yards and at smaller distances, at a moving object. "As a distinction, useful and honourable, this class will wear a green silk cockade in their caps!" As a further inducement to the acquirement of skill and its retention, a gold medal will be fired for once monthly by the first and second classes, six shots at 150 and six at 200 yards, the man who puts the greatest number of shots into the target to be presented with the medal, but he is to hold it no longer than he continues to be the best shot on the days of trial; the medal finally to become the property of the man who shall prove entitled to it, on six monthly trials, when a new one will be presented to the corps.

Occasionally these medals find their way to the auction rooms and, as a rule, command good prices. One appeared in Col. J. B. Gaskell's collection dispersed by Glendining and Co. on the 25th May, 1911. It bore the inscription, "Presented to Adjutant de Berenger for his skill in firing at the target at 200 yards distance, without a rest, and hitting the bull's-eye six times in seven shots, August 15th, 1811." It realised £5.

Capt. Barber's book concludes with "An extract from an address made to the Duke of Cumberland's Sharpshooters on their early formation, upon the subject of field duty."

Some time during the year 1804 the Sharpshooters presented their Commander with a silver cup surmounted with a figure of a member of the corps in uniform. Miss Augusta Beaumont, a granddaughter, kindly lent it for exhibition at the summer fête of the Victoria Rifles on June 28th, 1890. It bore the following inscription : "Vincit Amor Patriæ. To John Thomas Barber Beaumont, Esq., their Commander. The Duke of Cumberland's Sharpshooters unanimously voted and presented this Cup in testimony of their respect and as a tribute of gratitude for his indefatigable exertions. 1804. Laudumque Immensa Cupido."

The Sharpshooters very soon acquired a name for skill and efficiency with the rifle unsurpassed by other corps, and frequent references to them may be found in the newspapers of the day. Among the most expert was the Commandant, Major Barber,

APPENDIX I

concerning whose prowess it is related in an address on vellum presented to the regiment by his grandson, Capt. Spencer Beaumont, in 1886, and carefully preserved at the head-quarters in Davies Street. "So satisfied was he of the efficiency of his men that on one occasion, in Hyde Park, he held the target while the entire corps fired consecutively into it at the distance of 150 yards!"

Their superiority was due, according to a book published in 1808 and entitled *Scloppetaria: or Considerations on the Nature and Use of Rifled Barrel Guns*, etc., "By a Corporal of Riflemen," but ascribed by Col. T. F. Fremantle, in his *Book of the Rifle* (1901), to Col. Beaufoy, whom, he adds (page 178), was "a prominent member of the Duke of Cumberland's Sharpshooters." The "Corporal of Riflemen," whoever he was, writes: "Guns having been constructed on this plan (i.e. with a stronger or more rapid twist), they were first of all (we believe) adopted in the Duke of Cumberland's Sharpshooters, where they were found to answer so well that all their crack shots, and such as were fond of the sport, abandoned their old barrels, and procured others on the new plan, which was that of three-fourths. How long would have elapsed, before the other corps of the metropolis, made sensible of their error, would have exchanged their one-fourth for the three-fourths, was not left to the chance of time to determine: for at a match fired at about a year or a year and a half after their first pretty general introduction in the above-mentioned corps, the superiority of the three-fourths over all the smaller twists was too obvious to leave any doubt on the minds not only of the successful, but of the unsuccessful candidates also." The author concludes, "And it is too remarkable to be passed over in silence that the very person[1] who first gave the gunmaker the plans and ideas, which enabled him to strike out this improved manner of rifling, was himself among the number of the vanquished."

This great match is also commemorated by a coloured engraving of the time which is here reproduced.

The plate is inscribed:—

"London, Published June, 1808, by Random & Sneath, Sporting Gallery, Hart Street, Bloomsbury Square.

Painted by P. Reinagle, A.R.A., from a Sketch by Adjt. Random de Berenger.

The figure is engraved by G. Maile, and the Landscape by F. C. & G. Lewis.

To His Royal Highness The Duke of Cumberland,

This Plate representing Sharpshooters in Ambush, is most respectfully dedicated, With Permission, By His Royal Highnesses
Most humble and very obedient Servants,
Random & Sneath.

[1] Mr. Francis Delapierre of Hackney suggested the new method of rifling to Mr. Smith of Lisle Street, who made the guns for the D.C.S.S.

2 K

EXPLANATION. The Corps represented is that which has the Honor of bearing His Royal Highnesses Name. It was raised in 1803, under the care of its present Major (J. T. Barber, Esq.), and consisted of one company of Riflemen. In 1807 the same was increased to three companies whose expert firing and good Discipline leads to anticipate considerable augmentation. Their superiority as Marksmen was proved in November, 1805, in a Grand Trial of Skill with five other Rifle Corps each deputing six of its best shots and the following was the return :

	Hits.
The Duke of Cumberland's Corps	81
Honble Artillery Yagers	57
Hackney Riflemen	46
6th London Riflemen	37
North Briton Do.	33
Loyal Southwark Do.	21

The Shots selected by the D.C.S.S. were Major Barber, Capt. Reece, Adjt. Random de Berenger, Lieut. Silver, Serjt.-Major Pocock, & Corpl. Williams."

From another authority we learn that on this occasion Major Barber himself made the highest score (19). The match took place at Montpelier Gardens, Surrey.

A silver cup, the prize of the match, was exhibited at a summer fête, held by the Victoria Rifles, at the Drill Ground, Marlborough Place, St. John's Wood, on June 28th, 1890. It was lent among other relics and trophies by Miss Augusta Beaumont. In an inscription it gives further particulars of the contest, viz. " each man firing six shots at 100 and 150 yards off-hand, and at 200 and 250 yards resting. The target was a circle of 30 inches in diameter."

In after life the central figure of this plate, Charles Random de Berenger, attained considerable notoriety, being identified as the " Du Bourg or De Berenger," who played such a leading part in the Stock Exchange Hoax of 1814. Leaving London one Saturday night in February at a critical period of the war with France, he presented himself on Sunday night at the Old Ship Hotel at Dover, dressed as a staff officer, with despatches which announced the triumph of the Allies and the death of Bonaparte. The news, of course, sent up all the funds on the Stock Exchange on Monday morning to the vast profit of those who had Consols or Omniums to dispose of. Vast sums were sold in the course of the day,—not less, it is supposed, in all, than half a million ; but at length the non-arrival of the pretended French officer began to throw discredit on the tale. Omnium gradually declined from 33 to which it had risen to $28\frac{1}{2}$, only one point over the opening price. It is said that De Berenger left his postchaise at the outskirts of London and, taking a hackney coach, drove straight to a house in Green Street, then occupied by the famous Thomas, Lord Cochrane,

Charles Random De Berenger.
Adjutant, Duke of Cumberland's Sharpshooters.

APPENDIX I 499

afterwards tenth Earl of Dundonald, a man whose long life of adventure, exploit, and achievement is unique even in the naval annals of this country. Cochrane was not at home when his visitor arrived, in the uniform of the Cumberland Sharpshooters, but on his return recognised him as De Berenger with whom he had previously had some personal communication on certain professional topics in which both were interested. This visit made things look very black for Cochrane, and he was apprehended and sent for trial together with De Berenger, Cochrane-Johnstone, Cochrane's uncle, a man named Butt and others. They were tried before Lord Ellenborough and all convicted. Cochrane was sentenced to pay a fine of £1,000, to stand in the pillory for an hour, and to be imprisoned for a year. The pillory was remitted, but the imprisonment was inflicted and continued until the fine was paid under protest. Cochrane, on conviction, was expelled from the House of Commons, his name was struck out of the Navy and his Knighthood of the Bath cancelled. He, to the last, maintained his innocence, and ultimately all these indignities were revoked, but not until 1832 was he granted a full pardon.

De Berenger, who was sentenced to twelve months' imprisonment, beguiled his time in prison by writing his version of the hoax, under the title of *The Noble Stockjobber*. He afterwards opened an institution called the Stadium or " British National Arena for Manly and Defensive Exercises," on the site of Cremorne Gardens ; and he published a curious little book, *Helps and Hints How to Protect Life and Property*. It is claimed by his relatives that in his case also there had been a gross miscarriage of justice. De Berenger himself absolutely disclaimed any connection with the plot. His grandson in a letter to *The Times* in 1903 writes : " It is a noticeable and recorded fact that after his incarceration in the Marshalsea State Prison the Baron was visited and received by royalty and all the leading members of the nobility and literary circles of the day. Earl Cadogan, Count D'Orsay, Dickens and Cruikshank were his closest friends, all firmly convinced of his innocence, until the day of his death many years later."

It is not proposed here to give a full and detailed history of the Sharpshooters. Reviews and Inspections were things of frequent occurrence in those days, and in nearly all they duly played their part. To celebrate the birthday of their Royal patron (6th June) in 1804 the corps engaged Vauxhall Gardens for the accommodation of their members and friends and offered a number of prizes for rifle shooting and running. In common with the other Volunteers they took part in the rejoicings in connection with the King's Jubilee, in October, 1805, attending at St. Martin's Church, whence, having " listened to an excellent sermon," they marched to the park and fired a *feu de joie*. On one occasion (1804) when all the Light Infantry Companies of the Westminster, London and Southwark Volunteers were brigaded in Hyde Park we find it recorded

that "the Duke of Cumberland's Sharpshooters were the only corps in the neighbourhood of London absent!"
They still accumulated praise for their skill with the rifle. On the 18th April, 1805, " the admirers of military show were gratified with a most excellent treat in Hyde Park. Brigadier-General the Earl of Banbury, went to ' Buckdon Hill,' for the purpose of witnessing the expertness of the Duke of Cumberland's Sharpshooters in firing at a mark. They stood at a distance of 150 yards from a very small target, and though they were but few in number they may be said to have completely demolished it, it was so entirely perforated with the balls." Another account states that only three shots missed the target out of 67 fired.

Another historic contest of which we give a reproduction of a print published by Fores of Piccadilly, took place on the racecourse, Stamford, in August, 1811, between "five of the Hon. Artillery Yagers and five Nottingham Riflemen, which was won by the former by two shots. A second match afterwards took place between five of the Nottingham Riflemen and five of the Duke of Cumberland's Sharpshooters which was won by the latter by twelve shots a-head ; also beating the Artillery Yagers by six shots. The names of the five artillery gentlemen who shot were Beaumer, Garth, Davis, Waller and Broadhurst. The names of the five Gentlemen of the Duke of Cumberland's Sharpshooters were Bell, Henderson, Charlton, Lynch, and Fenton " (Bell's *Messenger*, September 1st, 1811).

In his *History of the H.A.C.* Raikes merely mentions the incident " reflecting credit on the Company (Yager) as in a late competition with a Society formed at Nottingham for the encouragement of rifle shooting, and who had challenged all England." The print reproduced bears the Legend, " The Challengers of All England Chop-Fallen : or the Cumberland Triumph." It also records, " The skill of the Competitors may be judged of by the following : First Match, Notts 21, Artillery Yagers 23. Second Match, Notts 18, Cumberland 31."

" N.B. The Notts took 2 hours and 40 minutes for their shots in order to drive the Cumberland into the night. The Cumberland fired theirs in 48 minutes, beginning at a quarter past five."

The following remarks are supposed to be made by the several figures depicted :—

" Those queer looking chaps are Robin Hood's men as they call themselves."

" Well, I always thought Robin Hood and his men had been gentlemen ! "

" Excellent Sharpshooters Pyes and Cumberland Nuts. I can't recommend the Nottingham Cakes, the company says they are rather sour ! "

" Why, Master Pyeman, your a wag, you had better take care what you say, the Colonel's a Magistrate."

RIFLE MATCH, 1811. DUKE OF CUMBERLAND SHARPSHOOTERS *v.* NOTTINGHAM RIFLEMEN.
"THE CUMBERLAND TRIUMPH."

APPENDIX I

" 'Pon my word, dat little Col. vat you call be very fine shoot indeed, you toss up de pin in de air and he shoot off de head, 'pon my vord, I be de Gun maker."[1]

" And the Trumpeter into the bargain it seems."

" It certainly must be oweing to the Belly Ache that I fired so bad. I never had such a belly ache in my life before. Griped all night I assure you."

" Why, I say, Col., that man's firing with a rest, damme if that's fair, they shant have the stakes."

" Twigg the two Slings to their Guns."

On the 10th June, 1811, a grand review took place on Wimbledon Common, before 100,000 spectators—" one of the grandest military spectacles ever witnessed," according to a contemporary journal. At 4 a.m., says the *National Register*, " the various volunteer corps in the metropolis were summoned to their respective parades by beat of drum, and the same sound brought forth everybody who could spare the time to see the show. At about six o'clock the Coldstream Regiment and the third battalion of Artillery set out from their parade in Birdcage Walk. The different corps of volunteers commenced their movements nearly at the same time. An immense concourse of people followed each of the regiments." About nine o'clock the troops reached the Common, and after halting for a short time the Guards and the Artillery proceeded to occupy the right of the field. Before the troops had reached their appointed stations His Royal Highness the Commander-in-Chief came upon the ground and was greeted with loud and repeated cheers. At eleven the volunteers of London and the environs arrived and formed up in close columns, the line extending from the Telegraph to the town of Wimbledon. The Corps were headed by their Patrons and Officers. His Royal Highness the Duke of Sussex headed the North Britons (the first London Scottish), Lord Duncannon the Mary-le-bone, and Lord Yarmouth the Duke of Cumberland's Sharpshooters. His Royal Highness the Prince Regent arrived on the right of the lines about twelve o'clock, his appearance being announced by a discharge of artillery. A royal salute followed, and the bands played " God Save the King." Accompanied by a numerous escort His Royal Highness proceeded down the line of volunteers, the Duke of York and the Duke of Cumberland riding on his right. His Royal Highness then occupied a station about the centre of the line. A *feu de joie* then ensued from the right all round the lines. " The troops fired in succession, almost instantaneously, producing an effect which words cannot describe. In the short space of four minutes 24,000 firelocks were discharged over a considerable tract of ground occupied by the troops. The *feu de joie* from the front rank was answered by the rear rank, and again repeated by the front rank. Three cheers with

[1] Fenton was a gunmaker carrying on business at Shoemaker Row. (*Scloppetaria*.)

caps in the air succeeded; the spectators joined in the joyful exclamations, while echo from the distant hills sent back the plaudits." The troops next passed in review before the Prince in a steady manner, and were then marched off the Heath. After the review the Prince, the Duke of York and the Duke of Cumberland proceeded to the neat and elegant cottage of Lord Yarmouth at Putney Heath to take refreshment. Lord Yarmuth had previously erected in his garden two superb marquees: the reception of his illustrious visitors, in which tables were spread in the most tasteful order with refreshments. An adjoining it was appropriated to the officers and attendants on the Royal Party. The Prince Regent and the Dukes of York and Cumberland were received on their arrival by a Guard of Honour, formed by the Duke of Cumberland's rifle corps on horseback! Thus early did the predecessors of the Victorias enact the rôle of Mounted Infantry.

A curious reference to the shooting exploits of the Sharpshooters is made by Jacob Larwood in his *Story of the London Parks*. He says, "Some years before this period (1775) a new Rifle Corps had been formed by the Duke of Cumberland, of Culloden celebrity, which was named after him the 'Cumberland Sharpshooters,' and these riflemen used to practise with ball in Hyde Park. In June, 1778, a massive earthen rampart was thrown up in the Park for this purpose; it was 20 feet high, 3 yards wide at the bottom and extended from Cumberland Gate in a westerly direction. Not very many years ago two stones were still remaining on the spot generally occupied by troops when practising at the target in front of this rampart. They were inscribed 'D.C.S.S.': his inscription, which might puzzle future antiquarians if they were to discover these stones, simply meant Duke of Cumberland's Sharpshooters." He may be right as to the stones, but he is lamentably wide of the mark concerning his dates and the nobleman after whom the regiment was named.

In June, 1814, a General Order for the disbandment of all Volunteers and for the return of their equipment to Government Stores was issued. It even was served upon the Honourable Artillery Company, but a week later the order so far as that body was concerned was rescinded. It has always been claimed that the Duke of Cumberland's Sharpshooters were also granted exemption, but reliable evidence upon the point is missing. The late Major Alfred Keeson in a *Memoir of the Victoria Rifles* (1882) states, "The Duke of Cumberland's Sharpshooters were very averse to sharing the general fate, for the love of the Rifle had become strong amongst them. Great efforts were made to win exemption from the fiat of general dissolution, but of course without avail, for the Government could not consistently make distinction in favour of any Corps. However, after a long correspondence with the authorities and the exertion of much influence their behalf, Mr. Ryder, the then Secretary of State, wrote a letter to the effect

APPENDIX I

that, although the Government could not afford them any official recognition, it would put no obstruction in the way of their continuing their association, so long as they did not obtrude themselves upon the public notice. As a matter of fact they became a Rifle Club ; but they retained amongst themselves the old regimental name, continuing to wear a uniform and meeting periodically for practice. It is very remarkable, as showing the hold the rifle gains upon the English mind, that throughout all the long years of peace the Cumberland Sharpshooters never lost their vitality. The crack of their rifles was to be heard in the summer afternoons, first at Wormwood Scrubbs and at a later date at Chalk Farm, where when a lad I frequently watched their practice, at what we should now deem the childish distance of 200 yards. The 300 seemed to be rarely attempted.

"At this period it was my lot to become acquainted with several of its old Members ; and, indeed, although never coming in contact with Major Barber Beaumont, I had, as a boy, several acquaintances who had had a personal knowledge, and always spoke of him as a man of unusual energy of character, one who had made his mark in the world even after the Volunteer movement had come to an end. Later in life I became acquainted with a veteran who had been one of the earliest recruits to the Duke of Cumberland's Sharpshooters, and he described to me the wonder of the Londoners at witnessing a kind of drill such as they had never seen before. . . . He told me that he had treasured up his old uniforms, and, oddly enough, it was mentioned in the Corps some few years ago that a specimen was still in existence. Although I heard of this I never for a moment suspected that the possessor was my old acquaintance, Corporal Hart, whom I had then lost sight of for many years. Nor was it until after his death that I became aware of the circumstance. Another of the old body was a sturdy little Scotchman named Wilson, and when a lad it was a great gratification to me to be allowed to see his rifles, of which he had many. Amongst them was the regulation one of the Cumberland Sharpshooters, upon which he appeared to set very great store."

The connection is recorded in similar terms in the memorials sent to public authorities in the attempt to gain official recognition in 1852–1853.

In a case of medals preserved at head-quarters is one having on the obverse the head of Barber Beaumont, and on the reverse "The Duke of Cumberland's Sharpshooters, the first Volunteer Rifle Corps in Great Britain was raised in 1803." On the edge is engraved, "Won by Mr. W. Moore at Chalk Farm, 26 Decr., 1839."

II

THE ROYAL VICTORIA RIFLE COMPANY

ALL authentic records of the D.C.S.S. cease with the general disbandment of the Volunteers in 1814, and their continued existence rests upon tradition and hearsay evidence. It is said that the surviving nucleus of the club into which they had passed "thought it would be more conducive to their prosperity if they sought a new and more popular name." The story is thus told in "the Address to the Laws of the Royal Victoria Rifle Company, originally made in 1835; severally revised and amended to the year 1846."

"This Society was founded on the 24th day of May, 1835, the birthday of our Most Illustrious Sovereign, Queen Victoria, by a party of gentlemen, principally connected with the Army and the Government, and residing in the neighbourhood of Earl's Court and Hammersmith, who made application to Her Royal Highness the Duchess of Kent, stating that they were desirous that Her Royal Highness with the Princess Victoria would be pleased to patronize it and sanction its being called the Royal Victoria Rifle Club."

The requisite permission was given in the following letter from Sir John Conroy, the Princess's secretary:

"KENSINGTON PALACE,
11th July, 1835.

SIR,—I have laid before the Duchess of Kent your letter of the 9th inst., stating that a party of gentlemen, residing in the neighbourhood of Earl's Court, Old Brompton, having formed a club for the purpose of rifle shooting, are desirous that her Royal Highness—with the Princess Victoria—would be pleased to patronize it, and sanction its being called the

'Royal Victoria Rifle Club.'

The Duchess of Kent commands me to request you will assure the Members of the Club, that Her Royal Highness is always happy to patronize the recreations of the Public,—and very readily accedes to their request.

I am, Sir, your most obedient servant,
JOHN CONROY.

Lieut. F. J. Dixon,
4 Earl's Court, Old Brompton."

This letter is carefully preserved at the Regimental Headquarters, 56 Davies Street, W. 1.

In consequence of a disagreement with Mr. I. Riviere, the

APPENDIX I

Treasurer of the Corps and the landlord of the ground at Kensal Green, in 1849 the club obtained from Lady Salisbury a lease of a new practice ground at Kilburn, where it had a rifle range of 400 yards, with a drill ground of 14 acres at a rental of £80 per annum.

Mr. Riviere appears not only to have been the Corps Treasurer, but also a member of the H.A.C.

As a proof that they considered themselves at this time, 1846, to be rather above the status of an ordinary rifle club, it may be mentioned that this book contains not only the laws and regulations of the club, but instructions for the use of the rifle, firing, manual and platoon exercises, bugle calls, field practice, firing regulations, etc., also particulars of the uniform and accoutrements to be worn by the members.

Coat.—A dark rifle green superfine or second cloth frock coat, single breasted, with stand-up collar, black horn buttons embossed with a death's head, the collar trimmed with black mohair cord to pattern, and the cuffs with narrow braid of the same material; officer's coats to be trimmed with broad braid, loops and frogs.

Trousers.—Of superfine or second cloth same colour as the coat, trimmed down the sides with black mohair oak-leaf lace, two inches wide.

Scales.—The shoulder scales to be bronzed, with a small silver bugle in the centre of a crescent; officers with plated scales, and a gilt bugle in the centre of the crescent.

Chaco.—Of black beaver, yeoman crown, ten inches across the top, and seven inches high from the centre, leather top, and leather V on each side; mohair cord and tassels, a small death's head, etc., on a silk rosette in front with a crown, and the letters R.V.R. underneath, all in silver or white metal; plain black leather fixed peak, bronzed lion's head, and scales, drooping horse hair plume, with bronzed socket, and plated ring; the officer's full dress a green feather plume.

Foraging Cap.—Of black oil skin (to stand up), ten inches across the crown, the band to be two inches wide, with a death's head, etc., in silver or white metal, on the front, black patent leather fixed peak.

Stock, rifle, sword, pouch, shoulder belt, waist-belt, ball bag and powder horn.

"About this time," says Major Keeson in his *Memoir*, "the political convulsions of 1848 having rendered the continuance of any semblance of military organisation by a private body a matter of some delicacy, unless conducted under official sanction, the club applied for and obtained from the magistrates of the County authority to assemble for drill and practice in the use of arms." This "licence"—also carefully preserved at head-quarters—is in the following terms:

"We, the undersigned, being Justices of the Peace for the

County of Middlesex and by the authority of an Act of Parliament passed in 60th year of the reign of his late Most Gracious Majesty, King George the 3rd, do hereby authorize the Officers of the Royal Victoria Rifle Company to drill and exercise the Members of the said Company in arms ; in order that they may be enabled from time to time to perfect the men under their command in the necessary rifle movements and practice, and for which this shall be their Warrant.

Given under our hands in the County of Middlesex this twentieth day of April, One Thousand Eight Hundred and Fifty.

    ROBERT GROSVENOR, 107 Park Street, Grosvenor Square.
    JOHN HALL, 68 South Audley Street, Grosvenor Square.
    W. APPS, The Hall, Pinner, Middlesex.

To Capt. Ellis,
    Commandant, Royal Victoria Rifle Company, Westbourn House, Westbourn Green, Harrow Road, Middlesex."

Another copy of the "Laws and Regulations" issued in 1850, shows that the title had been altered and extended to the "Royal Victoria Rifle Corps," by which name it was known until 1853. The book also contains the following :

DECLARATION

REQUIRED TO BE TAKEN BY MEMBERS ON ADMISSION.

"I do hereby declare that I am well affected to the Queen and Constitution ; and do solemnly engage, as long as I shall continue a Member of the Royal Victoria Rifle Corps, to conform to all rules and orders made for its government, to be obedient to my Officers and constant in attending to all my Military duties, and especially to promptly appear under arms whenever the Corps may be called upon for the purpose of assisting the civil power in maintaining tranquillity or suppressing riot.

In testimony of which I have subscribed my name in (this) the Roll book of the Corps."

The preface quotes a passage from the *Naval and Military Gazette* of the preceding year bearing upon the history of the corps : "We take this opportunity earnestly to impress upon those volunteer bodies existing, the advantage of at once setting about increasing their efficiency, by adding materially to their numbers and by more frequent drills and field exercise.

Of these bodies the Hon. Artillery Company of the City of London is the oldest ; the members of which are gentlemen of character, belonging to that city, and are divided into bodies of artillery and heavy and light infantry.

The other is entirely a rifle body (under the patronage of Her Majesty), denominated the Royal Victoria Rifle Corps, which has

APPENDIX I

existed for many years near London, the members of which are also of the highest respectability. They are thorough masters of their weapons, and will form the nucleus of a very efficient force."

The earliest use of the word " Corps " in connection with the Royal Victoria Rifles is in the Minute Book recording their transactions from the 12th July, 1848, to the 1st November, 1852. Under the first mentioned date it is recorded that " A detachment of the Royal Victoria Rifle Corps mustered on Fish Street Hill, in the City of London, at $\frac{1}{2}$ past 9 o'clock, a.m., for the purpose of proceeding to Erith for a day's Ball Practice, under the command of Captain Ellis." The detachment embarked at London Bridge on board the *Ruby* steamer at 10 o'clock, and arrived at Erith about half-past 11, were mustered on the pier and marched through the town to the Crown Inn, where they partook of a slight refreshment, and then proceeded to the shooting ground at the western extremity of the town, the detachment taking up its first position at 100 yards from the target. The prize to be contended for was a silver medal got up expressly for the occasion, having on one side a bust of Her Most Gracious Majesty Queen Victoria (the Patron of the Corps), with the words " Royal Victoria Rifle Corps, 1835 " round it, and on the obverse side the insignia of the corps, etc., encircled by a laurel wreath with the inscription " Erith Medal, 1848."

Dinner, it appears, had been ordered for 4 o'clock at the Pier Hotel, and at its conclusion Capt. Ellis, in a most eloquent, not to say a flowery, speech (carefully recorded at full length in the said Minutes), proposed the health of the Queen and Patron of the Corps. After this and other toasts had been duly honoured the firing roll was read by the Secretary, and Mr. Sinclair was declared to be the winner of the medal, Lieut. Clifford and Mr. Lee, both of whom had made a higher score, standing aside in his favour. Mr. Sinclair's thanks and comments are also preserved for the benefit of those interested in the early days of the Victorias, and " several other toasts were given and responded to, and many excellent songs sung, until the hour of eight, when the order was given to fall in and the detachment was marched to the head of the pier from whence it embarked on board the *Ruby* steamer for London Bridge."

The Erith Medal was competed for annually and monthly competitions for other medals were held. A large part of the book is taken up with details of the matches.

Another interesting entry appears under date of 24th November, 1848, when Capt. Ellis read a letter received by the Secretary from Messrs. W. A. Mearns and H. H. Brown, two of the recruits. The letter states, " We are young Members of the Royal Victoria Rifle Corps and trust we are committing no impropriety in representing to you that the irregular attendance of Members at Practice and the discontinuance of Drill can scarcely conduce to that state of efficiency both in numbers and discipline which should mark the only Volunteer Rifle Corps existing in England and the respect consequent thereon in which it should be held.

We humbly submit that it should be matter for consideration whether a more strict attendance at Practice and Drill would not be one of the greatest inducements to gentlemen to join the Corps to which we have the honour to belong."

Lieut. Christmas explained that as the place where the drills had hitherto been carried on was inconveniently small, and as the Committee had not been able up to that time to find a place suitable to their wants, the drill had been of necessity suspended, and he was instructed to convey that information to the writers of the letter.

III

Early Efforts to Obtain Recognition

The next phase, and the most important in the history of the Victorias, was the movement for the enrolment of Volunteer Corps in the middle of the nineteenth century. Inspired by a number of letters and communications published in the newspapers of the day somewhere about 1850, a feeling began to manifest itself throughout the country that a considerable increase to the National Defence had become a matter of pressing necessity. There are a host of claimants for the credit of reviving the Volunteer Force, but the point has never been satisfactorily settled; as they all had the same object in view it is safe to regard the honours as divided. The Victorias were certainly one of the earliest in the field, and from their unique position as a force actually in being, though admittedly a small one, possessing a drill ground, rifle range and an organisation of many years' standing, there is little doubt that their example and influence had a very appreciable effect in bringing the new force into existence.

Their first act was to order advertisements to be inserted in the public papers calling attention to the advantages of the Corps. Capt. Clifford was empowered to do this at a special meeting held on Tuesday the 20th January, 1852.

On February 3rd and on subsequent dates the following announcement appeared in *The Times*:

"Royal Victoria Rifles, established 24th May, 1835, under Royal authority, Practice Ground, Kilburn, Middlesex. The Members of the Corps are requested to hold themselves in readiness to Muster weekly instead of once a fortnight as hitherto. Gentlemen who feel at the present crisis the necessity of associating themselves together for the practice of the Rifle in order that they may be efficient to offer their services to the Government should circum-

Colour of the Royal Victoria Rifle Club, 1835.

APPENDIX I

stances render it necessary, have now an opportunity of joining the above Corps. For particulars apply to Capt. Ellis, 2 Warwick Crescent, Harrow Road ; Mr. Clifford, 82 Grosvenor Street ; Mr. Christmas, 34 South Audley Street ; and Mr. Lancaster, 151 New Bond Street."

At the meeting following the first appearance of the advertisements six new members were enrolled. It is significant that the meeting which authorised their publication was held exactly a week prior to the date (January 27th) on which the late Dr. (afterwards Sir John) Bucknill, by his own showing, first broached the plan to his Exeter friends which eventually led to the establishment of the Exeter and South Devon Rifles, and for which he ultimately received the honour of knighthood.

How the Victorias lost the precedence of being the earliest enrolled Volunteer Corps and how it happened that the Exeter and South Devon Rifles were accorded it is told in the following correspondence which is here given at some length as the incident referred to forms one of the most important in Volunteer annals and, moreover, it is the authority upon which many of the statements concerning the connection between the Sharpshooters and the Victoria Rifles rests.

(Extract from Minute Book of the Royal Victoria Rifles.)

At a Special Meeting of the Executive Committee of the Corps held in Oxford Street on Monday evening, 23rd February, 1852.

Present : Major Ellis, Commandant, in the Chair, Captain Clifford, Mr. Mann, Lieut. Christmas, Mr. Sinclair (Quartermaster), and Mr. George T. Lee and Mr. Julius Jones, Joint Honorary Secretaries.

The Chairman called the attention of the Committee to a letter published in *The Times* and other newspapers, relative to the formation of Rifle Clubs, and dated :

(Copy).

" WHITEHALL,

9th Feby., 1852.

SIR,

With reference to my letter to you of the 26th ult., I am directed by Secretary Sir George Grey to inform you that Her Majesty's Government are prepared in certain cases to advise Her Majesty to accept the services of Volunteer Rifle Corps provided that the proposed formation of such Corps is recommended by the Lord Lieutenant of the County and that the Members of the Corps undertake to provide their own arms and equipments and to defray all the expenses attending it except in the event of the Corps being assembled for active service.

It must be understood that such Corps will be subject to the provisions of the Act 44 Geo. 3rd, Cap. 54, and to such rules and regulations as may from time to time be made by Her Majesty under the authority of that or of any other Act relating to Volunteer Corps.

Any proposal for the formation of such Corps accompanyed by a statement of the intended number of Members, will, if transmitted to Sir George Grey by the Lord Lieutenant of the County receive the consideration of Her Majesty's Government.

I am, Sir, Your Obedient Servant,
(Signed) H. WADDINGTON."

Major Ellis reported that in consequence of the above letter thus publicly promulgated he had thought it necessary to memorialise the Government and bring to their notice the position in which the "Royal Victoria Rifles" stood with reference to any formations under Mr. Waddington's letter of the 9th February.

The memorial to the Government and a private letter to the Lord Lieutenant of the County which accompanied it were laid upon the table and ordered to be read by the Secretary and entered on the minutes.

(*Copy of Memorial to Government.*)

"No. 2 WARWICK CRESCENT,
WESTBOURNE TERRACE ROAD,
HYDE PARK,
20*th Feby.*, 1852.

MY LORD MARQUESS,

I beg on behalf of the Members of the 'Royal Victoria Rifles' (established under that title in the year 1835 by the patronage of Her Most Gracious Majesty) to render their services through your Lordship to Her Majesty's Government, as a permanent Volunteer Rifle Corps;—undertaking to provide their own arms and ammunition, and to defray all the expenses attending it, except in the event of the Corps being assembled for active service.

We have at present about fifty active members and are promised a very large accession on the Corps receiving the sanction of Her Majesty's Government.

We possess also a field of 14 acres at Kilburn, Middlesex, as an exercise and practice ground, upon which we have expended upwards of £300 in erecting a secure brick target embankment for Rifle practice and in other works.

With this memorial I have taken the liberty of sending a copy of the 'Laws and Regulations' by which the Corps is governed; and shall feel greatly obliged if your Lordship will forward it with this application to Sir George Grey.

I have further to express the hope of the Corps (that if through

APPENDIX I

your Lordship's kind interference in their behalf the Government should recommend to Her Majesty the continuance of the 'Royal Victoria Rifles' as at present established), that your Lordship will accept the command in order that they may be enabled under your Lordship's directions, to form a complete Battalion of not less than Eight Companies, of Sixty Rank and File each or such larger number of Companies as Her Majesty's Government may approve.

I have the honour to remain,
My Lord Marquess,
Your Lordship's most obedient,
And Most Humble Servant,
ROBERT ELLIS,
Major Commandant,
R.V.R.

To
The Most Noble,
The Marquess of Salisbury, K.G.,
&c. &c. &c."

(*Copy of a private letter from Major Ellis to the Marquess of Salisbury Lord Lieutenant of the County of Middlesex.*)

" No. 2 WARWICK CRESCENT,
WESTBOURNE TERRACE ROAD,
HYDE PARK,
20*th February*, 1852.

MY LORD MARQUESS,

In forwarding the accompanying Memorial :—I have to express the gratification felt by every Member of the 'Royal Victoria Rifles' in having the opportunity to place themselves under your Lordship's command, and their confidence that, one so capable of improving and carrying out the details of the Corps, will not unnecessarily change any part of its constitution or Laws which have for so many years worked so successfully.

Perhaps on receiving the reply of the Secretary of State for the Home Department Your Lordship will kindly allow a deputation to wait upon you for the purpose of receiving your Lordship's instructions as to carrying out and completing the formation of a MODEL RIFLE CORPS.

I have the honour to remain,
My Lord Marquess,
Your Lordship's Most Obedient,
And Most Humble Servant,
ROBERT ELLIS,
Major Commandant, R.V.R.

To
The Most Noble
The Marquess of Salisbury, K.G.
&c. &c. &c."

Major Ellis further reported the following answer received from the Marquess of Salisbury in reply to the above:

"HATFIELD,
21st Feb., 1852.

SIR,—I have the honour to acknowledge the receipt of your letter enclosing a Memorial rendering the services of the Royal Victoria Rifle Club to Her Majesty and expressing their wish to be formed into a permanent Rifle Corps of not less than eight companies:—I will as early as possible obtain the directions of Her Majesty's Government thereupon; and then request the favour of seeing a deputation from the Club.

I have the honour to be
Your Obedient Servant,
GASCOIGNE SALISBURY.

Robert Ellis, Esq."

It was resolved that the thanks of the Committee be given to Major Ellis and the Members of the Military Board for the prompt manner in which they had acted on behalf of the Corps.

At the next meeting of the Executive Committee of the Corps held at the Warwick Arms Hotel, on Monday, 8th March, 1852, Major Ellis read the following letter from the Marquess of Salisbury:

"LONDON,
1st March, 1852.

DEAR SIR,—I have the honour to acknowledge the receipt of your letter offering the services of the Royal Victoria Rifle Corps, established under the Volunteer Act—and to express my regret that circumstances have prevented me from submitting your proposal for the establishment of the Royal Victoria Rifle Corps to the Secretary of State at an earlier period. It will, however, be taken into consideration with the least possible delay, and I will forward his answer to you as soon as I receive it.

I have the honour to be, Dear Sir, Yours truly,
(Signed) GASCOIGNE SALISBURY.

(Under cover to G. T. Lee, Esq.
Hon. Secretary, R.V.R.)"

Another resolution passed by the Executive Committee ran: "That in the event of the Corps being permanently sanctioned by Her Majesty's Government a meeting of the Executive Committee be summoned at the earliest period to receive the Report of the Military Board as to the necessary steps to be adopted in future for the Government of the Corps."

APPENDIX I

The "circumstances" alluded to in the Marquess's letter which prevented the proposal being submitted to the Secretary of State at an earlier period, may be explained by the fact that on the very day the letter was written, February 20th, Lord John Russell's administration resigned and was succeeded by that of the Earl of Derby, Mr. Spencer Walpole taking the place of Sir George Grey at the Home Office.

In a subsequent letter, dated 15th March, 1852, Lord Salisbury writes Major Ellis, " I regret that the answer to the offer of the forming a Rifle Club under the Name of the Royal Victoria Rifle Corps which at your request I forwarded to the Secretary of State has not for the present been accepted. As the answer is couched in the most flattering terms I enclose an extract from it :

' Her Majesty's Government are highly sensible of the value and importance of having the assistance of Volunteer Rifle Corps, and in case of necessity they would willingly avail themselves of that assistance, but until some progress is made in the measure which they will have to submit to the consideration of Parliament with reference to the Militia, they have deemed it advisable that the formation of such corps should be suspended for the present, except in those cases where the late Government have actually sanctioned them or where it may be expedient for special reasons to make an exception. In the case of the County of Middlesex it does not appear that there is any immediate necessity for the formation of such corps, but I beg your Lordship will be so good as to thank the gentlemen who have made the applications submitted in your letters for the readiness they have shown in offering to come forward.'

It only remains for me to add my thanks to yourself and to the gentlemen with whom you act, not only for the zeal you displayed but for the manner personally obliging to myself in which you conveyed your offer."

To this Major Ellis replied (18th March, 1852).

" MY LORD MARQUESS,

I have the honour to acknowledge the receipt of your Lordship's letter announcing the unpleasant tidings that the services of the Royal Victoria Corps had not for the present been accepted.

On behalf of the members of the Corps I beg to tender to your Lordship our most grateful thanks for the trouble you have been so kind as to take in bringing our application to the notice of the Secretary of State ; I am afraid, however, that Mr. Walpole does not perfectly understand our position. We have virtually existed for forty-nine years, viz. from 1803 to the close of the Continental War as the Duke of Cumberland's Sharpshooters (under the Act 44 Geo. III, Cap. 54), the first Rifle Volunteer Corps established in

Great Britain, and from the peace to the present time, by the sanction of the late Earl of Harrowby (then Mr. Secretary Ryder), at the time the Volunteer Associations were disbanded ; and with the perfect knowledge of every subsequent Government as we have always openly mustered for drill and rifle practice once a fortnight during every year, and very often more frequently, and the Corps has ever been spoken of by the Public Press, as one which would at any time form the means of a very efficient Rifle Force.

We have during the number of years mentioned (at a great personal sacrifice to every individual member) maintained our practice in the field ; in the hope that the Government would be pleased at some period to recognize our claims to be permanently embodied under the title of The Royal Victoria Rifle Corps, a name we were graciously permitted to take by Royal favour in 1835, and especially as at this present time there is no force of the same description in the County of Middlesex.

I need scarcely express to your Lordship the very great disappointment we have experienced in being classed with the Rifle Clubs just forming ; we take, however, ground for hope in the expression of the Secretary of State ' that the formation of Rifle Corps should be suspended for the present, except in those cases where the late Government had actually sanctioned them or where it may be expedient for special reasons to make an exception.'

As your Lordship has been kind enough to take an interest in the success of our recent application, may I presume to further trespass on that kindness by requesting your Lordship will at any period which may best suit your convenience make the Secretary of State for the Home Department acquainted with our actual position and the hope we entertain (which we shall be loth to abandon) that in the words of his answer, we may be made an exception."

In a P.S. Major Ellis added, " I take this opportunity of stating that I have held a civil appointment under the Government for the last forty years and from which I retired about twelve months since with a compensation for my services."

On March 19th the Marquess wrote again appointing an interview to take place on the 22nd. Unfortunately no account of what took place at the meeting appears in the Minutes. On April 2nd Major Ellis reported that he had forwarded to the Marquess of Salisbury a medal which was struck in 1803 in commemoration of the establishment of the Duke of Cumberland's Sharpshooters and a copy of the Laws printed in 1805 by which it was governed, as also a medal struck in 1835 commemorative of the Corps being privileged to take the name of the Royal Victoria Rifles, which he trusted would be sufficient for the purposes required.

Nothing, however, came of the negotiations, the Government

APPENDIX I

threw cold water upon the patriotic aspirations of the people, and out of many applications for enrolment accepted that of Devon only. On March 26th Mr. Walpole, who had succeeded Sir George Grey, wrote to Earl Fortescue, the Lord Lieutenant of the County, saying that he was of opinion that Devonshire was a case in which an exception might properly be made from the general rules which the Government had thought it advisable to lay down with reference to the formation of Volunteer Corps, and that he had therefore laid the offer before the Queen, who had been graciously pleased to accept the same. Thus it was that the Exeter Corps which, unlike the Victorias, had no previous organization, uniform or headquarters, obtained official recognition, and that Devonshire took precedence of Middlesex in Volunteer history. The "Exeter and South Devon Rifles," consisting of two Companies, was notified in the *Gazette* of January 4th, 1853. Their first muster in uniform took place on the 6th October, 1852, when the oath of allegiance was taken by the 52 enrolled members. The claim of the Victorias to be the pioneers of the Volunteer Movement of 1852-3 is unquestionable, though the honour has never been officially accorded them.

The attempt to obtain official recognition was renewed towards the end of the year when the following representation was made to Viscount Hardinge at that time Commander-in-Chief of the Army :

"To the Right Honourable General Lord Hardinge, G.C.B., Commanding-in-Chief.

MY LORD,

We beg to submit to your Lordship's notice the Rules and Regulations by which The Royal Victoria Rifles are governed and the Declaration taken by each Member on joining (see page 2) and to state that the Royal Victoria Rifles always have been for Fifty Years a regularly constituted body under the Act of Parliament 44 Geo. 3rd, Cap. 54,—totally distinct from any of the newly proposed Rifle Clubs, and that they are a continuation of the Duke of Cumberland's Sharpshooters who have never ceased to Drill since then first established in 1803, providing their own arms and uniform and having a practice ground of fourteen acres.

They regret that from inadvertence and the apathy manifested towards all military bodies (until lately) they for a period neglected to report themselves, but they have always continued to exercise and Drill under the sanction of Magistrates as required by the Act of Parliament 60 Geo. 3rd Cap. 1.

Their numbers are considerably increasing and they now request Her Majesty's Government to appoint a Colonel, Lieutenant-Colonel, and frame such regulations and restrictions as Her Majesty's Government may see necessary in order to make the Corps useful and certain to be depended upon whenever their services may be required by the Country.

(Military Board, see page 20.)

ROBERT ELLIS	acting	Major.
WILLIAM WHITAKER	,,	Capt. and Adjt.
EDWARD CLIFFORD	,,	Capt. 1st Co.
JAMES CHRISTMAS	,,	Lieutenant.
HENRY JULIUS JONES	,,	,,
JOHN WILLIAM THOMAS	,,	,,

Board Room,
   Oriental Hotel,
      Vere Street.
December, 1852."

In due course the following reply was received :

"HORSE GUARDS,
1st Feby., 1853.

SIR,
    I have the honor by desire of the General Commanding-in-Chief to acknowledge the receipt of your letter of the 29th ultimo, respecting the "Royal Victoria Rifles"—Volunteer Corps—and to suggest that you should address yourself to the Secretary of State for the Home Department,
    I have the honor to be, Sir,
        Your most obedient humble Servant,
            (Signed) RICHARD AIREY.
William Whitaker, Esq."

In compliance with this suggestion a similar letter was addressed to Lord Palmerston, who replied on February 7th saying that he was not aware of the existence of the Royal Victoria Rifle Corps, but offering to receive a deputation at his house.

The following memorial was then addressed to his lordship :—

"To the Right Honourable the Lord Viscount Palmerston,
    Secretary of State for the Home Department.
MY LORD,
    We beg to submit to your Lordship's notice that the 'Royal Victoria Rifle Corps' was the first Volunteer Corps ever established in Great Britain, it was originally The Duke of 'Cumberland's Sharpshooters,' embodied in 1803, and was subjected to the provisions of the Act 44 Geo. 3, Cap. 54, and since the Peace has continued to Drill under the Authority of the County Magistrates according to Act of 60 Geo. 3, Cap. 1. A Book of the Rules and Regulations and a Medal struck on the occasion by their late Major Barber Beaumont are already in the possession of the Most Noble the Marquess of Salisbury.

APPENDIX I

The surviving members of this Corps were by Her Majesty's permission authorised to assume the Title of the 'Royal Victoria Rifle Corps' in 1835, and a Medal which is annually shot for by the Members is also in the possession of The Most Noble the Marquess of Salisbury.

The 'Royal Victoria Rifle Corps' at present consists of about sixty Members, but a great number would join immediately sufficient to establish a Regiment who only wait the recognition of the Corps by the Government.

It is now proposed that the Corps should consist of Ten companies of 100 rank and file each, but in this as in every other arrangement the Corps, being all loyal and well affected to Her Majesty's Government, are content to abide by their decision.

The Members of the 'Royal Victoria Rifle Corps' provide all their own arms, clothing, accoutrements and ammunition, and have established and maintained at great expense a ground of 14 Acres for Drill and Rifle practice, at Kilburn, as also private Drill twice a week at Allen's Riding School, Bryanston Square.

We also beg to bring to your Lordship's notice that several Militia Officers have joined as Honorary Members for the purpose of learning their Drill.

The Members of the 'Royal Victoria Rifle Corps' therefore hope they have strong claims on the Government to recognise them as an organised Military force, and that they may be permitted to retain the 'Title' so graciously conferred upon them by Her present Majesty in 1835.

Signed by order of the Officers and Members, 18th Feby., 1853.

WILLM. WHITAKER,
Late 16th Regmt.,
Acting Captn. & Adjutant,
Royal Victoria Rifles.

St. Alban's Hotel, Charles St.,
St. James'."

On March 24th a similar Memorial was addressed to the Marquess of Salisbury. It was not, however, until July 14th that success crowned the efforts of Major Ellis and his officers. On that date the Corps was enrolled as a Volunteer Corps, under the Act 44 Geo. 3, Cap. 54, and to mark the event a new Minute Book was started, the first entry in which runs as follows:

"Her Most Gracious Majesty has been pleased to accept the services, and approve of the offer for the formation of a Volunteer Rifle Corps under the provisions of the Act 44, Geo. 3rd, Chap. 54.

The Corps to consist of 300 men to be formed into 4 Companies of 75 men each, with 1 Lieut.-Colonel, 1 Major, 4 Captains, 4 1st Lieutenants, 4 2nd Lieutenants, 1 Adjutant, 1 Surgeon, under the style and title 'Victoria Rifles.'"

The following appointments appear in the *London Gazette* of the 4th August, 1853. Commissions signed by the Lord Lieutenant of the County of Middlesex.

"VICTORIA RIFLES.

The Most Noble Arthur Duke of Wellington, *Lieut.-Colonel* (Commandant).
The Right Hon. Earl of Perth and Melfort, *Major*.
William Whitaker, Esq., *Captain and Adjutant*.
Edward Clifford, Esq., *Captain*.
Fredk. Scipio Clarkson, Esq., *Captain*.
William Henry Sole, Esq., *Captain*.
Henry Cook, Esq., *Captain*.

The Most Noble Arthur Duke of Wellington, has been pleased to approve of the following uniform to be worn by the Officers and Privates of the Victoria Rifles :

OFFICERS : Dark Rifle Green Frock Coat ; Prussian Collar ; six Loops and Frogs upon the breast ; Trimmed Collar with ¾ inch braid ; Trimmed Sleeves ; Braided Skirts with Tassels.

Trousers : Rifle Green with two inch oak-leaf braid down the sides. For Private Parades, &c., a pair of dark Oxford Mixture.

Forage Cap : Rifle Green with oak-leaf band and black braided peak.

Sword belt of Black Morocco leather with Silver Lion's head clasp. Ornaments, silver bugle with crown over.

PRIVATES : Dark Rifle Green Frock Coat ; Prussian Collar, double row of braid round the Collar, down the breast, round the Cuffs, and up the back of skirts. Small shoulder knot with black silk ball.

Trousers to match with plain broad braid down the sides.

Forage Cap : Rifle Green, black braid round the cap and Peak. Ornaments Crown over Bugle (bronze).

Pouch, Ball-bag, and Powder horn. Sword with bronzed hilt, top and tip, with black leather scabbard.

By Order Will. Whitaker,
Captain and Adjutant."

It will be noticed that the word "Royal" which the Victorias had so proudly worn since the 24th May, 1853, is henceforth dropped from the Regimental title.

At this period the Corps numbered in its ranks many gentlemen of note. Among others may be mentioned the Earl of Ellesmere, Lord Garvagh, Viscount Hinton, Sir John Phillipart (Editor of the *Naval and Military Gazette*, who joined on May 24th, 1835), the Marquis of Stafford, and Capt. Whitaker (late 16th Regiment). Amongst those who had joined the Corps in its early days were Col. McDonagh (Guards, 1835), Count Villa (1835), the O'Gorman Mahon, M.P. (1838), and Baron Herteloup (1842).

APPENDIX I

IV

THE VICTORIA RIFLES
1ST MIDDLESEX RIFLE VOLUNTEERS

THE new Volunteer Regiment does not appear to have made much of a stir in the world. Many members of influence joined, but the public generally had not learned to take the Volunteers seriously, and no new formations were sanctioned even during the Crimean War and the Indian Mutiny which shortly followed. In 1854 the following advertisement appeared in *The Times* :

"The Minie Rifle.—Gentlemen who may desire Military Training with this favourite arm are invited to join the Victoria Rifles. Range of shooting ground at Kilburn, 400 yards."

In the following year there appeared in the pages of the *Illustrated London News* a picture of the range with the Guards practising shooting, and another of the Victoria Rifles on parade. In 1859 the demand for increasing the strength of the Nation's forces had grown to such dimensions that the Government could no longer withstand it, and on the 12th May the War Office authorised the establishment of Volunteer Rifle Corps, and soon throughout the length and breadth of the land Corps and Companies sprang into existence. Middlesex alone, apart from the City Regiments, contributed some 40 Corps. Of these the Victoria Rifles became the 1st Middlesex. It was at that time about 200 strong, the men thoroughly drilled, well practised with the rifle and with an efficient staff of Veteran Soldiers. Possessed of such a nucleus, with the advantage of a capital drill ground and rifle range within easy access of the City, men gathered fast, and permission was applied for and obtained to increase the establishment to eight Companies of 100 men each.

In all other respects than that of becoming the 1st Middlesex and of increasing the strength to eight companies the Victorias remained as before, permission to carry on under their old regulations being given in the following letter :

(*Seal of the Middlesex Lieutenancy.*)

"24 SPRING GARDENS, S.W.,
24*th October*, 1859.

MY LORD DUKE,

I am directed by the Lord Lieutenant to inform your Grace that Her Majesty, taking into consideration the special circumstances under which the Victoria Rifle Volunteer Corps was raised, and which does not therefore stand in the same position as those formed under the War Office Memorandum of 13th July last—does

not disallow the Rules submitted by your Grace for the Victoria Rifles.
I have the honour to be,
My Lord Duke, Your Grace's
Most obedient humble servant,
EDWARD NICHOLSON,
Clerk to the Lieutcy.

Lieut.-Colonel,
His Grace The Duke of Wellington,
&c. &c. &c."

One of the aspirants to the honour of being the founder of the Volunteer movement was Lieut. Hans Busk, author of *Rifle Volunteers: How to Organise and Drill Them; The Rifle and How to Use It; The Handbook to Hythe*, all of which ran to many editions, and of a number of other works, who had joined the Victorias in 1858 did much to popularise the regiment. What he thought of it he put on record in *The Rifleman's Manual*, 1858, which he dedicated to the Duke of Wellington, Lieutenant-Colonel Commandant.

"Selecting at random some forty names which have been added to the muster-roll during the past few weeks, I find among that number three Members of Parliament, fifteen Graduates of Oxford and Cambridge, five-and-twenty members of the Bar, a Captain in the Army, and some half dozen County Magistrates, &c. When men such as these—the majority of whom have attained high academic honours; whose eloquence graces the Senate, and whose brilliant abilities reflect a lustre on the professions they have embraced—are found uniting disinterestedly for the noblest purpose, not only without hope of personal advantage or emolument but at considerable inconvenience and expense, what further guarantee can be needed for the character of a Corps thus composed?"

In *Rifle Volunteers* (seventh edition) he gives the following estimate of the initial expense of joining the regiment:

	£	s.	d.
Tunic and Trousers (Superfine)	5	5	0
Undress Jacket (do.)	2	2	0
Forage Cap	0	15	0
Shako and Plume	2	2	0
Cross belt, with cartouch-box	1	15	0
Enfield Rifle (better finished than the common regulation arm), with sword bayonet and scabbard complete	5	5	0
The Members of this Corps wear a sword when they parade without rifle and bayonet, although this is not a requisite, the cost with belt being	4	10	0
Total	£21	14	0

The Recruit should also provide himself without fail with a regimental great coat or cloak; cost, five guineas.

APPENDIX I

"If to the above we add one guinea entrance fee and two guineas for the subscription for the first year, paid in advance, we shall find that each member disburses in the first instance nearly thirty pounds."

In spite of this formidable barrier recruits in plenty came along. Many of them joined with the idea of qualifying themselves for Commissions in other Corps, and in a short space of time it was currently reported that the Victoria Rifles had contributed upwards of 200 officers to the newly formed force. At one time eight of the Metropolitan Volunteer Regiments were commanded by officers who had served as privates in the Victorias.

It is not proposed here to give a detailed history of the regiment, but only to refer to the more important and unique events in its career. Unchecked prosperity was by no means its lot. With such heavy initial expenses recruiting began to fall off, but it was some years before the effect was appreciably felt.

A School of Arms was started in 1860 and continued to lead an active and successful existence right up to the outbreak of the great European War. In the year 1861 a notable incident occurred. Sergt. (afterwards Capt.) Alfred Savill Tomkins with a small party of congenial Vics got permission to set up a tent within the grounds of the National Rifle Association at Wimbledon, during the contest. They enjoyed their adventure greatly, and next year a larger party went down. The Victoria " Camp Fire " became a great institution, visitors were hospitably entertained and conviviality was in the ascendant. Other corps followed the example, and in process of time from this small beginning the N.R.A. Camp grew to what it now is at Bisley.

From 1864 to 1871 the Victorias ran a camp periodical yclept *The Earwig*. The editor was John Davison (J'ai dit) and its escutcheon bore the legend " Words not Deeds."

"As the Earwig yearly flies, flitting off on paper wing.
Multitudes distend their eyes and the assembled nations sing.
Earwig, happy, happy beast! Earwig, intellectual feast!"

In 1868 an " Earwig Prize " Competition was associated with the purchase of a copy.

In 1862 Sergt. Pixley won the Queen's prize, and in his honour a fête was held at the Drill Ground at Kilburn on Saturday, August 9th, three hundred bottles of champagne, the gift of the Colonel, the Duke of Wellington, being consumed. The band was in attendance, and archery, rifle shooting, football, quoits and other amusements indulged in.

In February, 1869, Major Barclay Greenhill, then Second in Command, sent out a solemn warning concerning " a supineness reigning amongst a great number of the Vics " and begging them not to " let the glorious old Corps die out for want of a little energy and determination." Apparently it had small effect, for on the 11th April, 1870, he issued a second circular, saying :

"As you are doubtless aware the Victoria Rifles have from various causes become reduced in numbers below the minimum of 360, entitling us to a Lieutenant-Colonel and the services of an Adjutant, principally from the number of gentlemen, considerably over 200, who have left us to obtain Commissions in the Army, Militia and other Volunteer Corps, besides those who have received civil appointments in India, China and Australia, and resignations from other causes. Recruiting has not kept pace with the resignations ; in consequence we are considerably below our proper strength, and an official notice has been received by the Lieut.-Col., His Grace the Duke of Wellington, from the War Office directing his attention to the fact. This notice has been forwarded to us by the Lieutenant-Colonel for our earnest consideration as to the best means to be adopted to fill up our ranks. At the request of the Lieutenant-Colonel to the War Office the time has been extended to the 15th June next—when failing in our endeavours we shall lose our Lieutenant-Colonel and the services of an Adjutant, and possibly be amalgamated with some other Corps. At all events some great alteration will be made in the constitution of the Corps, and I therefore address these few lines to you venturing to hope you will see the dangers impending over the Old Vics and endeavour by all means to enlist recruits and thus secure our present position as the 1st Middlesex Rifle Volunteers, our greatly esteemed Lieutenant-Colonel and our much respected Adjutant. As it is a critical time for all Volunteer Corps and the Government is nervously watching our doings, it is more important that the Victorias present as good a muster as possible at the forthcoming Review at Brighton, and I sincerely trust that everyone will make a point of attending. I hope you will seriously consider the observations contained in this letter. Now or never is the time to bring up the members to the proper state, and I have no doubt if we all stand together and do our best we shall save the glorious old ship from foundering.

I am, dear sir, yours truly,
BARCLAY GREENHILL,
Major, Victoria Rifles."

Every recognised mode of attracting recruits was tried, but tried in vain, and the "Appointed Day," June 15th, found the Victorias still far below the desired strength. Consequent upon this the Lieutenant-Colonel addressed the following letter to the members :

"LONDON, 2nd July, 1870.

GENTLEMEN.—The Victoria Rifles have fallen in numbers below the establishment which entitles them to a Lieutenant-Colonel and I have thought it right to resign that rank in consequence,

APPENDIX I

Major Greenhill now commands you, and I doubt not that you will henceforth find yourselves in abler hands than mine.

I cannot leave you without thanking you sincerely for the kindness and consideration with which you have ever treated me throughout our connection, and to assure you that your prosperity and high reputation will ever excite in my breast both pride and satisfaction. I have the honour to be, gentlemen,

Your affectionate well-wisher and obedient servant,

WELLINGTON."

The blow was very keenly felt by all ranks, and it was suggested that " on the occasion of the retirement of his Grace from the command of the Corps and of Captain Trew from the Adjutancy it would be a most fitting opportunity for the Corps to show its great respect to his Grace and its appreciation of the services rendered by Captain Trew to the Victoria Rifles and the Volunteer Service generally, by presenting them with Testimonials." A committee was at once formed under the Presidency of Major Greenhill and with Lieutenant Stanley George Bird as Hon. Sec., for carrying into effect the suggestion.

By the express wish of the Duke the proposal to present him with a testimonial was withdrawn, but that to Capt. Trew was proceeded with, the presentation taking place following a committee meeting held at Head-quarters, Marlborough Place, in the month of August, and consisting of a silver pint mug suitably inscribed together with a cheque for one hundred pounds.

It had been his Grace's custom during the years he held command of the regiment once a year to entertain the officers at dinner at Apsley House, the members being invited to attend a reception or soirée following the dinner. "The princely hospitalities of Apsley House," records Major Keeson in his little brochure, " which were so frequently extended to both Officers and Men of the Corps, will never be forgotten by those who were so fortunate as to share in them." We should think not glancing at the menu card of one of these functions :

(Taken at random. Some are much more elaborate.)

Diner du 5 Août, 1863.

Potages : Tortue liée. Printanier.
Poissons : Saumon, Sauce Italienne.
Turbot, Sauce Hômards.
Cromeskis de Volailles.
Côtelettes d'Agneau, Concombres.
Poulet Sauté Financier.
Paté Chaud de Foie-gras.
Quenelles de Gibier.
Hanche de Venaison.
Bœuf roti.
Buffet : Milk Punch.

SECOND SERVICE.

Levreaux piqués rôtis.

Petits Pois à la Francaise.
Salade de Hômards.
Gelée Macédoine.
Pouding à la d'Orleans.
Petit Savarin.
Croutes au Fromages.

Although, as is well known, it was not customary for a rifle regiment to carry colours, in the year 1860 the lady friends of the Victorias subscribed for and worked with their own hands a handsome set of colours—the Queen's and the regimental. They were presented in that year by the Duchess of Wellington. They still remain in the possession of the regiment. So also do a pair of silver bugles " elaborately finished and enclosed in neat and suitable cases, subscribed for by the wives of the members of the Corps as a mark of their appreciation and the warm interest felt for this great national movement." These were presented on the 11th August, 1860, at Kilburn, by the Duchess of Wellington, the Victorias being mustered in great force. The bugles were the workmanship of Messrs. Antoine and Courtois, the celebrated musical instrument manufacturers of Paris.

In 1867 the Corps acquired the old Archery Ground in Marlborough Place, St. John's Wood, with a spacious armoury, mess and dressing-rooms, etc. The first parade on the new ground took place on the 19th October in that year. In the following December it became a rallying place for the Special Constables enrolled on account of the Fenian scare. The arms were distributed quietly at night time, wrapped in blankets, to members of the Corps living in the neighbourhood. An order to remove all private arms was issued to the members on 8th January, 1868.

In April, 1871, the regiment was armed with the short, breech loading Snyder rifle. Up to that time they had used the muzzle-loading Metford rifle. In the same year a contingent took part in the first autumn manœuvres. Both these events arose out of the German victory over France.

In 1878 the shako was abolished, and the Army pattern helmet adopted.

On the occasion of the opening by Queen Victoria of the People's Palace on the 14th May, 1887, the Victoria Rifles, along with the Grenadier Guards and the Tower Hamlets Volunteers, formed the Guard of Honour. The People's Palace arose out of the Beaumont Trust, so called after the former founder of the Duke of Cumberland's Sharpshooters, Major J. T. Barber Beaumont, who designed and erected at a cost of £5000, the Beaumont Institution in

APPENDIX I

Beaumont Square, Mile End, containing a spacious hall, with a fine organ, for concerts and lectures ; a library ; a museum of natural history, committee and class-rooms, etc. At the same time Mr. Beaumont invested the sum of £13,000 in the names of trustees and guardians of the property, to apply the income arising therefrom to the maintenance of the Institution. In 1883 an endeavour was made to extend the scheme, and a meeting was held in January at the Mansion House at which Sir Edmund Currie and the Lord Mayor explained that the intention was to "provide wholesome, improving recreation and education for something like a million of souls who were without the means of getting either." Apparently the object was not immediately obtained, for on June 23rd, a couple of years later, another meeting was held at the Mansion House, when, in pursuance of a resolution moved by the Prince of Wales and seconded by the Earl of Rosebery, it was decided to make an appeal to the country for funds to carry out the scheme of the Beaumont Trustees, and to provide intellectual improvement and rational recreation and amusement for the inhabitants of East London. The sum of £100,000 was asked for, and with the aid of large contributions from the Drapers' and other City Companies, and with £12,000 found by the Trustees of the Institute, was soon forthcoming. The connection of the founder of the Trust with the Victoria Rifles was brought to the notice of Queen Victoria and the Duke of Cambridge, who were both very interested in the fact, and the Victorias were accorded the honour of being included in the Guard of Honour, though not until opposition on the part of the Army Officials had been overcome through the express wishes of Her Majesty.

In January, 1863, a suggestion was made that to make rifle shooting more attractive to the rank and file a Rifle Club should be formed, and on the 16th of the month the first competition took place. The name first adopted was that of "The Gorilla Vics," which only three months later was changed to that of "Our Club." The object, says the rules, was "to promote good fellowship among the members of the Victoria Rifles and the interchange of ideas upon shooting matters."

The club was to consist solely of members of the Corps and there were to be eight meetings a year, the last in July (or August) to be held in the country, "each meeting to be preceded by a dinner." The dinner was to take place at seven o'clock at a price not exceeding five shillings per man, "exclusive of beer, wine and attendance." Wine of the value of three shillings per man was to be placed on the table, after which each member paid for that which he was pleased to order. The only toast to be proposed was "The Queen," and no subject was to be discussed which in the opinion of the chairman would be likely to interfere with or disturb the harmony and good fellowship of the meeting. For the first few years the meetings were held at the Eyre Arms Hotel, St. John's

Wood, and then a change was made to the Café Royal, where the club continued to meet right up to the spring of 1914. In the course of time the rules were made more elastic, admitting "Members (Active or Honorary) of the Victoria and St. George's Rifles, and of such other gentlemen connected with the Corps as may be proposed as Honorary Members on behalf of the Committee." A Prize Fund was instituted, and team and other competitions organised. At the 25th Anniversary Dinner held on the 9th May, 1888, Colonel Stanley George Bird presented a handsome old Sheffield Plate Candelabra on behalf of the old members, and its fellow was purchased out of the club's funds. Amongst other trophies the club possesses are a team Challenge Cup, the highest Aggregate Cup, the President's Bowl, a replica of the Team Cup presented by Mr. Thomas Gellatley, then the "Father" of the club, at the Jubilee Dinner held in May, 1913, to take the place of the first one upon which it had become impossible to inscribe further names, and a silver mounted ballot box made of wood from the house of Sir Walter Raleigh, Effra River, Brixton Hill, presented by Col. Stanley Bird in 1868. During the war no meetings were held, but a shoot followed by a dinner took place at Bisley on 20th June, 1922.

Another matter upon which the Victorias pride themselves is the establishment of a Mounted Infantry Contingent. The first attempt was made as far back as December, 1859, when a circular was issued stating "the formation of a Mounted Company, in connection with the Victoria Rifles, having been thought desirable and approved of by His Grace the Duke of Wellington, it is necessary that a sufficient number of names of those gentlemen who are willing to join the same be immediately forwarded to Captain and Adjutant Trew, Orderly Room, Kilburn, to justify His Grace in preferring a petition to the Lord Lieutenant for power to form such Company." Apparently sufficient names were not forthcoming, for nothing further was heard of the matter. Better success attended the efforts of Lieut. T. E. Phillips, who in October, 1882, succeeded in forming a small but very efficient troop of Mounted Infantry. At successive meetings of the Royal Military Tournament Lieut. Phillips and Sergts. Nash and Sandeman distinguished themselves, taking a number of prizes.

On the retirement of Lieut. Phillips in May, 1889, the following Battalion Order was issued: With reference to the resignation of Lieut. Phillips, "The Commanding Officer (Col. Bircham) cannot allow the occasion to go by without expressing his deep regret at the loss the regiment has sustained in it. Lieut. Phillips has not only done himself but the regiment infinite credit by the raising of the Mounted Infantry, and the care and attention he has at all times given to it. He can fairly claim to have been first in the field in this department, and the way the name of the regiment has been so worthily represented and upheld by him and others in public competitions at the Agricultural Hall and elsewhere is due to his energy and perseverance in a great measure. The C.O. takes this opportunity of expressing to Lieut. Phillips his thanks for his devotion and good services."

The next to take up the running was Captain Wyndham Dickins, who was so successful that in December, 1900, he was able to announce " The Mounted Infantry Company is now up to full strength of a Field Service Company, viz. 141, for which number the Special Capitation Grant is given, therefore any men wishing to join must have their names registered on the waiting list from which vacancies will be filled." Separate quarters were secured in Queen's Terrace, St. John's Wood, having a private entrance into the Barrack Square of the Royal Horse Artillery in Ordnance Road, where instruction was given by the Sergeant-Major and the Rough-Riding Corporal in the R.H.A. Riding School.

This splendid force was ruthlessly torn from the Victoria and St. George's Rifles by the transformation of the Volunteers to the Territorial Force in 1908. A similar fate befell an equally efficient Cyclist Section.

V

THE ST. GEORGE'S HANOVER SQUARE VOLUNTEERS
THE OLD ST. GEORGE'S

THE inhabitants of the Parish of St. George, Hanover Square, have ever been among the first to respond with men or money or both to all National appeals for aid, and from very early times militant organisations of some kind have been associated with the locality. In Rowlandson's *Loyal London Volunteers* (Ackerman, 1799) it is stated that " On the 7th of December, 1792, Mr. Edward Foster called a meeting of the inhabitants and they resolved to arm for the protection of each other and the bringing to justice such persons as disturbed the peace, or acted in any way contrary to the laws of the land, or to the interests of the Sovereign."

Following closely upon this meeting another was held, this time in the Festino Rooms, Hanover Square, and was numerously attended by the " nobility, gentry and others." A subscription was raised and a considerable number of men enrolled. On 12th March, 1794, the Royal approval was promulgated in the following terms : " His Majesty having signified his pleasure to me (Sir George Yonge, Secretary of War), that Commissions be presented to him for the following gentlemen to be Officers in the Volunteer Companies to be associated in the Parish of St. George, Hanover Square, but not to take rank in the Army except during the time of the said Companies being called out into active service, viz. :

Commissions dated 1794, March 5.

To be Captains, Edward Foster Esq., John Tyler Esq., Samuel Wild Esq., Nathaniel Payne Fitch Esq., John Mitchell Esq.

To be Lieutenants, Thomas Russell, gent., (John) Higgenbotham, gent., — Wall, gent., (James) Carr, gent.,— Witburn, gent.

To be Ensigns, (Thomas) Anderton, gent., — Coup, gent.,— Starr, gent., — Deering, gent., — Bellamy, gent.

On January 5th, 1795, Edward Foster was appointed Lieut.-Colonel Commandant and Captain John Tyler, Major. Promotion respectively to Colonel and Lieut.-Colonel followed on March 2nd, 1797."

According to Rowlandson, who gives two plates of the uniform of the St. George's, Hanover Square, Volunteers, one (No. 9) at the "Shoulder Arms" and the other (No. 11) at "Charge Bayonets" (2nd Motion), "in 1796 additions were made to the Corps ; and in 1797 four more Companies, to form a Regiment, and two Flank Companies ; but in April, 1798, after the result of a Court of Inquiry, his Majesty was pleased to appoint the Earl of Chesterfield Colonel, and the Hon. Henry Stanhope Lieut.-Colonel, in the room of Col. Foster and Col. Tyler, who resigned. At this time the Regiment was advanced in number to **630** Rank and File, 21 Drums, 30 Sergeants, 3 Field Officers, 7 Captains, 20 Subalterns, and 5 Staff."

Their place of arms and parade were in North Audley Street. A set of Colours was presented to them by Field Marshal Sir George Howard on February 9th, 1795, the ceremony taking place in Hyde Park.

The uniform consisted of blue, long-tailed coats, double-breasted, with bright red facings ; cocked hat for battalion company, white breeches, black gaiters up to the knee, with white metal buttons, black velvet stocks, leather pigtails, red and white hackle feathers, twelve inches long, and bright-barrelled firelocks. The grenadiers wore the bearskin caps, with patch of red cloth behind and white chain ornaments. The Light Infantry Company had leather helmets with a green feather attached. They were called the "Light Bobs."

The Motto of the Corps was then *Pro Rege, Lege, et Patria*, and the "St. George and Dragon" was the principal ornament on the pouches. The officers' breastplate bore the King's Arms, chased on an oval gilt plate.

The men were found with clothing, arms, and ammunition, and were paid for their attendance on field days, reviews, or ball practice, and also for mounting guard, which was taken in turn by the whole Corps, about twenty on each night with one commissioned Officer. It is worthy of note that the men on guard rendered frequent assistance in cases of fire.

In Rowlandson's book is another plate, No. 53, "The St. George's, Hanover Square, Armed Association," the figure standing at the "Make Ready" as a centre rank. Of this body he says : "This Association was instituted in June, 1798, when they resolved to serve without pay, to assist the Civil Magistrates in suppressing any Riot, Tumults or hostile Force, within the Parish of St.

St. George's Hanover Square Volunteers
Rowlandson's "Loyal London Volunteers," 1792.

APPENDIX I

George's, Hanover Square ; and to provide clothes and accoutrements at their own expense. Their Quarterly Committee consists of the Officers and six Non-commissioned Officers and Privates, appointed by the majority of the Corps. There is also a body of Inhabitants belonging to this Association, who are not trained to the use of Arms, but ready to assist in such manner as may be judged most useful."

Officers : Capt. — Boodle ; Lieut. — Tombling ; Ensign — Storey.

Dress : Helmet ; bear-skin, red feather tipped white.

Breastplate, oval, with cypher, S.G.H. in centre of Garter ; above the Crown, with the word ASSOCIATION under it.

Cartouch Box : S.G.H. in cypher within a Garter, inscribed ASSOCIATION and radiated with a Star ; the crown above.

Buttons : cypher, S.G.H.A. under the Crown ; the whole encircled with the Garter.

Half boots.

Of the Old St. George's under the year 1794 Mr. Cecil Sebag-Montefiore says in his *History of the Volunteer Forces*, 1908 :

" Prompted by this patriotic feeling numerous bodies of the citizens came forward with offers of personal service to the Government. The first of these bodies to be enrolled was the five Associated Companies of St. George's, Hanover Square, concerning whom the following letter was addressed by Sir George Yonge (Secretary at War) to Henry Dundas (Secretary of State for War) on March 26th. The letter is of interest as showing the circumlocutory method employed at this date in furnishing arms to Volunteer Associations.

" His Majesty having been pleased to approve of the offer made by the inhabitants of the Parish of St. George's, Hanover Square, to form five associated Companies, each to consist of 3 Sergeants, 3 Corporals, 2 Drummers, and 60 Private Men, under Officers to be Commissioned by His Majesty, on the terms approved by His Majesty's Confidential Servants, and communicated by Lord Amherst to the Deputy Lieutenant of the County of Middlesex, I have the honour to acquaint you therewith, and am to desire you will be pleased to receive and transmit His Majesty's Commands to the Master General and Board of Ordnance that the Arms, &c., undermentioned[1] with a proportionate quantity of Ammunition may be issued out of H.M.'s stores for the use of the said Corps and the expense thereof charged to the Estimate of Ordnances for Parliament."

In February, 1799, the whole Corps took the oath of Fidelity, and were freshly enrolled to serve under a General Officer in the London District whenever called upon. At the great Review held by the King in Hyde Park on June 4th, 1799, the St. George's were the strongest on the ground, numbering 641 of all ranks. The Earl

[1] " 15 Halberts ; 10 Drums with pairs of Sticks, &c. ; 315 Complete Stands of Arms." Letter Books of the Secretary at War and the Secretary of State for War, known as the " Secretary's Common Letter Books."

of Chesterfield was in command. The St. George's, Hanover, Square, Armed Association was also present with a strength of 97 under Captain Boodle. The congratulations of H.R.H. to the several Corps concerned were issued in a Special Order to the St. George's.

The Volunteers of that day were paid somewhat more liberally, if we may judge by an order dated St. George's Parade, August 24, 1799, for £1000, being " three months' allowance to the St. George's, Hanover Square, Volunteer Regiment, commanded by Colonel the Earl of Chesterfield for pay, &c. &c., to the non-commissioned officers, drummers, privates, from the 25th of May to the 24th of August."

In October, 1801, was signed the Treaty of Amiens declaring peace between Great Britain, Holland, France and Spain, and the St. George's, together with all other Volunteer Corps, were disbanded. This state of things, however, did not last long, for on May 18th, 1803, Great Britain again declared war on France and volunteers in all parts of the country eagerly responded to the new call to arms, close upon 400,000 men being enrolled to meet the vast army assembled by Bonaparte upon the heights of Boulogne for the invasion of England. Amongst the first to offer themselves were the St. George's, Hanover Square, under their former Officers, the commissions of the latter bearing date 26th May, 1803. The Earl of Chesterfield was once more in command with Lord John Thynne as Lieutenant-Colonel. In the volume for 1803 of the Home Office Military Entry Books appears the following entry :

"On April 2nd the Marquis of Titchfield forwarded to Lord Hobart proposals for re-embodying three of the best known London Volunteer Corps of Infantry which had been disbanded at the Peace. These were the St. George's Volunteers, the St. James's Volunteers, and the Bloomsbury Association, respectively commanded by Lord Chesterfield, Lord Amherst, and Mr. Samuel C. Cox. The terms proposed for the St. George's Corps were the same as those granted during the late war, viz. 4000 pounds per annum while embodied, full pay for an adjutant, and clothing every third year ; the establishment being 10 Companies of 60 rank and file each."[1]

[1] The following details of the establishment proposed for this Corps are of interest as showing the composition of a first-rate London Corps of Volunteer Infantry at this period :

No. of Companies	10
Rank and File per Company	60

Colonel	1	Brought forward	32
Lieut.-Colonel	1	Quartermaster	1
Major	1	Sergeant-Major	1
Captains	7	Sergeants	30
Capt.-Lieutenant	1	Corporals	30
Lieutenants	11	Drum-Major	1
Ensigns	8	Drummers	20
Adjutant	1	Privates	600
Surgeon	1		
	32		715

GENERAL ORDERS

Horse Guards, June 4th 1799.

His Royal Highness the Commander in Chief has his Majesty's particular commands to communicate to the several corps of Volunteers assembled this morning in Hyde Park, the great satisfaction with which his Majesty witnessed their regularity and military appearance, and the striking manifestation of their cordial and affectionate attachment to his Majesty. It is peculiarly pleasing to his Majesty to observe the effects of the unwearied diligence and attention of the Officers, & of the zeal & alacrity of the Volunteers composing this truly respectable force, which entitle them to the strongest expressions of his Majesty's approbation, and which gratify the just sentiments of national pride, in the same proportion in which they add to the public security. His Majesty cannot express the satisfaction he has received on this occasion, without the pleasing recollection of the principles of attachment to the Constitution under which these corps have been formed; and without considering their appearance and conduct on this day as a proof of their firm determination to support his Majesty in transmitting it with its blessings unimpaired to their posterity. His Royal Highness has peculiar pleasure in making known his Majesty's gracious sentiments on an occasion so acceptable to his feelings, and he requests the respective Commanding Officers to take the earliest opportunity of communicating them to the several corps, seen by his Majesty this morning.

(Signed)

Frederick F.M.
Commander in Chief.

SPECIAL ORDER OF THE DAY, 4TH JUNE, 1799.
ENGRAVED AND ISSUED TO THE ST. GEORGE'S VOLUNTEERS.

APPENDIX I

That well-known war correspondent, the late Mr. H. H. S. Pearse, in an article in the *Graphic* of July 8th, 1899, in connection with the Centenary Review of Volunteers, mentions a memorandum book kept by the Regimental Adjutant Capt. Walter " and now in the custody of Major G. S. Beeching." He quotes extracts to show that although the St. George's, like most other Volunteer Corps, drew " allowances for field days and guard duties it was apparently not on a scale very ruinous to the State, as we find from an entry in Captain Walter's memorandum book that 495 men of the St. George's Regiment were paid for a review, at which the King was present, the magnificent sum of fivepence each ! They had, however, beer tickets in addition, to the value of sixpence, and one of these bearing the Adjutant's initials ' F.A.W.' has been preserved to this day. Another entry in that book is interesting if not curious. It records how the Adjutant, returning from a field day, found that the armourers had been ' from three in the afternoon till night playing cards and drinking.' To one apparently simple event this Officer evidently attaches some grave meaning. The fact that ' Captain Vincent called to intimate his having wrote to Lord Chesterfield his resignation ' is set down with three big notes of exclamation."

Lieut. Frederick Augustus Walter was gazetted Adjutant on May 26th, 1803, the day when the regiment was reconstituted. He is said to " have earned the affection and respect of the Regiment, and it is recorded that having met with an accident in the execution of his duties, a sum of nearly £700 was voted to him as a testimony to his professional ability and the esteem in which he was held, and at his death a monument was erected to his memory in the burial ground of St. George, Bayswater Road."

As we now know the Volunteers were not called upon to repel invasion, but they practised steadily to perfect themselves in the use of arms. The St. George's met for this purpose at the back of Norfolk Street, Middle Row, Park Lane. Various alterations were made in the uniform which now consisted of scarlet jackets and deep crown felt hats with small tops, and to mark their early enrolment they had on their buttons " St. George, No. 1 Regiment," the figure 1 being surmounted with a crown. The officers wore blue pantaloons and Hessian boots with silk tassels. On the occasion of the Jubilee of King George III, October 29th, 1805, it is recorded :

" The (Old) St. George's Volunteers paraded at 10 o'clock, and marched to St. George's Church, preceded by their excellent band, in rich and elegant new clothing for the occasion ; each (nearly 500) wore a sprig of laurel in his cap, which had a pleasing effect. After a most animating discourse by the Rector there was a collection at the doors for charitable purposes, to which the Corps liberally subscribed. The Regiment, on coming out of church, formed into companies, during which time the band formed in front of the Church and played 'God Save the King,' at the conclusion of which the immense number of spectators gave three hearty cheers. The Regiment then marched back to their Parade to receive their arms and ammunition, and repaired to their alarm post (Grosvenor Square), where they trooped their colours in a grand style of military parade; they then marched into Hyde Park and fired a *feu-de-joie* with great exactness and rapidity, giving three cheers after each repeated three rounds; the band playing, drums beating, &c., gave the whole a truly grand effect. The Regiment then returned to their parade, and after lodging their arms, &c., were plentifully regaled with good old English cheer of roast beef and plum-pudding, &c., provided for them by their officers, to which the Commanding Officer (Major Harrison) added a sufficient quantity of punch to drink ' Health and prosperity to the best of kings.' "

In those days Reviews were of frequent occurrence and seem to have been very popular. The St. George's apparently were always to the fore and numerous references to their skill and smartness may be found in papers of the time. Upon the abdication of Napoleon in 1814 the Volunteers were again disbanded after final Reviews in Hyde Park on Saturday the 18th and Monday the 20th of June, in the presence of H.R.H. the Prince Regent, The Emperor Alexander of Russia, the King of Prussia, Prince Schwartzenberg, Prince Blücher and an immense concourse of people. The St. George's attended on the second day and received the following letter in reference to the event :

"Horse Guards, 21 *June*, 1814.

My Lord,

The Commander-in-Chief commands me to inform you that H.R.H. the Prince Regent has been graciously pleased to express his regret that the third line in which the Corps under your Lordship's command was stationed at the Review of yesterday, from the confined space of the ground and the pressure of the increasing crowd was not passed by the Royal Procession while in Line. H.R.H. was highly gratified by the appearance of your Regiment when it passed in open column, which the Prince Regent is desirous should be particularly expressed to the Officers and Men under your Lordship's command. Yours &c.,

Wm. Wynyard, Adjt.-General.

To
    Col. the Earl of Chesterfield or Officer Commanding
        the St. George's Volunteers."

About this time there was another body of Volunteers having its head-quarters in the neighbourhood of Hanover Square, namely the Duke of Gloucester's Regiment. This was also embodied on the 30th of July, 1803, with Richard Viscount Chetwynd as Colonel,

APPENDIX I

Edward Boodle Lieutenant-Colonel, 7 captains, 8 lieutenants and 5 ensigns. An adjutant (John Burrows), a quartermaster (John Tombling) and a surgeon. The names Lieut.-Col. Boodle and the quartermaster leads to the assumption that this was the old St. George's, Hanover Square, Armed Association of 1798, mentioned by Rowlandson, revived. It was often called the New St. George's in contemporary journals and confused with the St. George's proper.

VI

THE ST. GEORGE'S RIFLES
6TH MIDDLESEX R.V.C.

ONE of the earliest of the 40 Middlesex Corps which followed the publication of the War Office letter of May 12th, 1859, was the St. George's, which became the 11th Middlesex R.V.C. By advertisement in the daily papers a general meeting of the inhabitants of the parish of St. George's, Hanover Square, was summoned, and was held at the Board Room, Mount Street, Grosvenor Square, on Saturday, June 25th. The call was heartily responded to; in a short time some hundreds of men were enrolled and a lengthy list of subscriptions was announced from those who could not give active support. The first muster of the new regiment took place on August 24th. Regarding this the *Illustrated London News* says : " On Wednesday evening the members of the St. George's, Hanover Square, Volunteer Rifle Corps, amounting to several hundreds, mustered in the grounds of Burlington House, Piccadilly, for drill and training. Amongst the Volunteers are several of the principals of large establishments in the locality, and the sons of some noble families residing in the district. The training will be continued every Monday, Wednesday and Friday, the Volunteers mustering at six o'clock in the evening. After having become proficient in the Manual and Platoon exercises the Corps will proceed to Kilburn for rifle practice."

In their search for a Commanding Officer they approached Lieut.-Gen. Sir Harry Smith, of South African fame, who replied to the Secretary, Mr. Robert W. Ollivier, 19 Old Bond Street :

" SIR,—I have the honour to acknowledge your letter of the 22nd inst. (November) submitting the prospectus of the St. George's Volunteers with a request from the Committee that I should take command. While fully sensible of the honour, my position in the Army must prevent it. No man in England has a higher opinion of the rifle volunteer movement than I, and no General Officer has ever found the well-armed people of a gallant nation more formidable in the field."

Eventually the choice settled upon the Hon. Charles Hugh

Lindsay (late Grenadier Guards). On January 14th, 1860, he was appointed Major Commandant, and shortly afterwards upon the increased establishment of the regiment, Lieutenant-Colonel. At a dinner held upon St. George's Day, 1861, Sir Hamilton Seymour presented him in the name of the St. George's Rifles with a handsome sword and an address expressive of the approbation and esteem of all under his command. This sword, in July, 1917, found its way back to the Regiment as a present from a member of the Q.V.R. Old Comrades Association, a member of a West-end firm of gunmakers in whose possession it had lain for many years. Inquiry of the relatives of Col. Lindsay elicited the information that all knowledge of its whereabouts had long been lost, and the weapon was duly handed to the Duchess of Rutland, his daughter.

At a meeting of the council of the National Rifle Association at Willis's Rooms on Monday, 27th May, 1861, Col. Lindsay announced that it was the intention of the members of the St. George's Rifles to present a challenge vase for competition among the various battalions of Volunteers in Great Britain to be shot for under the special auspices of the National Rifle Association. The design and artistic appearance of the vase, he added, would be such as to create considerable interest, and this statement of his has been fully borne out by the fact that ever since it has been regarded second only in importance to that of the Queen's (now the King's) Prize, and annually secures nearly as large a number of entries. When first competed for in 1862 its value was estimated at £250, and four additional prizes were offered, viz. a gold and enamelled jewel of St. George to the winner of the vase, a similar silver enamelled jewel to the second best shot, a bronze cross to the third, and a photograph of the vase and jewels to the battalion to which the winner belonged. The shooting at the first competition was of an exciting nature and resulted in a tie between Leete of the Queen's Westminster R.V. and Corpl. Ferguson of the 1st A.B. Inverness, with 30 out of a possible 40, the distances being 200 and 500 yards, 5 shots at each. On shooting off the following day Ferguson won the vase and gold jewel and Leete the silver jewel. Pte. Henery of the St. George's R.V. was the winner of the bronze cross. In 1865 "The Dragon Cup" was added to the prize list, the competition being divided into two stages, 7 shots at 500 and 7 at 600 yards, the Cup going to the winner of the 2nd stage. In 1874 the 2nd stage was abolished, and the winner of the challenge vase took the dragon cup.

In their history of the N.R.A. Cols. Humphrey and Freemantle say, under date of 1881, " The St. George's Vase had from its first establishment been under the control of Col. the Hon. Charles H. Lindsay, its original promoter, and a small Committee representing the donors, the St. George's Rifles, who received all the entries and provided the Prize List, and handed to the N.R.A. a donation, at this time £200 out of the surplus, the N.R.A. defraying all the

APPENDIX I 535

expenses of conducting the competition. Various members, at their head Col. Alexander Wilson of Bannockburn, afterwards a member of the Council, expressed in print their dissatisfaction with this arrangement and a wish to see the accounts. Col. Lindsay, feeling aggrieved at the remarks which had been made, threatened to withhold the St. George's Vase after the current year unless the remarks were withdrawn ; thereupon Col. Wilson promptly undertook in that event to give a St. Andrew's Vase to make good the deficiency, and a memorial asking to see accounts was signed by a large number of Competitors. The Council gave diplomatic consideration to the matter and expressed their opinion that the Vase was the property of the St. George's Rifles ; consequently Col. Lindsay undertook not to withhold it, and when it should be won out and out, to hand over to the Council the balance due to the fund on condition that a vase of like value should be provided for future competition."

The incident apparently terminated to the satisfaction of all concerned, for we learn from the same authorities that " very complete records of the accounts and history of the competition were made for the first and later years and were preserved in elaborately illuminated volumes now in the possession of the N.R.A., and annually shown in the Exhibition Tent at Bisley." On the death of Col. Lindsay the control of the St. George's Vase and its fund devolved upon Col. Stanley Bird. At his generous invitation the Vase and its fund, amounting to £908, were handed over to the Association on the condition that the competition for the St. George's Vase and Dragon Cups should be continued, and that another St. George's Vase should be provided in place of that which had been hitherto competed for, whenever it should be won outright. The Council presented to the St. George's Rifles, by the hands of the Duke of Westminster, a Cup of the value of £100 in commemoration of the long connection which had existed between the Corps and the N.R.A.

Field-Marshal E. Blakeney, G.C.B., Governor of Chelsea Hospital, was appointed Honorary Colonel of the 11th Middlesex on 20th March, 1868.

The old Colours belonging to the Volunteer Corps of St. George's Parish, Westminster, from 1795 to 1814, under the command of the Earl of Chesterfield, were found in a lumber room of Chesterfield House, Mayfair, when that mansion was bought by the Duke of Abercorn in 1870. Lord Chesterfield, with great propriety, presented them to the existing St. George's Rifle Volunteer Corps (raised in 1859) under the command of Col. the Hon. C. H. Lindsay, M.P. On Saturday, June 18th (1870), the Colours were formally presented to the Corps by Lord Elcho, who had been invited to perform the ceremony at a parade in the ground of the Duke of York's Royal Military School, Chelsea. Lord Elcho was accompanied by Lady Elcho and by Col. Muller, Commandant of the

Royal Military Asylum, Col. Adams, Deputy Governor, and other officers. The Boys of the Royal Military School formed a Guard of Honour. A large number of Soldiers, Volunteers, Chelsea Pensioners, and others witnessed the proceedings.

The original Colours were presented to the St. George's by Field-Marshal Sir George Howard in Hyde Park, on February 9th, 1795. They remain a valued trophy of the regiment, and were taken from their secure resting-place to meet once more the public gaze at the Royal Centenary Review of Volunteers by H.R.H. the Prince of Wales (King Edward VII), in July, 1899.

When the Volunteer Regiments were renumbered in 1880, the St. George's became the 6th Middlesex.

For many years the St. George's had to put up with anything but suitable Head-quarters, always remaining, however, in close contiguity with the Square from which they derived their name. About the year 1888 an effort was made to secure a more satisfactory habitation, and supported by gifts and promises from residents in the neighbourhood they set about building the handsome home they now occupy. His Grace the late Duke of Westminster presented a noble site in Davies Street, Berkeley Square, at a peppercorn ground rent for 200 years, and the building was erected thereon at a cost of £16,000. It comprises a spacious drill hall, armoury, Morris-tube and revolver range. Officers' and Sergeants' rooms, general mess room, together with all necessary offices, and secure to every individual, whether officer or private, at a moderate cost all the convenience and comfort of a West-end club. Of these advantages a large number of honorary members avail themselves. The building was opened on December 6th, 1890, by Her Grace the Duchess of Westminster.

VII

The Victoria and St. George's Rifles
The South African War
The Imperial Service Company
The Centenary

The Victoria and St. George's Rifles

For many years the Victorias and the St. George's had worked in close association, and on several occasions, particularly upon the retirement from the command of the Victorias of Col. A. H. Bircham (formerly of the K.R.R.C. and late adjutant of the St. George's), in 1899, there had been talk of amalgamation, but the Victorias were loth to give up their independence and contrived to maintain it until June, 1892. On the 3rd of that month the following notice appeared in the *London Gazette* :

APPENDIX I

MEMORANDUM

"Her Majesty the Queen having been pleased to approve of the 1st and 6th Middlesex Rifle Volunteer Corps being formed into one Corps, from June 1, 1892, and of the New Corps being designated the '1st Middlesex (Victoria and St. George's) Rifle Volunteer Corps,' it is hereby notified that the Officers, at present holding commissions in the 1st and 6th Corps respectively, will be considered to have received commissions of the same rank and date in the new consolidated Corps."

The War Office establishment was 8 companies, but for purposes of interior economy the regiment was told off into 9 companies, " A," " B," " C," " D," " E," and " F " being the St. George's, and " G," " H," and " I " the Victorias. In other ways the changes were few and unimportant, no friction resulted, and from the first the amalgamation proved advantageous to both Corps. One change was referred to later on in a Regimental Order. It is worthy of record. "The gorgeous and expensive uniform of the old Victoria Rifles has been superseded by the neat and serviceable pattern of the K.R.R."

The commanding officer at that time was Col. Stanley George Bird, who had at the age of 22, in May, 1859, six days after the authorised establishment of the Volunteer force, joined the Victoria Rifles as a private. Within twelve months he had received his first stripe, and after four years' service as a non-commissioned officer was appointed an ensign. In 1866 he was promoted to lieutenant, and in 1871 got his company. In 1878 Capt. Bird was offered and accepted the vacant majority of the St. George's, and in 1885, upon the resignation of Col. Lindsay, succeeded him in the command. At the time of the amalgamation the St. George's being short of officers the vacant commissions were filled by members of the Victoria Rifles, in which regiment it had always been the custom to serve through the ranks to a commission.

The adjutant at that time was Major W. Pitcairn Campbell, King's Royal Rifle Corps, which he had joined in Canada in March, 1876. In the Nile Campaign for the rescue of Gen. Gordon in 1884 Capt. Campbell was selected to command a detachment of Mounted Infantry, and was present at the battles of Abu Klea, Gubat, Metemneh and the subsequent operations. On his return to England in 1885 he was appointed Adjutant of the 1st Battn. K.R.R., and in September, 1889, he was appointed Adjutant of the St. George's R.V. Major Campbell strove hard to make the amalgamation a success, but in 1894 his time was up and he had to rejoin his regiment. Now, as Lieut.-Gen. Sir Wm. Pitcairn Campbell, K.C.B., he is Honorary Colonel of Queen Victoria's Rifles.

On the 9th June the new regiment had its first public parade when it was inspected in Hyde Park by Col. Sterling, Coldstream Guards, commanding the North London Brigade.

In the Battalion Orders for 19th October, 1892, appeared the following : (1) "Regimental Title. The Commanding Officer is pleased to inform the Regiment that H.R.H. the Commander-in-Chief, has conferred a great honour on the 1st Middlesex Rifle Volunteers. He has sanctioned it being appointed the 1st Volunteer Battalion of the King's Royal Rifle Corps. The Victoria and St. George's Rifle Corps is now the premier Volunteer Battalion of a Regiment which deservedly stands second to none in the British Army."

(2) "Extract from Confidential Report. It is with much pleasure that the Major-General Commanding receives so satisfactory a report upon this Battalion, and he desires to express his gratitude to Col. Bird, and Lieut.-Col. Hart, the Adjutant and all ranks of the Corps, for the way in which the wishes of the authorities have been accepted and cordially carried out, with the result that the Battalion, as it now stands, is in a satisfactory and creditable state of efficiency, and in a fit condition to take its place in the defence of the country. The Major-General hopes next year to hear that the Battalion is completed to its establishment, and that at future Inspections there will be no members absent without leave." (They were then 89 below the authorised establishment.)

Referring to the new title the *Volunteer Service Gazette* stated " By the action of the Duke of Cambridge in making the 1st Middlesex R.V. the premier Volunteer Battalion of the K.R.R.C., as this Regiment is admittedly the most distinguished one in the service—no less than 30 ' honours ' being credited to it, and H.R.H. being the Colonel-in-Chief, the compliment was an exceptionally high one. The wisdom of his Royal Highness's choice, however, has been abundantly proved and the parent Corps has every reason to be proud of its Volunteer off-shoot."

At the beginning of 1899 Col. Stanley Bird resigned the command of the regiment. The news was conveyed to all ranks in Battalion Orders, 18th February :

(1) "The following War Office letter dated 9th January, 1899, is published for information :

Sir,—I am directed by the Secretary of State for War to acknowledge the receipt of your letter of the 5th inst., submitting the resignation of Colonel S. G. Bird, Commanding the Victoria and St. George's Rifle Volunteer Corps, which will be submitted for Her Majesty's acceptance in due course.

The Secretary of State has received this resignation with regret, and has desired me to thank Colonel Bird, on behalf of himself and the Commander-in-Chief, for his long, useful, and faithful service, not only in his own Corps, but in the interests of the Volunteer Force generally. I have the honour to be, Sir,

Your obedient servant,

(Signed) T. K. Kenny,

I.G.A.F.

APPENDIX I

(2) Farewell Order by Colonel Stanley G. Bird, V.D.

After forty years' service in the Victoria and St. George's Rifles, the time has now come when I have to sever my connection with the Corps ; but before doing so I wish to tender my deep thanks to the Officers, Non-commissioned Officers and Men, past and present, for the support they have, one and all, given me on all occasions, which has made the command one of great pleasure to me.

I wish also to testify to the discipline, harmony, and admirable *esprit de corps* which has throughout existed in the Regiment, all of which qualities have tended to make my command one of the happiest periods of my life, to which I shall look back with ineffaceable pride and satisfaction.

The maintenance of the prestige of the Corps has been my constant aim, and in this I have always received the loyal co-operation and support of all members. Under younger hands the old Regiment must, and will go on and prosper ; and that it may do so is the earnest prayer of their old Colonel.

(3) Lieut.-Col. and Hon. Col. S. G. Bird, resigns his Commission, also is permitted to retain his rank, and to continue to wear the Uniform of the Corps on his retirement.

In drawing attention to the above notification in the *London Gazette* of the 17th inst., the Commanding Officer cannot refrain from testifying to the great loss the Regiment has sustained by the retirement of Col. Stanley Bird, who has faithfully served his Queen and country for no less than 43 years. He was one of the first to join the great Volunteer movement at its inauguration, and he has seen it pass through many phases.

During his long connection with this Regiment, some very important changes have taken place. Owing to his energetic and tactful action, the amalgamation of the Victoria and St. George's Rifles was consummated. Both these Battalions held very high positions in the Volunteer service and were justly proud of their traditions, and both were naturally very loth to lose any of their privileges ; but by judicious handling all friction was avoided, and the united Regiment we now have shows conclusively that a very great and beneficial change was successfully accomplished.

No less than four different weapons have been in use since Col. Bird joined the force, the old muzzle-loader, Snider, Martini-Henry, and Lee-Metford. The gorgeous and expensive uniform of the old Victoria Rifles has been superseded by the neat and serviceable pattern of the King's Royal Rifles.

It was mainly owing to his initiative, and through the kindness of the Duke of Westminster, that we now possess our splendid Head-quarters, probably the best in England. Colonel Bird also devoted much time outside our Regiment for the good of the Volunteers. He was the founder of the Commanding Officers' Institute, and its present Hon. Secretary ; a body that has done much service in bringing the Force more in touch with the War Office. He was Honorary Secretary to Sir James Whitehead's Fund for Equipping the London Battalions, and he was elected on the Council of the National Rifle Association, when the St. George's Prize was handed over to their custody, and he is also a member of the Governing Body of the United Service Institute.

Owing to ill-health the last three years Colonel Bird has not been able to join in the many social and enjoyable functions connected with Volunteering, but when he was present with us his amiable and kindly disposition rendered him most popular amongst all ranks, and the Commanding Officer feels certain that he is only acting as the mouthpiece of every man in the Battalion when he wishes Colonel Bird may have long life in the enjoyment of his well-earned repose."

On the 14th June, 1899, Colonel Stanley Bird was appointed Honorary Colonel of the Regiment. He was succeeded in the command of the Victoria and St. George's Rifles by his brother, Col. Charles Bird, formerly in the Victorias, which he left as a corporal at the same time as his brother, and was appointed to the command of a company.

The South African War

The C.I.V.

In October of the same year the Boers delivered their ultimatum to the British and thereafter commenced the South African War. Col. C. Bird promptly offered the services of the Victoria and St. George's to the Government, and was told that it was not intended to employ the Volunteers outside their proper sphere of Home Defence. He then issued a notice that members of the regiment could, however, show their interest by trying to help their more fortunate comrades who had been sent to the front. "Three Battalions of the Regiment to which we are affiliated have been mobilised for service, and this will entail great distress upon the wives and children left behind, especially of men married off the strength of the Regiment. The Victoria and St. George's being the 1st V.B. of the King's Royal Rifles, it is proposed that a subscription should be raised in the Regiment for their relief, and all present and old members of the Regiment are invited to help."

The fund proved eminently successful, upwards of £500 being subscribed by November 16th.

However, things did not go quite as they were expected and following the "Black Week" in December the Volunteers got their first chance of proving their use in the field. The City Imperial Volunteers, a composite battalion from all the London Corps, and the Imperial Yeomanry were formed, and further calls made for "Service Companies" to the Regular Battalions at the front. Forty-four men under Capt. R. B. Shipley, who was given

APPENDIX I

command of " E " Company, formed the contingent to the C.I.V., while another thirty-five joined the Service Company of the K.R.R.

Shortly before their departure Col. Bird addressed a letter to Sir Arthur John Bigge, the Queen's private Secretary, narrating the history of the old Victoria Rifles, and enclosing a copy of Sir John Conroy's letter of 11th July, 1835 ; Col. Bird stated that the first detachment of the Victoria and St. George's was about to leave for South Africa, and concluded : " During all these years no opportunity has arisen, but now that a call to arms has been made the Regiment has responded with alacrity and enthusiasm. All ranks that bear this honoured name, now join with me in humbly approaching Her Majesty and assuring her of their unswerving loyalty and devotion to her Throne and Person. The first detachment of 39 included in the City of London Imperial Regiment under Capt. R. B. Shipley, a respected Burgess of the Royal Borough of Windsor, leaves for South Africa on Saturday next." To this the following gracious reply was made :

" OSBORNE,
Jan. 11, 1900.

SIR,—I am commanded to convey to you and all ranks of the 1st Middlesex, Victoria and St. George's Volunteer Rifle Corps, the thanks of the Queen for their assurance of loyalty and devotion expressed in your letter to me of the 9th inst.

The Queen is gratified to think that the Corps which in its earlier formation was identified with the Duchess of Kent and Herself is now among those which have responded enthusiastically to the Call to Arms.

Her Majesty sends her best wishes to the detachment which is about to sail for South Africa.

I am, Sir, Yours very faithfully,
ARTHUR BIGGE.

Colonel C. Bird,
    Commanding 1st Middlesex,
        Victoria and St. George's V.R.C."

" Swearing in " for the new regiment began on New Year's Day, 1900, and by the 12th some 1300 men were fully equipped and ready for embarkation. On that day all ranks received the Freedom of the City of London, in the evening attended a farewell service at St. Paul's, and supper in the Inner Temple, and on the following morning marched through the streets from Bunhill Row to Nine Elms amid the greetings of an enormous crowd. Arrived at Southampton 250 rank and file, under Col. Cholmondeley, proceeded on board the *Briton*, and a similar number, under Capt. Shipley (Victoria and St. George's) on the *Garth Castle*. The rest of the regiment followed a week later in the *Ariosto*, *Gaul* and *Kinfaun's Castle*.

In describing his first experiences Capt. Shipley wrote : " We left Cape Town on Feb. 20th, after hanging about there for nearly three weeks, and arrived at Orange River Camp after a somewhat tedious journey. Except for 20 miles north of Cape Town the country through which the line passes is without doubt the most utterly desolate and uninteresting land it has ever been my lot to set eyes on. Absolutely nothing but mile after mile of sandy waste, with stones and rocks strewn around, the monotony only broken by the everlasting kopje. . . . My Company has been guarding the railway bridge most of the time since we have been up here. It is an iron girder structure nearly 500 yards long, and besides trains we have to work all the wheeled traffic, ox wagons, convoys, etc. So I am a species of railway station master and cattle driver. In the day time there is nothing much to do except to hang about in case of a breakdown, and at night we have six groups out on N. side and four South. I just have sufficient men to do the work, one night in bed and one on duty. Thank goodness it usually is fine. Last night we had a thunder storm and were nearly washed out of our tents, the groups having a badish time. The whole C.I.V. Regiment is scattered all over the shop."

It was not until the end of March that the Battalion was consolidated, and on the 31st it left Orange River Camp in two special trains for Naauwpoort, where a week was spent in Battalion training and in shelter trench exercise. On Easter Monday, April 16th, Lord Roberts began his march upon Bloemfontein, the C.I.V. starting from Springfontein. Up to that time they had only seen some desultory fighting. Bloemfontein was reached on St. George's Day, the C.I.V. being inspected the following afternoon by Lord Roberts, who expressed himself as pleased with the appearance and steadiness of the men.

On Sunday, April 29th, writes Capt. Shipley : " We left Glen Camp in the afternoon having cut the baggage down to minimum, leaving kits behind ; marched 8 miles N.E. and bivouacked. Monday, turned out at 4.30 and lay out, advancing slowly as supports to Camerons who attacked big Kopje but Boers did not stand so we did not come under fire ; marched 10 miles. This was the beginning of ' Bobs' ' general advance N. Tuesday, 4.30 a.m., our Brigade turned due E. and marched 13 miles joining Broadwood's Cavalry Division, then on again another 10 miles and relieved Ian Hamilton's Brigade which was having a warm time against 5000 Boers. It was an exciting afternoon as we hoped to cut the Boers off but did not succeed. It was scorching hot and we had practically no water except the one bottle per man. The Boers saw us coming some miles off and scooted. We then became part of Ian Hamilton's Division. As we (we were advanced guard) advanced we could watch the shells of the Boers and of our own side bursting ; there were a few spent bullets whizzing about but no harm was done. Tuesday, we had a day's rest as Ian

APPENDIX I 543

Hamilton's men were rather done having been out 12 days from Bloemfontein and fought on seven days out of them. General Hamilton came down in the morning and Mackinnon introduced me to him. He gave us a most interesting resumé of the fighting they had been doing and was glad we had turned up as we did. We heard that the Boers had split up, some going N. to Brandfort and the majority of them to Winburg. Wednesday, we were up early and after the latter. We marched 17 miles; I had two companies under me as escort to two 5 in. naval guns, each drawn by 20 oxen. It was rather a trying job as the cattle went slowly and therefore had to keep going, so we got no halts when the others halted. Still we got into camp early, near a delicious spring of water and within five miles of the Boers. Next morning early we were after them again, but the General had news from the cavalry that they had slipped off early and were taking up a position on Impediment Hill. The General refused to go for a frontal attack and determined to turn the enemy's right flank. We went for about 7 miles over the open veldt leaving the hill about 2 miles on our right; the Boers were in force on the Scouts' end but our cavalry and M.I. kept out of range until they reached a point where the Boers opened fire on them from a Creuzot gun and pompom. Our Brigade was leading and the Sussex were ordered to attack the Hill to the left of the road where the pompom was, the cavalry going round to the extreme left to turn the position. The C.I.V. were in support of the Sussex, my company third. We halted in extended order when we were about 600 yards behind the front line and lay down for nearly an hour awaiting the attack. Several shells burst over us, but no damage was done. It was grand fun watching the Boers leaving the south end of Impediment Hill and rushing to our flank, building stone sangars and strengthening others, and then our batteries took up positions in some mealy patches and made ripping practice. Through our glasses I was watching about 30 Boers; some were collecting rocks and building a sangar under a tree. Our gunners spotted them and sent a shell plumb into that tree and out scuttled about five Boers. Another lot had just completed a sangar when they got two shells into them and a lot bolted out; two rushed along to another sangar and ran into another shell just as it burst. I only saw one afterwards—he jumped about six feet and turned like a rabbit hit hard. We then advanced and our guns soon shifted the Boer Artillery, and the Sussex took the smaller hill to the left. The C.I.V. were then ordered to right form and attack Impediment Hill. My company (C) was in the 3rd line and a battery took up a position behind us and plumped a number of shells on the top close to a gun embrasure and into a deserted Kaffir kraal which was on top. The Boers never stood but cleared with the exception of about a dozen snipers, who luckily did no damage. When we reached the top we found it clear and about 500 Boers galloping away about 1500 yards right front.

We shoved a few volleys into them but with little result beyond wounding some horses. We had a magnificent view from the top. About three miles away in front were the Boer guns slowly retiring and parties taking up positions to cover their retreat ; then away seven miles right front the Boer main convoy about five miles long wending its way down to a drift on the Winburg road. It was most tantalising and made one want to get at them. I had orders to stay on the hill with my company until all our brigade transport had passed, which took about three hours, and we then marched down to camp about five miles getting in at 7 p.m. It was altogether a most interesting day. The Sussex had one officer and 3 men wounded, and the cavalry lost one officer and 2 men killed and several wounded. We captured a Boer ambulance with 4 wounded and one doctor in it and we found 70 wounded Boers in Winburg supposed to have been wounded in this action.

On Saturday we were up early and after them again and expected they would make a stand at a drift where we had to cross the Vet River, but when we came to the top of a hill overlooking the drift we could see the Beggars trekking N. and N.E. out of Winburg. So the General sent a flag of truce into Winburg about 8 miles off. The Staff Officer who took in the flag had rather a rough time on arrival in the town as some German artillerists wanted to shoot him, but the Boer General (Botha) would not let them molest him. The Landrost had received a message from Steyn's government to deliver up the town so we entered in triumph." This was on May 5th.

Writing about this time, Rfn. H. H. Lewis says : " We have been having a pretty rough time of it, nothing but continual long marching and very often on very short rations. We started from Bloemfontein, entered Winburg (May 5) and are now leaving here (Kronstadt), I hope for Pretoria. We have not seen any tents for nearly a month, but luckily it has been dry weather, otherwise we should be rather miserable. We are at present on $\frac{3}{4}$ rations which means three biscuits a day and a little meat which we cook ourselves. Not much to do 20 miles in marching order, is it ? "

On May 29th there was a biggish fight at Doorn Kop (the hill where, on January 1, 1896, Dr. Jameson surrendered), the casualties to the C.I.V. resulting in one officer and 11 men wounded. " This happy result," says Col. Mackinnon, *Journal of the C.I.V.*), " being in great measure due to the intelligent manner in which the men had learnt to take cover. When one saw the bullets skipping through, and in front of, and behind the ranks, one thought that not a man could escape being hit."

Pretoria fell on June 5th and the C.I.V. took part in the march past of the troops before Lord Roberts in the big square in the middle of the town, the ground being kept by the Guards Brigade. Col. Mackinnon, Commanding C.I.V., next day issued the following order to the battalion :

C.I.V. CONTINGENT.
FIRST MIDDLESEX (VICTORIA AND ST. GEORGE'S), V.R.C.

APPENDIX I

"In congratulating the Battalion on the splendid march they have made, which commenced at Springfontein on Easter Monday, 16th April, and terminated in the creditable and soldier-like parade before the Field-Marshal Commander-in-Chief in Pretoria yesterday, the Commandant publishes for information the following figures: The march has lasted for fifty-one days; forty of which have been marching days, the distance covered was 523 miles, which gives an average of over 13 miles per marching day."

Further high praise was bestowed upon the regiment by the Commander-in-Chief in the Army Orders of June 7th:

"The newly-raised battalion of the City of London Imperial Volunteers marched 500 miles in fifty-one days, only once having two consecutive days' halt. It took part in twenty-six engagements with the enemy."

Gen. Ian Hamilton's testimony was brief but only foreshadowed what Londoners proved themselves capable of in the Great War that was to come fourteen years later: "With such troops I could go anywhere and do anything."

On June 11-12th took place the battle of Diamond Hill. The Boers were known to be holding strong positions to the south-east of Pretoria, and Gen. Ian Hamilton's force, with which was the C.I.V., was sent out to drive them back. The attack on the Hill was made by the Sussex on the left, the C.I.V. in the centre, and the Derbys on the right, with the Camerons four miles in rear. Subsequently the 1st Battalion Coldstream Guards arrived and extended on the right. Towards the close of day on June 12th the firing died down and it was found that the Boers had quitted their second and strongest position. This was the most desperate fight the C.I.V. had in the war, their attack having to be made across a wide open expanse, and in consequence they suffered some casualties. The news was transmitted to London by the following dispatch from Lord Roberts.

"PRETORIA RESIDENCY, Thursday.
(*June* 14, 1900.)

The following Casualties occurred in the City Imperial Volunteers during the fighting on the 11th and 12th:

Killed: Lieut. Alt and 752 Pte. G. E. Ives.
Dangerously wounded: Three.
Severely wounded: Three.
Slightly wounded: Eighteen.
Please inform the Lord Mayor the battalion greatly distinguished itself."

In response the following telegram was dispatched to Col. Mackinnon, Commanding C.I.V.: "Most cordial congratulations on Field-Marshal's generous praise to Battalion. The City very proud of their regiment, but deeply grieved at your losses and wounded. Convey latter sympathy and wire their progress.—ALFRED NEWTON, Lord Mayor."

The C.I.V. did not see much fighting after this. The regiment had suffered somewhat from the long march and the ranks were depleted by wounded and sick. From July 5th to 24th they were resting at Heilbron, though during the last few days their rest was disturbed by De Wet, who had broken through the cordon and harassed them for some nights, also capturing a convoy with new clothing and equipment intended for their use. A wire was received on July 23rd from the Chief of the Staff ordering Col. Mackinnon at once to remove all the garrison and supplies to Krugersdorp. The operation was safely performed though it took two days to do it. Many days were spent in fruitless chase after De Wet, and occasionally that elusive gentleman did some of the chasing. On August 23rd the regiment was back at Pretoria, where it marched past Lord Roberts in the big square. On September 23rd news came that the battalion was to return home, and preparations for the journey commenced. Entraining began on October 2nd, and on the 7th the whole regiment embarked on the *Aurania* for England, which was reached on the 29th.

London was prepared to give them a hearty welcome home, but what actually took place may without exaggeration be described as a scene of wild enthusiasm. The streets were lined with battalions of the Metropolitan Volunteer Regiments, but at one place the crowd broke through and mingled in the ranks of the C.I.V. At once all military formation was swept away, including the troops intended to guard the line of route, and the C.I.V. struggled along in twos and threes to their destinations in the City, some of them taking hours to get there. The Victoria and St. George's gave their contingent a "Welcome Home" Dinner at the Holborn Restaurant on November 10th, Col. Charles Bird being in the chair. Supporting him were Col. the Earl of Albemarle, who commanded the infantry of the C.I.V., Col. Stanley Bird, the Hon. Col. of the Victoria and St. George's V.R.C., and Capt. Shipley who was in charge of the detachment. Col. Mackinnon put in an appearance at a later stage of the evening. There were also present the contingent who were going out to Australia as part of the bodyguard of the Duke and Duchess of York under Lieut. A. R. Davies.

The names of Capt. Shipley and Clr.-Sergt. F. Judge were mentioned in a special dispatch from Earl Roberts, dated September 4th, 1901, for meritorious service. Two members alone of the 42 men of the regiment who served with the C.I.V. failed to return, viz. Ptes. E. C. Day and G. E. Halford, both of whom died on service.

The following letter was received by Col. Bird :

APPENDIX I

"*S.S. Aurania,*
14.10.00.

DEAR COLONEL BIRD,

I cannot say enough for the good work Shipley has done throughout our campaign. He has been an ideal company commander and has given me most complete satisfaction. I have specially brought him to the notice of the F.M. Commanding-in-Chief as having stood out conspicuously among the Captains.

Colour-Sergeant Judge has also done all his duties conspicuously well and I have nothing but good to say of him.

Sergt. Marsh has been a great help to the Company, and is a very reliable man, and Corporal Millett has also done out of the way well.

Where so many have done their duty there is difficulty to select a few, but the above have come specially under my notice, and I think you will like to hear of them.

Yours very truly,

HENRY MACKINNON."

Capt. Shipley was also accorded a very hearty reception upon his return to Windsor. Flags were displayed, maroons were fired, and Mr. Alfred Barber, the Mayor, and several members of the Corporation of the Royal Borough, took part in the welcome. Capt. Shipley was presented by the burgesses with a ruby and diamond ring and an illuminated address.

The year 1900 was also memorable for the fact that the battalion at home was stationed at Bullswater Camp, Pirbright, for 28 days' training, pay at army rates being issued to all ranks for the actual days in camp, including the days of arrival and departure. This special Emergency Camp, the first of its kind, lasted from July 21st to August 17th. In connection with it the following Special Order was issued to all ranks by Col. C. Bird :

" It is with great confidence that the Commanding Officer appeals to all ranks to make this Emergency Camp a distinct success. During the last few days some doubt has been raised by the Public Press as to the feasibility of the scheme proposed by the War Office. The Premier Volunteer Corps of the Home District, and the oldest Volunteer Corps of England, must not belie its ancient traditions, but must willingly make every sacrifice to uphold the *esprit de corps* of which the Regiment has always been so justly proud. If any Rifleman who has sent in his name finds that through unforeseen circumstances, beyond his control, he cannot possibly attend the camp, he *must*, without fail, apply for leave and state fully the reasons of his inability to attend, but the Commanding Officer feels certain that everyone in the Regiment will do his level best to fulfil all the requirements laid down by Her Majesty's Government."

Just prior to this it had been decided to adopt a new head-dress—black slouch hat with cock's feathers. They were issued in time for the camp and proved very useful, the summer being an unusually hot one.

K.R.R.C. SERVICE COMPANY

The Victoria and St. George's sent as a first contingent to the King's Royal Rifles Special Service Company: Lieut. R. fF. Davies, Sergt.-Instructor A. Freeman (an old K.R.R. man), Sergts. G. F. Richardson and F. R. Brooke and 27 men. They left Southampton on March 16th in the s.s. *Tagus*. Writing on April 3rd, Lieut. Davies says: "We expect to reach Cape Town to-morrow so I will try and give you a short account of our voyage. We have had a most calm voyage ever since we left the Bay, and I think our men have been very happy although, I suppose, rather bored with the monotony of it. Our detachment is considered the smartest on board, which causes us to lose many of our best men as they are taken for other duties. Two Sergeants and a private have been made ship's police and are very smart. Brooke is one of the Sergts. They gave him Lance rank at the depot. You should really see some of the Yeomanry at drill; it is too funny. They know absolutely nothing and the officers bring their drill books on to parade and then can't get the words of command right. We do not yet know what is to happen to us to-morrow. We hope to go on to Durban by this boat. Duties on board ship are not very heavy, I have had to do officer of the watch 3 times during the voyage, and we only get about one drill every three days as there is no room for more. We of course have a muster parade every day at 10 a.m."

Rfn. G. C. Randle supplies some further information about the voyage. "The inoculation for typhoid and enteric fever was a terrible time for us and happened three days before ' crossing the Line.' We were punctured in the abdomen on the left side, and some fluid injected. Four hours after you begin to feel effects, first as though somebody had kicked you in the stomach with a very heavy boot, then you start to stiffen and inflame all up your side to the arm, your head is splitting, you gradually double up, and by the time you go to bed you have all the symptoms of the fever. It takes three days to get the fever off you." Crossing the Line was carried out with all the good old ceremonies of King Neptune and his staff. They also witnessed an impressive funeral at sea, one of the West Kent's dying on the voyage.

At Cape Town the contingent was transhipped to the Nile, which was described as "dirty, rotten and foul." Durban was reached without incident and the contingent took train straight to Pietermaritzburg in open trucks, and as there was a thunderstorm the men got properly wet through. They left Pietermaritzburg at eleven o'clock the next night and arrived at Ladysmith at seven

APPENDIX I

in the morning. In the afternoon they proceeded to Modder Spruit, where they joined the 2nd Battalion K.R.R. commanded by Major the Hon. E. J. Montagu Stewart-Wortley, C.M.G., D.S.O. As the battalion had been through the famous siege of Ladysmith it was kept out of the fighting line for some time, though the training as usual was pretty intensive. Early in May Capt. Warren, of the 2nd London Rifles, who was in command of the company, succumbed to an attack of dysentery, and was succeeded in the command by Lieut. "Bobby" Davies, of the Victoria and St. George's V.R.C., who was subsequently promoted to Captain.

The company was moved to Sunday's River Bridge on May 17th. "This is a most charming place," writes Lieut. Davies, "with plenty of water and vegetation, so different from Modder Spruit. There are several pools in the streams round where you can get a grand swim, which is delightful; it was most pleasant to find such a nice place after our march, which was very trying, the dust getting up in places like a regular fog. The Commanding Officer was very pleased with our Coy., as I was able to report when we halted on our arrival that all the men were present, which was extremely creditable after covering 25 miles in the day. We were the only Co. who could do so, in fact 9 men were still missing the next morning."

The company remained with the 2nd Battalion K.R.R.C. until July 18th when the following was published in Battalion Orders :

"INGOGO. *July* 18*th*, 1900.

10.—VOLUNTEER COMPANY.

The Volunteer Company attached to this Battalion having been ordered to proceed to join the 3rd Battalion, the Commanding Officer wishes to place on record his appreciation of the excellent spirit which they have shown and of the good work they have performed while with the 2nd Battalion. In wishing them every good luck he trusts that the comradeship and mutual interest which has arisen may continue in future, and he hopes that on the completion of the Campaign they will convey to the Battalions they represent the assurance of their comrades in the Regular Battalion that their assistance has been greatly appreciated and will always be welcomed.

By Order.

(Signed) H. R. GREEN, Capt. and Adjt.

2nd K.R. Rifles."

By request of Major the Hon. E. J. Montagu Stewart-Wortley, Lieut. Davies forwarded a copy of the order to Col. Charles Bird. The Service Company were never in any big action, but continued to carry out with tact and ability very necessary and arduous duties on the lines of communication. From time to time fresh drafts were furnished from Regimental H.Q. to South Africa. On January 4th, 1901, Lieut. Davies wrote Col. Bird as follows ;

"SUNDAY'S RIVER BRIDGE, NATAL.

The section wishes me to thank you for your very kind telegram of New Year's wishes. The company is now all split up guarding bridges. After we left the 3rd Battn., at the beginning of November, they sent us to Colenso to guard the big bridge over the Tugela, but just before Christmas they split us up; Wyld with 30 men stayed at Colenso, and I came here with 30 more, and I have to look after two posts between here and Ladysmith—one of 14 men at Elandslaagte and another of 14 at Modder Spruit. I find it deadly dull all by myself but spend a good part of my time looking after these places. Sergt. Brooke has just rejoined after three and a half months' wandering about. He was sent from Heidelberg to Cape Town in the month of September in charge of some Boer prisoners, and on the way back was collared and detained at various places, until at last he wrote to me and I managed by wiring the authorities to get him back. When we are going to leave this country is still an unknown quantity, and I don't suppose now, that we shall get away before the end of February. All the men out here are, I think, very well. Cleeves (V.) is still at Maritzburg doing light duty as he practically lost the use of one arm after enteric, but he is getting it right again now. Hawes (S.E.) has dropped into a very good billet in the office of the Military Governor at Johannesburg; he has got his discharge from the Coy., and I believe his salary to start with is £20 a month. The fellows here had a great time at Christmas as the men at the Elandslaagte colleries sent them up any amount of luxuries. I hope you all had a happy Christmas and that the New Year may be a prosperous one. With very best wishes from us all, believe me,

Yours very sincerely,
ROBERT FF. DAVIES."

Early in May, 1901, the Special Service Company received orders to return home after fourteen months' experience of active soldiering with the celebrated King's Royal Rifle Corps. The Victoria and St. George's contingent was amongst the earliest to reach London, arriving at Waterloo shortly after two o'clock on the afternoon of Saturday, June 1st. Here a crowd was awaiting them, attracted thither by the presence of the Regimental Band and members of the Corps in walking out order. Accompanied by these and an enthusiastic following, though the numbers were not so great as on the occasion of the return of the C.I.V., the contingent marched direct to the H.Q. in Davies Street, where they were greeted by Col. Bird, the officers and men of the regiment. On June 20th another "Welcome Home" dinner was held, this time at Davies Street, Col. Bird being again in the chair. Of the original draft only four men were missing: Rfn. S. E. Bradley, who had died on active service; Rfn. A. G. Guthrie, invalided home and dying from an attack of enteric fever; a third was in hospital at Ladysmith, and a fourth had been given a commission in Baden Powell's Police.

Imperial Representative Corps. November, 1899. Victoria and St. George's V.R.C.

APPENDIX I

Regimental records show that among the members of the Victoria and St. George's R.V. who had volunteered for active service, 10 had joined the Sharpshooters, 13 Paget's Horse, 18 other units of the Imperial Yeomanry, and one the Duke of Cambridge's Own Middlesex Regiment.

THE IMPERIAL REPRESENTATIVE CORPS

A signal honour was paid to the Victoria and St. George's R.V.C. in October, 1900, though, much to the chagrin of the members, it was subsequently considerably modified. On the 17th of the month the following Regimental Order was issued :

SPECIAL BATTALION ORDER

(By Col. Charles Bird, V.D., Commanding.)

HEAD-QUARTERS,
17th October, 1900.

Her Majesty having signified her pleasure to send out detachments representing the respective branches of the Army as a Guard of Honour for the Opening Ceremony of the first Parliament of the Australasian Commonwealth, the Commanding Officer has the great pleasure to announce that the Victoria and St. George's Rifles have been selected to represent the whole of the Volunteer Force of Great Britain, and he feels certain that all ranks and all old Members and friends of the Regiment will feel gratified that such a distinguished honour has been conferred on the Battalion to participate in this historical and unique function.

A Detachment consisting of 1 Captain, 1 Subaltern, 4 Sergeants, 1 Bugler, and 49 Rank and File, will leave England for Australia in the middle of November, and will be absent probably over 3 months.

Officers will hold Army rank.

Riflemen will be sworn in and attested as soldiers for the time being.

Army pay and allowance to all ranks.

Sea Kit and White Helmets will be issued in addition to ordinary uniform.

All ranks must have been efficient during 1900.

Preference as far as possible will be given to bachelors.

Riflemen willing to go will parade at Head-quarters on Friday evening the 19th inst., at 8 p.m. Drill order.

Captains commanding companies will furnish a list of 8 men per company, including mounted infantry, by 10 o'clock, on Monday, 22nd inst., and the names of those selected by the War Office will be announced as soon as possible.

By order,
E. GRAHAM SNOW, Major & Adjt.
1st Mx. (V. & St. G.) V.R.C.

The wide publicity given to this announcement aroused considerable excitement in Devonshire, and loud protests were made at the War Office at the selection of a London regiment in preference to the 1st Devon R.V., which claimed to be, in circumstances told elsewhere in this volume, the oldest Volunteer Corps. Yielding to popular clamour the Army authorities cancelled their first order and compromised the matter by substituting for the single company of the Victoria and St. George's a combined company of 2 officers and 28 Rank and File of the 1st V. B. Devon Regt. and 1 officer and 23 men of the 1st Middlesex. Lieut. A. R. Davies was appointed by Col. Bird to command the latter.

The other contingents of the Imperial Representative Corps were supplied from the following regiments :

Cavalry :
    Royal Horse Guards.
    1st Dragoon Guards.
    7th Hussars.
    21st Lancers.

Royal Regiment of Artillery :
    Royal Horse Artillery, " V " Battery.
    Royal Field Artillery, 10th Battery.
    Royal Garrison Artillery.

Guards :
    Grenadiers, Coldstream, Scots and Irish.

Royal Engineers.

Highland Regiments :
    Black Watch.
    Highland Light Infantry.
    Seaforth Highlanders.
    Cameron Highlanders.
    Highland Light Infantry Band.

Rifles :
    Scottish Rifles.
    K.R.R. Corps.
    Royal Irish Rifles.
    Rifle Brigade.

Fusiliers :
    Northumberland F.
    Royal F.
    Royal Welsh F.
    Royal Irish F.

Line Regiments :
    Royal West Surrey.
    East Kent.
    Somersetshire L.I.
    Duke of Cornwall's L.I.

APPENDIX I

Line Regiments:
 A.S.C.
 A.O.C.
 R.A.M.C.
 Army Pay Department.
Militia:
 4th Norfolk.
Yeomanry:
 Royal Wiltshire.

A total strength of 44 officers, 957 men and 4 R.H.A. guns. Lieut.-Col. W. G. Crole Wyndham, 21st Lancers, was in command, with Capt. A. H. Wood, 2nd Battalion Scottish Rifles as adjutant. The contingent sailed from Southampton on November 12th.

Reporting to Col. Bird on Christmas Day, 1900, from Sydney, Lieut. Davies says: " As we are at last on land once more I write a few lines to let you know how we are getting along. First of all we are all very fit, except, I am sorry to say, Waller, who has a bad go of dysentery; he is doing well, but won't be able to take any part in the show here or elsewhere I am afraid.

We have most excellent quarters here (Agricultural Grounds), the large show buildings being turned into barrack rooms, large and airy; every man has a spring mattress bed, sheets, blankets, etc. The meals are top hole, 4 or 5 courses for breakfast, goodness knows how many for dinner, men to wait on them and outside the ground everyone pressing our unfortunate fellows to drink. Considering the awful temptation the men are very good.

All the infantry except the Guards, with the cavalry, are here. The Gunners and Guards being in the Victoria Barracks, about ½ mile away; they are in some ways better off, the barracks being permanent and as good as any of ours at home. The Officers' quarters are first class, good Mess and Ante-rooms. The permanent Corps are quartered there.

We are all very glad to get away from H.M.S. Transport *Britannic*; she is not quite the sort for the job. One gets very tired of the food—so little change in it. I fear our men would have done rather badly if they had had no money to buy extras from the canteen; also the water supply is bad.

We had a very hot march up here on Saturday. It is only about 3 miles from the Quay, but in Marching Order it was trying. Of course, we are told it was a cool day; if that is so I fear we shall have many casualties on the 1st when we tramp about 7 miles in our Sunday best. From here, which we leave on 14th, we go to Brisbane, Hobart, Melbourne, Adelaide, Fremantle, and stay about two days at each. There is a chance of our going to New Zealand. If we do I suppose we shall not be home until the middle of April, otherwise we ought to get back about the 3rd week in March.

The Adjutant told me the other day he was very pleased at the way our fellows behave. I can only add that they are indeed first class, taking their share of duties right well. Cowell (Corpl. H. W.) and Howden (Rfn. J. B.) did very well in the skill at arms competition ; our team won the cock fighting and with better luck we might have had a chance for the tug-of-war. There is an I.R.C. paper which gives all our doings ; I am bringing copies home with me. Of course we had a great reception here and at Fremantle. We all send our good wishes to you all for the New Year."

Wherever they went, the Imperial Troops (there was a contingent from India in addition to those before enumerated) received an enthusiastic welcome, the citizens turning out as one man to watch them marching past or displaying their skill at arms. Unhappily the death of Queen Victoria on January 22nd cast a gloom over the later proceedings in connection with the inauguration of the Australian Commonwealth, and the tour which commenced under such brilliant prospects terminated with the return to England of the Imperial Representative Corps almost unnoticed.

Writing from Marlborough Barracks, Dublin, the Commander, Lieut.-Col. W. G. Crole Wyndham, 21st Lancers, to Col. Bird, says : " I hope you will allow me to express my appreciation of the detachment of the 1st Middlesex which accompanied the Imperial Representative Corps to Australia. The men were an excellent lot and their conduct and bearing throughout the trip was all that could be desired. They were well commanded by Lieut. Davies. 28th April, 1901."

Centenary Celebrations

The year 1903 proved to be one of the most important in the history of the Victoria and St. George's Rifles. First some very important changes were made in the personnel of the staff. The *London Gazette* published the following announcements :

" Lieut.-Col. and Hon. Col. Charles Bird, V.D., resigns his commission with permission to retain his rank and wear the prescribed uniform on retirement, dated 30th January, 1903."

" Major and Hon. Lieut.-Colonel F. P. Ococks to be Lieut.-Colonel and to command under paragraph 55a, Volunteer Regulations, dated 3rd March, 1903."

Major W. M. Tanqueray, V.D., was appointed to the right half battalion, and Major G. M. Weekley to the left half battalion. Capt. E. Northey, 1st K.R.R.C., having been selected for the Adjutancy of the regiment took over the duties from Major E. G. Snow from the 23rd April.

Col. Ococks' first duty was to issue a farewell order upon the retirement of Colonel Bird :

" In a term of service extending over 26 years, he evinced a keen interest in Volunteer work, and more especially during the four years of his command he devoted himself with untiring energy and self sacrifice to the increased demands upon his time occasioned by the

APPENDIX I

exigencies of the war. One will always remember that during the dark days of that period, when a call was made upon the Volunteer Force to assist in defending the existence of our Empire, how readily our late C.O. responded to that call by immediately offering himself for service at the front, and by issuing an order to his Battalion, which, as many will recollect, resulted in no less than 200 men volunteering to follow their C.O.'s example. Those selected both for the C.I.V. and for the Service Company must always retain a lively recollection of the kindly interest taken by Colonel Charles Bird in their welfare previous to sailing and during the time they were in South Africa.

Again it was mainly owing to Colonel Bird's initiative that a fund was opened in our battalion, resulting in a sum of nearly £1,000 being handed to the K.R.R.'s for the benefit of those of the regiment who had suffered from the war.

These and similar instances of the keen interest Colonel Bird displayed in his work connected with the Victoria and St. George's Rifles go to prove how great a loss has been sustained by our battalion.

In his retirement the C.O. on behalf of all ranks wishes Colonel C. Bird Long Life, Happiness and the Best of Everything." ,

At a meeting of officers held at head-quarters on March 11th, it was decided that a presentation be made to Col. Bird on his retirement from the regiment after his many years of active and devoted service. Subscriptions were invited from members of the officers' mess, and at a mess dinner held on May 6th, Col. Bird was presented with a handsome china cabinet.

On June 5th the Commanding Officer invited every officer to attend His Majesty's Levee on June 12th. The Levee, which was held at Buckingham Palace, was the first following King Edward's Coronation. Many of them availed themselves of the opportunity and were duly presented by Col. Stanley Bird, C.B., the Hon. Colonel of the Regiment.

On Thursday, July 2nd, Lieut.-Gen. Lord Grenfell attended at the head-quarters in Davies Street to unveil a memorial to those members of the regiment who had served in South Africa. The memorial was the gift of Col. Charles Bird, V.D., late commanding officer, and consists of two marble tablets on which are inscribed no fewer than 150 names of members of the corps who went to South Africa, and served in the King's Royal Rifles, the City Imperial Volunteers, the Imperial Yeomanry and other corps. Each tablet bears the regimental badge of the Victoria and St. George's Rifles. Among those present at the ceremony were Col. Stanley Bird, C.B., honorary colonel of the regiment ; Lieut.-Col. Page Ococks, the officer commanding, and a number of other officers and men of the corps as well as their friends. A guard of honour was mounted by the regiment and the band was in attendance. In opening the proceedings Col. Charles Bird referred to the good services of the men of the battalion who volunteered to go out to South Africa, and said that, as the tablets record, out of their number five died and one was killed in action. He hoped that in time of trouble the country would be able to rely on the Volunteers for service. Lord Grenfell then unveiled the memorial. On behalf of the regiment, Col. Stanley Bird thanked Lord Grenfell, who, in reply, remarked that he had lately been sitting on the Royal Commission on the Auxiliary Forces, and part of his duty was to elicit from some of the officers who had been present in South Africa during the war their opinion as to the conduct of the Volunteers. It was a great pleasure to him, who had been associated for some years with the Volunteer Service, to hear the high terms in which every officer, from Lord Roberts downwards, spoke of the conduct of the Volunteers. The thanks of the country were due to those men who gave up, at great inconvenience, their civil duties, and he was glad to think that there was the permanent record which he had just unveiled of their services. Col. Ococks thanked Col. Charles Bird for his gift to the battalion, and the proceedings closed.

The year marked the centenary of the formation of the Duke of Cumberland's Sharpshooters, and great preparations were made to celebrate the event. Application was made to King Edward to honour the regiment by inspecting it, and the request was graciously acceded to. The inspection took place in the most superb weather in the gardens of Buckingham Palace, at six o'clock, the regiment forming up at 4.30 outside the head-quarters, 56 Davies Street, under the command of Col. Ococks, the other Field Officers being: Lieut.-Col. Tanqueray, Major Weekley and the Adjutant, Capt. Northey. The notice for the parade had been very short, but nevertheless there was a strong muster, 580 men including a number of mounted infantry and cyclists (both dismounted for the occasion) being present. Headed by the brass and bugle bands the regiment marched to the Palace, the route being lined by interested spectators. A large proportion of the men wore the South African Medal, and, wearing the smart Colonial hat and black feathers, excited admiration as they marched proudly through the leading thoroughfares. On reaching the garden front of Buckingham Palace the regiment formed up in a line of eight companies facing the saluting base, which was marked by a Royal Standard in front of the grand entrance. In attendance upon the King were Col. the Earl of Kintore, A.D.C. (Lord in Waiting), Vice-Admiral Sir John Fullerton (Groom in Waiting), Col. A. Davidson and Capt. G. Holford (Equerries in Waiting), Major-Gen. Sir A. E. Turner (Inspector-Gen. of Auxiliary Forces), Major-Gen. Oliphant (Commanding the Home District), with his staff, and Col. Sir Howard Vincent (A.D.C. in Waiting). His Majesty was received with a Royal Salute and then made a close inspection of the line. At the conclusion of the inspection the battalion marched past, and, after reforming in column

APPENDIX I

of double companies on the original alignment, advanced in Review Order, and gave a Royal Salute. The King then addressed the officers and men, complimenting them upon their appearance and on the long and creditable record of the corps. Col. Ococks on behalf of the battalion thanked His Majesty for the honour he had done them in inspecting them, and the battalion, taking the time from the Officer Commanding, gave three cheers for the King and marched past His Majesty in column of fours on leaving the garden. Col. C. Bird, late Commanding Officer of the Regiment, and Lieut.-Col. H. F. Dickins, the veteran Quartermaster and Treasurer of the regiment, had the honour of being presented to His Majesty.

In celebration of the Centenary a dinner was held at the Hotel Cecil on July 11th, Gen. Sir Redvers Buller, V.C., Col.-Commandant of the King's Royal Rifle Corps, presiding. There was a large gathering of members of the regiment, " Old Vics " and " Old Georges " and other guests. Among the latter were Major-Gen. Sir H. Trotter, Major-Gen. Sir A. E. Turner (Inspector-Gen. of Auxiliary Forces), Brig.-Gen. Eyre Crabbe, C.B., Col. Sir Edward Ward (Permanent Under Secretary of State for War), Col. the Hon. H. Legge, M.P., Capt. Jessell, M.P., Col. the Hon. Henniker-Major, etc.

The loyal toasts having been given by the Chairman and drunk with enthusiasm, Sir Redvers Buller proposed the toast of " The Victoria and St. George's Rifles." He said there was in these days a good deal of misplaced importance attached to what was called regimental *esprit de corps*, but they could depend upon it they would never be wrong in honouring those who in old days had ventured for their own beloved country nobly to dare and to die. It was a great thing for any regiment to be able to look back, as that regiment could, on 100 years of patriotic service. It was not merely the fact that a soldier came forward to offer his services to his country, but it was most praiseworthy that a man should come forward at a time when the example brought others forward to help them. It was not only what they did individually, but what they inspired others to do. The regiment had found a company for the City Imperial Volunteers and had sent out most valuable and most worthy representatives of English fighting men to battalions abroad. He conceived that in that they had fulfilled the whole duty of a Volunteer regiment, which surely was that men with other and more peaceful occupations should use their hours of leisure to perfect themselves for the protection of their country's interest, and, as he knew, nobly was that regiment represented by those they sent out to the Cape. He did not think he could give them higher or truer praise than that. Looking back through the past 100 years they found that their predecessors were banded together as a Volunteer corps, and when there was no longer any necessity for such a corps they had maintained their patriotic endeavour by organising themselves into a company of Sharpshooters. They could not have a more valuable or more material lesson. It was what they wanted now. Whatever else was required of Volunteers, it was undoubtedly required that they should do all they could to keep up their powers of rifle shooting. They could do much as a Volunteer regiment. They had the chance of setting to a great extent an example to the youth of England. They were passing at the present moment through a great change in the ideals of national education. Where in the past it was considered the whole duty of man to be instructed in the three R's, there were now those who had discovered that there was much more importance in the three H's, which meant that they should train their heads, their hands and their hearts. Education was to be practical—not merely a question of training the mind and not the body, or rather the memory and not the body, but they had to train the whole mind, for the mind should have full power over the man. A man had to take the physical action which the mind told him was necessary. Their gymnastic exercises, their marches and their Volunteer training generally were of true educational importance to all of them. They had a fine record for 100 years, and they should keep themselves ready in body as well as in mind. They should be ready not only to think, but to act in accordance with their thoughts. To do that was not so difficult as people thought. All the basis of drill could be taught in a gymnasium. He congratulated the regiment, whose work was a magnificent example of what a regiment could do.

Lieut.-Col. Ococks in reply stated that the Victoria and St. George's Rifles were proud of their position as the 1st Volunteer Battalion of that most distinguished Corps, the King's Royal Rifles. In mentioning some of the outstanding incidents in the history of the regiment he said it was on that very date, July 11th, in 1835, that permission was granted for the then Rifle Club to call itself the " Royal Victoria Rifle Club." As the letter of her Majesty to Col. Bird on the eve of the departure of the C.I.V. contingent, showed, the late Queen, whose honoured name they had borne for 68 years, had not forgotten the regiment.

Lieut.-Col. W. M. Tanqueray proposed " Our Guests," and Major-Gen. Sir A. E. Turner in responding said he had the command of the King to express His Majesty's best wishes for the success of their banquet and for their future prosperity. His Majesty said, further, that he was much pleased with everything he saw during his inspection of them on the previous Saturday. He had been much struck with the steadiness of the battalion on parade, their general appearance, and the smartness with which they marched past, and His Majesty again added, " I hope their numbers will be kept up." Col. Stanley Bird, C.B., then gave the " Health of the Chairman," and Sir Redvers Buller having replied the company dispersed.

The great banqueting hall of " the Cecil " was crowded with the diners. The galleries and private *loges* were occupied by brilliantly

APPENDIX I

gowned ladies. The band of the regiment played during dinner and, as may be imagined, the scene was a very fascinating and beautiful one. *Camaraderie* and good fellowship reigned supreme. The two centre tables were reserved for old members of the two regiments, Mr. Thomas Gellatley presiding over the " Old Vics," and Major G. S. Beeching, V.D., over the " Old St. George's."

In congratulating all concerned on the success attending the Centenary celebrations, Col. Ocoks in a Regimental Order of July 18th, concluded, " Do not let us forget these grand records of the past, but try by the energy of our present actions to build up a no less glorious future. The future prosperity of the regiment depends on the efforts now made by each individual member to keep up that high state of efficiency of which we have always been so proud, and every Rifleman must do all in his power by personal influence and example, not only to attract fresh numbers, but also to induce those now serving to continue their service as long as possible. Only by these means can we obey His Majesty's twice-expressed wish, which is to us a command, ' Keep up your numbers.' "

Words as applicable in 1923 as they were in 1903.

Capt. Northey, K.R.R.C., having been promoted to Major on the 3rd of August, 1904, vacated his appointment as Adjutant on the 30th September following. Although he had not been very long with the Victorias all ranks were much attached to him and, in the words of a Regimental Order, " joined with the Commanding Officer in thanking Major Northey for the great interest he has taken, not only in his work as Adjutant, but in all matters associated with the welfare of the battalion, and also in wishing him success in his future career." The wish was gratified. The late Adjutant is now Major-Gen. Sir Edward Northey, K.C.M.G., C.B., late Governor and Commander-in-Chief of the East Africa Protectorate and High Commissioner for the Zanzibar Protectorate. His successor was Capt. R. Johnstone, as usual from the K.R.R.C. He commenced his duties on the 1st January, 1905, Major V. W. F. Dickins being Acting Adjutant in the interim.

The Honorary Colonel of the Regiment, Col. Stanley George Bird, C.B., V.D., died at Tunbridge Wells on the 18th April, 1905. His brother and successor in the command of the regiment, Col. Chas. Bird, died seven days later at Monte Carlo. It was decided to commemorate the long connection with the Victoria's and St. George's of Col. S. G. Bird by placing a memorial tablet in the Drill Hall. Subscriptions varying from one shilling to one guinea, in order that all ranks might join in it, were invited, with the result that on the afternoon of December 7th, 1907, a handsome marble and brass tablet was affixed to the wall of the Drill Hall and unveiled by Major-Gen. Sir W. Pitcairn Campbell, Adjutant of the Regiment, at the time of the amalgamation of the Victoria's with the St. George's. The inscription runs as follows :

Colonel Stanley George Bird, C.B., V.D.,
Joined 19th May, 1859, Captain 8th May, 1871,
Colonel Commanding, 24th January, 1885,
Honorary Colonel of the Battalion, 14th June, 1899,
which latter position he held at the time of
his Death, 18th April, 1905.

This Tablet is erected by old Friends and Comrades
as a Token of their Esteem and Regard,
Also in Appreciation of the many Years of Zealous Work
Devoted to the interests of the Volunteer Force,
and to this Battalion in particular.

Major-Gen. Herbert Francis, Lord Cheylesmore, was appointed to the Honorary Colonelcy, dated 31st July, 1905.

The coveted King's Prize, a gold medal and badge and a cheque for £250, was won at the N.R.A. Meeting at Bisley in 1906 by Capt. Robert fF. Davies, with a record score—324, this being the third occasion on which a member of the Victoria's had carried it off, viz. :

    1862.   Sergt. Stewart Pixley.
    1887.   Capt. R. O. Warren.
    1906.   Capt. R. fF. Davies.

On the 3rd March, 1907, Col. Ococks relinquished the command of the battalion and was succeeded by Major and Hon. Lieut.-Col. W. M. Tanqueray, V.D. Major and Hon. Lieut.-Col. G. M. Weekley, V.D., was appointed to the command of the Right Half Battalion, and Capt. and Hon. Major R. B. Shipley to the Left Half Battalion.

VIII

THE ST. GILES'S AND ST. GEORGE'S (BLOOMSBURY) VOLUNTEERS

BLOOMSBURY, like most of the London parishes, has had a long and honourable association with the various Volunteer Corps that have from time to time sprung up for the protection of the country from invasion. Amongst the earliest to bear the name was the " Bloomsbury and Inns of Court Volunteers," raised in June, 1797, and resuscitated in April, 1803, when the war broke out afresh. Its Commander was Lieut.-Col. Samuel Compton Cox, who retained the position until the general disbandment of Volunteers in 1814. This regiment, however, must not be confounded with the Bloomsbury's proper, being generally spoken of as the " Inns of Court Volunteers " or the " Devil's Own," to use the name the King is said to have conferred on them at the great Review in 1803. The

APPENDIX I

present Inns of Court O.T.C. have long since appropriated them as their ancestors. In the plan of the still earlier Review in Hyde Park on 4th June, 1799, they are given the 6th post, with a muster of 604 under Lieut.-Col. Cox. On the same plan appears the name of the St. George's, Bloomsbury, with a muster of 51 under Capt. East. We have been unable to identify either the Captain or his regiment. No mention is made of the latter in Rowlandson's book, which is certainly peculiar, for there is plenty of evidence that the editor did his utmost to make his list of regiments as complete as possible. For instance, to Plate No. XXXIV, "Cheap Ward Association," appears the following note : " The Proprietor, with all due respect, begs leave to observe, that he is prevented, by the following letter, from communicating to the Public the principles by which the Members of the Cheap Ward Association were united : ' Sir, I am directed to communicate to you, that the Committee of the Cheap Ward Association have taken your letter (requesting answers to several questions respecting the regulations of the Corps) into consideration : It was resolved, that it was not necessary to answer the same. I have the honour to be, Sir, Your obedient Servant, SAMUEL CULME WEST, Secretary. *May* 10*th*, 1799.' "

When the Peace of Amiens came to an end in 1803 we are on surer ground, for it is on record that " At a very numerous meeting of the Joint Vestry of the Parishes of St. Giles in the Fields and St. George, Bloomsbury, held in the Vestry Room of St. Giles in the Fields, on Tuesday, the 2nd day of August, 1803 : Mr. Alex Stewart, Churchwarden, in the Chair :

It was resolved unanimously, ' That this Vestry will ever feel an ardour equal to that of the most zealous of His Majesty's most loyal and patriotic subjects, to encourage, promote and join in such measures as may be most effectual for chastising and repelling from our native land an arrogant and ferocious enemy, who insolently threatens to invade it, and involve its hitherto free and happy inhabitants in the wretched misery and slavery with which that enemy has overwhelmed every country and people where he has procured an entrance, either by open hostility, or treacherous offers of fraternity ; both leading to the same fatal goal ! And as the Legislature of our country has now passed an Act (which received the Royal Assent on the 27th of July last)[1] for providing for the General Defence and Security of the Realm in case of invasion, this Vestry consider it to be their most incumbent duty to forward the intentions of that Act by every means in their power ; and that they cannot do so more effectually than by a short explanation of what will be expected from the inhabitants of these Parishes, in common with all their fellow subjects, in pursuance of it, in order that a prompt compliance with its several provisions may be carried into the fullest effect in these Parishes ; and so as to ensure, with the least possible delay, what under the present emergent circumstances

---

[1] 43 Geo. III, Cap. 121.

is the most desirable—the strong and ready means of complete defence and protection against invasion and plunder.

In order to give facility and promptitude to these means of defence, the Committee, appointed by this Vestry, will arrange a plan for the more easily and quickly procuring returns of lists of the persons who are liable to be called upon in these Parishes to be 'trained and exercised,' as intended by the said Act, and can never doubt that, in such a cause, they will be called upon in vain. Forms of returns will be delivered at the houses of the inhabitants. The Act has imposed a considerable weight of duty on the Constables; but having required that they shall be aided and assisted in making out the lists (as well as in other important matters) by the Ministers, Churchwardens and other Parochial Officers in every Parish, this Vestry fully rely on the exertions, as well of the Ministers and Churchwardens, as on those who are designated by the words 'other parochial officers,' including the Sidesmen, Overseers of the Poor, and Collectors of the Poor's Rate, in doing their utmost, not only by assisting in making out the notices to the inhabitants, but in procuring returns of the Lists with as much dispatch as possible; And the Vestry most earnestly exhort the inhabitants in general to consider that, as all the people in this our country are engaged in one common cause, they ought cheerfully and readily to concur in any measure that may tend to save unnecessary trouble to those whose peculiar duty it is to be instrumental in calling them into action, for the protection and preservation from irretrievable ruin of Themselves, their Relatives, their Friends, their Neighbours, their Constitution, their Country! against an inveterate, a rapacious and desolating enemy! an enemy that has and will continue to set every religious and moral principle at naught or make them bend to his convenience or rapacity.

Resolved, That the thanks of this Vestry be given to the Churchwardens for their promptitude in causing this Meeting to be convened as soon as a copy of the Act could be obtained from the King's Printer.

Resolved, That the thanks of this Vestry be given to those inhabitants of these Parishes who have taken an active part in adopting measures for forming a Volunteer Corps.

ALEX. STEWART, Chairman.

Resolved, That the thanks of this Vestry be given to the Chairman for his great attention to the important business of this Meeting."

Apparently the services of the Corps were accepted before this meeting was held, for a number of officers were gazetted the very next day. From a list appearing in 1807 we take the following:

Lieut.-Col. Com. Sir John Nicholl	3 Aug., 1803.
Lieut.-Col. A. H. Sutherland	5 May, 1804.
Major Robert Ward	17 Dec., 1803.

APPENDIX I

Captains John Fernandez	17 Aug., 1803, Adjut.
James Henry Arnold	17 Sept., 1803.
John Legh	do.
John Dynely	do.
T. W. Carr	18 do.
W. H. Hartley	17 Dec., 1803.
Wm. Coningham	3 Jan., 1804.
Augustus Gostling	5 May
Benjamin Gostling	do.

There are also given the names of 15 Lieutenants, 4 Ensigns; Wm. Gurney, Chaplain; John Page, Paymaster; John Cook, Physician; Richard Ogle, Surgeon; and Robert Banks, Quartermaster.

The O.C., Sir John Nicholl, was a Member of Parliament, D.C.L., and the King's Advocate-General.

The 19th October, 1803, was set apart as a General Fast, and all the Volunteers attended a Church Parade. The St. Giles's and St. George's, after attending divine service at St. Giles's Church, proceeded at once to the Toxopholite ground behind Gower Street, where they received their colours among thousands of spectators. On the 26th of the month King George III reviewed in Hyde Park 12,401 Volunteers and on the 28th 14,676 more. By fortuitous coincidence the St. Giles's and St. George's, the St. George's, Hanover Square, and the Duke of Cumberland's Sharpshooters were all present on the latter occasion. The parade strength of the St. Giles's and St. George's is given as 603, which shows a very rapid development.

According to a notice in *The Times* of February 15th, 1804, "At a very numerous meeting of the St. Giles's and St. George's Bloomsbury Volunteers in the Museum Gardens on Monday, the Commanding Officer having explained to them their right of resignation, the several companies unanimously requested their respective Captains to inform the Commanding Officer that it was their fixed determination not to lay down their arms until the security of the country should be permanently established; and also desired that such their determination should be immediately communicated to the Lord Lieutenant of the County." What was the occasion of this demonstration does not appear, and it can only be surmised that some official ineptitude may have occurred to increase the difficulties of the Volunteers or to discourage their efforts.

A contemporary journal of the day (*The Times* of 30th July, 1806) records that "the third anniversary of the acceptance of the St. Giles's and St. George's, Bloomsbury Corps, falling in 1806 on Sunday, the 3rd of August, it was celebrated on the Monday by the members in a manner at once creditable to themselves and to the institution. At half-past six in the morning the Corps, 300 strong, met in their drill ground at the

British Museum, where their excellent Colonel, Sir John Nicholl, explained to them the new military regulations which the Legislature had lately adopted by the Training Bill and the consequent arrangements he had made to suit the convenience of the Corps, and give the fullest effect to that assistance which the volunteer system is capable of affording to the military strength of the country. Provided with haversacks and canteens for a necessary refreshment, the Corps marched to the Heath at Brixton Causeway, taking their route across Westminster Bridge, and by their strength and military appearance, after three years' service, excited no small admiration. Upon their arrival at Brixton Heath, the second section of each company was marched forward and the Colonel himself having assumed command of them took up a strong position behind a raised causeway with trees, and prepared to annoy his antagonist by throwing out a few open files under shelter of an old building to the left, and on a small eminence to the right. Lieutenant-Colonel Sutherland with the main body began the attack in great order, advancing his skirmishers to drive in those of his comparatively small, though formidable foe, and to harass him in flank, when after a few volleys he advanced to the charge. The enemy on this commenced an excellent retreat under the fire of his skirmishers and again strongly secured himself in the mouth of the road leading from the Heath to Dulwich. Retiring again he was supposed to have run quite off and Lieutenant-Colonel Sutherland's men continued their route no longer dreading their enemy; when, upon turning a corner of the road, he was found most formidably drawn up in line, and at the same moment a party which lay in ambush began a heavy and well-directed fire from the adjoining trees and hedges; surprised but not confounded by this new and desperate stratagem, Lieutenant-Colonel Sutherland immediately availed himself of the great width of the road and deployed into line. His skirmishers advanced to cut off the party in ambush, and after a volley he fell upon the enemy with a *British charge*, who having thrown his whole strength into the last effort, could no longer fly but yielded to superior force.

The victors and prisoners then marched to Montpelier Gardens, where an excellent dinner refreshed them after the labours of the day, which even a very heavy rain in only a slight degree checked. Col. Sir John Nicholl, in giving the several patriotic toasts which followed, introduced each with such ennobling sentiments, or such happy sallies of humour and gaiety, that they were drank with enthusiasm. When Lieut.-Col. Sutherland gave the health of their Colonel, the love and respect which every member of the Corps bears him could not for a moment be restrained, but resounded in long and repeated acclamations.

Soon after seven the drum again beat to arms, and the Corps returned to town, after a day which animated the attachment of the members to each other, their love to their Colonel, and devotion

APPENDIX I

to their King and Country, and was unsullied by one disgraceful action."

The St. Giles's and St. George's Bloomsbury Volunteers continued to drill and practise in much the same way until the peace of 1814 when the general disbandment of these Corps took place. Their attendance at the numerous reviews which took place in the intervening years may be frequently traced in the journals of the time.

1859

Among the forty corps of Middlesex which so quickly followed the publication of the War Office letter of May 12th, 1859, was the St. Giles's and St. George's, Bloomsbury, which when the regiments came to be numbered was given the 37th place. The earliest reference to its formation appears in the following account of a meeting taken from the columns of the *Standard* of December 23rd, 1859:

"Last evening a meeting for the formation of a rifle corps for the parishes of St. Giles and St. George, Bloomsbury, was held at the Music Hall, Store Street; Mr. Churchwarden Harvey in the chair. The meeting became a numerous one soon after its commencement.

A letter was read from Sir S. M. Peto, M.P. for Finsbury, forwarding a donation of £10, and in the course of which he expressed a warm concurrence in the movement.

The Chairman opened the proceedings by stating that the result of the preliminary efforts to the present time had been very gratifying, the subscriptions amounting to £437 (applause). In adopting the principle of national rifle corps they were only carrying out the great principles of every-day life that pointed out the propriety of providing for the security of our lives and property, and all the circumstances of the present time suggested and justified this great and national movement.

Lieut.-Colonel Kennedy proposed the first resolution, to the effect 'that the organization of volunteer corps was a prudent and desirable measure as a constitutional and permanent addition to our national defences.' That we had occasion to establish national defences was beyond the shadow of a doubt. England could not pretend to cope with other European nations in the extent of our standing army. Although our territories would justify us in having fivefold the standing army of any nation in Europe, yet the most powerful line of defence was our navy (applause), and he was happy to find that the Government of the country were supplying that great desideratum. He admitted that the chance of being attacked on our own shores was very improbable, but what he did feel most was the fear of the disaster of a national panic in all our great commercial and industrial circles, arising out of the mere apprehension of an invasion. This fear had tended much during the last five years to stagnate our commercial enterprise and energy; and it was his conviction that thorough and complete preparation at all times for any such emergency, come from what quarter it might, would tend to dissipate this disastrous feeling. They all wished for peace, but we must put ourselves in a position that no one could attack us with impunity. However much they might be led to entertain no fear or apprehension of the intentions of the present Emperor of the French, he differed from those who contended that a volunteer force would not cope with an army of the line.

The Rev. Mr. Dibdin, in seconding the resolution, said it was because he was a clergyman and a man of peace that he supported the resolution. Religion itself justified war; so did the Bible and the Articles of the Church of England.

Mr. Maskelyne, of the British Museum, supported the resolution, and intimated that a rifle corps would be formed in connection with that noble institution.

Dr. Hodgkin, of the Society of Friends, rose to enter his protest against the proposition. He need not say that the principle of rifle corps was opposed to the views of the Society of Friends as being inconsistent with the spirit of Christianity. The speeches at meetings of rifle corps recently had exhibited a general feeling of hostility to our French neighbours. Now, he had lately been from the north to the south of France, and he felt bound to say that, having come into communication with Frenchmen, he had found them exceedingly courteous, and if feelings of hostility did exist they existed mainly in the minds of the aged, and if Young England and Young France did their part there would be no necessity for France to come over here in any way to injure us. It has been stated that we were not arming for France, but for any other people; and yet could anyone say that the Kaffirs or the Moors were coming to us? (loud laughter). No, it must be from some apprehension that the French were coming (interruption and cries of 'no, no'). Why raise a force which was to be equivalent to one-tenth of the capable men of the country, and incur such enormous expense for this, in his view, unchristian object? (murmurs and disapprobation). He would rather hold out to France the olive branch than the rifle (oh, oh). There were many things that Young England and Young France could do, and that would be far better for both of them. He would entreat those who were contemplating entering a rifle corps to consider it. It was only to be regretted that laudable and useful objects were overlooked; there were our poor to be fed and our narrow streets to be widened, and we had great difficulty in raising the means. Why not imitate the French and improve our streets and towns? (disturbance and cries of 'Question,' and 'What have improvements to do with rifle corps?'). He would entreat them to consider what good they

APPENDIX I

might accomplish with the money to be expended in rifle corps. If such a military spirit had been engendered in so short a time what would that spirit become if fostered for two or three years? In conclusion he entered his earnest protest against the movement. The resolution was then put and carried with but one dissentient.

Mr. Robert Kenyon moved the next resolution: "That this meeting declares its approval of proceedings hitherto taken by the Committee of the inhabitants towards the enrolment of a rifle corps within the parishes, and pledges itself to the support and furtherance of the measure."

Mr. N. Brydges seconded the resolution, and it was carried unanimously.

The Rev. E. Bayley, rector of St. George's, Bloomsbury, proposed the next resolution: 'That it seems desirable to this meeting that the corps to be raised in these parishes should form part of one of the Middlesex corps.' This country had too long built upon the capital of its bravery and success in past battles, and this had tended to engender a feeling of apathy with reference to preparation for the present. No one knew in what the approaching congress might result, and a watchful preparation was indispensable.

Mr. Rogers, Q.C., seconded the motion in a humorous speech, expressing a hope that measures would soon be adopted to enable our working men to join in the movement.

The resolution was then put and carried with applause.

Mr. Malcolm Corrie next proposed: 'That the managing Council or Committee be allowed, at their discretion, to admit as members of the corps such effective men as might be prepared to pay the admission fee and annual subscription, their uniform, etc., to be provided, so far as possible, out of the funds of the corps.' He had reason to believe that the feeling described by Dr. Hodgkin was not shared by all the Society of Friends, and that there were men amongst them that, in the event of invasion, would enrol themselves in rifle corps. Mr. Steddall seconded the motion and it was carried unanimously.

Thanks were then voted to the chairman for his ability in presiding, and the meeting separated."

Other meetings were held, and with the assistance of leading residents of the district, including Dr. Richards, father of Mr. Samuel Smith Crosland Richards, one of the first captains and subsequently a Commanding Officer of the Corps, Mr. G. B. Gregory, M.P., Mr. John William Jeakes, the first Commanding Officer, Mr. Malcolm Corrie, the first Major, Mr. J. Peacock, and many other staunch supporters, the project was duly carried into effect.

At a meeting of the St. Pancras and North Middlesex V.R.C. held at the Vestry Hall, Camden Town, on December 28th, Mr. Shoolbred called attention to the resolution moved by the Rev. Mr. Bayley and quoted above, "That they should amalgamate with one of the Middlesex Corps," and he moved that a deputation should wait upon the St. Giles's and St. George's, with a view to a mutual arrangement. The resolution was carried *nem. con.*, but the Bloomsbury's, we believe, did not entertain the idea of joining the St. Pancras Corps. Application was made to the Foundling Hospital by Mr. Steddall for permission to use their famous ground for drill purposes such as had been granted to the Volunteers of 1803, and this was readily granted, and, in addition, shortly after, accommodation for the head-quarters of the corps was placed at its disposal in the hospital.

As had happened forty-five years earlier, some little confusion was brought about by another corps which had its head-quarters at 14 Queen Square, Bloomsbury, and also adopted the district title. This was the 19th Middlesex, the corps of the Working Men's College, in Great Ormond Street. The President and Captain-Commandant was Thomas Hughes, the author of *Tom Brown*, under whose care it prospered until it reached a maximum strength of ten companies. It was looked upon and prided itself upon being thought one of the best of the Metropolitan artisan corps. In the great review held in Hyde Park on June 23rd, 1860, it was the last battalion of the 1st Division to pass before the Queen. The late George Augustus Sala in his account of the spectacle says " their step was regular, and their front accurate as if it had been ruled by a line." Of the Victoria's he says," The Duke (Wellington) rode at the head of the Victoria Rifles, of which corps he is the colonel. His Grace was loudly cheered, his services in bringing this fine regiment into an effective state being well known and appreciated. The men have been admirably drilled, and appear ready to take the field at any moment. . . . They fully sustained their reputation ; as did also the Volunteers of Lord Ranelagh's brigade, and the splendid St. George's Corps, headed by Col. Lindsay and the Adjutant, Horton Ives." (This, of course, should be Gordon Ives, the Second in Command of the Regiment.)

It has frequently been stated in articles dealing with Volunteer history that the Bloomsbury Rifle Volunteers were founded by the author of *Tom Brown's Schooldays;* the foregoing shows how the error originated.

We now leave the narrative to Major R. M. P. Willoughby, one of the officers who came over with the Bloomsbury's at the time of the amalgamation. " The Commanding Officer's First Annual Report, a copy of which may be seen in the British Museum Library, together with succeeding copies, and is written by Major J. William Jeakes, Commanding, and issued from 35 Bernard Street, Russell Square, mentions that Major Jeakes headed the subscription list with £100 and £20 for the band fund. This report shows that, beginning as a single company, scarcely 60 strong, the corps had in the first twelve months expanded into an effective force of four companies each nearly 100 strong, and records obligations owed to,

APPENDIX I

among others, Captain Barnett, R.N., and the Committee over which he had presided, and referring in grateful terms to the assistance given, as half a century ago it had been given to their predecessors by the Foundling Hospital; it further mentions that the corps had a volunteer band of 20 musicians and also projected a joint rifle range of 750 yards with the 20th Middlesex at Willesden.

The corps received the formal designation of the 37th Middlesex Rifle Volunteer Corps (27th May, 1861) and in 1866, Lieut.-Colonel Robert Steddall succeeded Lieut.-Colonel Malcolm Corrie, the second Commanding Officer, in command of the regiment, a position he retained for the next 15 years. A Report for 1869 by Lieut.-Colonel Steddall, issued from the Foundling Hospital, states that the corps then consisted of 8 companies, 180 recruits and a total strength of 700; there were 653 efficients, 79 marksmen, and the figure of merit was second only to one other regiment in the county. 'No paper or fictitious men are permitted to be borne on the rolls.' This report also records the presentation by the Duke of Bedford, throughout a generous benefactor of the Corps, of a magnificent cup bearing his name, for which the companies of the present regiment still annually compete.

At the end of its first decade the Bloomsbury's were thus well on their feet, no longer drilling as best they might with Russian muskets captured in the Crimea (as one of the original members told the present writer was at first the case), and an efficient and leading Metropolitan corps, a position it ever maintained as worthy representatives of its Bloomsbury forbears. It claimed, too, to be the exclusive representative of those forbears. As previously stated, another corps with head-quarters in the district had assumed the title 'Bloomsbury Rifle Volunteers,' and representations were made by the 37th as to its sole right to bear such a designation. The offenders were thereupon ordered to drop the title, and formal authority was given by the Secretary of State to the 37th Middlesex Rifle Volunteers bearing the special designation of the 'St. Giles's and St. George's Volunteer Corps.' This title it bore from thenceforth (1863) though it was usually known for short as the 'Bloomsbury Rifles.' In 1880 the Corps was renumbered as the 19th Middlesex, which curiously enough was the number of the Working Men's College Corps which had arrogated to itself the title of 'Bloomsbury.' The incident has led to many an error being made by persons unacquainted with it.

The St. Giles's and St. George's links with the past proved of substantial use when the need for new head-quarters had become acute and enabled it to lay claim to a sum of money which had belonged to their predecessors of the same name, a claim which was allowed by the High Court as a contribution towards the building fund. A considerable sum had been accumulated by the former corps, the income from which had, after the cessation of its military activities, been applied for the benefit of its surviving members in need of assistance. By the year 1877 the last of these had died out, and in accordance with an earlier scheme, under which the fund had meanwhile been administered by local residents under the direction of the two Rectors, it became applicable ' in or towards the raising or maintaining of such a Volunteer Corps or Association ' as might thereafter be raised 'similar to the aforesaid Volunteer Corps known as the G.G.B. or St. Giles and St. George Bloomsbury Volunteer Corps '—subject to the approval of the Court. Application was accordingly made (See proceedings in Chancery, In the Matter of the G.G.B. etc., 1877), and an affidavit filed by Colonel Steddall setting out the history of the existing Corps and the circumstances in which it was formed, and submitting that ' the fund now belongs to and ought to be paid over to the Officer for the time being Commanding the 37th Middlesex Volunteers Rifle Corps as the undoubted successors of the G.G.B. or St. Giles and St. George Bloomsbury Volunteer Corps.' This claim was allowed, and the fund, amounting to some £2,000 paid over, and with this and private advances (in particular by Lieut.-Colonel Smith Richards, subsequently to succeed Colonel Steddall in the command) fine head-quarters in Chenies Street were built at a cost of over £11,000. There the Bloomsbury's remained until, with the coming of the Territorial Force, the local connection ceased upon amalgamation with the Victoria's and St. George's Rifles in May, 1908, as the 9th County of London Regiment, Queen Victoria's Rifles."

The history of the Bloomsbury Rifles was much that of other Metropolitan corps. It always maintained a very high state of efficiency, as was evidenced by the reports of the authorities of the War Office, and it would be no exaggeration to say that for steady and serviceable work it was second to none. The drill was kept at a perfection which was attained by few other corps, and reports of Inspecting Officers frequently expressed their high approval of its smartness. In shooting it ranked high ; not only was the average good but many of its marksmen earned special distinction at Wimbledon and Bisley. In the old days it ran a private camp at Wimbledon and copper tokens were issued to those who wished to obtain entry. One specimen in the editor's possession has the monogram "G.G.B." with the words round "37th Middlesex R.V. Camp," and on the reverse a large figure 2 and above it " Two Shillings." It bears the imprint "W. J. Taylor, Medallist, London." According to Lieut.-Cols. Humphry and Fremantle (*History of the National Rifle Association*), in 1864 there was a camp paper, *The G.G.B. Magazine*, which was produced by the St. Giles's and St. George's, Bloomsbury, Rifle Corps, a rival to the Victoria's *Earwig*, but it had a much shorter existence.

" The Bloomsbury Rifles," says Major Hale, " was practically the first corps to form a detachment to march to Brighton for the review, I think, 1871. I had been made Sergeant and had numerous

APPENDIX I 571

friends in the company. Some of them wanted to walk down to Brighton during the Easter holiday for the Monday. It was suggested we should do so in uniform and I was to take a sort of charge of them. I told them the consent of Captain Steddall, my company commander, would have to be obtained. When I asked for it, he said, ' if they want to march see how many we can get and I will take command, but must ask permission.' He spoke to Colonel (then Major) Richards, who said, ' put a notice up in the Orderly Room and see how many names you get.' This was done, and the number obtained was 75, so Major Richards said, ' We will take the drums with us.' The ultimate parade state was between 115 and 120. Major Richards commanded. We went partly by train and marched the rest. Archibald Forbes, the celebrated War Correspondent, wrote an account of our march for the *Daily News*. These marching detachments afterwards developed into Marching Columns."

During the Boer War the 19th Bloomsbury Rifle Volunteer Corps duly supplied its quota for active service. A tablet now at the head-quarters of the Q.V.R., 56 Davies Street, but formerly at the old regimental home in Chenies Street, records that Lieut. C. P. Grindle and 39 men joined the C.I.V. ; 58 the Imperial Yeomanry ; 2 the K.R.R.C. ; and 29 the R.A.M.C.

The complete list of Commanding Officers, from the raising of the regiment in 1859 to the amalgamation in 1908, is as follows :

Lieut.-Col. J. W. Jeakes, 1860–1863.
Lieut.-Col. Malcolm Corrie, 1863–1866.
Lieut. Col. Robert Steddall, 1866–1880.
Lieut.-Col. S. S. C. Richards, 1880–1898.
Lieut.-Col. B. W. Hardcastle, 1898–1904.
Lieut.-Col. A. S. Barham, 1904–1908.

IX

TERRITORIALS

9TH BATTALION, COUNTY OF LONDON QUEEN VICTORIA'S REGIMENT

THE Territorial and Reserve Forces Act, 1907 (7 Edward VII, Cap. 9), received the Royal Assent on the 2nd August, 1907, and came into operation on the 1st April, 1908. The Victoria and St. George's (1st Middlesex) R.V.C. and the St. Giles's and St. George's (Bloomsbury) 19th Middlesex R.V.C. went to sleep on March 31st and woke the morning following to find themselves Territorials and members of one regiment. The 1st and the 19th Middlesex were no more and in their stead was to rise the " 9th Battalion, County of London (Queen Victoria's) Regiment." The enforced amalgamation at first gave rise to a great deal of heart-burning. The Bloomsbury's regretted the loss of their local connections and traditions, the Victoria's and St. George's the loss of their splendid detachment of 150 Mounted Infantry men who were turned into Yeomanry, and a strong Cyclist Section who were attached to the 25th County of London (Cyclists), and they both felt the loss of many men over 40 years of age who in the past had done so much in keeping up the *esprit de corps* of the Volunteers.

The Officer Commanding the Victoria and St. George's at that time was Lieut.-Col. W. M. Tanqueray, V.D., and he was appointed to take command of the combined regiment. The remaining officers were posted as follows :

London Gazette.

" *9th Battalion, County of London (Queen Victoria's) Regiment ;* the undermentioned officers, from the 1st Middlesex (Victoria and St. George's) Volunteer Rifle Corps, are appointed to the battalion, with rank and precedence as in the Volunteer Force. Dated 1st April, 1908 :

Major and Honorary Lieutenant-Colonel George Mitchell Weekley.
Major and Honorary Lieutenant-Colonel (Honorary Captain in the Army ; Lieutenant, Reserve of Officers) Reginald Burge Shipley. (To be supernumerary.)
Captain and Honorary Major James Ernest Wild Harrison.
Captain and Honorary Major (Lieutenant, Reserve of Officers) Vernon William Frank Dickins.
Captain William Palmer Wilton.
Supernumerary Captain (Honorary Captain in the Army) Robert fFinden Davies. (To remain supernumerary.)
Captain Thomas Prior Lees.
Captain Stephen Victor Shea.
Captain Daniel O'Connell Finigan. (To be supernumerary.)
Captain Harry Arthur Fenton. (To be supernumerary.)
Captain Owen Alfred Howell. (To be supernumerary.)
Lieutenant Reginald Woodruff Cox.
Lieutenant Herbert Flemming.
Lieutenant Reginald Geoffrey Warren.
Second Lieutenant Leslie Howard Marten.
Second Lieutenant Randall Walter Henderson.
Quartermaster (Quartermaster and Honorary Major, retired pay) Alfred Wynn.

The undermentioned officers, from the 19th Middlesex (St. Giles's and St. George's) Volunteer Rifle Corps, are appointed to the

APPENDIX I

battalion, with rank and precedence as in the Volunteer Force. Dated 1st April, 1908 :

Major (Captain, Reserve of Officers) Andrew Reginald Berry.
Major Percy Edward Langworthy Parry. (To be supernumerary.)
Captain George Tolley.
Captain Wilfrid Watson Parker. (To be supernumerary.)
Captain Roland Moffatt Perowne Willoughby.
Captain Samuel John Merton Sampson.
Quartermaster and Honorary Captain Claud Scott."

On Saturday, May 9th, an " amalgamation parade " to cement the unity of the two battalions was held in Hyde Park. The parade took the form of an inspection, and only the men who had signed on for service as Territorials were eligible to muster, others being unrecognised officially unless they signed before June 30th. Nearly 500 men were present out of the 1009 of the new establishment. There was a large gathering to witness the inspection, including Major-General Lord Cheylesmore, Hon. Col. ; Major-Gen. Codrington, commanding the 1st London Division to which the battalion belonged, and other officers. The Victoria and St. George's were the first to arrive, marching in at Grosvenor Gate from the Headquarters in Davies Street while the Bloomsbury's entered the park from the Marble Arch, the band playing for the last time the old Regimental March, " Ninety-five." They carried with them their ancient pair of Colours, and the commander of the new 3rd London Brigade, Col. F. J. Maxse, Coldstream Guards, did them the honour to lead them on to the ground. The two battalions formed up facing each other and Col. Tanqueray took command. The two corps acknowledged each other with a general salute and then forming into line were told off into 8 companies according to the new order, the right half being the Victoria's and the left half the Bloomsbury's. The men moved to the right for marching past, and to the " March Past " of the K.R.R.C. (the old 60th) the united battalion swung past the Brigadier in splendid fashion, the machine-gun detachment and the bearer company bringing up the rear. After a short address from the General Commanding the Division upon the amalgamation the battalion marched off as the newly christened Queen Victoria's Rifles. At the end of the year, October 31st, the regimental strength was returned at 538. Unfortunately the regiment was unable to keep up its numbers ; when Col. Shipley took over the command in December, 1912, the strength was 650, or 370 below its establishment. Nevertheless officers and men persevered to make themselves fit and efficient in every way. Both in Musketry and Field training the system pursued was a great improvement over that of the old Volunteers, and it was not the fault of the Territorials but of the nation itself that almost every single battalion was below strength. The Queen Victoria's kept up their old practice of holding a Musketry Camp on the range at Stanmore as well as attending the Training Camp annually in August. They did not perhaps make history in those days but they prepared themselves for the day that was to come, and when it did come they were not found wanting.

Col. Tanqueray relinquished the command on the 4th February, 1911, on completion of his period of service. He was succeeded by:

Lieut.-Col. A. R. Berry, T.D., 1911–1912.
Lieut.-Col. R. B. Shipley, C.M.G., T.D., 1912–1915.
Lieut.-Col. V. W. F. Dickins, D.S.O., V.D., 1915–1920.
Lieut. P. E. Langworthy Parry, D.S.O., O.B.E., T.D., 1921-1923.

Honorary Colonels

Major-Gen. Herbert F., Lord Cheylesmore, K.C.V.O., 1905–1913.
Lieut.-Gen. Sir Wm. Pitcairn Campbell, K.C.B., 1913–1922.

Regimental Care Committees

In the course of the history of the battalion during the Great War many references have been made to the comforts, etc., sent to the men at the front by the Old Comrades Association. In addition to that organisation, which was founded early in 1913, there were other Committees formed after the outbreak of war for the purpose of seeing that the men had regular supplies of food, clothing and other necessaries. In August, 1914, the Q.V.R. Ladies' Guild was started by a number of the officers' wives, under the Presidency of Mrs. R. B. Shipley and Mrs. O'Shea as Honorary Secretary. Quantities of shirts, socks, mittens, Balaclava helmets and similar articles reached the men from this source, and were found very useful during the exceptionally wet winter of 1914–1915.

Following the Battle of the Somme in July, 1916, when for the first time men of the Q.V.R. were taken prisoners, a Prisoners' of War Help Committee was established, the executive being:

Mrs. Vernon Dickins, President.
S. A. Sampson, Esq., Hon. Treasurer.
Mrs. G. Culme-Seymour, Hon. Sec.
R. Flemming, Esq.   Committee.
Mrs. Berry   ,,
Mrs. R. fF. Davies   ,,
Mrs. Langworthy Parry   ,,

Later in the year the Central Prisoners of War Committee was formed, and the Q.V.R. Committee found it necessary in order to carry on their good work to become an authorised Care Committee and to register under the War Charities Act. The name was now

APPENDIX I

changed to that of " Queen Victoria's Rifles (9th County of London Regiment) Prisoners' of War Care Committee." Mr. Robert Flemming, an uncle of Capt. H. Flemming, who died of wounds on May 7th, 1915, died in the month of September, 1916, whereupon Mr. F. Shore, who had gone out as C.Q.M.S. with the 1st Battalion in 1914 and was so severely wounded on 5th January, 1915, was elected to serve on the Committee in his stead. On the 31st Aug., 1917, Mrs. Berry and Mrs. Culme Seymour retired from the Committee, and thenceforth Mrs. Vernon Dickins filled the dual position of President and Secretary. A call for subscriptions was readily responded to, upwards of £800 being received by February, 1917. In their Second Report, February, 1918, the Committee allude to the increase in the number of prisoners and also in the cost of food parcels, from 7s. to 8s. per parcel. Every prisoner was sent 3 parcels per fortnight, or 78 per annum, which at 8s. per parcel cost £31 4s. per annum. An additional allowance of £4 17s. 6d. for bread or biscuits raised the annual cost per prisoner to £36 1s. 6d. At a subsequent date the cost of the parcels was raised to 10s. Some of the prisoners were sent to Holland or Switzerland and a few were returned home.

The total amount received by the Committee from August, 1916, to February, 1919, was £4795 4s. 2d., and the total expenditure was £4660 5s. 11d., the cost of administration being £83 14s. 7d. During the same period 8000 different articles of clothing were packed and sent out, under the supervision of Mr. F. Shore.

On Saturday, February 8th, 1919, the repatriated Riflemen were entertained to tea and a concert at Davies Street, when the orchestra of the Prince's Theatre volunteered their services during the meal, and afterwards a number of artists, under the direction of Ex-Rfn. Trussell, Q.V.R., provided a highly enjoyable concert.

The good work done by the Committee was much appreciated both by the prisoners and by the contributors to the Fund, and the best thanks of all past and present members of the Q.V.R. are due to Mrs. Vernon Dickins, President and Secretary, Mr. Sampson, Treasurer, and all the members of the Committee. It is satisfactory to know that sufficient funds were raised by voluntary subscriptions among the friends of the regiment without having to apply to the Central Committee for any help whatever.

QUEEN VICTORIA'S RIFLES

Roll of Honour

Officers

1915

1st Jan.	Lieut. Fargus, F. B. A. Killed in action. Messines.
21st April.	Major Lees, T. P. Killed in action. Hill 60.
21st April.	Capt. Fazakeley Westby, G. B. J. Killed in action. Hill 60.
21st April.	2nd Lieut. Summerhays, D. L. Killed in action. Hill 60.
7th May.	Capt. Culme Seymour, G. Killed in action. Hill 60.
7th May.	Capt. Flemming, H. O. Died in London of wounds received at Wieltje, near Ypres, 23rd April.
10th Sept.	Capt. Holms, J. C. Killed in action. Carnoy.

1916

2nd May.	Capt. Cornfoot, D. H. H. Died in France from illness.
18th June.	Capt. Bolton, F. W. Died in England from illness contracted in France.
1st July.	Capt. Cox, H. E. L. Killed in action. Gommecourt.
1st July.	Capt. Houghton, P. S. Killed in action. Gommecourt.
1st July.	Capt. Cunningham, R. W. Killed in action. Gommecourt.
1st July.	2nd Lieut. Meeking, N. A. Killed in action. Gommecourt.
1st July.	2nd Lieut. Lane, E. A. J. A. Killed in action. Gommecourt.
1st July.	2nd Lieut. Fielding, F. W. Killed in action. Gommecourt.
1st July.	2nd Lieut. Simmonds, P. G. Killed in action. Gommecourt.
1st July.	2nd Lieut. Cary, R. H. Killed in action. Gommecourt.
1st July.	2nd Lieut. Mason, O. T. Killed in action. Gommecourt.
12th July.	2nd Lieut. Fleetwood, C. P. Died of wounds (as prisoner of war) received at Gommecourt on 1st July.
9th Sept.	Capt. Davies, R. fF. Killed in action. Leuze Wood.
9th Sept.	Capt. Woods, G. Killed in action. Leuze Wood.
9th Sept.	2nd Lieut. Sim, N. Y. Killed in action. Leuze Wood.
24th Sept.	2nd Lieut. Rumsey, A. C. Died of wounds received at Leuze Wood and Combles.

Memorial to the Fallen and Roll of Honour, The Drill Hall, 56 Davies Street, W. 1.

APPENDIX I

24th Sept.	2nd Lieut. Ord-Mackenzie, D. A. Killed in action. Near Leuze Wood and Combles.
27th Sept.	Capt. Eccles, J. D., M.C. Died of wounds received at Leuze Wood on 9th Sept.
2nd Oct.	2nd Lieut. Gutteridge, R. H. Killed in action. Les Bœufs.
7th Oct.	2nd Lieut. Maddock, O. L. Killed in action. Les Bœufs.
8th Oct.	2nd Lieut. Ludlow, L. Killed in action. Les Bœufs.
8th Oct.	2nd Lieut. Warren, A. R. Wounded and missing (death accepted). Les Bœufs.
8th Oct.	2nd Lieut. Dowdswell, C. V. Killed in action. Les Bœufs.
10th Oct.	2nd Lieut. Parslow, A. J. Died of wounds received. Les Bœufs.

1917

24th March.	Lieut.-Col. Berry, A. R. Died of pneumonia in France.
12th April.	2nd Lieut. Smith, R. S. Killed in action.
14th April.	2nd Lieut. How, H. J. Killed in action.
22nd April.	2nd Lieut. Saxby, G. S. Died of wounds.
23rd April.	2nd Lieut. Hunter, A. D. Killed in action.
1st May.	Capt. Blackwood, H. S. Died of wounds.
9th July.	2nd Lieut. Thornton, H. B. Killed in action.
13th July.	2nd Lieut. Long, A. G. H. Died of wounds.
14th July.	2nd Lieut. Caley, P. R. Died of wounds.
13th Aug.	Capt. Symes, E. D., M.C. Killed in action.
13th Aug.	2nd Lieut. Bate, M. C. T. Killed in action.
16th Aug.	2nd Lieut. Brown, J. W. Killed in action.
16th Aug.	2nd Lieut. Goundry, J. F. Killed in action.
9th Sept.	2nd Lieut. Wightwick, S. Died of wounds.
12th Sept.	Capt. Walker, H. S. Died of wounds received at St. Julien.
26th Sept.	Capt. Griffith, G. F. Killed in action.
26th Sept.	2nd Lieut. Browett, R. Killed in action.
26th Sept.	2nd Lieut. Marshall, J. Missing.[1]
26th Sept.	2nd Lieut. Rolason, L. N. Killed in action.
27th Sept.	2nd Lieut. Blackburne, H. D. Killed in action.
20th Nov.	2nd Lieut. May, J. H. Killed in action.
23rd Nov.	Capt. Brand, D. W. McL. Died of wounds (attd. from Middlesex Regiment).
23rd Nov.	Capt. Clarke, A. B., R.A.M.C., attd. 9th Q.V.R. Killed in action.
30th Dec.	Lieut. McCallum. Missing, believed drowned.[1]
10th Dec.	2nd Lieut. Leete, F. E. Died of wounds.

[1] Omitted from War Office List.

1918

23rd March.	2nd Lieut. Bristow, P. H.	Killed in action.
28th March.	2nd Lieut. Newland, G. M.	Killed in action.
30th March.	2nd Lieut. Astill, E. W. D.	Killed in action.
24th April.	2nd Lieut. Plummer, S. A.	Killed in action.
25th April.	Capt. Hadden, A. R.	Killed in action.
25th April.	Lieut. Easterbrook, H. G.	Died of wounds.
25th April.	Lieut. Brown, S. S.	Killed in action.
30th May.	2nd Lieut. Prince, W. F. J.	Drowned whilst attd. R.A.F.
24th Aug.	Capt. Ralls, F. H., M.C. and bar.	Died of wounds.
27th Aug.	Lieut. Garside, F. G.	Killed in action.
30th Aug.	2nd Lieut. Vanderlinde, M. J. T.	Killed in action.
1st Sept.	Lieut. Brandram, T. C.	Died of wounds.
3rd Sept.	2nd Lieut. Haselgrove, B. T.	Died of wounds.
22nd Sept.	Lieut. Sedgeley, H. F.	Killed in action.
22nd Sept.	2nd Lieut. Sanctuary, C. R.	Killed in action.
22nd Sept.	2nd Lieut. Hunt, L. G.	Killed in action.
27th Sept.	2nd Lieut. Prince, J. C. B.	Killed in action.
29th Sept.	2nd Lieut. Lacey, G. H.	Died of wounds.
4th Nov.	2nd Lieut. Moore, F. H. B.	Killed in action.
5th Nov.	2nd Lieut. Smith, H. R., M.C.	Killed in action.

Q.V.R. GIVEN COMMISSIONS IN OTHER REGIMENTS

LONDON REGIMENT.

(1st)	Chichester, Wm. George Cubit, Lieut.	Killed in action.		15.9.16
(2nd)	Gretton, Horace Edward, Capt.	,,	,,	16.8.17
,,	Winterbourne, Frank Thos., Capt.	Drowned.		10.10.18
,,	Wright, J. G. W., 2nd Lieut.	Killed in action.		11.5.17
(3rd)	Todman, C. V., Lieut.	Drowned.		3.8.18
(6th)	Lawrence, Harold Roy, 2nd Lt.	Died of wounds.		12.12.17
,,	Perry, Leslie Roy, 2nd Lieut.	Killed in action.		15.9.16
(10th)	Chubb, Theodore, 2nd Lieut.	,,	,,	17.2.17
,,	Greenwood, Cecil James, Lieut.	,,	,,	9.8.18
,,	Hunt, H. H., 2nd Lieut.	,,	,,	26.10.18
,,	Morbey, J. S., 2nd Lieut. (attd. R.A.F.).	Died.		8.8.18
(12th)	Charles, Cecil Arthur, 2nd Lieut.	Died of wounds.		22.9.18
(15th)	Stoneman, Wm. Thos., 2nd Lieut.	,,	,,	26.7.17
(17th)	Sheppard, Hubert, 2nd Lieut.	,,	,,	9.12.17
(19th)	Foulds, Maurice Frank, 2nd Lt.	Killed in action.		30.10.17
,,	Ward, Fred., M.C., Capt.	,,	,,	8.12.17

APPENDIX I

(20th)	Thornton, Reginald George, 2nd Lieut.	Killed in action.	5.9.17
(21st)	Carr, Wm. Parsons, Lieut.	,, ,,	13.12.17
(22nd)	Reid, Alexander, 2nd Lieut.	,, ,,	15.2.17
(24th)	Rich, Austin Fredk., 2nd Lieut.	,, ,,	27.12.17

MIDDLESEX REGIMENT.
- Askew, Cyril Horace, 2nd Lieut. Killed in action. 9.4.17
- Asser, Harold Edward, 2nd Lieut. ,, ,, 1.7.16
- Broom, Fredk. J.M., 2nd Lieut. ,, ,, 7.6.17
- Boreham, Harry Pendry, 2nd Lt. ,, ,, 16.4.18
- Colcott, Ernest Harry, 2nd Lieut. ,, ,, 11.9.16
- Devereux, Frederick Herbert ,, ,, 31.7.17
- Linsell, Johnson Hugh, 2nd Lieut. ,, ,, 25.9.15
- Lorenzen, Otto Hans Herman, 2nd Lieut. Died of wounds. 16.9.16
- Maisey, Albert Henry, 2nd Lieut. ,, ,, 16.2.17
- Morrison, Robert Vernon, 2nd Lt. Killed in action. 13.5.17
- Targett, George Henry, Lieut. ,, ,, 18.9.18

MACHINE GUN CORPS.
- Davis, Edward Bernard, 2nd Lt. Killed in action. 21.7.17
- Jones, Ernest Hugh, 2nd Lieut. ,, ,, 26.10.17
- Warner, Wm. Henry, 2nd Lieut. ,, ,, 21.8.18
- Yates, Alec. James, D.C.M., 2nd Lt. ,, ,, 28.3.18

TANK CORPS.
- O'Shea, Dermot Timothy, 2nd Lt. Killed in action. 10.8.18

BEDFORDSHIRE REGIMENT.
- Baden, Reginald, 2nd Lieut. Killed in action. 26.6.16

WORCESTER REGIMENT.
- Robertson, Frank, Capt. Died of wounds. 25.6.15

ROYAL WEST SURREY (QUEEN'S) REGIMENT.
- Budge, Preston Fredk., T/Lieut. Killed in action. 8/9.5.17 (attd. R. Berk. R.)
- Maisey, Alfred George, 2nd Lieut. ,, ,, 12.5.17
- Pope, Wm. Archer, Capt. Died of wounds. 7.10.16
- Saltmarshe, Oliver Edwin, Lieut. Killed in action. 1.7.16

ESSEX REGIMENT.
- Hill, Eric Battley, 2nd Lieut. Died. 19.11.16
- Holmes, Aubrey, 2nd Lieut. Killed in action. 1.7.16
- Wiltshire, H. J. A., 2nd Lieut. ,, ,, 19.4.17

EAST SURREY REGIMENT.
(11th)	Caffyn, C. McC. H. M., Lieut.	Killed in action.	28.3.17
	Dranklin, Wm. Joseph, 2nd Lt.	,, ,,	5.10.16
	Scott, Victor William, Lieut. (attd. R.F.C.)	,, ,,	16.3.18
(14th)	Holgate, Harold Arthur, 2nd Lt.	,, ,,	25.9.16

N. Staffs. Regiment.

Ede, E. D., 2nd Lieut.	Died of wounds.	13.6.18
Williamson, Harold Godwin, 2nd Lieut.	Killed in action.	1.7.16

Devonshire Regiment.

Skardon, Herbert John, Lieut.	Died of wounds.	31.10.18

Oxford and Bucks L.I.

Birch, Walter Robt., Capt.	Killed in action.	7.10.16

R.A.S. Corps.

Hartree, Eric Mursell, Lieut. (attd. R. Berks.)	Killed in action	8.8.18
Reynolds, Percy Basil, Capt.	Died.	4.12.18

Somerset L.I.

Scott, William Francis, 2nd Lt.	Killed in action.	1.7.16

R.F.A.

Belcher, Frederic Percy, Capt. (A/Major).	Died of wounds.	5.8.18
Cross, Leslie, Lieut.	,, ,,	30.9.15
Wright, N. J. R., 2nd Lieut.	Killed in action.	15.9.14

R.H.A.

Bennett, Henry Richard, Lieut.	Died.	4.1.18

Manchester Regiment.

Gossling, Donald Foley, 2nd Lt.	Died of wounds.	10.6.17
Rose, R. A., 2nd Lieut.	Killed in action.	2.8.17

Norfolk Regiment.

Brown, W. J. H., Capt.	Killed in action.	4.9.16

Durham Light Infantry.

Target, Noel Alexander, Lieut.	Killed in action.	4.8.16

Royal Fusiliers.

(7th)	Elliott, Walter, 2nd Lieut.	Killed in action.	13.11.16
	Withall, John, 2nd Lieut.	,, ,,	7.10.16

Royal Berkshire Regiment.

Haase, E. G. L., 2nd Lieut.	Killed in action.	3.7.16

West Riding Regiment (Duke of Wellington's).

Kitchen, Harold Rosslyn, Lieut.	Killed in action.	27.9.16

West Yorkshire Regiment.

Walton, Francis, J. G., 2nd Lt.	Killed in action.	1.7.16

K.O.Y.L.I.

Midgley, E. R., 2nd Lieut.	Killed in action.	15.11.15
Woollett, Wm. Charles, Capt.	,, ,,	16.9.16

Liverpool Regiment.

Varndell, Leslie John, 2nd Lieut.	Died of wounds.	18.9.16

APPENDIX I

THE BUFFS (East Kent Regiment).
    Sankey, Cecil Martin, M.C.,   Killed.   15.5.18
    2nd Lieut. (attd. R.F.C.).

ROYAL FLYING CORPS.
    Vick, K. J., 2nd Lieut.   Killed.   5.7.17

ROYAL WELCH FUSILIERS.
    Jones, T. G., Lieut.   Killed in action.   20.4.17

ROYAL IRISH RIFLES.
    Wale, Clifford Hardwicke, 2nd Lt.   Killed in action.   19.1.16

ROYAL WARWICKSHIRE REGIMENT.
    Coatsworth, Alfred Henry, 2nd Lieut.   Died of wounds.   8.9.16

GLOUCESTER REGIMENT.
    Beale, R. A., 2nd Lieut.   Killed in action.   15.3.17
    Quint, H. J., 2nd Lieut.   ,,   ,,   24.9.18

SOUTH WALES BORDERERS.
    Hall, C. E. Lyon, Lieut.   Killed in action.   7.7.16

LINCOLNSHIRE REGIMENT.
    Bowen, Leslie Harold, Lieut.   Killed in action.   22.12.15
    Cooper, Clarence Edwards Nooth, Lieut.   ,,   ,,   16.9.16
    Stephens, Ernest Stanley, 2nd Lt.   ,,   ,,   6.7.17

LEICESTER REGIMENT.
    Hussey, Frank Wm., Lieut.   Killed in action.   24.9.18

NORTHERN CYCLIST BATTALION.
    Dixon, C. Lieut. (attd. R.A.F.)   Killed in action.   19.9.18

HAMPSHIRE REGIMENT.
    Wilde, Arthur Wm., 2nd Lieut.   Killed in action.   21.1.16

MONMOUTH REGIMENT.
    Taylor, Francis Henry, 2nd Lt.   Killed in action.   30.11.17

IRISH GUARDS.
    Hamilton, Archibald James Rowan, Lieut.   Died of wounds.   21.10.15

LANCASHIRE FUSILIERS.
    Robinson, James Vernon, Lieut.   Died of wounds.   13.8.18

WARRANT OFFICERS, NON-COMMISSIONED OFFICERS, AND RIFLEMEN

(Reproduced from the List of Members of the 9th London Regiment who died in the Great War, 1914–19. By permission of the Controller of His Majesty's Stationery Office.)

EXPLANATION OF ABBREVIATIONS

"b." .. .. "born."	"d. of w." .. .. "died of wounds."
"e." .. .. "enlisted."	"k. in a." .. .. "killed in action."
"d." .. .. "died."	"F. & F." .. .. "France & Flanders."

When the place of enlistment is followed by the name of another place in brackets, the latter represents the deceased soldier's place of residence.

Abbs, James Arthur, e. London (Kennington), 4010, Rfn., k. in a., F. & F., 1/7/16.
Ablewhite, Charles, b. Lincs, Boston, e. London, 392055, Rfn., k. in a., F. & F., 15/12/17.
Adams, Francis Charles, b. Dartmouth, Devon, e. Hammersmith (Croydon), 6844, Rfn., d. of w., F. & F., 20/2/17.
Adams, Jack Atlee, b. Bloomsbury, e. London (Kilburn), 4802, Rfn., k. in a., F. & F., 9/9/16.
Adamson, Gordon Victor, b. York, e. London (Watford), 4211, Rfn., d., Home, 3/5/15.
Adderson, Fred, b. Crimplesham, Norfolk, e. London (Notting Hill), 392240, Rfn., d. of w., F. & F., 16/4/17.
Adler, Edgar Cyril, b. Uxbridge, Middx., e. London (Littlehampton), 392375, Rfn., d. of w., F. & F., 9/6/17.
Airey, George William, b. Ipswich, e. Mill Hill (Edmonton), 393529, Rfn., k. in a, F. & F., 25/7/18, formerly 6211, 11th London Regt.
Akers, George Henry, b. Highgate, e. London (Holloway), 392117, Sgt., d., F. & F., 13/11/18.
Albert, Arthur Frederick, b. Marylebone, e. London (Paddington), 391793, Rfn., d. of w., F. & F., 9/4/18.
Alder, Harold Basil, b. Leyton, e. London (Westcliff-on-Sea), 891, A/Sgt., d. of w., F. & F., 25/5/15.
Aldis, Arthur Robert, b. Brixton, e. London (Camberwell), 393996, Rfn., k. in a., F. & F., 24/10/17.
Allam, Albert Jonathan, b. Holloway, e. Fulham (Tufnell Park), 393224, Rfn., k. in a., F. & F., 25/8/18, formerly 3215, 25th London Regt.
Allen, Sydney John, e. London (Thornton Heath), 3123, Cpl., k. in a., F. & F., 1/7/16.
Allsop, Frank, e. London (E. Finchley), 2532, Rfn., k. in a., F. & F., 1/1/15.

APPENDIX I

Alwin, Arthur Ernest, e. London (Plumstead), 2250, Rfn., k. in a., F. & F., 5/1/15.
Anderson, Arthur Walter, b. Battersea, e. London (Fulham), 7044, Rfn., k. in a., F. & F., 9/10/16, formerly 3039, 25th London Regt.
Anderson, David, e. Stratford (Manor Park), 415204, Rfn., k. in a., F. & F., 3/5/17, formerly 7920, 7th London Regt.
Andrews, Frederick Arthur, e. London (Chelsea), 391881, Rfn., k. in a., F. & F., 3/5/17.
Angus, Andrew, e. Motherwell, 393738, Rfn., k. in a., F. & F., 14/4/17, formerly 5420, 8th London Regt.
Ansell, Arthur Roland, e. London (Erith, Kent), 393591, Rfn., k. in a., F. & F., 14/4/17, formerly 4524, 2nd London Regt.
Ansley, Arthur, b. Southall, e. Southall (Southall), 393874, Rfn., k. in a., F. & F., 24/1/17, formerly R/419, 8th Middx. Regt.
Appleton, Sydney, e. London (Lymm, Cheshire), 415278, Rfn., k. in a., F. & F., 28/11/17, formerly 375138, 8th London Regt.
Armstrong, William Henry, b. Kentish Town, e. London (Hampstead), 390313, Sgt., k. in a., F. & F., 8/9/17.
Arnett, Walter James, b. Farnham Royal, Bucks, e. London (Letchworth), 393739, Rfn., k. in a., F. & F., 7/9/17, formerly 5696, 8th London Regt.
Arnold, John, b. Eastbourne, e. London (Kennington), 393558, Rfn., k. in a., F. & F., 14/4/17.
Arthur, Charles, b. St. Pancras, e. London (Hampstead), 1770, Rfn., k. in a., F. & F., 5/1/15.
Arthur, Herbert Frederick, b. Lewisham, e. Fulham (Lewisham), 393263, Rfn., k. in a., F. & F., 28/3/18, formerly 878, 25th London Regt.
Ascott, Charles Edward, b. Leeds, e. Leeds, 393119, Rfn., d. of w., F. & F., 25/3/18.
Ashby, John Stanley, e. London (Highbury), 4769, Rfn., k. in a., F. & F., 1/7/16.
Ashton, Frederick Henry, e. London (Walworth), 3655, Rfn., k. in a., F. & F., 1/7/16.
Ashton, Harry Stephen, b. Kensington, e. London (Notting Hill), 5125, Rfn., k. in a., F. & F., 9/9/16.
Astill, Reginald, b. Brixton, e. London (Carshalton), 2010, Rfn., k. in a., F. & F., 1/7/16.
Astle, Percy, b. Winshill, Derby, e. Litchfield (Winshill), 415123, Rfn., d., F. & F., 3/11/18, formerly C/6980, 18th K.R.R.C.
Atchison, Sidney John Lyell, e. London (Brixton), 3227, Rfn., k. in a., F. & F., 1/7/16.
Atkins, Frederick Charles, e. London (Kilburn), 4188, Rfn., k. in a., F. & F., 1/7/16.
Atkins, Frederick Robert, e. London (Highgate), 2333, Cpl., k. in a., F. & F., 1/7/16.
Atkins, Leslie, b. Walsall, Staffs, e. London (W. Hampstead), 4915, Rfn., k. in a., F. & F., 1/7/16.

Attridge, Frederick, b. High Roothing, Essex, e. Chelmsford (Gt. Dunmow), 6629, Rfn., k. in a., F. & F., 9/10/16, formerly 2635, 5th Essex Regt.
Avant, Francis Frederick William, e. Hornsey (Muswell Hill), 7835, Rfn., k. in a., F. & F., 9/9/16, formerly 5089, 7th Middx. Regt.
Avila, Leonard Frederick, e. London (W. Norwood), 2181, Rfn., k. in a., F. & F., 4/12/14.
Avis, Albert William, e. London (Ebury Bridge), 392388, Rfn., k. in a., F. & F., 14/4/17.

Baggarley, Ernest Sidney, b. Lambeth, e. London (Camberwell), 1394, Rfn., k. in a., F. & F., 1/7/16.
Baggs, William Arthur Hillary, b. Rangoon, India, e. London (Cricklewood), 5927, Rfn., k. in a., F. & F., 9/9/16.
Bailey, Frederick James, e. London (W. Kensington), 4433, Rfn., k. in a., F. & F., 1/7/16.
Bailey, John, e. Woolwich (Woolwich), 393592, Rfn., k. in a., F. & F., 21/3/17, formerly 5841, 11th London Regt.
Baker, Frederick, b. Kensington, e. London (Willesden), 392520, Rfn., k. in a., F. & F., 12/9/18.
Baker, Frederick Henry John, e. London (St. John's Wood), 391813, Bugler, k. in a., F. & F., 24/5/17.
Baker, Henry James, b. Clapham, e. London (Upper Norwood), 391944, Rfn., k. in a., F. & F., 27/8/17.
Baker, William Godfrey, e. London (Brondesbury), 2123, Rfn., k. in a., F. & F., 1/7/16.
Baker, William Edward, b. Marylebone, e. London (St. John's Wood), 4856, Rfn., d. of w., F. & F., 13/10/16.
Bangs, Leonard Edward, e. London (Tottenham), 3963, Rfn., d. of w., F. & F., 5/7/16.
Bansor, Arthur, b. Woking, Surrey, e. Enfield Town (Enfield), 303804, Sgt., k. in a., F. & F., 24/8/18, formerly 2182, 7th Middx. Regt.
Barnes, Arthur Herbert, b. Shoreditch, e. London (Haggerston), 392741, Rfn., k. in a., F. & F., 14/4/17.
Barnes, George Henry, b. Clerkenwell, e. London (Islington), 393593, Rfn., k. in a., F. & F., 14/4/17.
Barnes, Sydney, George e. London (Brixton Hill), 2738, Rfn., d. of w., F. & F., 4/7/16.
Barnes, Walter Fred, b. Slough, Bucks, e. London (N. Kensington), 6693, Rfn., k. in a., F. & F., 9/10/16, formerly 6682, 6th Essex Regt.
Barnett, Samuel Munday, e. Camberwell (E. Dulwich), 393097, Rfn., k. in a., F. & F., 14/4/17.
Barr, Harry Edwin, e. London (Harrow Road), 4015, Cpl., d. of w., F. & F., 22/1/17.

APPENDIX I 585

Barry, John, b. Whitehaven, Cumberland, e. Carlisle (Whitehaven), 7720, Rfn., k. in a., F. & F., 9/10/16, formerly 23848, Border Regt.
Bartlett, Anthony, b. Beer, Devon, e. London (Kilburn), 391838, L/Cpl., k. in a., F. & F., 26/9/17.
Bartlett, Herbert, e. London (Putney), 415264, Rfn., k. in a., F. & F., 1/9/18, formerly 3273, 18th London Regt.
Bartlett, Stephen Harold, b. W. Kensington, e. London (W Kensington), 1236, Rfn., k. in a., F. & F., 1/7/16.
Bartlett, Thomas John, e. London (Hendon), 391124, Cpl., k. in a., F. & F., 26/9/17.
Barton, David William, b. Lambeth, e. Kingston-on-Thames (Brixton Hill), 395115, Rfn., d. of w., F. & F., 26/8/18.
Barwise, John Thomas, b. Newby West, Cumberland, e. Carlisle (Cummersdale), 7719, Rfn., k. in a., F. & F., 9/10/16, formerly 23931, Border Regt.
Bassett, Henry Edward, e. London (Kilburn), 3912, Rfn., k. in a., F. & F., 1/7/16.
Bassett, Philip James, e. London (Kilburn), 4963, Rfn., k. in a., F. & F., 1/7/16.
Bastin, Sidney Horace, e. London (Putney), 4642, Rfn., k. in a., F. & F., 1/7/16.
Batchelor, James Alexander, b. Marylebone, e. London (Walthamstow), 5795, Rfn., k. in a., F. & F., 9/10/16.
Batchelor, William Thomas, b. Islington, e. London (St. Pancras), 391436, Cpl., k. in a., F. & F., 29/11/17.
Bateman, Arthur George, b. Marylebone, e. London (St. John's Wood), 392829, Rfn., k. in a., F. & F., 14/4/17.
Bateman, Frederick Charles, e. Uxbridge (Uxbridge), 392875, Rfn., d. of w., F. & F., 17/4/17, formerly 5113, 5th Essex Regt.
Bates, Horace Edward, e. London (Luton, Beds), 392299, Rfn., d. of w., F. & F., 22/4/17.
Baumgartner, Arnold Werner, e. London (Cricklewood), 391298, Rfn., k. in a., F. & F., 22/3/18.
Bayley, Felix Guy, e. London (New Cross), 4757, Rfn., k. in a., F. & F., 1/7/16.
Bayley, Leonard Robert, b. Kilburn, e. London (New Cross), 4683, Rfn., k. in a., F. & F., 25/9/16.
Beale, Albert James, e. London (Highams Park), 3861, Rfn., k. in a., F. & F., 1/7/16.
Beare, Cecil Charles, e. London (Southampton), 2819, L/Cpl., k. in a., F. & F., 25/4/15.
Beattie, James John, e. London, 392326, Rfn., k. in a., F. & F., 27/5/17.
Beaumont, George, e. London (Watford), 3777, Rfn., k. in a., F. & F., 1/7/16.
Beecham, William Stanley, b. Marylebone, e. London (Pimlico), 392303, Rfn., k. in a., F. & F., 25/4/18.

Beedham, Reginald William Joseph, b. Maida Vale, e. London (Kensal Rise), 391957, Rfn., d. of w., F. & F., 17/10/18.
Beer, Robert Frank, e. London (Pimlico), 2469, Rfn., d. of w., F. & F., 6/2/17.
Beer, John Albert Edward, b. Newmarket, e. London (Kilburn), 392422, Rfn., k. in a., F. & F., 26/3/17, formerly 298, 26th London Regt.
Behennah, Alfred Dunn, b. Cornwall, e. London, 390117, Rfn., k. in a., F. & F., 8/7/17.
Belham, William Nathaniel, b. Camberwell, e. London (New Malden), 4680, Rfn., d., 21/6/15.
Bell, Norman, e. London (Lee), 2519, Sgt., k. in a., F. & F., 9/10/16.
Bell, Robert Morton, e. London (Clapton), 3480, Rfn., k. in a., F. & F., 1/7/16, M.M.
Bell, Sidney John, b. Deal, e. London, 1393, Rfn., k. in a., F. & F., 25/10/15.
Bennett, Philip Hood, b. Ham Common, Surrey, e. London (Shepherd's Bush), 6044, Rfn., d. of w., F. & F., 10/10/16.
Bentman, Leonard, e. London (Marylebone), 5304, L/Cpl., k. in a., F. & F., 21/1/17.
Bernstein, Charles Nathaniel, b. Holloway, e. Kilburn (Willesden), 393106, Rfn., k. in a., F. & F., 14/4/17.
Bettle, William Henry, b. Tooting, e. London, 1672, L/Cpl., k. in a., F. & F., 1/7/16.
Bezer, William Dudley, e. London (Lee), 2425, L/Cpl., k. in a., F. & F., 1/7/16.
Bigg, Richard Maskell, b. Deptford, e. London (Ladywell), 4827, Rfn., k. in a., F. & F., 9/9/16.
Biggs, Sydney, e. London (Brixton), 4637, Rfn., k. in a., F. & F., 1/7/16.
Bignall, Charles, b. Chiswick, e. London (Chiswick), 1645, Rfn., k. in a., F. & F., 1/7/16.
Birbeck, Alfred William, e. London (Leytonstone), 3574, Rfn., k. in a., F. & F., 9/10/16.
Bird, Albert, e. Hounslow (Hampton), 7864, Rfn., k. in a., F. & F., 9/10/16, formerly 3429, 8th Middx. Regt.
Bird, Charles Edward, b. Edmonton, e. London (Edmonton), 5682, Rfn., k. in a., F. & F., 25/9/16.
Birtles, William Robert, e. London (Forest Gate), 3575, Rfn., k. in a., F. & F., 1/7/16.
Biscoe, Frank, e. London (Kingston-on-Thames), 3946, Rfn., d. of w., F. & F., 19/3/16.
Bishop, Sidney, e. London (Hornsey Rise), 2838, Rfn., k. in a., F. & F., 1/7/16.
Bishop, Frederick, e. London (Westminster), 393232, Rfn., k. in a., F. & F., 16/8/17, formerly 1816, 25th London Regt.
Bishop, Percy, e. London (Manor Park), 393454, Rfn., k. in a., F. & F., 14/4/17, formerly 6116, 11th London Regt.

APPENDIX I 587

Bisley, Horace, e. London (Kilburn), 392010, L/Cpl., k. in a., F. & F., 12/5/17.
Bittles, Leslie Victor, e. London (Brentwood), 393058, L/Cpl., d. of w., F. & F., 23/9/17, formerly 16, 25th London Regt.
Blackburn, John Edward, b. Holloway, e. London (Walthamstow), 394276, Rfn., k. in a., F. & F., 14/4/17 to 19/4/17, formerly 5601, 11th London Regt.
Blackman, Alfred Charles, e. London (Mile End), 392486, L/Cpl., d. of w., F. & F., 2/5/17.
Blackshaw, Charles Frederick, e. London (Dalston), 4794, Rfn., k. in a., F. & F., 1/7/16.
Blake, George Henry, b. Cardiff, e. London (Battersea), 391730, Rfn., k. in a., F. & F., 26/9/17.
Blanden, Lewis, b. Norfolk, e. London (Marylebone), 1598, Rfn., k. in a., F. & F., 19/12/15.
Blew, William Humphreyson, e. London, 3589, L/Cpl., d. of w., Home, 12/9/16.
Bliss, Joseph, b. Banbury, Oxford, e. London (Leamington), 4714, Rfn., k. in a., F. & F., 9/10/16.
Bloyce, Albert Edward Victor, b. Blackheath, e. London (Sydenham), 415259, Rfn., d. of w., F. & F., 27/9/17, formerly 594709, 18th London Regt.
Blunkett, Walter, b. Egham, e. London (Cattlestone), 391414, Rfn., k. in a., F. & F., 13/8/17.
Boggis, Frank, e. London (Whitney), 3149, L/Cpl., k. in a., F. & F., 1/7/16.
Bohle, Charles Christopher John, b. St. George's-in-the-East, e. London (Bermondsey), 393050, L/Sgt., k. in a., F. & F., 20/5/18.
Boismaison, John William Petit, e. London (London, N.), 3594, Rfn., k. in a., F. & F., 9/9/16.
Boncey, Richard Walter, e. London (Fulham), 7488, Rfn., k. in a., F. & F., 24/1/17, formerly 5842, 11th London Regt.
Bond, Harold, e. London (Harrow Rd.), 2486, Rfn., k. in a., F. & F., 1/7/16.
Bond, Sydney George, b. Paddington, e. London (Cricklewood), 390026, Rfn., k. in a., F. & F., 27/9/18.
Bonham, Alfred George, e. London (Brixton), 392471, Rfn., k. in a., F. & F., 14/4/17.
Bonner, George Edward, e. London (Tottenham), 5801, Rfn., k. in a., F. & F., 28/2/17.
Booth, Albert, e. London, 3753, Rfn., k. in a., F. & F., 1/7/16.
Borsberry, Thomas Frederick, b. Deptford, e. London (Deptford), 390116, Sgt., k. in a., F. & F., 6/3/17.
Bouldstridge, Victor Edward, e. London, 392691, Rfn., k. in a., F. & F., 14/4/17.
Bourne, William George, b. Warehorne, Kent, e. London, 392104, Rfn., k. in a., F. & F., 25/8/18.

Bowden, Clarence Ralph, b. Shaftesbury, Dorset, e. London (Blackfriars), 2269, Rfn., k. in a., F. & F., 5/1/15.
Bowden, John Humphrey, b. Marylebone, e. London (Paddington), 392111, L/Cpl., d. of w., F. & F., 10/4/18.
Bowden, James Robert Morris, e. London (Kensington), 392988, Rfn., k. in a., F. & F., 14/4/17, formerly 6684, Essex Regt.
Bower, Augustus Joseph, b. Langton Maltravers, Dorset, e. London (Clapham), 390007, Sgt., k. in a., F. & F., 24/4/18.
Bower, Herbert William, e. Norwich (Norwich), 392906, Rfn., k. in a., F. & F., 14/4/17, formerly 23784, Norfolk Regt.
Bowie, David John, b. Blairdrummond, Perthshire, e. London (Cromwell Rd., S.W.), 392206, Rfn., k. in a., F. & F., 28/3/18.
Bowles, William James, b. Barnet, Herts, e. London (King's Cross), 391375, Rfn., k. in a., F. & F., 25/4/18.
Bowyer, Morton Alfred, b. Weston Colville, Cambs, e. London (Cambridgeshire), 392006, L/Cpl., k. in a., F. & F., 25/4/18.
Box, William, e. London (Watford), 3796, Rfn., d. of w., F. & F., 11/9/16.
Boyd, Christopher Henry, e. Woolwich (Brixton), 392656, Rfn., d. of w., F. & F., 15/4/17.
Bradish, Leonard Michael, e. London (Stoke Newington), 3792, Rfn., k. in a., F. & F., 2/10/16.
Brand, Thomas Richard, b. Brompton, London, e. London (Kilburn), 1927, Rfn., d. of w., F. & F., 5/1/15.
Bray, Albert, b. Stepney, e. London (Plaistow), 394184, Rfn., k. in a., F. & F., 27/9/17.
Bray, Cecil Herbert, b. Harringay, e. London (Seven Kings), 2081, Rfn., k. in a., F. & F., 17/7/15.
Breed, Albert, e. London (Greenwich), 3616, Rfn., k. in a., F. & F., 1/7/16.
Bremner, Alexander Wilfred, b. London, e. London (Highbury), 391041, Rfn., d. of w., F. & F., 22/9/17.
Brent, Clifford Herbert, b. Alexandra Park, Middx., e. London (Hornsey), 2786, Rfn., k. in a., F. & F., 9/9/16.
Brewer, Alfred Verney, e. London (Bayswater), 4407, Rfn., k. in a., F. & F., 1/7/16.
Brewer, Stanley Edward, b. Malden, Essex, e. Malden (Heybridge), 6633, Rfn., k. in a., F. & F., 9/10/16, formerly 3344, Essex Regt.
Bridgman, Walter, b. Regent's Park, e. London (King's Cross), 4551, Rfn., k. in a., F. & F., 9/10/16.
Brinton, Robert Cecil, e. London (Isleworth), 2376, Rfn., k. in a., F. & F., 24/4/15.
Briscoe, Oliver George, e. London (Balham), 393230, Rfn., d. of w., F. & F., 15/4/17, formerly 3064, 25th London Regt.
Brittenden, Frederick, e. London (Deal), 390735, Sgt., d., W. Africa, 28/10/18.
Brooker, Horace Bryan, e. London (Weybridge), 2301, Rfn., k. in a., F. & F., 21/4/15.

APPENDIX I

Brookes, Herbert Ernest Victor, e. London (Catford), 390970, Rfn., d., F. & F., 10/12/17.
Brooks, William Raymond, e. London (Palmer's Green), 3268, L/Cpl., k. in a., F. & F., 21/4/15.
Brown, Arthur Hutchinson, b. Market Rasen, Lincs, e. London (Peckham), 392327, Rfn., k. in a., F. & F., 3/9/17.
Brown, Ernest Edward, e. London (Chelsea), 392248, Rfn., k. in a., F. & F., 14/4/17.
Brown, Herbert Albert, e. London (Pimlico), 5623, Rfn., k. in a., F. & F., 20/7/16.
Brown, Tom, b. Paddington, e. London (Paddington), 394252, Cpl., d. of w., F. & F., 26/4/18.
Browning, George, b. Brighton, e. London (Enfield Court), 3983, Rfn., k. in a., F. & F., 9/9/16.
Brownscombe, Lionel, e. London (Harrow), 2679, L/Cpl., k. in a., F. & F., 1/7/16.
Brunning, Charles James, e. Woolwich (Greenwich), 393764, Cpl., k. in a., F. & F., 14/4/17, formerly 5046, 20th London Regt.
Bryanton, Herbert, b. Knightsbridge, e. London (Fulham), 4370, Rfn., k. in a., F. & F., 9/10/16.
Buckeldee, Frank Lewis, b. Spalding, Lincs, e. London (Paddington), 390915, Rfn., d. of w., F. & F., 30/11/17.
Buckett, Robert Frank, e. London (Henley), 4732, Rfn., k. in a., F. & F., 1/7/16.
Buckland, Richard Julian, e. London (Stoke Newington), 2222, Cpl., k. in a., F. & F., 1/7/16.
Bull, Charles, e. London (Tottenham), 3614, Rfn., k. in a., F. &. F., 1/7/16.
Bullen, John Byford, b. Lewisham, e. Blackheath (Bromley), 393749, Rfn., k. in a., F. & F., 16/8/17, formerly 4866, 20th London Regt.
Bunney, George Thomas, b. Clerkenwell, e. London (London), 392687, Rfn., k. in a., F. & F., 14/8/17.
Burfoot, Robert, e. London (Woolwich), 393561, Rfn., k. in a., F. & F., 14/4/17, formerly 6109, 12th London Regt.
Burgess, Edward Cecil, b. London (Marylebone), e. London (Streatham), 455, Sgt., k. in a., F. & F., 16/10/15, D.C.M.
Burke, Edward Henry Mansell, e. London (Finchley), 393073, Rfn., k. in a., F. & F., 16/8/17, formerly 3001, 28th London Regt.
Burley, Ernest Leonard, e. London (Clapham), 2829, Sgt., k. in a., F. & F., 1/7/16.
Burrell, Francis Mark, b. St. Pancras, e. London (Harrow), 392360, L/Cpl., d. of w., F. & F., 24/9/18.
Burrows, George Henry, e. London (Southall), 7893, Rfn., k. in a., F. & F., 9/9/16, formerly 4713, 8th Middx. Regt.
Burt, Albert Victor, e. London (Marylebone), 391355, Rfn., d., Balkans, 29/10/18, formerly 4155, 9th London Regt.

Burt, John Alexander, e. London (Ealing), 2825, Cpl., k. in a., F. & F., 1/7/16.
Burton, Ernest Francis, b. Stratford, e. London (Cambridge), 391847, L/Cpl., k. in a., F. & F., 27/9/17.
Burton, Joseph Thomas, e. London (Paddington), 7333, Rfn., d. of w., F. & F., 23/1/17, formerly 5652, 11th London Regt.
Butcher, William Harold, e. Portsmouth (Portsmouth), 419015, Rfn., k. in a., F. & F., 11/8/18, formerly 1739, R. E. (T.F.).
Butler, Edmund Hearn, e. London (Southwark), 391910, Cpl., k. in a., F. & F., 26/5/17.
Butler, Walter John, e. London (Ilford), 3779, L/Cpl., k. in a., F. & F., 1/7/16.
Butler, Bertram Allen, e. Manchester (Bournemouth), 419082, Rfn., k. in a., F. & F., 12/10/18, formerly 3868, 6th Manchester Regt.
Butterwick, Alexander Middleton, e. London (Kew), 3636, Rfn., k. in a., F. & F., 13/7/15.

Caddy, George John, b. Stoke Newington, e. London (Bethnal Green), 392704, L/Cpl., k. in a., F. & F., 20/5/18, formerly 6390, 4th London Regt.
Cade, Charles Albert, e. London (Bayswater), 2392, Rfn., k. in a., F. & F., 29/5/16.
Calder, Roy Grant, e. London (East Sheen), 3859, Rfn., d. of w., F. & F., 15/7/16.
Call, Thomas Romney Robinson, b. Fulham, e. London (Southfields), 392021, Rfn., k. in a., F. & F., 27/9/17.
Callaghan, Joseph, b. Bethnal Green, e. London (Bethnal Green), 415009, Rfn., k. in a., F. & F., 26/9/17, formerly 5480, A.S.C.
Calthorpe, William, b. Lowestoft, e. London (Mile End), 394568, L/Cpl., d. of w., F. & F., 26/9/18, formerly 8117, R. W. Kent Regt.
Camp, Robert George, e. London (Hampstead), 6058, Rfn., k. in a., F. & F., 9/10/16.
Canby, Thomas Barton, e. London (Crouch End), 3687, Rfn., d. of w., F. & F., 26/6/15.
Candler, Harold Cornell, e. London (Hammersmith), 3969, Rfn., k. in a., F. & F., 1/7/16, formerly 3123, 12th London Regt.
Card, Reginald Oscar, e. London (Walthamstow), 2433, Rfn., k. in a., F. & F., 1/7/16.
Carmichael, Ernest Clarence, b. Stamford Hill, e. London (Stamford Hill), 394261, Cpl., k. in a., F. & F., 9/8/18.
Carrington, Frank Golding, e. London (Regent's Park), 391723, Rfn., d. of w., F. & F., 19/5/18.
Carrington, William John, e. London (Regent's Park), 5974, L/Cpl., k. in a., F. & F., 21/1/17.
Carter, Matthew, b. Sutton Courtney, Berks, e. London, 391659, Rfn., k. in a., F. & F., 14/4/17.

APPENDIX I

Casiraghi, Gilbert, b. Hastings, e. London (Kentish Town), 392970, Rfn., k. in a., F. & F., 25/4/18, formerly 4853, Essex Regt.
Cattell, Henry, e. London (Hounslow), 390710, Rfn., k. in a., F. & F., 27/9/17.
Cattermoul, Frank William, e. London (Kensington), 393442, Rfn., k. in a., F. & F., 14/4/17, formerly 6039, 11th London Regt.
Cave, William Edwin, b. Hampstead, e. Mill Hill (Cricklewood), 394102, Rfn., k. in a., F. & F., 10/10/17.
Cecil, Arthur Edward, b. East Ham, e. London (Forest Gate), 539, L/Cpl., k. in a., F. & F., 9/10/16.
Chambers, George, b. Mile End, e. London (Leytonstone), 415241, Rfn., k. in a., F. & F., 15/7/18.
Chambers, James Arthur Leslie, e. London (Paddington), 391191, Rfn., d. of w., F. & F., 4/5/17.
Champ, Philip, b. London, e. London (Finsbury Park), 391478, Sgt., k. in a., F. & F., 25/8/18.
Chapman, Edgar Arthur, b. Hornsey, e. Hornsey (Tottenham), 393857, Rfn., k. in a., F. & F., 14/4/17, formerly 4912, 7th Middx. Regt.
Chapman, Jack Courtenay, e. London (Kettering), 392180, Rfn., k. in a., F. & F., 14/4/17.
Chapman, William Henry, b. Marylebone, e. London (Lavender Hill), 391961, Cpl., k. in a., F. & F., 27/9/17, M.M.
Chappell, Albert Ernest, e. London (Chelsea), 392031, L/Cpl., k. in a., F. & F., 26/9/17.
Charton, Jean Christian, b. Dalston, e. London (W. Acton), 4762, Rfn., k. in a., F. & F., 25/9/16.
Chedgey, Percy James, e. London (Lutterworth, Leicester), 391118, Sgt., d. of w., F. & F., 22/3/17.
Chennell, Edgar John, e. Mill Hill (Crouch End), 393087, Rfn., k. in a., F. & F., 11/4/17.
Chennell, Leslie Francis, b. Hornsey, e. London (North Finchley), 393088, Rfn., d. of w., F. & F., 21/3/18.
Chick, Albert George, e. London (Hendon), 390621, Sgt., d. of w., F. & F., 20/4/17.
Child, Harold William, e. Birmingham (Streatham), 6051, Rfn. k. in a., F. & F., 9/10/16.
Chivers, Alfred Theodore, e. London (Parsons Green), 392108, Rfn., k. in a., F. & F., 27/9/17.
Chivers, Frederick James, b. Battersea, e. London (Battersea), 392675, Rfn., d. of w., F. & F., 17/4/17.
Choppen, Albert John, b. Marylebone, e. London (Marylebone), 390004, Sgt., k. in a., F. & F., 26/9/17.
Church, William Reginald, e. London (Rothwell, Northants), 392152, L/Cpl., d. of w., F. & F., 24/8/18.
Churchward, Thomas Joseph, b. Beccles, e. London (Blackfriars), 1968, Rfn., k. in a., F. & F., 25/9/16.

592 QUEEN VICTORIA'S RIFLES

Clack, Alfred Walter, b. Kentish Town, e. Hounslow (Willesden), 395154, Rfn., k. in a., F. & F., 23/9/18.
Claridge, Arthur Henry, e. London (London, E.), 3223, Rfn., k. in a., F. & F., 1/7/16.
Clark, Charles Clifford, b. King's Cross, e. London (Clapham), 3217, Rfn., k. in a., F. & F., 1/7/16.
Clark, Frederick William, b. Clapham, e. Kingston-on-Thames (Thornton Heath), 394520, Rfn., k. in a., F. & F., 4/7/18.
Clark, Guy, e. London (Chippenham, Wilts), 2771, Rfn., k. in a., F. & F., 29/4/15.
Clark, James Richard, b. St. Pancras, e. London (Clapham), 1578, Rfn., k. in a., F. & F., 1/1/15.
Clark, Leonard Harry Hudson, b. Paddington, e. London (Cheltenham), 392019, Rfn., k. in a., F. & F., 27/9/17.
Clark, Leslie William, b. Handley Castle, Worcester, e. Chelmsford (Colchester), 393031, Rfn., d. of w., F. & F., 8/5/17, formerly 2212, Essex Regt.
Clark, Reginald Cann, e. London (Finchley), 392395, Rfn., d. of w., Home, 29/6/18.
Clark, Tom, b. Bow, e. London (Leytonstone), 394101, Rfn., d. of w., F. & F., 27/4/18.
Clark, William, e. Chelmsford, 6605, Rfn., k. in a., F. & F., 25/9/16, formerly 3301, Essex Regt.
Clarke, Stanley Percival, e. London (Catford), 3194, Rfn., k. in a., F. & F., 1/7/16.
Clarke, Alfred Algernon, e. Enfield (Oxford), 7796, Rfn., k. in a., F. & F., 9/9/16, formerly 3323, 7th Middx. Regt.
Clarke, Basil Heathcote, e. London (Muswell Hill), 2336, Rfn., k. in a., F. & F., 6/3/15.
Clayton, Walter John, e. London (Ditton Hill, Surrey), 2267, A/Sgt., k. in a., F. & F., 21/4/15.
Clegg, Harry Edwin, e. London (Harringay), 3378, Rfn., k. in a., F. & F., 24/4/15.
Clements, Norman Harlow, b. Chiswick, e. London (Brixton), 394514, Rfn., k. in a., F. & F., 10/8/18.
Climpson, George Clements, b. Maidstone, e. London (Maidstone), 4623, Rfn., k. in a., F. & F., 23/11/16.
Clough, George William, e. London (Hendon), 390596, Sgt., k. in a., F. & F., 16/8/17.
Cocks, Harold Hornsby, e. London (W. Ealing), 3848, Rfn., k. in a., F. & F., 1/7/16.
Cocquerel, Marcel, e. London, 3934, Rfn., k. in a., F. & F., 1/7/16.
Coe, William, b. Booton, Norfolk, e. Dunbar (Dunbar), 392903, Rfn., d. of w., F. & F., 28/11/17, formerly 24527, Norfolk Regt.
Coel, William Henry, e. London (Willesden), 390442, Rfn., d., F. & F., 22/10/18.
Coggin, Sydney John, b. Lambeth, e. London (Blackfriars), 393943, Rfn., k. in a., F. & F., 8/9/17.

APPENDIX I 593

Cohen, Lewis, b. St. Botolph's, Middx., e. London (Maida Vale), 391330, Rfn., d. of w., F. & F., 1/3/17.
Cole, David, b. Marylebone, e. London (Paddington), 391879, Rfn., d., Home, 3/9/18.
Cole, Reuben Garrett, e. London (Chelsea), 4875, Rfn., k. in a., F. & F., 1/7/16.
Coleman, Thomas James, e. Chelmsford (Chelmsford), 392915, Rfn., k. in a., F. & F., 11/4/17, formerly 3009, Essex Regt.
Coles, Cecil Frederick Gottlieb, e. London (Forest Hill), 390653, Sgt., d. of w., F. & F., 26/4/18.
Coles, George Francis, b. Shoreditch, e. London (Bethnal Green), 394085, Rfn., d. of w., F. & F., 24/9/18.
Collier, Sydney Clarence, b. Islington, e. London (Islington), 392030, L/Cpl., k. in a., F. & F., 27/9/17, M.M.
Colling, William, e. London (E. Dulwich), 390607, Sgt., k. in a., F. & F., 26/9/17.
Collins, Arthur Henry, b. Plaistow, e. London (Plaistow), 393307, Rfn., d. of w., F. & F., 15/4/18, formerly 5134, 11th London Regt.
Collis, Alfred, e. Derby (Chesterfield), 415243, Rfn., k. in a., F. & F., 14/8/17, formerly 81160, 5th London Regt.
Collis, Leonard Alfred, e. London (Wandsworth), 4343, Rfn., k. in a., F. & F., 1/7/16.
Collison, Edgar, e. Woolwich (Plumstead), 393595, Rfn., d. of w., F. & F., 7/5/17, formerly 6003, 11th London Regt.
Coltman, Norman Owen, b. Leicester, e. London (Brixton), 392801, Rfn., k. in a., F. & F., 22/11/17.
Colyer, Ernest, e. Barnet (Barnet), 7801, Cpl., k. in a., F. & F., 9/9/16, formerly 3423, 7th Middx. Regt.
Comley, Charles James, b. Battersea, e. London (Battersea), 393988, Rfn., d. of w., F. & F., 26/8/17.
Connolly, Thomas, b. Kildare, Ireland, e. London (Kildare), 7672, Rfn., k. in a., F. & F., 15/9/16, formerly 5457, 8th London Regt.
Connor, Robert William, b. Westminster, e. London (E. Stepney), 419007, Rfn., k. in a., F. & F., 25/4/18, formerly 5063, 18th London Regt.
Conquest, Louis Joseph, b. Watford, e. London (Watford), 3982, Rfn., k. in a., F. & F., 1/7/16.
Cook, Albert Bertie, e. Chelmsford (Colchester), 6703, Rfn., k. in a., F. & F., 2/10/16, formerly 2598, Essex Regt.
Cook, Harry Field, e. London (W. Dulwich), 390446, W.O. Class 2, k. in a., F. & F., 14/4/17.
Cook, John Albert, e. Chelmsford, 392974, L/Cpl., k. in a., F. & F., 14/4/17, formerly 2540, Essex Regt.
Cook, William Arthur, b. Lambeth, e. London (Stockwell), 7674, Rfn., d. of w., F. & F., 22/9/16, formerly 5684, 8th London Regt.
Cooke, John Percy Rice, e. London (Richmond), 3363, Rfn., d. of w., F. & F., 11/9/15.

2 Q

Cookson, John, b. Blackpool, e. Blackpool (Marton), 419032, Rfn., k. in a., F. & F., 17/7/18, formerly 3729, 4th L.N. Lancs Regt.
Cooper, Frank, b. Leicester, e. London (Bayswater), 3437, Rfn., k. in a., F. & F., 1/7/16.
Cooper, Harry, e. Chelmsford (Braintree), 6707, Rfn., k. in a., F. & F., 2/10/16.
Cooper, Harry, b. Fulham, e. London (S. Norwood), 1592, Rfn., d. of w., F. & F., 2/7/16.
Cooper, William, b. Shepherd's Bush, e. London (Bayswater), 391741, Rfn., k. in a., F. & F., 24/4/18.
Cooper, William, b. Camberwell, e. London (Streatham), 2043, Cpl., k. in a., F. & F., 1/7/16.
Copas, Herbert Alfred, e. London (W. Acton), 392561, Rfn., k. in a., F. & F., 29/4/17.
Copestake, Cecil Charles, b. New Cross, e. London (Forest Gate), 6879, Rfn., k. in a., F. & F., 26/1/17.
Coppen, Archibald James, e. Chelmsford (Danbury), 303033. L/Cpl., k. in a., F. & F., 14/4/17, formerly 2089, Essex Regt.
Cork, Graham, b. Kilburn, e. London (Fulham), 394056, Rfn., k. in a., F. & F., 27/9/17.
Cork, James, e. London (Barnsbury), 393459, Rfn., k. in a., F. & F., 14/4/17, formerly 5190, 11th London Regt.
Corrigan, George Edward, e. London (Bromley by Bow), 415135, Rfn., k. in a., F. & F., 3/5/17, formerly 5614, 10th London Regt.
Cosgrove, William George, e. London (Stamford Hill), 3505, L/Cpl., k. in a., F. & F., 2/11/16.
Coulter, Edward Stanley, b. India, e. London (Willesden), 576, Sgt., k. in a., F. & F., 14/9/15.
Coulton, William Whiting, e. London (Barnsbury), 390796, L/Cpl., k. in a., F. & F., 26/5/17.
Court, Albert Gordon, e. London (Bracknell, Berks), 391111, Sgt., d. of w., F. & F., 5/11/18.
Cousins, Arthur Edwin, e. London (Eatonford, Hunts), 391955, Rfn., k. in a., F. & F., 26/9/17.
Cowing, John Henry George, b. Westminster, e. London (Vauxhall), 393980, Rfn., k. in a., F. & F., 13/8/17.
Cox, Charles Mortimer, b. Willesden, e. London (Willesden), 4434, Rfn., k. in a., F. & F., 25/9/16.
Cox, Edward Albert, e. Camberwell (Kennington), 7431, Rfn., k. in a., F. & F., 24/1/17, formerly 6231, 11th London Regt.
Cox, Frederick Geoffrey, b. Brixton, e. London (Clapham), 969, Cpl., k. in a., F. & F., 1/7/16.
Cox, Ronald Owen Harvey, e. London (Westminster), 3849, Rfn., k. in a., F. & F., 1/7/16.
Cox, William, b. Bermondsey, e. London (Walworth), 394095, Rfn., d. of w., F. & F., 8/9/17.
Crabtree, Ernest, b. Illingworth, e. London (Southall), 390717, A/Sgt., k. in a., F. & F., 14/8/17.

Crack, Lionel Thomas, b. London, e. London (Westminster), 392314, Rfn., k. in a., F. & F., 27/9/17.
Craig, Joseph Kerr, b. Walton, Liverpool, e. Kingston-on-Thames (S. Norwood), 394641, Rfn., k. in a., F. & F., 2/9/18.
Cresswell, Ernest Alan, e. London (Hampstead), 2206, A/Cpl., k. in a., F. & F., 4/6/15.
Crombie, William George, e. London (Fulham), 393402, Rfn., k. in a., F. & F., 11/4/17, formerly 5622, 11th London Regt.
Crook, Walter William, e. London (Clapham Common), 390943, Rfn., k. in a., F. & F., 14/4/17.
Crookbain, Charles Benjamin, b. Bethnal Green, e. London (Bethnal Green), 415201, Rfn., k. in a., F. & F., 16/8/17, formerly 6832, 7th London Regt.
Cross, Alfred, b. Southend, e. Chelmsford (Broomfield), 6606, Rfn., d. of w., F. & F., 12/10/16, formerly 2068, Essex Regt.
Cross, Charles Sidney, e. London (London), 2900, Rfn., k. in a., F. & F., 1/7/16.
Cross, Sydney, e. London (S. Hackney), 2872, Rfn., k. in a., F. & F., 9/10/16.
Curths, Herman Morton, e. London (Chiswick), 2864, Rfn., k. in a., F. & F., 1/7/16.
Curtis, Ernest Victor, b. Bethnal Green, e. London (Finsbury), 391842, Rfn., k. in a., F. & F., 8/9/17.
Curtis, Herbert John, e. Colchester, 392972, Rfn., k. in a., F. & F., 25/4/18, formerly 3412, Essex Regt.
Curtis, Harry Leon, b. Wandsworth, e. London (Hanwell), 6613, Rfn., k. in a., F. & F., 9/10/16, formerly 5114, Essex Regt.
Curtis, William Henry, b. Bethnal Green, e. Hackney (Bethnal Green), 415136, Rfn., k. in a., F. & F., 16/8/17, formerly 1418, 10th London Regt.
Cusack, William, b. Marylebone, e. London (Fulham), 393538, Rfn., d. of w., Home, 11/10/17, formerly 6068, 11th London Regt.
Cuthbert, George Richard, e. London (Islington), 4805, Rfn., k. in a., F. & F., 1/7/16.
Cuthbert, Henry Albert, e. London (Harlesden), 3625, Rfn., k. in a., F. & F., 1/7/16.

Dady, Joseph Alfred, b. Lakenham, Norfolk, e. Norwich, 392878, Rfn., k. in a., F. & F., 14/8/17, formerly 24433, Norfolk Regt.
Daintree, William, e. London (Battersea), 393539, Rfn., k. in a., F. & F., 14/4/17, formerly 5684, 11th London Regt.
Dale, Harold Cortley, e. London (Willesden), 392158, Rfn., d. of w., F. & F., 29/4/17.
Daniel, Alfred Charles, b. Beckenham, Kent, e. Camberwell (Sydenham), 394535, Rfn., k. in a., F. & F., 1/9/18.
Dann, Frederick William, e. London (Walthamstow), 4209, Rfn., k. in a., F. & F., 1/7/16.

Darvill, Alfred, b. Ropley, Hants, e. London (Ropley), 391802, Rfn., d. of w., F. & F., 21/9/17.
Davey, Reginald James, e. London (Canning Town), 3511, Rfn., k. in a., F. & F., 1/7/16.
Davies, Bertrand, b. Pembroke, e. London, 1925, Rfn., d., F. & F., 1/7/16.
Davies, Edwin William, e. London (Westminster), 392851, Rfn., d. of w., F. & F., 2/5/17.
Davies, Kenneth Middleton, e. London (Brockley), 2984, Rfn., k. in a., F. & F., 1/7/16.
Davies, John Sewell, e. London (London), 2065, Rfn., k. in a., F. & F., 24/4/15.
Davies, Richard, e. London (Lavant), 2980, A/Cpl., d. of w., Home, 16/1/15.
Davies, William Evan, e. London (Paddington), 5898, Rfn., k. in a., F. & F., 9/10/16.
Davis, Archibald, e. London, 392383, L/Sgt., k. in a., F. & F., 14/4/17.
Davis, Arthur Henry, e. London (Barnsbury), 393378, Rfn., k. in a., F. & F., 14/4/17.
Davis, John North, b. Epping, e. London (Epping), 394733, Rfn., k. in a., F. & F., 1/9/18.
Davis, Sidney Charles, e. London (Bermondsey), 2449, Rfn., k. in a., F. & F., 30/5/16.
Davison, George Reginald, e. London (Harrow-on-Hill), 3803, Rfn., k. in a., F. & F., 1/11/16.
Dawkes, Albert Edward, b. Queen's Park, e. London (Queen's Park), 1358, L/Cpl., k. in a., F. & F., 1/7/16.
Dawson, Harry, e. London (Westminster), 391005, Rfn., k. in a., F. & F., 16/8/17.
Day, Albert Victor, b. Needham, Norfolk, e. Norwich (Norfolk), 6594, Rfn., k. in a., F. & F., 9/10/16.
Day, Frank, e. London (Clapham Junction), 392819, Rfn., k. in a., F. & F., 14/4/17.
Day, Vivian, e. London (Acton Green), 393379, Rfn., k. in a., F. & F., 14/4/17, formerly 2958, 11th London Regt.
Defriez, Ernest James, e. London (Camberwell), 7337, Rfn., k. in a., F. & F., 21/1/17, formerly 6202, 11th London Regt.
Dengate, William, e. London (Clapham), 3408, L/Cpl., k. in a., F. & F., 1/7/16.
Dennis, Edward Arthur, e. London (Stratford), 391019, Rfn., k. in a., F. & F., 25/4/18.
Dennis, Frank, b. Westminster, e. London, 391865, Rfn., k. in a., F. & F., 26/9/17.
Dennis, Frederick, e. Hornsey (New Southgate), 393858, Rfn., k. in a., F. & F., 14/4/17, formerly 4918, 7th Middx. Regt.
Denny, Arthur Martin, b. Wimbledon, e. London (W. Ealing), 5600, Rfn., d. of w., Home, 29/10/16.

APPENDIX I

Dew, James Robert John, b. St. Pancras, e. London (Marylebone), 391321, Rfn., d., Home, 17/11/18.
Dewey, Cecil Wilfred, e. London (Wallington, Surrey), 390976, Rfn., k. in a., F. & F., 3/9/17.
Dickins, George Charles, e. Camberwell (Battersea), 415285, Rfn., k. in a., F. & F., 1/9/18, formerly 375621, 8th London Regt.
Dickson, Reginald Harry, b. Forest Gate, e. London (Camden Town), 392855, Rfn., d. of w., F. & F., 5/6/17.
Divers, John, e. Fulham (Richmond), 7056, Rfn., k. in a., F. & F., 9/10/16, formerly 2009, 25th London Regt.
Dix, George Henry, b. Walworth Rd., e. London (Bermondsey), 415338, Rfn., k. in a., F. & F., 25/4/18, formerly 1974, 22nd London Regt.
Dix, Ivan Chester, e. London (Bayswater), 4824, Rfn., d. of w., F. & F., 10/7/16.
Dixon, George Stanley, e. London (Grimsby), 2628, Rfn., d. of w., F. & F., 5/1/15.
Dixon, Robert Henry Charles, b. Walworth, e. London (Maida Hill), 4472, Rfn., d. of w., F. & F., 17/10/16.
Dockery, Thomas Edwin, e. Camberwell (Camberwell), 393098, Rfn., k. in a., F. & F., 14/4/17, formerly 6851, 9th London Regt.
Dodge, John Wilks, e. London (Kew), 392449, Rfn., d. of w., F. & F., 22/4/17.
Doggrell, John Stanley, e. Camberwell (Bermondsey), 393463, Rfn., k. in a., F. & F., 14/4/17, formerly 6157, 11th London Regt.
Dollin, Henry Rickon, e. London (Tufnell Park), 392791, Rfn., k. in a., F. & F., 1/5/17.
Donaldson, William Herbert Ross, e. London (Gateshead), 394409, Rfn., d., F. & F., 2/2/17, formerly 5612, 8th London Regt.
Donovan, William Richard, e. London (Balham), 3126, Rfn., d. of w., F. & F., 6/6/15.
Dore, Frederick Henry, b. Battersea, e. London (Bermondsey), 1313, L/Cpl., d. of w., F. & F., 29/4/15.
Dore, William John, b. Canning Town, e. Stratford (Canning Town), 394322, Rfn., d., F. & F., 7/5/17.
Dorman, Stanley Meredith, e. Barnet (Tottenham), 7797, Rfn., k. in a., F. & F., 9/9/16.
Double, Charles Frederick, b. St. Pancras, e. London (King's Cross), 392562, Rfn., d. of w., F. & F., 6/5/17.
Dovey, Alfred Thomas, e. London (Regent's Park), 390834, Rfn., d. of w., F. & F., 27/5/17.
Downie, Hubert Barnett, e. London (Teddington), 3040, Rfn., k. in a., F. & F., 1/7/16.
Downie, Thomas Smith, e. London (Paddington), 393540, Rfn., d. of w., F. & F., 11/4/17.
Dowsett, Albert George, e. London (Plaistow), 419009, Rfn., d. of w., F. & F., 25/8/18, formerly 2238, 7th London Regt.

Drake, Henry Alfred, e. London, 4720, L/Cpl., k. in a., F. & F., 1/7/16.
Drew, Albert Jeremiah, e. London, 392811, Rfn., k. in a., F. & F., 14/4/17.
Drew, Edward, e. London (Islington), 393172, Rfn., k. in a., F. & F., 24/5/17, formerly 2408, 12th London Regt.
Drew, Frederick John Staunton, b. Dublin, e. London, 415054, Rfn., k. in a., F. & F., 8/9/18, formerly 5721, 11th London Regt.
Drew, Herbert Harold, e. Norwich (King's Lynn), 392880, Rfn., k. in a., F. & F., 14/4/17, formerly 24944, 10th Norfolk Regt.
Drury, Frederick, e. London (Willesden), 391926, Rfn., k. in a., F. & F., 24/5/17.
Dullam, Reginald William, b. Barnstaple, Devon, e. London (Westminster), 1731, Rfn., k. in a., F. & F., 1/7/16.
Dunn, Hardinge Slather, b. Hampstead, e. London (Paddington), 1611, Rfn., d. of w., F. & F., 5/1/15.
Dunn, Lionel Eric, b. Battersea, e. London (Clacton-on-Sea), 391882, Rfn., k. in a., F. & F., 25/8/18.
Durrant, Herbert Frank, b. Brighton, e. London (Westminster), 394338, Rfn., k. in a., F. & F., 26/3/17, formerly 5183, 12th London Regt.
Dutson, Arthur Charles, e. Hounslow (Staines), 7876, Rfn., k. in a., F. & F., 26/11/16, formerly 1154, 8th Middx. Regt.
Dymond, Stanley William, e. London (Tottenham), 5714, Rfn., d. of w., Home, 24/9/16.
Dyson, Harry, b. Southport, Lancs., e. Southport (Southport), 418005, Rfn., d. of w., F. & F., 1/11/17, formerly 2022, R.A.S.C.

Earthy, Wilfred, e. London (Hersham), 4329, Rfn., k. in a., F. & F., 1/7/16.
East, Henry George, e. London (Queen's Park), 3627, Rfn., k. in a., F. & F., 28/5/16.
Easton, Claude Edgar, e. London (Richmond), 4749, Rfn., k. in a., F. & F., 1/7/16.
Ebers, Leonard Charles, b. Newington, e. London (Walworth), 1804, Rfn., k. in a., F. & F., 17/12/14.
Edmonds, Frederick, b. Lambeth, e. Camberwell (Brixton), 393951, Rfn., k. in a., F. & F., 16/8/17.
Edmondson, Edward Tepper, b. Norwood, e. London (Tooting Common), 3347, Rfn., d. of w., F. & F., 4/7/16.
Edwards, Charles, e. London (Enfield), 394871, Rfn., k. in a., F. & F., 25/8/18.
Edwards, Edward, b. Neasden, e. London (Neasden), 4457, L/Cpl., k. in a., F. & F., 9/10/16.
Edwards, Leoline Arthur, e. Hampton Court (Twickenham), 7874, L/Cpl., k. in a., F. & F., 9/10/16, formerly 3772, 8th Middx. Regt.

APPENDIX I 599

Edwards, Thomas, b. Hornsey, e. London (Bromley), 1863, Rfn., k. in a., F. & F., 1/7/16.
Eggleton, Harold George, e. London (Wimbledon), 3750, Rfn., d. of w., F. & F., 2/4/15.
Egner, William, e. Stratford (Upton Park), 392621, Rfn., d. of w., F. & F., 16/4/17, formerly 6374, 7th London Regt.
Eisele, George John, b. Marylebone, e. London (Westminster), 5210, Rfn., k. in a., F. & F., 9/9/16.
Eisenegger, Albert Eugene, b. Chelsea, e. London (Kentish Town), 391196, Cpl., d. of w., F. & F., 13/8/17.
Elliott, Claude, e. London (Aldershot), 3305, Rfn., k. in a., F. & F., 7/4/15.
Ellis, Frederick Henry, b. St. Pancras, e. London (Euston), 391945, Rfn., k. in a., F. & F., 8/9/17.
Ellis, Matthew George, b. Gt. Yarmouth, e. London (Fulham), 394049, Rfn., d. of w., F. & F., 19/5/18.
Elliston, Percy Loweth, b. Dalston, e. London (Bermondsey), 393959, Rfn., k. in a., F. & F., 27/9/17.
Elms, Frederick Gilbert, b. Plumstead, e. London (Plumstead), 1370, Rfn., k. in a., F. & F., 1/7/16.
Elsey, Henry Joseph, e. London (Chelsea), 391825, Rfn., k. in a., F. & F., 26/9/17.
Emery, Reginald Stuart, e. London (St. Margarets), 2057, Rfn., d. of w., F. & F., 6/12/15.
English, George Ellis, e. London (South Wold), 391739, Rfn., k. in a., F. & F., 10/4/17.
Etherington, Frank Henry Charles, e. London (Camberwell), 393202, Rfn., d. of w., F. & F., 23/5/17.
Evans, Arthur, e. London (Hackney), 392746, Rfn., k. in a., F. & F., 14/4/17.
Everest, Albert, e. London (Putney), 2238, Rfn., k. in a., F. & F., 1/7/16.
Everidge, Frederick Alderman, b. Marylebone, e. Hammersmith (Hampstead), 392539, Rfn., d. of w., F. & F., 13/9/17.
Exon, Thomas Frederick, b. Croydon, e. London (Streatham), 4515, Rfn., d. of w., F. & F., 11/10/16.

Fairall, John Herbert, b. St. Pancras, e. London (Ealing), 140, W.O., Class 2, k. in a., F. & F., 24/8/15.
Faire, Eric Leslie, b. Marylebone, e. London (Putney), 7016, Rfn., k. in a., F. & F., 9/10/16, formerly 3561, 25th London Regt.
Farley, Frank, e. London (Brixton), 393446, Rfn., k. in a., F. & F., 14/4/17, formerly 6074, 11th London Regt.
Farmer, Frank Arthur, e. London (Seven Kings), 2395, Rfn., d. of w., F. & F., 1/5/15.
Farmer, Leonard Arley, b. East Ham, e. London (Seven Kings), 390455, L/Cpl., d. of w., F. & F., 4/7/18.

Farmer, Frederick William, e. London (Kilburn), 391448, Rfn., k. in a., F. & F., 23/9/18.
Farnsworth, John, b. Chelmsford, e. Chelmsford (Little Waltham), 6640, Rfn., k. in a., F. & F., 25/9/16, formerly 1537, 5th Essex Regt.
Farquharson, Stanley James, e. London (S. Kensington), 3723, Rfn., k. in a., F. & F., 1/7/16.
Farrar, Howard Alan, b. Stroud, Glos., e. Cheltenham (London), 1474, A/Cpl., k. in a., F. & F., 24/4/15.
Farrow, Albert John, e. Walthamstow (Walthamstow), 393111, Rfn., k. in a., F. & F., 14/4/17.
Farthing, George Ernest, b. Dovercourt, e. Dovercourt (Dovercourt), 6641, Rfn., k. in a., F. & F., 9/10/16, formerly 2029, Essex Regt.
Faulks, Edwin Alfred, e. London (Putney), 393275, Rfn., k. in a., F. & F., 14/4/17, formerly, 1819, 25th London Regt.
Fay, Edward, b. Newington, e. London (Walworth), 393209, Rfn., k. in a., F. & F., 26/9/17.
Felton, Edwin, e. London (W. Hampstead), 4036, Rfn., k. in a., F. & F., 1/7/16.
Fewster, Arthur Leslie, b. Hull, Yorks, e. London (Barking), 394649, Rfn., k. in a., F. & F., 2/9/18. M.M.
Field, Leslie George, b. Paddington, e. London (W. Croydon), 392280, Rfn., d. of w., F. & F., 8/9/18.
Fielder, Cecil Buckler, b. Finchley, e. London (E. Finchley), 1231, W.O., Class 2, k. in a., F. & F., 1/7/16.
Fielding, George Henry, e. London (Hanwell), 2111, Rfn., k. in a., F. & F., 1/7/16.
Finlinson, Wilkinson, b. Aikton, Cumberland, e. Carlisle (Drumburgh), 393780, Rfn., d. of w., F. & F., 29/6/17, formerly 23941, 10th Border Regt.
Finn, Daniel Patrick, e. London (Donnybrook), 393610, Rfn., d. of w., Home, 30/4/18, formerly 4144, 8th London Regt.
Fippard, Herbert John, b. Paddington, e. London (Maida Hill), 2087, Cpl., k. in a., F. & F., 4/6/15.
Fisher, Alfred Frederick, b. Tottenham, e. London (Edmonton), 391925, Rfn., k. in a., F. & F., 25/4/18.
Fisher, Herbert James Benjamin, e. London (Kensington), 391197, L/Sgt., k. in a., F. & F., 26/9/17.
Fisher, Henry Matthew, e. London (Islington), 415077, Rfn., k. in a., F. & F., 22/5/17, formerly 3276, 11th London Regt.
Fisher, Joseph, b. Shepherdess Walk, e. London (Kensington), 2128, L/Sgt., k. in a., F. & F., 9/9/16.
Fisher, Tom James Turner, b. Stoke Newington, e. London (Forest Gate), 392870, Rfn., d. of w., F. & F., 10/11/17.
Fisher, Wilfred, e. London (Harlesden), 2551, Rfn., k. in a., F. & F., 21/4/15.

APPENDIX I

Fitzgerald, George Maurice, b. Islington, e. London (Islington), 7646, Rfn., k. in a., F. & F., 25/9/16, formerly 5682, 8th London Regt.

Flaunty, Joseph Peate, e. Woolwich, 7461, Rfn., d. of w., F. & F., 23/1/17, formerly 6422, 12th London Regt.

Fleming, George Stephen, b. Maidstone, e. London (Camberwell), 392859, Rfn., k. in a., F. & F., 16/8/17.

Fletcher, Henry William, e. London (Chelsea), 2958, L/Cpl., d. of w., F. & F., 20/9/16.

Follett, Harry Arthur, b. Croydon, e. London (Richmond), 391539, L/Cpl., k. in a., F. & F., 25/4/18.

Ford, Edgar Allen, e. Hornsey (Wood Green), 7794, Rfn., k. in a., F. & F., 9/9/16, formerly 3111, 7th Middx. Regt.

Ford, Ernest John, b. Mortimer West, Hants, e. London (St. George's), 5617, L/Cpl., d. of w., F. & F., 10/9/16.

Ford, Percy Gordon, e. London (Finchley), 3250, Rfn., k. in a., F. & F., 24/4/15.

Foster, George, e. London (Kentish Town), 393367, Rfn., d. of w., Home, 13/4/17, formerly 5167, 11th London Regt.

Foucar, Clement Auguste, b. Rangoon, India, e. London, 1931, Rfn., k. in a., F. & F., 21/4/15.

Fowler, George, b. Lambeth, e. Camberwell (Lambeth), 415014, Rfn., k. in a., F. & F., 27/9/17, formerly 5292, 10th London Regt.

Fox, Sidney Herbert, e. London (Rayleigh), 3590, Rfn., k. in a., F. & F., 31/5/16.

Foxley, Roland Rayment, b. London, e. Mill Hill (Tottenham), 394504, Rfn., d., F. & F., 4/5/18.

Foxwell, Christopher John, b. Deptford, e. London (Rotherhithe), 391974, L/Cpl., d. of w., F. & F., 1/9/18.

Frampton, Herbert Francis, b. Burnley, Lancs, e. London (Camden Town), 4849, Rfn., d., Home, 6/3/16.

Francis, Charles Edward, e. London (Peckham), 2664, L/Cpl., k. in a., F. & F., 20/9/16.

Francis, Wallace Henry, e. London (Alberbury, Salop), 393672, Cpl., d., E.E.F., 25/10/18, formerly 5536, 8th London Regt.

Franklin, George Washington, b. Poplar, e. London (Islington), 6393, Rfn., d. of w., Home, 15/2/17.

Franks, Leslie Bastin, b. Ipswich, e. London (Coulsden), 4882, L/Cpl., d. of w., F. & F., 30/7/16.

Freeman, Frederick William, b. Chatteris, e. Chatteris, 5896, Rfn., k. in a., F. & F., 25/9/16.

Freeman, George Thomas Laurence, b. Peshawar, e. Canterbury, 392542, Rfn., d. of w., F. & F., 26/4/18.

Freeman, Richard Henry Hawtin, e. London (Stanmore), 393632, Rfn., k. in a., F. & F., 24/8/18, formerly 5086, 8th London Regt.

French, Joseph James, e. London (Nr. Kilburn), 391338, Rfn., d. of w., F. & F., 20/8/17.
Friday, Edward, b. St. Pancras, e. London (Camden Town), 393369, Sgt., k. in a., F. & F., 14/4/17, formerly 1264, 11th London Regt.
Frier, David Anthony, e. Hammersmith (Westbourne Park), 5874, Rfn., k. in a., F. & F., 20/7/16.
Froment, Archibald Walter, e. London (Forest Gate), 4280, Rfn., k. in a., F. & F., 1/7/16.
Frost, Alexander William, e. London (Walthamstow), 4819, Rfn., k. in a., F. & F., 1/7/16.
Fryer, Edwin Samuel, e. London (Newington Green), 2902, Rfn., k. in a., F. & F., 18/12/14.
Fulcher, Harold Arthur, b. Hackney, e. London (S. Hackney), 392035, A/Cpl., k. in a., F. & F., 8/9/18.
Fuller, Herbert William, e. London (Highbury), 2781, Rfn., k. in a., F. & F., 1/7/16.
Furse, Maurice, e. London (Epsom), 3101, L/Cpl., k. in a., F. & F., 1/7/16.
Furst, Edward, b. Westminster, e. London (Lewisham), 5899, Rfn., d. of w., F. & F., 16/9/16.
Fusier, Victor, b. Battersea, e. London (Clapham), 1525, Rfn., k. in a., F. & F., 5/4/15.

Gabriel, Herbert Henry, e. London (Camden Town), 3540, Rfn., k. in a., F. & F., 1/7/16.
Gale, Cyril Francis, b. Shepherd's Bush, e. London (W. Kensington), 1911, Sgt., k. in a., F. & F., 9/9/16.
Galley, Ruben George Edwin, b. Walworth, e. London (Rickmansworth), 2067, Rfn., k. in a., F. & F., 1/1/15.
Gallop, Harry, b. Bristol, e. London (Tottenham), 391956, L/Cpl., k. in a., F. & F., 24/4/18.
Gammie, John Henry, b. St. John's Wood, e. London (Streatham), 5455, Rfn., k. in a., F. & F., 9/10/16.
Gardiner, Arthur Frank, e. London (Clapton), 7019, Rfn., k. in a., F. & F., 9/10/16, formerly 221, 25th London Regt.
Garratt, Hubert George, b. Tulse Hill, e. London (Streatham), 391990, Cpl., d. of w., F. & F., 25/8/18. M.M.
Garratt, Robert Charles, b. Frettenham, Norfolk, e. Norwich (Frettenham), 393661, Rfn., k. in a., F. & F., 22/11/17, formerly 5511, 8th London Regt.
Garrod, Herbert, e. London (Rochester), 3243, Sgt., k. in a., F. & F., 21/12/16.
Gathercole, Herbert Edward, e. London (Streatham), 2455, L/Cpl., d., F. & F., 26/3/16.
Gathercole, Walter, e. Norwich (Norfolk), 393047, Rfn., d. of w., F. & F., 4/5/17, formerly 24889, Norfolk Regt.

APPENDIX I 603

Gawthorn, Albert Augustus, e. London (Lewisham), 390769, Rfn., d. of w., F. & F., 28/5/17.
George, Henry William, b. Bow, e. London (Plaistow), 394343, Rfn., d. of w., F. & F., 4/5/17, formerly 6134, 12th London Regt.
Ghem, Charles Edward, b. Highbury, e. London (Highbury), 394172, Rfn., k. in a., F. & F., 17/6/17.
Gibb, George William, e. London (Earlsfield), 393933, Rfn., k. in a., F. & F., 30/10/17, formerly 3361, 10th Middx. Regt.
Gibbon, Charles Robertson, b. Edinburgh, e. London (Maida Vale), 392748, Rfn., k. in a., F. & F., 14/4/17.
Gibbons, Frederick Arthur, e. London (Paddington), 3993, Rfn., k. in a., F. & F., 1/7/16.
Gibbons, Reginald Lionel, b. Paddington, e. London (Paddington), 1053, Rfn., k. in a., F. & F., 24/4/15.
Gibbs, Alfred Arthur, b. Stanmore, e. Watford (Bushey, Herts), 394942, Rfn., d. of w., F. & F., 27/9/18.
Gidley, Geoffrey Dameral, e. London (Chiswick), 3005, L/Cpl., d. of w., F. & F., 30/5/16.
Gilders, Clifford Edward, e. London (Goodmayes), 3110, L/Cpl., k. in a., F. & F., 1/7/16.
Gill, Harry, b. Wakefield, e. London (Mile End), 394098, Rfn., d. of w., F. & F., 28/9/17.
Gillate, Geoffrey, b. Camberwell, e. London, 1957, Rfn., k. in a., F. & F., 29/4/15.
Gladman, Alfred Mitchell, b. Hackney, e. London (Dalston), 4847, Rfn., k. in a., F. & F., 9/10/16.
Gladman, Edwin John, b. Paddington, e. London (Queen's Park), 4857, Rfn., k. in a., F. & F., 9/10/16.
Glover, Frederick, e. London (Chelsea), 4632, Rfn., k. in a., F. & F., 1/7/16.
Glover, Horace, George William, e. London (Lambeth), 4789, Rfn., k. in a., F. & F., 28/5/16.
Gobener, William, e. London (Yiewsley), 3997, Cpl., k. in a., F. & F., 9/9/16.
Godier, William Edward, b. Shoreditch, e. London (Bethnal Green), 392701, Rfn., d. of w., F. & F., 17/12/17.
Golder, Spencer Kingsland, e. London (Harrow), 3345, Rfn., k. in a., F. & F., 9/9/16.
Good, Eric Arnold, e. London (Hornsey), 3853, Rfn., d. of w., F. & F., 30/5/16.
Goodfellow, Arthur, e. London (Westbourne Grove), 4121, L/Cpl., k. in a., F. & F., 1/7/16.
Goodhind, Jeffrey, e. London (Kentish Town), 391195, Rfn., k. in a., F. & F., 14/4/17.
Goodridge, Alfred Herbert, b. Camden Town, e. London (Putney), 391409, Rfn., d. of w., Home, 20/11/18.

Goodwin, Arthur Herbert, e. London (East Dulwich), 393086, Rfn., k. in a., F. & F., 29/4/17.
Goodwin, Charles, e. Woolwich (Plumstead), 393466, Rfn., k. in a., F. & F., 14/4/17, formerly 6077, 11th London Regt.
Goodworth, Cyril James, b. Islington, e. London (Highbury), 1612, Rfn., k. in a., F. & F., 21/4/15.
Gore, Harold Thomas, e. London (Brockley), 2426, Rfn., d. of w., F. & F., 27/4/15.
Gough, William, e. London (Brondesbury), 2290, Rfn., k. in a., F. & F., 5/1/15.
Gould, Frederick Henry William, e. London (Barnsbury), 392713, Rfn., d. of w., E.E.F., 2/2/18.
Gower, Lawrence, e. London (Clapham), 393600, Rfn., k. in a., F. & F., 14/4/17, formerly 6150, 11th London Regt.
Gowers, Albert Marks, b. Walthamstow, e. London (Walthamstow), 393447, Rfn., k. in a., E.E.F., 23/12/17, formerly 5663, 11th London Regt.
Grafham, James Arthur, e. Ashford (Egham, Surrey), 392841, Rfn., d. of w., F. & F., 22/3/17.
Graham, Herbert Henry, b. Crockenhill, e. London (Crockenhill), 391870, Cpl., d. of w., Home, 31/5/18.
Graham, Sydney Harold, e. London (Turner's Hill), 3734, Rfn., d. of w., F. & F., 6/7/16.
Gray, Arthur Stanley, e. London (Cookham, Berks), 4303, Rfn., k. in a., F. & F., 14/9/16.
Gray, Edward, James, e. London (Marylebone), 2698, Rfn., d. of w., F. & F., 1/5/15.
Gray, John Charles, b. Hammersmith, e. London (Pimlico), 391939, Rfn., k. in a., F. & F., 15/4/18.
Green, Cyril John, b. Wimbledon, e. London (Wimbledon), 7538, Rfn., k. in a., F. & F., 9/9/16, formerly 5421, 8th London Regt.
Green, Edward Oscar, e. Colchester (Mersea), 392922, Rfn., k. in a., F. & F., 24/12/17, formerly 2899, Essex Regt.
Green, Henry Peter, e. London (Marylebone), 3923, Rfn., d. of w., F. & F., 29/5/16.
Green, John Arthur, b. Brockley, e. London (Neasden), 1945, L/Cpl., k. in a., F. & F., 1/7/16.
Green, Stanley Frederick, b. Lincoln, e. Peterborough (Peterborough), 394429, Rfn., k. in a., F. & F., 9/4/18.
Green, Walter John, b. Brighton, e. London (Sydenham), 391383, Rfn., d. of w., F. & F., 8/9/17.
Greenland, Sidney, b. Islington, e. London (Holloway), 394174, Rfn., k. in a., F. & F., 24/4/18.
Greenleaf, Godfrey Charles, b. Southampton, e. London (Lambeth), 1854, Rfn., k. in a., F. & F., 21/4/15.
Gregory, Albert James, e. London (Addlestone), 3871, Rfn., k. in a., F. & F., 1/7/16.

APPENDIX I

Gretton, Douglas, Wilfred, e. London (Goodmayes), 2401, Rfn., k. in a., F. & F., 1/7/16.
Griffiths, William Henry, e. London (St. George's), 392284, Rfn., k. in a., F. & F., 26/5/17.
Guilfoy, John, b. Clapham, e. London (Battersea), 392195, Rfn., k. in a., F. & F., 16/8/17.
Gunnell, Archibald Cecil, b. Windsor, e. London (Watford), 1745, Rfn., d., F. & F., 15/7/15.
Gunnell, Arthur Revely Williams, e. London (Chiswick), 2760, Rfn., k. in a., F. & F., 1/7/16.
Gunnell, George Alfred James, b. Nunhead, e. London (Harringay), 392074, Rfn., k. in a., F. & F., 3/9/17.
Gunning, William Henry, b. Bethnal Green, e. London (St. Luke's), 392847, Rfn., k. in a., F. & F., 1/12/17.
Gurney, Henry Thomas, e. Hornsey (Wood Green), 7788, L/Sgt., k. in a., F. & F., 9/9/16, formerly 3257, 7th Middx. Regt.

Hagen, Charles Macdonald, e. London (Maida Vale), 4070, Rfn., k. in a., F. & F., 1/7/16.
Hagger, Harold, e. Peterboro (Chelmsford), 393007, Rfn., k. in a., F. & F., 24/3/17, formerly 3366, Essex Regt.
Haines, Charles Samuel, b. Lambeth, e. London (Kennington), 4356, Rfn., k. in a., F. & F., 9/9/16.
Haines, William, e. London (Walworth), 391594, Rfn., k. in a., F. & F., 16/8/17.
Hairby, Frank, e. London (Croydon), 3844, Rfn., k. in a., F. & F., 1/7/16.
Hale, Frederick Thomas, e. London (Leytonstone), 2466, Rfn., k. in a., F. & F., 21/4/15.
Hall, Charles James Howard, e. London (Regent's Park), 4601, Rfn., d. of w., F. & F., 2/7/16.
Hall, Henry Stewart, e. London (Brixton), 3288, Cpl., d., F. & F., 12/2/17.
Hall, Stanley Alfred, e. London (Forest Hill), 3368, Rfn., k. in a., F. & F., 24/4/15.
Hallett, Frank William Marmaduke, e. London (Brondesbury), 3885, Rfn., k. in a., F. & F., 27/5/15.
Halls, Frederick James, e. London (Silvertown), 393468, Rfn., k. in a., F. & F., 14/4/17, formerly 5578, 11th London Regt.
Halse, Horace Leslie, b. Stoke Newington, e. London (Ealing), 1438, Rfn., k. in a., F. & F., 9/9/16.
Hammerton, Charles William, b. Windsor, e. London (Windsor), 5335, Rfn., k. in a., F. & F., 9/10/16.
Hancock, Ernest James, b. Camberwell, e. London (Brockley), 393693, Rfn., d. of w., F. & F., 29/12/17, formerly 5588, 8th London Regt.
Hancock, Frederick Martin, e. London (Harlesden), 390375, Rfn., k. in a., F. & F., 14/4/17.

Handley, Wilfred, b. Hull, Yorks, e. London (Neasden), 1942, Rfn., k. in a., F. & F., 1/7/16.
Hanks, Percy George, e. London (Hornsey), 7906, Rfn., d. of w., F. & F., 10/9/16, formerly 2494, 10th Middx. Regt.
Hannam, William Alfred, e. London (St. George's), 4528, Rfn., k. in a., F. & F., 1/7/16.
Harding, James, e. London (Prescott), 415233, Rfn., k. in a., F. & F., 27/9/18, formerly 5280, 8th London Regt.
Hardwick, Donald Oscar, e. London (Leyton), 391048, L/Cpl., d. of w., F. & F., 2/5/17.
Hardwick, Frank Alfred, b. Harringay, e. London (Bowes Park), 1472, L/Cpl., k. in a., F. & F., 21/4/15.
Harman, Reginald John, b. Betchworth, e. London, 1655, Rfn., k. in a., F. & F., 1/7/16.
Harrington, Henry Charles, e. London (Westminster), 2716, Rfn., k. in a., F. & F., 1/7/16.
Harris, Delme Alfred, e. London (London), 4810, Rfn., k. in a., F. & F., 1/7/16.
Harris, Gilbert Norwood, e. London (Ealing), 2830, Rfn., k. in a., F. & F., 1/7/16.
Harris, Oscar Jeffrey, e. London (Tufnell Park), 7643, Rfn., k. in a., F. & F., 26/1/17, formerly 5673, 8th London Regt.
Harris, Reginald, e. London (Hounslow), 4867, Rfn., k. in a., F. & F., 1/7/16.
Harrison, Herbert, e. Norwich (Fakenham), 6651, Rfn., k. in a., F. & F., 13/11/16, formerly 24555, Norfolk Regt.
Harrison, William Septimus, b. Byker, Newcastle, e. Newcastle (Heaton), 7552, Rfn., k. in a., F. & F., 9/10/16, formerly 5464, 8th London Regt.
Harrold, Samuel Henry, e. London (Battersea), 4513, L/Cpl., k. in a., F. & F., 1/7/16.
Hart, Harold George, b. Collingham, Newark, e. London (Richmond), 1767, Rfn., k. in a., F. & F., 7/1/15.
Hartwright, Harold Ivor Vincent, b. Guildford, e. London (St. George's), 391903, Rfn., k. in a., F. & F., 27/9/17.
Harvey, Francis Philpott, e. London (Highbury), 390544, L/Sgt., k. in a., F. & F., 27/9/17.
Harvey, John Delby Alexander, e. London (Dulwich), 2967, Rfn., k. in a., F. & F., 1/7/16.
Harvey, Thomas Brown Jackson, b. Hampstead, e. London (Stoke Newington), 394143, Rfn., k. in a., F. & F., 13/6/17.
Haskey, George Thomas, e. London (Barnsbury), 415290, Rfn., k. in a., F. & F., 4/11/18, formerly 375609, 8th London Regt.
Hassett, Ernest Edwin, e. London (Golder's Green), 2565, Sgt., k. in a., F. & F., 1/7/16.
Hatcher, Edward William, e. London (Thornton Heath), 3442, L/Cpl., k. in a., F. & F., 1/7/16.

APPENDIX I

Hawker, Thomas George, b. Camberwell, e. London (Islington), 415274, Rfn., k. in a., F. & F., 23/9/18, formerly 8357, 18th London Regt.
Hawkins, George, e. London (Gosport), 393622, L/Sgt., d. of w., F. & F., 26/8/17, formerly 5034, 8th London Regt.
Hawkins, Hermin Archibald, b. Islington, e. Paris (Paris), 392552, Rfn., k. in a., F. & F., 16/8/17.
Hayman, Harold Watts, e. London (Cheshunt), 3754, Rfn., k. in a., F. & F., 1/7/16.
Haynes, Alexander George, e. Hackney (Dalston), 394347, Rfn., k. in a., F. & F., 3/5/17, formerly 6174, 12th London Regt.
Hayter, Percy Frank, b. Islington, e. London (Islington), 393368, W.O., Class 2, d. of w., F. & F., 20/8/17, formerly 144, 11th London Regt.
Hazzard, Reginald, Stephen, b. Twickenham, e. London (Knightsbridge), 1613, Rfn., k. in a., F. & F., 1/7/16.
Head, Arthur Ernest, e. London (Teddington), 393905, Cpl., k. in a., F. & F., 14/4/17, formerly 3786, 8th Middx. Regt.
Heal, William Thomas, b. Camberwell, e. London (Camberwell), 394046, Rfn., d. of w., F. & F., 21/10/17.
Hedges, Alfred Joseph, e. London (Bayswater), 391771, Rfn., k. in a., F. & F., 26/9/17.
Hedges, Arthur James, e. London (Pimlico), 4460, Rfn., k. in a., F. & F., 1/7/16.
Hedges, Harry, b. Marylebone, e. London (Queen's Park), 392798, Rfn., d. of w., F. & F., 8/9/18.
Heir, William John Henry, b. Islington, e. Fulham (Islington), 5941, Rfn., d., Home, 9/4/16, formerly 320, 26th London Regt.
Heis, Henry, b. East Ham, e. London (Upper Clapton), 393695, Rfn., k. in a., F. & F., 2/12/17, formerly 5591, 8th London Regt.
Hemsley, Laurence George, e. London (Twickenham), 2548, L/Cpl., d. of w., F. & F., 1/6/16.
Henderson, Thomas Thorpe, b. Kentish Town, e. London (Cricklewood), 392214, L/Cpl., d. of w., F. & F., 3/9/18.
Henry, Leslie, b. Clapham, e. London (Kennington), 2137, Rfn., k. in a., F. & F., 2/10/16.
Herbert, Charles, b. Twyford, e. London (Wargrave), 391831, Rfn., k. in a., F. & F., 26/9/17.
Herford, Francis Mackay, e. London (Golder's Green), 2294, Rfn., k. in a., F. & F., 24/4/15.
Hermann, Julius, e. London (Whitechapel), 6874, Rfn., k. in a., F. & F., 25/9/16, formerly 2269, R.A.S.C.
Herron, William Arthur, b. St. Pancras, e. London (Wembley), 4520, Rfn., k. in a., F. & F., 9/10/16.
Hersant, Stanley James, b. St. Pancras, e. London (St. Pancras), 394047, Rfn., k. in a., F. & F., 25/8/18.
Hewitt, James, e. London (Dilworth) 393715, Rfn., k. in a., F. & F., 3/5/17, formerly 5665, 8th London Regt.

Hickman, Francis, e. Bocking, 6727, Rfn., k. in a., F. & F., 9/10/16, formerly 3474, Essex Regt.
Hickman, Frank Henry Charles, e. London (Leytonstone), 2117, Sgt., k. in a., F. & F., 1/7/16. M.M.
Higgins, Tom, b. Pontypool, e. Pontypool (Pontnewydd), 419041, Rfn., k. in a., F. & F., 24/9/18, formerly 3274, 2nd Mon. Regt.
Higgins, William John, b. St. Luke's, London, e. London (Islington), 415272, Rfn., k. in a., F. & F., 25/8/18, formerly 5769, 18th London Regt.
Higgs, Francis William, e. London (King's Cross), 391312, Rfn., d. of w., F. & F., 30/11/17.
High, Walter Henry, e. London (Maida Vale), 393542, Rfn., d. at Sea, 30/12/17.
Hilburn, Laurance Geoffrey, e. London (Chiswick), 4387, Rfn., k. in a., F. & F., 1/7/16.
Hill, Francis William, b. Birmingham, e. London (Shepherd's Bush), 1916, Rfn., k. in a., F. & F., 24/4/15.
Hill, Victor George, e. London (Hammersmith), 390772, L/Sgt., k. in a., F. & F., 25/8/18.
Hillier, Harry Thomas, e. Camberwell (W. Norwood), 392866, Rfn., d. of w., F. & F., 13/5/17.
Hindry, Albert William, e. London (Marylebone), 4043, Rfn., k. in a., F. & F., 1/7/16.
Hinkins, Harry, e. Bermondsey, 394018, Rfn., k. in a., F. & F., 6/11/18.
Hitchcock, Charles Edward, b. Deptford, e. Deptford, 392708, Rfn., k. in a., F. & F., 25/8/18.
Hobbs, John Edward, e. London (Holloway), 394293, Rfn., k. in a., F. & F., 14/4/17, formerly 6048, 12th London Regt.
Hobrough, Alfred Charles, e. Colchester (Colchester), 6765, Rfn., k. in a., F. & F., 9/10/16, formerly 3159, 5th Essex Regt.
Hobson, William, b. Sheffield, e. Seaford (Carlisle), 393785, Rfn., d. of w., F. & F., 13/8/17, formerly 23934, Border Regt.
Hodnett, Edwin Roy, e. London (Ilford), 3801, Rfn., d. of w., F. & F., 1/7/16.
Hodson, George Frederick, e. London (Reading), 4678, Rfn., d. of w., F. & F., 2/7/16.
Hoellen, Alfred Ernest, b. Fulham, e. London (Fulham), 1259, L/Cpl., d. of w., F. & F., 5/1/15.
Hogben, Stephen Henry, b. Camden Town, e. London, 392527, Rfn., k. in a., F. & F., 27/9/18.
Holes, Alfred Edward, b. Stevenage, e. Eastleigh (Stevenage), 419016, Rfn., k. in a., F. & F., 25/4/18, formerly 2152, R.A.M.C.
Holland, William, e. Hornsey (Hornsey), 393855, Rfn., d. of w., F. & F., 24/4/17, formerly 4867, 7th Middx. Regt.
Hollingshead, William, b. Paddington, e. London (Edgware Rd.), 390005, L/Cpl., k. in a., F. & F., 19/7/18.

Holloway, Alfred Carl Richard John, b. London, e. London (Stanford), 391418, Cpl., k. in a., F. & F., 8/9/18.
Holmes, Samuel Creighton, e. London (Paddington), 391652, Rfn., d. of w., F. & F., 30/3/17.
Holt, Edmond, b. Halifax, e. London (Kennington), 391980, L/Cpl., k. in a., F. & F., 26/9/17.
Holt, Thomas, b. Littleborough, e. London (Stratford), 392290, Rfn., k. in a., F. & F., 8/7/17.
Honess, Frederick, b. Tunbridge Wells, e. London (Clapham), 392853, Rfn., k. in a., F. & F., 14/4/17.
Honiatt, William Frederick, b. Shepherd's Bush, e. London (Shepherd's Bush), 391657, Rfn., k. in a., F. & F., 20/5/18.
Hook, Henry Preston, e. London (Bexley Heath), 3352, Rfn., k. in a., F. & F., 1/7/16.
Hooker, Henry Arthur, b. High Barnet, e. London (Hanwell), 4488, Rfn., k. in a., F. & F., 1/7/16.
Hooper, Charles Edwin, b. Plumstead, e. London (Manor Park), 393543, Rfn., k. in a., F. & F., 16/8/17.
Hooper, Frederick Arthur, e. London (St. John's Wood), 2349, L/Sgt., k. in a., F. & F., 31/5/15.
Hooper, Sydney John, b. Plumstead, e. London (St. John's Wood), 391837, L/Cpl., k. in a., F. & F., 23/9/17. M.M.
Hopkin, Thomas Frank, e. Woolwich (Harlesden), 6103, Rfn., d. of w., F. & F., 24/1/17.
Hopkins, Reginald Thomas, b. Northbrook, Worcester, e. London (Barnes), 1824, Rfn., d. of w., F. & F., 5/1/15.
Hopkinson, William Ewart, e. London (E. Sheen), 3386, L/Cpl., d. of w., F. & F., 6/6/15.
Horne, Stanley Frank, e. London (Palmer's Green,) 3095, Rfn., d. of w., F. & F., 27/4/15.
Hoskin, William, e. London (Lee), 2351, Rfn., k. in a., F. & F., 6/3/15.
How, William John, e. London (Stepney), 393724, Rfn., d. of w., F. & F., 17/4/17, formerly 5702, 8th London Regt.
Howard, Alfred, e. London (Kilburn), 390335, Rfn., k. in a., F. & F, 14/4/17.
Howard, Thomas Lionel, e. London (Clapham), 3656, Rfn., k. in a., F. & F., 30/5/16.
Howell, Walter, e. Chelmsford (Tooting), 6773, Rfn., d. of w., F. & F., 30/9/16, formerly 3175, Essex Regt.
Howlett, James Henry, e. London (Uxbridge), 392212, Rfn., k. in a., F. & F., 14/4/17.
Howlett, Percy Alfred, e. Putney (High Wycombe), 393244, Rfn., k. in a., F. & F., 14/4/17, formerly 2163, 25th London Regt.
Hubbard, Stanley William, e. Camberwell, (Herne Hill), 394704, Rfn., k. in a., F. & F., 1/9/18.
Hudson, Charles, e. Woolwich (Woolwich), 7709, L/Cpl., k. in a., F. & F., 24/1/17, formerly 5143, 20th London Regt.

Hudson, John, e. London (Putney), 392437, Rfn., k. in a., F. & F., 14/4/17.
Hughes, George Wacker, e. London (Kensington), 393176, Rfn., k. in a., F. & F., 22/9/17.
Hughes, Herbert Stanley, b. Shepherd's Bush, e. London (Hammersmith), 394401, Rfn., k. in a., F. & F., 24/4/18.
Hulett, Arthur Henry, b. U.S.A., e. London (Old Ford), 6009, Rfn., k. in a., F. & F., 23/12/16.
Hull, Bertram, b. Studham, Bedford, e. Bedford (Studham), 7910, Rfn., k. in a., F. & F., 9/10/16, formerly 3/8739, Bedford Regt.
Humberstone, Frederick George, b. Kilburn, e. London (Notting Hill), 6699, Rfn., d. of w., F. & F., 5/10/16, formerly 6700, Essex Regt.
Humphrey, Gerald Henry, e. Hornsey (Finsbury), 393865, Sgt., k. in a., F. & F., 13/10/18, formerly 5037, 7th Middx. Regt.
Hunt, Charles, b. St. Mark's, e. London, 4306, Rfn., k. in a., F. & F., 9/10/16.
Hunt, James, b. Westminster, e. Fulham (Kennington), 393281, Rfn., k. in a., F. & F., 16/8/17, formerly 1987, 25th London Regt.
Hunter, Frederick Charles, e. London (St. George's), 3998, Rfn., k. in a., F. & F., 1/7/16.
Huntley, Frank Morley, b. Lambeth, e. Camberwell (Clapham), 393151, Rfn., k. in a., F. & F., 3/5/17.
Hurle, Thomas Henry, b. Southwark, e. London (Walham Green), 391839, Rfn., d. of w., F. & F., 30/4/18.
Hurley, Isaac, e. Kingston-on Thames (Kennington), 395088, Rfn. d. of w., F. & F., 25/8/18.
Hurling, Herbert William, b. Lincoln, e. Mill Hill (Finchley), 415248, Rfn., d. of w., F. & F., 14/8/17.
Hussey, Albert Alfred, b. Walworth, e. Camberwell (Loughborough), 394193, Rfn., k. in a., F. & F., 27/9/17, formerly 6564, 11th London Regt.
Hutchings, Henry James, e. London (Seven Kings), 391149, L/Sgt., k. in a., F. & F., 25/8/18. M.M.
Hutchinson, Alfred James, b. Islington, e. Camberwell (Brixton), 393954, Rfn., k. in a., F. & F., 26/9/17.
Hutchison, Edwin Douglas, e. Camberwell (East Dulwich), 393142, Rfn., k. in a., F. & F., 13/8/17.
Hyde, Edward Henry, e. Stratford (East Ham), 7389, Rfn., k. in a., F. & F., 24/1/17, formerly 6044, 11th London Regt.
Hyde, Harold Frederick, e. Ealing (Hanwell), 7900, Rfn., k. in a., F. & F., 9/10/16, formerly 4831, 8th Middx. Regt.
Hyde, Oswald Charles Bird, b. Paddington, e. London (W. Hampstead), 4955, Rfn., d. of w., F. & F., 19/10/16.
Hygate, Richard, e. Camberwell (E. Dulwich), 393571, Rfn., k. in a., F. & F., 3/5/17, formerly 6434, 12th London Regt.

APPENDIX I 611

Hymes, John S., e. London (Brixton), 394311, Rfn., d. of w., F. & F., 29/5/17, formerly 4468, 12th London Regt.
Hyne, Sidney Frank, b. Mill Hill, e. London (Hendon), 7511, Rfn., k. in a., F. & F., 9/10/16, formerly 4577, 8th London Regt.

Igglesden, Albert Charles Henry, e. London (Streatham), 390456, L/Cpl., k. in a., F. & F., 21/9/18.
Inwards, Victor Joseph, e. London (Kennington), 390948, L/Cpl., k. in a., F. & F., 23/9/18.
Isaac, Ernest William, b. Westminster, e. London (Marylebone), 394312, Rfn., k. in a., F. & F., 30/10/17, formerly 5293, 12th London Regt.
Ives, Arthur Frank, e. London (Edmonton), 2800, A/Cpl., d. of w., F. & F., 31/5/16.

Jackman, Richard Washington, b. Finsbury, e. London (Islington), 415170, Rfn., k. in a., F. & F., 16/8/17, formerly 6579, 10th London Regt.
Jackson, Edward, e. London (Edmonton), 2357, Rfn., k. in a., F. & F., 23/10/15.
Jackson, Frederick George, e. Frinton-on-Sea (Kirby Cross), 392931, Rfn., k. in a., F. & F., 14/4/17, formerly 3189, Essex Regt.
Jackson, Harold Edward, e. London (Harrow), 390748, Cpl., k. in a., F. & F., 14/4/17.
Jackson, William Frederick, e. London (Camden Town), 391379, Rfn., k. in a., F. & F., 24/5/17.
Jacomb, Frederick, e. London (Mortlake), 391428, Rfn., d. of w., F. & F., 30/12/17.
James, Jerald, e. London (Newbridge), 393628, Rfn., k. in a., F. & F., 16/8/17, formerly 5051, 8th London Regt.
Jamieson, Ernest, b. Hornsey, e. London (Queen's Park), 1551, Rfn., d. of w., F. & F., 13/5/15.
Jannings, George Herbert, e. London (Cricklewood), 2205, Rfn., d. of w., F. & F., 2/3/15.
Jarvis, Frank, b. Sheerness, e. London (E. Dulwich), 4991, Rfn., k. in a., F. & F., 9/10/16.
Jarvis, Victor George, b. Clerkenwell, e. London (Clerkenwell), 393382, Rfn., d. of w., F. & F., 26/4/18, formerly 1545, 11th London Regt.
Jaundrill, William George, b. Chelsea, e. Camberwell (Battersea), 7579, Rfn., k. in a., F. & F., 9/9/16, formerly 5521, 8th London Regt.
Jeeves, Frank Cyril, e. London (Epsom), 4062, Rfn., k. in a., F. & F., 1/7/16.
Jefferies, Walter Henry George, e. London (Willesden), 3610, Rfn., k. in a., F. & F., 1/7/16.
Jefferson, Alfred, e. London (Willesden), 390353, Rfn., k. in a., F. & F., 15/7/18.

Jeffery, Herbert William, e. London (Tottenham), 391217, Sgt., k. in a., F. & F., 27/9/17.
Jellyman, Herbert William, b. Cannock, e. London (Cannock, Staffs), 5859, Rfn., d. of w., F. & F., 24/9/16.
Jenkins, Walter Joseph, e. London (Shepherd's Bush), 7880, Rfn., k. in a., F. & F., 9/9/16, formerly 2919, 10th Middx. Regt.
Jennings, George Henry, e. London (Kentish Town), 3542, Rfn., k. in a., F. & F., 1/7/16.
Jennings, Sidney Neville, b. Clapham, e. London (Loughborough Park,) 1811, A/Cpl., d., Home, 9/8/15.
Jermy, Robert, b. Blofield, e. Norwich (Baconsthorpe), 392969, Rfn., k. in a., F. & F., 4/7/18, formerly 24381, Norfolk Regt.
Jervis, Francis, b. Hampstead, e. London (W. Hampstead), 810, A/Cpl., d. of w., F. & F., 6/3/15.
Jessep, George Davie, e. London (Tufnell Park), 3472, Rfn., k. in a., F. & F., 1/7/16.
Jessup, Frederick Ernest, e. London (Stoke Newington), 4246, L/Sgt., k. in a., F. & F., 9/9/16.
Johnson, Arthur Fanner, b. Forest Gate, e. London (Leytonstone), 394294, Rfn., k. in a., F. & F., 14/4/17, formerly 5740, 12th London Regt.
Johnson, Guy Frank, e. London (Regent's Park), 392131, Rfn., d. of w., F. & F., 17/4/17.
Johnson, Harry, b. Southwark, e. Camberwell (Bermondsey), 394024, Rfn., k. in a., F. & F., 26/9/17.
Joiner, Charles, e. London (Nelson's Square), 3857, Rfn., k. in a., F. & F., 24/4/15.
Jolley, Leslie Harold, b. Cambridge, e. London (Walham Green), 1960, Sgt., k. in a., F. & F., 1/7/16.
Jones, Stephen James, b. Wandsworth, e. London (Streatham), 4698, Rfn., d. of w., F. & F., 29/9/16.
Joy, George Thomas, b. Finsbury, e. London (Holborn), 392085, Rfn., d. of w., F. & F., 31/5/17.
Joyce, John George, e. London (Battersea), 393109, Rfn., k. in a., F. & F., 3/5/17, formerly 6862, 9th London Regt.
Jupp, William Thomas, e. London, 391058, Rfn., k. in a., F. & F., 24/8/18.

Kedgley, Arthur William, b. Islington, e. London (Balham), 4774, L/Cpl., k. in a., F. & F., 9/9/16.
Kellaway, Henry William, b. Portsmouth, e. London (Streatham), 4401, Rfn., k. in a., F. & F., 9/10/16.
Kelleher, Frederick, b. Marylebone, e. London (St. John's Wood), 391525, Rfn., k. in a., F. & F., 28/8/18.
Kelly, James, e. London (Holloway), 394295, Rfn., k. in a., F. & F., 14/4/17, formerly 6149, 12th London Regt.
Kemp, Robert Oscar, b. Colchester, e. Colchester (Colchester), 6657, Rfn., d. of w., F. & F., 28/9/16, formerly 2125, 5th Essex Regt.

APPENDIX I

Kempe, Charles Brett, e. London (Finchley), 3319, Rfn., d. of w., F. & F., 2/7/16.
Kerr, Oliver, John Whiston, e. London (Harlesden), 2790, Rfn., k. in a., F. & F., 1/7/16.
Kettle, Alfred, b. Millwall, e. London (Stepney), 394183, Rfn., d. of w., Home, 20/9/17, formerly 7010, 11th London Regt.
Kettle, William George Burnet, e. London (Acton), 2435, Rfn., k. in a., F. & F., 1/7/16.
Kevan, Frederick Joseph, b. Cheshire, e. London (Feltham), 393670, Rfn., k. in a., F. & F., 3/9/17, formerly 5531, 8th London Regt.
Kew, William James, e. London (Canonbury), 392245, Rfn., k. in a., F. & F., 3/5/17.
Kibbey, Robert Edwin, b. S. America, e. London (Forest Gate), 392321, Rfn., k. in a., F. & F., 22/9/18.
Kidby, Arthur, e. London (Hoddesdon, Herts), 2894, Rfn., k. in a., F. & F., 3/3/15.
Kidby, George Frederick, e. London (Hoddesdon), 391267, Rfn., d. of w., F. & F., 30/8/18.
Kiely, Thomas Daniel, e. London (Lambeth), 6527, Rfn., k. in a., F. & F., 22/1/17.
Kight, Douglas, e. London (Earl's Court), 4347, Rfn., k. in a., F. & F., 1/7/16.
Kimmons, Percy Reginald, b. Norfolk, e. Norwich (Wisbech), 6655, Rfn., k. in a., F. & F., 9/10/16, formerly 24487, Norfolk Regt.
King, Charles Henry, b. Teddington, e. Camberwell (Upper Norwood), 393717, Rfn., k. in a., F. & F., 14/8/17, formerly 5670, 8th London Regt.
King, Ernest, e. Brightlingsea, 392995, Rfn., k. in a., F. & F., 17/6/17.
King, Ernest Edward, b. Hammersmith, e. London (Norwood), 393716, Rfn., k. in a., F. & F., 14/4/17, formerly 5669, 8th London Regt.
King, Frank Walter, e. Fulham (Clapham), 7066, Rfn., k. in a., F. & F., 9/10/16, formerly 2024, 25th London Regt.
King, John Frederick, b. Lambeth, e. London (Norwood), 390127, Rfn., k. in a., F. & F., 17/6/17.
King, John Wilfred, b. Clapham, e. London (Clapham), 1256, Rfn., d. of w., F. & F., 27/4/15.
King, Reginald William, b. Leeds, e. London (Leeds), 391834, L/Cpl., k. in a., F. & F., 27/9/17.
Kingham, Leslie, b. Finchley, e. London (Finchley), 7640, Rfn., k. in a., F. & F., 25/9/16, formerly 5667, 8th London Regt.
Kingsbury, Clarence, b. St. Paul's, e. Halstead (Halstead), 6610, Rfn., k. in a., F. & F., 9/10/16, formerly 2020, Essex Regt.
Kingston, George William, e. London (Uxbridge), 392220, Rfn., k. in a., F. & F., 14/4/17.
Kirby, George Harry Edgar, b. Marylebone, e. London (London), 1485, Cpl., k. in a., F. & F., 9/10/16.

Kirkby, George William, e. Fulham (Wandsworth), 393245, Rfn.,
k. in a., F. & F., 14/4/17, formerly 3083, 25th London Regt.
Kirsch, Cecil, e. London (Walthamstow), 2400, Rfn., k. in a., F. &
F., 3/4/15.
Kissane, John, e. London (Stoke Newington), 393707, Rfn., d. of w.,
F. & F., 4/5/17, formerly 5643, 8th London Regt.
Kleiner, David, b. Russia, e. Hounslow (Fulham), 395147, Rfn.,
k. in a., F. & F., 24/4/18.
Kneale, William Carran, b. Ramsay, I. of M., e. London, 1547, Rfn.,
d. of w., F. & F., 5/1/15.
Knight, Alfred Henry, e. London (Chelsea), 4523, Rfn., d. of w.,
F. & F., 21/9/16.
Knight, John, e. Tallow (Tallow), 393611, Rfn., k. in a., formerly,
8299, 9th London Regt.
Knight, William, b. Smisby, Derby, e. Burton-on-Trent (Burton-on-Trent), 394096, Rfn., k. in a., F. & F., 13/8/17, formerly
8299, 9th London Regt.
Knowles, Edward, e. London (Paddington), 391290, Rfn., d. of w.,
F. & F., 1/10/17.

Lahee, Terence, b. Enfield, e. London (Winchmore Hill), 1984, Cpl.,
k. in a., F. & F., 1/7/16.
Lambert, Ambrose, e. London (St. Paul's Churchyard), 2226, Cpl.,
k. in a., F. & F., 9/9/16.
Lambert, Christopher, e. London (Ramsgate), 391784, Rfn., k. in a.,
F. & F., 14/4/17, formerly 4909, 9th London Regt.
Lane, Walter Ernest, e. London (King's Cross), 392721, Rfn., k. in
a., F. & F., 14/4/17, formerly 6408, 9th London Regt.
Langford, James, e. London (Hindley), 7504, Rfn., d. of w., F. & F.,
3/10/16, formerly 4064, 8th London Regt.
Langston, Leslie Charles, e. London (Ealing), 3949, Rfn., k. in a.,
F. & F., 1/7/16.
Lanston, Robert Frederick, b. Holloway, e. London (Holloway),
7537, Rfn., k. in a., F. & F., 2/10/16, formerly 5413, 8th London
Regt.
Lapworth, Charles Werrell, b. Paddington, e. London (Paddington),
391348, Rfn., k. in a., F. & F., 26/9/17, formerly 4142, 9th
London Regt.
Larkin, Reginald Harry, e. London (S. Croydon), 2890, Rfn., k. in a.,
F. & F., 1/7/16.
Lathan, Arthur Herbert, b. Heigham, Norfolk, e. Norwich (Norwich), 6662, Rfn., k. in a., F. & F., 9/10/16, formerly 23898,
Norfolk Regt.
Laurence, Harry George, b. Marylebone, e. London (St. John's
Wood), 392456, Rfn., d. of w., F. & F., 16/8/17, formerly 5986,
9th London Regt.
Lawrence, Ernest Arthur, e. London, 392320, Rfn., k. in a., F. &
F., 26/5/17, formerly 5819, 9th London Regt.

APPENDIX I

Lawrence, William Stephen, b. Wantage, e. London (Chelsea), 393355, Cpl., k. in a., F. & F., 15/6/17, formerly 5204, 11th London Regt.

Lay, George, e. London (Hammersmith), 7369, Rfn., k. in a., F. & F., 24/1/17, formerly 6032, 11th London Regt.

Laycock, Benjamin Herbert, e. London (Westbourne Grove), 4575, Rfn., k. in a., F. & F., 1/7/16.

Laycock, William Morris, b. Islington, e. Wood Green (Palmer's Green), 394616, Rfn., k. in a., F. & F., 1/9/18.

Layland, George James, b. Cheshire, e. London (Fulham), 1871, Rfn., d., F. & F., 20/7/16.

Leach, James Richard, e. Camberwell (Peckham), 393605, Rfn., k. in a., F. & F., 14/4/17, formerly 6192, 11th London Regt.

Leach, William Nesbeth, b. Brixton, e. London, 390149, A/L/Cpl., k. in a., F. & F., 21/9/18, formerly 1739, 9th London Regt.

Leaver, Thomas Clinch, e. London (Westminster), 3565, Rfn., k. in a., F. & F., 25/9/16.

Lee, Edward, e. Canning Town (Canning Town), 415146, Rfn., k. in a., F. & F., 16/8/17, formerly 5221, 10th London Regt.

Lee, Harry Watson, b. Worcester, e. London, 390243, Rfn., k. in a., F. & F., 11/4/17, formerly 1964, 9th London Regt.

Lee, Henry Joseph, b. Upton Park, e. Hackney (Walthamstow), 415063, Rfn., k. in a., F. & F., 7/11/17, formerly 6041, 12th London Regt.

Lee, William Oscar, b. Norwich, e. Norwich (Norwich), 6663, Rfn., k. in a., F. & F., 9/10/16, formerly 24330, Norfolk Regt.

Leech, Edmund James, b. Homerton, e. Stratford (Manor Park), 394486, Rfn., k. in a., F. & F., 21/9/18.

Leech, William Leonard Boghurst, e. London (W. Ealing), 3407, Rfn., d. of w., Home, 14/5/15.

Leon, Charles Henry, b. Kensington, e. London (Barnsbury), 392789, Rfn., k. in a., F. & F., 8/8/18, formerly 6486, 9th London Regt.

Lester, Alfred Edward, b. London, e. London (East Ham), 2749, Rfn., d. of w., Home, 21/12/16.

Lester, Charles Thomas, e. London (Harrow), 4197, Rfn., k. in a., F. & F., 9/10/16.

Leverington, James, e. London (Nunhead), 4577, Rfn., k. in a., F. & F., 1/7/16.

Leverson, David Edward, e. London (S. Tottenham), 3272, L/Cpl., k. in a., F. & F., 1/7/16.

Le Voi, Edward, b. Kilburn, e. London, 1581, Rfn., k. in a., F. & F., 9/9/16.

Levy, Daniel, b. Finsbury, e. London (King's Cross), 4947, Rfn., k. in a., F. & F., 9/10/16.

Levy, Godfrey, e. Stratford (Notting Hill), 415193, Rfn., k. in a., F. & F., 22/12/17, formerly 5570, 17th London Regt.

616 QUEEN VICTORIA'S RIFLES

Lewington, Edmund, e. Stratford (Plaistow), 7392, Rfn., k. in a., F. & F., 24/1/17, formerly 6144, 11th London Regt.
Lewis, Arthur, b. Hammersmith, e. London (S. Kensington), 392028, Rfn., k. in a., F. & F., 27/9/17, formerly 5267, 9th London Regt.
Lewis, Harold, e. Camberwell (Peckham), 393545, Rfn., d. of w., F. & F., 29/11/17, formerly 6190, 11th London Regt.
Lewis, John, e. London, 415042, Rfn., k. in a., F. & F., 14/4/17, formerly 5643, 12th London Regt.
Lewis, Richard Frank, e. London (New Cross), 2513, L/Cpl., k. in a., F. & F., 1/7/16.
Lewis, Victor Hudson, e. London (Shepherd's Bush), 3822, Rfn., k. in a., F. & F., 1/7/16.
Lewsey, George, e. London (Paddington), 4541, Rfn., k. in a., F. & F., 1/7/16.
Lewthwaite, Stanley Basil, b. Didcot, e. London (Willesden), 391975, Rfn., d. of w., F. & F., 22/7/17, formerly 5184, 9th London Regt.
Lightfoot, Sydney Herbert, e. London (Sutton), 2494, Rfn., k. in a., F. & F., 9/9/16.
Lilley, John, b. Ashstead, e. London, 391973, Rfn., k. in a., F. & F., 27/9/17, formerly 5181, 9th London Regt.
Linton, John Henry, b. Seaton, e. Whitehaven (Workington), 7740, L/Cpl., k. in a., F. & F., 26/12/16, formerly 23839, Border Regt.
Lipscombe, Leslie, e. London (Edgware), 2438, Rfn., k. in a., F. & F., 28/5/15.
Little, Herbert John Albert, e. London (Mitcham), 4825, Rfn., k. in a., F. & F., 1/7/16.
Little, James, e. London (Walthamstow), 393310, Rfn., k. in a., F. & F., 14/4/17, formerly 5213, 11th London Regt.
Little, John William, b. Cumberland, e. Carlisle (Kirk Bampton), 7739, Rfn., k. in a., F. & F., 9/9/16, formerly 23936, Border Regt.
Little, Ronald Henry, b. Merton, e. Camberwell (Brockley), 394627, Rfn., k. in a., F. & F., 20/8/18.
Lloyd, John, b. Holloway, e. London (Holloway), 393803, Rfn., k. in a., F. & F., 6/9/17, formerly 2005, 7th Middx. Regt.
Long, Arthur Henry, e. London (City), 4137, Rfn., k. in a., F. & F., 1/7/16.
Long, Charles Herbert, e. Camberwell (Brockley), 415295, Rfn., k. in a., F. & F., 30/8/18, formerly 375593, 8th London Regt.
Longhurst, Reginald, e. London (Camberley), 392505, Rfn., k. in a., F. & F., 14/4/17, formerly 6049, 9th London Regt.
Longman, Leslie Lionel, b. Surrey, e. Croydon (Thornton Heath), 394478, Rfn., d. of w., F. & F., 25/8/18.
Lott, William James, e. London (Paddington), 391230, Rfn., k. in a., F. & F., 14/4/17.

APPENDIX I 617

Love, Alan, e. London (W. Ealing), 392310, Rfn., d. of w., F. & F., 23/5/17, formerly 5807, 9th London Regt.

Love, William, b. Ealing, e. Ealing (Ealing), 392389, Rfn., k. in a., F. & F., 24/4/18, formerly 5902, 9th London Regt.

Loveland, George Alfred, b. Dulwich, e. Camberwell (Dulwich), 394724, Rfn., k. in a., F. & F., 2/9/18.

Lovelock, Sidney James, e. London (Stockbridge), 2284, Rfn., k. in a., F. & F., 9/9/16.

Loven, William Edward, b. Colchester, e. Colchester (Colchester), 392934, Rfn., d., F. & F., 20/1/18, formerly 2796, 5th Essex Regt.

Lowes, Andrew Robinson, e. London (Lee), 2509, Rfn., k. in a., F. & F., 9/2/15.

Lowry, Edwin Alexander, b. Kilburn, e. London (Hampstead), 394087, Rfn., k. in a., F. & F., 10/8/18, formerly 8290, 9th London Regt.

Lowry, Philip Archibald Nicholas, e. London (Kilburn), 392399, Rfn., k. in a., F. & F., 14/4/17, formerly 5915, 9th London Regt.

Lucas, Frederick, e. London (Watford), 3300, L/Cpl., k. in a., F. & F., 1/7/16.

Lucas, Joseph Thomas, e. Southwark (Lambeth), 7130, Rfn., k. in a., F. & F., 24/1/17, formerly 5350, 11th London Regt.

Lyons, Alfred Stanley, b. Halstead, e. London (Colchester), 5675, Rfn., k. in a., F. & F., 25/9/16.

Mackey, John, e. Stranmer (Glenluce), 393640, L/Sgt., k. in a., F. & F., 14/4/17, formerly 5454, 8th London Regt.

MacPherson, Alexander, e. London (Boat of Garton), 393705, Rfn., d. of w., Home, 14/6/17, formerly 5637, 8th London Regt.

Mahony, Joseph Seward, e. London (Lisson Grove), 4400, Rfn., k. in a., F. & F., 9/10/16.

Maidment, Alfred Sydney, b. Marylebone, e. (Wharncliffe Gardens), 8422, Cpl., k. in a., F. & F., 1/7/16.

Maile, Edmund Frank, e. Norwood (W. Norwood), 393093, Rfn., k. in a., F. & F., 14/4/17, formerly 6845, 9th London Regt.

Maisey, Frank Douglas, e. London (Dalston), 2326, Rfn., k. in a., F. & F., 21/4/15.

Makepeace, William John, b. Marylebone, e. Harrow (Harrow), 7610, Rfn., k. in a., F. & F., 9/10/16, formerly 5585, 8th London Regt.

Mallett, Horace, e. London (St. Paul's Churchyard), 390968, Cpl., k. in a., F. & F., 26/9/17, formerly 3554, 9th London Regt.

Mancer, Alfred Henry, b. London, e. London (Vauxhall), 393575, Rfn., d. of w., Home, 23/6/17, formerly 5975, 12th London Regt.

Mandy, William George, e. London (Fulham), 4969, Rfn., k. in a., F. & F., 1/7/16.

Manktelow, Thomas William, b. Islington, e. London (Islington), 390132, W.O. Class 2, k. in a., F. & F., 24/8/18, formerly 1705, 9th London Regt. D.C.M.
Mann, Harold Arthur Gordon, e. London (Woodford), 392266, Bugler, k. in a., F. & F., 27/9/17, formerly 5756, 9th London Regt.
Manning, Charles, b. Burton, e. Burton (Burton-on-Trent), 393386, Rfn., k. in a., F. & F., 13/8/17, formerly 5308, 11th London Regt.
Marchant, Vivian John Barker, e. London (Knightsbridge), 3373, Rfn., k. in a., F. & F., 1/7/16.
Marlow, Alexander George, e. London (Walworth), 4662, Rfn., k. in a., F. & F., 1/7/16.
Marriott, Archibald Quarrington, b. Bow, e. London (St. John's Wood), 1375, Rfn., k. in a., F. & F., 19/12/15.
Marriott, Henry John, e. London (Pentonville), 393546, Rfn., k. in a., F. & F., 14/4/17, formerly 4087, 11th London Regt.
Marsh, Harold Belsey, e. London (Alexandra Park), 3977, Rfn., k. in a., F. & F., 1/7/16.
Marshall, Frank, e. London (Maidenhead), 3458, Rfn., k. in a., F. & F., 30/5/16.
Marshall, John, e. Woolwich (Plumstead), 393479, Rfn., k. in a., F. & F., 3/5/17, formerly 5551, 11th London Regt.
Martin, Cecil, b. Southborough, e. London, 1980, Rfn., k. in a., F. & F., 1/1/15.
Martin, Cuthbert Charles Woodham, e. London (Beckenham, Kent), 7517, Rfn., k. in a., F. & F., 25/9/16, formerly 4883, 8th London Regt.
Martin, Harold William, b. Clayham, e. Woolwich (Bexley Heath), 394587, Rfn., k. in a., F. & F., 4/9/18.
Martin, William Frederick, b. Paddington, e. London (North Kensington), 393606, Rfn., k. in a., F. & F., 15/4/18, formerly 6123, 11th London Regt.
Mason, Cecil Sidney, e. London (Anerley), 2064, Rfn., k. in a., F. & F., 4/9/15.
Massey, Frank, b. West Ham, e. Stratford (Leytonstone), 415260, Rfn., k. in a., F. & F., 27/9/17, formerly 594748, 18th London Regt.
Massey, Henry Thomas, e. Stratford (Forest Gate), 415210, Rfn., k. in a., F. & F., 16/8/17, formerly 7934, 7th London Regt.
Mathias, Sam, e. Hawley (Kent), 393526, Rfn., k. in a., F. & F., 26/6/18, formerly 6089, 11th London Regt.
Matson, Andrew, e. London (Canonbury), 393387, Rfn., k. in a., F. & F., 14/4/17, formerly 2896, 11th London Regt.
Matthew, Ernest, b. Paddington, e. London, 8457, L/Cpl., k. in a., F. & F., 1/7/16.
Matthews, Archibald Henry, b. Kensington, e. London (Kensington), 1875, Cpl., k. in a., F. & F., 1/7/16.

APPENDIX I 619

Matthews, James Victor, b. London, e. London (Holland Park), 390021, Sgt., k. in a., F. & F., 30/9/17, formerly 1357, 9th London Regt.

Maunder, William John, b. Islington, e. London (Harrow), 4381, Rfn., k. in a., F. & F., 9/9/16.

May, Reginald Charles, e. Chelmsford (Chelmsford), 6664, Rfn., k. in a., F. & F., 2/10/16, formerly 2715, Essex Regt.

May, Sidney Charles, e. London (Marylebone), 391737, Rfn., k. in a., F. & F., 14/4/17, formerly 4822, 9th London Regt.

Mayne, Harry William, e. London (Walworth), 393345, Rfn., k. in a., F. & F., 27/9/17, formerly 5244, 11th London Regt.

Maytum, Percy Charles, b. Snodland, Kent, e. West Ham (Chatham) 392896, Rfn., k. in a., F. & F., 21/10/17, formerly 4909, Essex Regt.

McGarr, John, e. Carlisle (Manchester), 393700, Rfn., k. in a., F. & F., 3/5/17, formerly 23917, Border Regt.

McGrath, James Henry, b. Battersea, e. London (Battersea), 5731, Rfn., k. in a., F. & F., 9/9/16.

McKechnie, James Agamemnon, b. Aberdeen, e. Stratford 7028, Rfn., k. in a., F. & F., 9/10/16, formerly 3743, 25th London Regt.

McNeill, Archibald, e. Oban (Appin), 393696, Rfn., k. in a., F. & F., 14/4/17, formerly 5593, 8th London Regt.

McSweeney, William, e. Rotherhithe (Rotherhithe), 394019, Rfn., d. of w., F. & F., 3/9/17, formerly 8085, 9th London Regt.

Meachen, Ernest, b. Yaxham, e. Norwich (Norfolk), 6667, Rfn., k. in a., F. & F., 9/10/16, formerly 24333, Norfolk Regt.

Mead, George, b. Caulfield, e. Bardfield (Lindsell), 393037, Rfn., k. in a., F. & F., 8/9/18, formerly 1958, Essex Regt.

Measures, Arthur Richards, e. London (New Cross), 3914, Rfn., k. in a., F. & F., 1/7/16.

Mercer, Burvill, e. London (Streatham), 4045, Rfn., k. in a., F. & F., 1/7/16.

Mercer, Charles Ellis, e. London (Ticehurst), 393676, Rfn., d. of w., F. & F., 19/4/17, formerly 5550, 8th London Regt.

Mersh, William Richard, b. Stepney, e. London (Ratcliffe), 415021, Rfn., k. in a., F. & F., 6/6/17, formerly 5077, 10th London Regt.

Merten, Harold Leonard, b. Islington, e. London (East Finchley), 391547, L/Cpl., k. in a., F. & F., 8/9/18, formerly 4461, 9th London Regt.

Messiter, Claude Malin, b. Birmingham, e. Birmingham (Hall Green), 7027, Rfn., k. in a., F. & F., 2/10/16, formerly 3835, Worcester Yeo.

Methofer, William Arthur, b. St. Pancras, e. London (Regent's Park), 1805, Rfn., d. of w., F. & F., 5/1/15.

Mettem, Percy Charles, b. Caversham, e. London (Marylebone) 415175, Cpl., k. in a., F. & F., 24/4/18, formerly 6569, 10th London Regt.

Mexson, Walter Percy, e. London (Notting Hill), 2459, Rfn., k. in a., F. & F., 9/9/16.
Miles, Reginald Charles, e. London (Streatham), 392217, Rfn., d. of w., F. & F., 11/4/17.
Miller, Frank, b. Nottingham, e. London (Kettering), 392200, Rfn., k. in a., F. & F., 28/3/18, formerly 5648, 9th London Regt.
Milligan, Alfred Edward, b. Islington, e. London (Forest Gate), 394991, Rfn., k. in a., F. & F., 23/9/18.
Mills, Arthur Charles, e. Stratford (Cubitt Town), 393767, Rfn., k. in a., F. & F., 14/4/17, formerly 5075, 20th London Regt.
Mills, George William, b. Littlehampton, e. London (Peckham), 392044, Cpl., k. in a., F. & F., 27/9/17, formerly 5287, 9th London Regt.
Ming, Ronald Eustace, b. West Hampstead, e. London (Muswell Hill), 392349, Rfn., k. in a., F. & F., 27/9/17, formerly 5852, 9th London Regt.
Mitchell, Harold Hildige, e. London (Wembley), 2175, L/Cpl., k. in a., F. & F., 1/7/16.
Mogford, Leslie Wells, e. London (London), 2734, Rfn., k. in a., F. & F., 1/7/16.
Moncur, George Clark, e. London (St. John's Wood), 3457, L/Cpl., k. in a., F. & F., 25/4/15.
Montague, Percy Robert, b. Paddington, e. London (Willesden), 391848, Rfn., k. in a., F. & F., 1/9/18, formerly 5003, 9th London Regt.
Montgomery, Eli John, b. Battersea, e. London (Battersea), 1246, Rfn., k. in a., F. & F., 9/10/16.
Moorcroft, Harry, b. Quarndon, Derby, e. London (Quarndon), 7543, Rfn., k. in a., F. & F., 9/9/16, formerly 5432, 8th London Regt.
Moore, George Arthur, e. Norwich (Gt. Yarmouth), 392939, Cpl., k. in a., F. & F., 14/4/17, formerly 24543, Norfolk Regt.
Moore, Harry, b. Kensington, e. London (Hyde Park), 391688, Rfn., k. in a., F. & F., 12/7/17, formerly 4740, 9th London Regt.
Morey, Charles William, e. Hornsey (Hornsey), 7799, Rfn., k. in a., F. & F., 9/9/16, formerly 3391, 7th Middx. Regt.
Morgan, Charles Howlett, b. Harringay, e. London (Harringay), 390125, Rfn., k. in a., F. & F., 28/3/18, formerly 1686, 9th London Regt.
Morgan, Lorenzo, b. Marylebone, e. London (London), 931, L/Cpl., k. in a., F. & F., 1/1/15.
Morrill, Edward George, b. Fulham, e. London (London), 392313, Rfn., k. in a., F. & F., 27/9/17, formerly 5812, 9th London Regt.
Morris, George Edward, e. London (Ealing), 3335, Rfn., k. in a., F. & F., 1/7/16.
Morrison, George Herbert, e. London (Crouch End), 3561, Rfn., k. in a., F. & F., 31/5/16.

APPENDIX I

Mott, Henry, e. London (Shepherd's Bush), 7442, Rfn., d. of w., F. & F., 31/1/17, formerly 5766, 11th London Regt.
Moult, Clifford, e. London (Hampstead), 2631, Rfn., k. in a., F. & F., 9/10/16.
Mourant, Roland Walter, e. London (London), 2355, L/Cpl., k. in a., F. & F., 1/1/15.
Moynihan, Bernard John, e. London (Edgware Rd.), 390864, Rfn., k. in a., F. & F., 10/8/18, formerly 3360, 9th London Regt.
Moynihan, Garrett Thomas, b. Marylebone, e. London (Edgware Rd.), 3364, Rfn., k. in a., F. & F., 9/10/16.
Mudd, John Reginald, b. Walthamstow, e. Stratford (Walthamstow), 394656, Rfn., k. in a., F. & F., 25/4/18.
Mumford, Henry Walter, e. Manchester (Forest Gate), 392448, Rfn., k. in a., F. & F., 29/4/17, formerly 5977, 9th London Regt.
Murray, Alexander Bolton, b. Hornsey, e. London (Seven Kings, Essex), 1460, Sgt., k. in a., F. & F., 1/7/16.
Musk, William Albert, b. Windsor, e. London (Feltham), 5218, Rfn., k. in a., F. & F., 9/10/16.
Mussenden, Leonard Lawson, b. Dulwich, e. London (Knightsbridge), 1646, L/Cpl., k. in a., F. & F., 1/7/16.
Myall, Edward Henry, e. London (Plaistow), 3087, Rfn., k. in a., F. & F., 1/7/16.
Myatt, Walter Cecil, b. St. John's Wood, e. London (Bloomsbury), 5904, Rfn., k. in a., F. & F., 9/10/16.
Myddleton, Harold Whalley, b. Blackburn, e. London (Thornton Heath), 392119, Rfn., k. in a., F. & F., 20/5/18, formerly 5411, 9th London Regt.

Nash, Frank Branch, e. London (Watford), 3827, Rfn., k. in a., F. & F., 1/7/16.
Nash, Frederick Richard, e. London (Regent's Park), 390953, Cpl., k. in a., F. & F., 28/3/18, formerly 3529, 9th London Regt.
Naylar, Percy, b. Maidenhead, e. London (Brompton), 390001, Sgt., k. in a., F. & F., 14/8/17, formerly 1269, 9th London Regt.
Needham, Louis Alfred, b. Balham, e. London (Lewisham), 391583, Rfn., d., Home, 17/3/17, formerly 4534, 9th London Regt.
Needham, Leslie Alfred, e. London (West Kilburn), 2742, Rfn., k. in a., F. & F., 21/4/15.
Needs, James Henry, e. Hackney (South Hackney), 415058, Rfn., k. in a., F. & F., 10/9/18, formerly 5149, 11th London Regt.
Neldrett, Frederick Charles, e. Hornsey (Tottenham), 7774, Rfn., k. in a., F. & F., 9/9/16, formerly 2694, 7th Middx. Regt.
Nelmes, Joseph, b. Islington, e. London (East Croydon), 392545, L/Cpl., k. in a., F. & F., 14/8/17, formerly 6100, 9th London Regt.
Nelson, Stephen Henry, e. London (Ratcliffe), 7115, Rfn., k. in a., F. & F., 24/1/17, formerly 5139, 11th London Regt.

Neville, Arthur Charles, b. Dalston, e. Stratford (Walthamstow), 415214, Rfn., k. in a., F. & F., 12/5/18, formerly 7941, 7th London Regt.
Newbold, William, b. Highgate, e. London (Highgate), 1698, Rfn., k. in a., F. & F., 1/7/16.
Newland, Harold Hooper, e. London (Holloway), 392780, Rfn., k. in a., F. & F., 26/3/18, formerly 6477, 9th London Regt.
Newling, Roland, e. London (Chiswick), 2364, Rfn., k. in a., F. & F., 24/4/15.
Newman, Frank, e. Clacton-on-Sea (Great Bentley), 6734, Rfn., d. of w., F. & F., 11/10/16, formerly 3187, Essex Regt.
Newton, Leslie, b. Marylebone, e. London (Chiswick), 4641, Rfn., k. in a., F. & F., 9/9/16.
Newton, Russell, e. London (Tottenham), 4263, Rfn., k. in a., F. & F., 1/7/16.
Nicholls, Joseph Edward, e. Lambeth (Brixton), 393052, Rfn., k. in a., F. & F., 14/4/17, formerly 6793, 9th London Regt.
Nicholls, Harold Stevenson, b. Penge, e. Kingston-on-Thames (North Croydon), 394748, Rfn., d. of w., F. & F., 2/9/18.
Nicholls, Harry Bertie, b. Pimlico, e. London (Hampstead), 1979, Rfn., k. in a., F. & F., 17/12/14.
Nichols, William Robert, b. Bow, e. Stratford (Walthamstow), 394265, Rfn., k. in a., F. & F., 10/4/18, formerly 5357, 11th London Regt.
Noakes, Frederick John, e. Woolwich (Plumstead), 7370, Rfn., k. in a., F. & F., 21/1/17, formerly 5904, 11th London Regt.
Noakes, Vivian Frederick, e. London (Muswell Hill), 2634, Rfn., k. in a., F. & F., 9/10/16.
Noble, Francis, b. Haxley, e. London (Castleford), 7622, Rfn., k. in a., F. & F., 25/9/16, formerly 5615, 8th London Regt.
Noble, Harold Edwin John, e. London (Stroud Green), 392519, Rfn., k. in a., F. & F., 14/4/17, formerly 6066, 9th London Regt.
Norman, Arthur Louis, e. London (Acton Hill), 3483, Rfn., k. in a., F. & F., 1/7/16.
Norris, Harry, e. Hounslow (Hanwell), 393930, A/Cpl., k. in a., F. & F., 25/8/18, formerly 4845, 8th Middx. Regt.
Nugent, Alfred Harry, b. Camberwell, e. London (East Dulwich), 5734, Rfn., k. in a., F. & F., 9/10/16.

O'Connor, Patrick, b. Marylebone, e. London (Edgware), 4883, Rfn., k. in a., F. & F., 1/10/16.
Odell, Charles, e. London (Elstree), 3519, Rfn., d., Home, 7/12/15.
Oldham, George, b. Monte Video, e. London (Walthamstow), 392282, Cpl., k. in a., F. & F., 10/8/18, formerly 5777, 9th London Regt.
Orpet, Walter Oswald, b. Islington, e. London (Highbury), 1484, L/Cpl., k. in a., F. & F., 25/10/15.

APPENDIX I

Orton, William Thomas, b. Hammersmith, e. London (Barnes), 5457, Rfn., k. in a., F. & F., 9/10/16.
Oulds, Albert Ernest, b. Tooting, e. London (Tooting), 4509, Rfn., k. in a., F. & F., 9/10/16.

Packer, Harold Arthur, b. Wandsworth, e. Fulham (East Dulwich), 393252, L/Cpl., k. in a., F. & F., 25/4/18, formerly 3021, 25th London Regt.
Packman, George Farrel, b. Foots Cray, Kent, e. Woolwich (Sidcup), 7717, Rfn., d. of w., F. & F., 25/9/16, formerly 5235, 20th London Regt.
Page, Arthur Cyril, b. Brixton, e. Wandsworth (Putney), 394497, Rfn., k. in a., F. & F., 21/9/18.
Palmer, Henry John, e. London (St. George's), 392482, Rfn., k. in a., F. & F., 14/4/17, formerly 6020, 9th London Regt.
Pannett, Joseph, e. London (Newark, U.S.A.), 4591, Rfn., k. in a., F. & F., 1/7/16, formerly 4591, 9th London Regt.
Parfitt, George Henry, e. London (St. Pancras), 392857, Rfn., k. in a., F. & F., 14/4/17, formerly 6569, 9th London Regt.
Parish, Eric, b. Lambeth, e. Hendon (Hendon), 392599, Rfn., k. in a., F. & F., 27/9/17.
Parish, William Charles, e. London (Harlesden), 4270, Rfn., k. in a., F. & F., 30/5/16.
Parkinson, John Albert, e. London (Camden Town), 4066, Rfn., k. in a., F. & F., 9/10/16.
Parmiter, Alfred Dunstan, b. Rotherham, e. London (Tooting), 391359, L/Cpl., k. in a., F. & F., 8/9/17, formerly 4159, 9th London Regt.
Parsons, Alfred John, b. Camberwell, e. London (Camberwell), 7540, Rfn., k. in a., F. & F., 9/9/16, formerly 5423, 8th London Regt.
Parsons, Frank, b. Chertsey, e. Fulham (Chertsey), 7032, Rfn., k. in a., F. & F., 9/10/16, formerly 3098, 25th London Regt.
Parsons, Frederick Charles, b. Peckham, e. London (Winchmore Hill), 1782, Rfn., k. in a., F. & F., 1/7/16.
Parsons, Frederick William, e. London (Streatham), 3172, Sgt., k. in a., F. & F., 1/7/16.
Parsons, Harold Cope, e. London (Carshalton), 390946, Cpl., k. in a., F. & F., 24/6/18, formerly 3514, 9th London Regt.
Parsons, Ivor Willie, e. London (Laken Heath), 2941, Rfn., k. in a., F. & F., 21/7/16.
Parsons, James William, b. Hampstead, e. London (Hornsey), 1183, Rfn., k. in a., F. & F., 20/4/15.
Parsons, William Edwin, b. Chelsea, e. Camberwell (Wandsworth), 393990, Rfn., k. in a., F. & F., 27/9/17, formerly 8054, 9th London Regt.
Parsons, William Joseph, b. Cubitt Town, e. Stratford (Cubitt Town), 415182, Rfn., k. in a., F. & F., 9/8/18, formerly 6601, 10th London Regt.

Passmore, William John, b. Glams, e. Swansea (Swansea), 418016, L/Cpl., d., F. & F., 14/12/17, formerly 2114, R.A.M.C.
Patch, Albert William, e. London (Kentish Town), 7533, Rfn., k. in a., F. & F., 9/10/16, formerly 5087, 8th London Regt.
Patey, Sydney Edward, e. London (Hampstead), 2955, L/Cpl., k. in a., F. & F., 1/7/16.
Pavord, Arthur, e. London (Clapham), 3985, Rfn., k. in a., F. & F., 1/7/16.
Payne, Walter Alfred, e. London (Regent's Park), 394062, Rfn., k. in a., F. & F., 1/3/17.
Peachey, Albert Alexander, b. Battersea, e. London (Upper Tooting), 415065, Rfn., k. in a., F. & F., 14/4/17, formerly 5731, 12th London Regt.
Peacock, Francis Harry, e. Chelmsford (Dunmow), 6672, Rfn., d. of w., F. & F., 25/1/17, formerly 3156, Essex Regt.
Peagam, Walter Enness, e. London (New Cross), 2759, L/Sgt., k. in a., F. & F., 1/7/16.
Pearce, Charles, b. Willesden, e. Camberwell (Rotherhithe), 394017, Rfn., k. in a., F. & F., 20/6/17.
Pearce, Percy, b. Hoathley, Sussex, e. London (Hoathley), 391966, Cpl., k. in a., F. & F., 25/4/18.
Pearson, Sydney John, e. London (Seven Kings), 3384, Rfn., k. in a., F. & F., 21/4/15.
Peet, Charles Herbert, b. Enfield, e. New Barnet (New Barnet), 392558, Rfn., k. in a., F. & F., 14/4/17.
Peffer, Robin Charles, e. London (Harringay), 2022, Rfn., k. in a., F. & F., 9/9/16.
Peirce, William Alec, e. London (Harringay), 3994, Rfn., d. of w., F. & F., 17/7/16.
Penn, Henry George, e. London (Kentish Town), 394060, Rfn., k. in a., F. & F., 26/5/17.
Penn, Walter Edward, e. London (Camberwell), 393550, Rfn., d., F. & F., 12/5/17.
Penney, George Arthur, e. London (Willesden), 2814, Rfn., k. in a., F. & F., 1/7/16.
Penney, Henry John, e. Putney (Brixton), 7074, Rfn., d. of w., F. & F., 22/10/16, formerly 2594, 25th London Regt.
Penrose, William Henry, b. Hull, e. Whitley Bay (Whitley Bay), 7593, Rfn., d. of w., F. & F., 15/9/16, formerly 5551, 8th London Regt.
Peppin, Fred, e. London (Pimlico), 394330, Rfn., d. of w., F. & F., 7/5/17, formerly 5201, 11th London Regt.
Perkins, Walter George, b. Croydon, e. London (Croydon), 7590, Rfn., k. in a., F. & F., 25/9/16, formerly 5545, 8th London Regt.
Perrott, Alfred George, e. London (Peckham), 3186, L/Cpl., k. in a., F. & F., 1/7/16.
Perry, John Frederick, e. London, 393155, Rfn., k. in a., F. & F., 16/8/1

APPENDIX I

Perry, Samuel, b. Highwood, Essex, e. Chelmsford (Willingale), 6670, Rfn., k. in a., F. & F., 9/10/16, formerly 2638, 5th Essex, Regt.
Perry, Horace Smith, e. London, 3124, Rfn., d. of w., F. & F., 27/4/15.
Peters, Arthur James, b. Brixton, e. London (Stockwell), 7516, Rfn., k. in a., F. & F., 25/9/16.
Phillips, Sidney George, e. Melksham (Melksham), 7657, Rfn., k. in a., F. & F., 14/9/16, formerly 5713, 8th London Regt.
Picking, Robert, b. Windsor, e. London (Lillington St., S.W.), 1419, Rfn., k. in a., F. & F., 25/10/15.
Playfair, Victor Hamilton, b. Clacton-on-Sea, e. London (Beckenham), 1879, L/Cpl., d., Home, 26/2/17.
Pocock, Harold Francis, e. London (Streatham), 390473, A/Cpl., k. in a., F. & F., 16/10/18.
Pogson, Frank Woodhead, b. Loughborough, Leicester, e. London (Chesterfield), 392020, Rfn., k. in a., F. & F., 27/9/17.
Poole, Norman, e. London (Stroud Green), 3863, Rfn., k. in a., F. & F., 1/7/16.
Poore, John Donald, b. Camberwell, e. East Ham (Peckham), 393311, Rfn., d. of w., Home, 20/4/18, formerly 5171, 11th London Regt.
Potter, Augustin Tudor, e. Whitstable, 6048, Rfn., d. of w., F. & F., 23/1/17.
Potter, Ernest Victor, b. Marylebone, e. London (Maida Vale), 391876, Rfn., k. in a., F. & F., 12/5/18.
Potter, John Robert, b. Reading, e. London (Fulham), 2653, Rfn., k. in a., F. & F., 9/10/16.
Potts, Arthur George, e. London (Fulham), 393909, L/Cpl., k. in a., F. & F., 14/4/17, formerly 3011, 10th Middx. Regt.
Potts, Thomas Charles, e. London (Richmond), 390741, Sgt., d. of w., F. & F., 25/8/18.
Powell, Sydney, b. Chelsea, e. London (Kilburn), 4691, Rfn., k. in a., F. & F., 1/10/16.
Power, Hugh William, b. Brixton, e. London, 1631, Rfn., d. of w., F. & F., 26/3/15.
Power, Alfred Edward, b. London, e. Woolwich (Woolwich), 415035, Rfn., k. in a., F. & F., 26/9/17, formerly 6035, 11th London Regt.
Prance, William Charles, e. London (Willesden), 3056, Rfn., d. of w., F. & F., 30/9/15.
Pratt, William, b. St. Pancras, e. London (King's Cross), 391341, Rfn., d. of w., F. & F., 28/9/17.
Preece, Charles Albert, b. Liverpool, e. Chelmsford (St. Albans), 6675, Sgt., d. of w., F. & F., 14/10/16, formerly 2265, Essex Regt.
Preece, Frank John, b. Hythe, e. London (Twickenham), 1894, A/Cpl., k. in a., F. & F., 1/7/16.

Price, Charles Benjamin, e. London (Twickenham), 5805, Rfn., k. in a., F. & F., 8/10/16.
Price, George Leslie, b. Lewisham, e. Camberwell (Lewisham), 7691, Rfn., k. in a., F. & F., 9/10/16, formerly 4931, 20th London Regt.
Price, Harold, b. Stroud, Glos., e. London (East Ham), 391921, Rfn., k. in a., F. & F., 8/9/17.
Price, Rowland, e. London (Brixton), 4567, Rfn., k. in a., F. & F., 1/7/16.
Prince, Lancelot, b. Wimbledon, e. London (Finsbury), 393077, Rfn., k. in a., F. & F., 18/8/18, formerly 7197, 28th London Regt.
Privett, Arthur Edward, b. Aldershot, e. London (Petersfield), 391952, Rfn., k. in a., F. & F., 23/9/18.
Prockson, Frederick, e. London (Bethnal Green), 393580, Rfn., k. in a., F. & F., 14/4/17, formerly 5959, 12th London Regt.
Prowse, Frederick George, b. Queen's Park, e. London (Willesden), 391154, Rfn., k. in a., F. & F., 28/3/18.
Pryer, Andrew, e. Woolwich (Abbey Wood), 393753, Rfn., k. in a., F. & F., 15/8/17, formerly 4910, 20th London Regt.
Pudge, Cecil Halliwell, e. Fulham (Norbury), 7076, Rfn., k. in a., F. & F., 9/10/16, formerly 3069, 25th London Regt.
Pulford, Arthur Lewis, b. Chelmsford, e. Clacton-on-Sea (Clacton on-Sea), 6673, Rfn., k. in a., F. & F., 9/10/16, formerly 3003, Essex Regt.
Puplett, John Edward, e. London (W. Hampstead), 2920, Rfn., k. in a., F. & F., 9/6/15.
Purkis, Harry William, e. London (Barnes), 2586, Rfn., k. in a., F. & F., 24/4/15.

Quibell, Stephen William, e. London (Watford), 391289, Rfn., k. in a., F. & F., 26/9/17.
Quinton, Gerald Horace, e. London (Bayswater), 4109, Rfn., k. in a., F. & F., 9/9/16.

Ramage, Sydney George, b. Leyton, e. Stratford (Walthamstow), 392493, Rfn., k. in a., F. & F., 12/9/18.
Ramsay, William, b. Hutchisontoun, Glasgow, e. London (Glasgow), 7666, Rfn., k. in a., F. & F., 9/10/16, formerly 5766, 8th London Regt.
Ramus, Ernest, b. Willesden, e. London (Brondesbury), 1599, Cpl., k. in a., F. & F., 1/7/16.
Ratcliff, Frederick Charles, b. Dalston, e. London (Dalston), 391522, Bugler, d. of w., F. & F., 31/8/18, formerly 4408, 9th London Regt.
Rawlings, Thomas, e. Clacton-on-Sea (Beaumont), 6780, Rfn., k. in a., F. & F., 9/10/16, formerly 3096, 2/5th Essex Regt.

APPENDIX I

Rayner, Frank Edward, e. London (Ealing), 6107, Rfn., d. of w., F. & F., 23/1/17.
Read, Frederick, b. Knightsbridge, e. London (Chelsea), 391995, Rfn., k. in a., F. & F., 27/8/18, formerly 5225, 9th London Regt.
Redgell, Arthur Sidney, e. London (Paddington), 392670, Sgt., k. in a., F. & F., 14/4/17, formerly 6354, 9th London Regt.
Redgell, Percival John, b. Marylebone, e. London (London), 1541, Sgt., k. in a., F. & F., 26/5/16.
Reed, Alfred Richard, e. London (Westminster), 3900, Rfn., k. in a., F. & F., 1/7/16.
Rees, David Mansell, b. Highgate, e. London (St. John's Wood), 5023, Rfn., d., Home, 18/4/16.
Reeves, Arthur John, b. London, e. Attleborough (Wymondham), 392379, Rfn., k. in a., F. & F., 15/8/17, formerly 5889, 9th London Regt.
Reeves, Frank, b. Leytonstone, e. London (Leytonstone), 415329, Rfn., d. of w., F. & F., 26/8/18, formerly 2901, 7th London Regt.
Reeves, Herbert John, b. Bow, e. Chelsea (Manor Park), 415271, L/Cpl., k. in a., F. & F., 30/12/17, formerly 5742, 18th London Regt.
Regal, Frederick, e. London (Kilburn), 4861, Rfn., k. in a., F. & F., 1/7/16.
Reid, George, e. London (London), 3577, Cpl., k. in a., F. & F., 24/1/17.
Reilly, Patrick, e. Navan (Navan), 393629, Rfn., k. in a., F. & F., 14/4/17, formerly 5058, 8th London Regt.
Renwick, Norman, e. London (Leytonstone), 2866, Rfn., k. in a., F. & F., 1/7/16.
Rest, William John, e. London (Pimlico), 392417, Rfn., k. in a., F. & F., 14/4/17, formerly 5936, 9th London Regt.
Reynolds, John Richard, e. London (New Cross), 3613, Rfn., k. in a., F. & F., 24/4/15.
Rhodes, Frederick Robert, b. Bermondsey, e. London (Mile End), 394267, Rfn., d. of w., F. & F., 13/8/17, formerly 5363, 11th London Regt.
Rich, Frederick James, b. Portslade, e. Camberwell (Clapham), 394200, Rfn., k. in a., F. & F., 20/6/17, formerly 6967, 11th London Regt.
Richards, Ernest Edward, b. Forest Hill, e. Lewisham (Forest Hill), 7714, Rfn., d. of w., F. & F., 3/10/16, formerly 5200, 20th London Regt.
Riddle, Wilfred Hedley, b. Lewisham, e. London (St. John's Wood), 392434, Rfn., d. of w., F. & F., 28/8/17, formerly 5960, 9th London Regt. M.M.
Ridgeway, Ralph Stanley, e. London (Watford), 2879, Rfn., k. in a., F. & F., 27/2/15.
Ridler-Rowe, Wallace Buffett, b. Bridgewater, Som., e. London (Lambeth), 1666, Rfn., k. in a., F. & F., 1/7/16.

Riley, Clifford, e. London (Hendon), 3776, Rfn., k. in a., F. & F., 1/7/16.
Riley, Harry Axon, b. Morecombe, Lancs, e. Fulham (Bradford), 415255, Rfn., k. in a., F. & F., 16/8/17, formerly 305461, 5th London Regt.
Roberts, John, b. Belfast, Ireland, e. Stratford (West Ham), 419012, Rfn., d. of w., F. & F., 23/10/18, formerly 595945, 18th London Regt.
Roberts, John Arthur, b. Chelmsford, e. Chelmsford (Chelmsford), 392949, Rfn., k. in a., F. & F., 25/8/18, formerly 2097, Essex Regt.
Robertson, Arthur Douglas, e. London (Harlow), 3850, Rfn., d. of w., Home, 14/8/16.
Robertson, Douglas Alexander, e. London (Fulham), 391667, Rfn., d. of w., F. & F., 6/5/17, formerly 4706, 9th London Regt.
Robins, Gilbert, b. Honiton, Devon, e. London (Edgware), 4633, Rfn., k. in a., F. & F., 9/9/16.
Robinson, Cyril, b. Ashford, Kent, e. London (Corringham), 394606, Rfn., k. in a., F. & F., 27/9/17.
Robinson, Henry Alfred, e. London (Southfields), 4549, Rfn., k. in a., F. & F., 1/7/16.
Robinson, Thomas Joseph, e. London (Leytonstone), 3968, Rfn., k. in a., F. & F., 16/12/15.
Rogan, John, e. York (Leeds), 393660, Sgt., k. in a., F. & F., 14/4/17, formerly 5508, 8th London Regt.
Rogers, Vallack Thomas, b. Devonport, e. London (Kensington), 5906, Rfn., k. in a., F. & F., 25/9/16.
Roots, Henry Arthur James, b. Paddington, e. London (St. Peter's Park), 390122, Rfn., k. in a., F. & F., 14/4/17, formerly 1680, 9th London Regt.
Roper, Fred, b. Queen's Park, e. London (Kilburn), 391352, L/Cpl., d. of w., F. & F., 30/4/18, formerly 4150, 9th London Regt.
Rose, George Albert, b. Paddington, e. London (Paddington), 4667, Rfn., k. in a., F. & F., 1/10/16.
Ross, Arthur, b. Walworth, e. Camberwell (Camberwell), 394041, Rfn., k. in a., F. & F., 18/8/17, formerly 8107, 9th London Regt.
Ross, Charles Lawes, e. London (Aldershot), 390833, Sgt., k. in a., F. & F., 12/7/17, formerly 3306, 9th London Regt.
Ross, Francis William, e. London (Hornsey), 2627, Rfn., k. in a., F. & F., 9/9/16.
Rowe, Charles Edward, b. Dovercourt, Essex, e. Dovercourt (Dovercourt), 6783, Rfn., k. in a., F. & F., 9/10/16, formerly 2116, 5th Essex Regt.
Rowe, John Lovell, e. London (W. Hampstead), 3196, L/Cpl., d., Home, 3/2/15.
Rowland, Frederick George, b. Strand, e. London (Tottenham), 394625, Rfn., k. in a., F. & F., 26/9/17.

APPENDIX I

Rowland, William George, b. London, e. London (Notting Hill), 1807, Rfn., k. in a., F. & F., 1/7/16.
Rowlands, James Gwynne Vaughan, b. Pembroke, e. London (Haverford), 393080, Rfn., k. in a., F. & F., 27/9/17, formerly 5450, 28th London Regt.
Rudge, Frank Percy, e. London (Edgware Road), 3699, Rfn., k. in a., F. & F., 1/7/16.
Rush, Arthur James, b. Islington, e. London (Highbury), 393635, Rfn., k. in a., F. & F., 24/8/18, formerly 5412, 8th London Regt.
Rushen, Reginald John, e. Ealing (Ealing), 393911, L/Cpl., k. in a., F. & F., 22/9/17, formerly 4601, 8th Middlesex Regt.
Rushworth, Samuel Anderson, e. London (Wood Green), 2792, Rfn., k. in a., F. & F., 3/3/15.
Russell, Alfred Cushing, b. Marylebone, e. London (Chelsea), 5578, Rfn. k. in a., F. & F., 9/10/16.
Russell, William Denman, b. Brondesbury, e. London (Hampstead), 392012, Rfn., k. in a., F. & F., 24/4/18.
Russell, William Mark, b. Lambeth, e. London (Bloomsbury), 7177, Rfn., k. in a., F. & F., 21/1/17, formerly 2051, 11th London Regt.
Ryall, Gaston Albert, b. London, e. London (Hammersmith), 415227, Rfn., k. in a., F. & F., 17/8/18, formerly 33466, 7th London Regt.
Ryde, Alfred Edward, b. Bournemouth, e. London (Bournemouth), 391911, L/Cpl., k. in a., F. & F., 6/5/17, formerly 5095, 9th London Regt.

Sabberton, Ernest Frederick Edward, b. Norwich, e. London (Norwich), 5661, Rfn., k. in a., F. & F., 9/10/16.
Saberton, Henry James, e. Camberwell (Battersea), 393107, Rfn., k. in a., F. & F., 3/5/17, formerly 6860, 9th London Regt.
Saddleton, Sydney, e. London (Ealing), 3004, Cpl., k. in a., F. & F., 1/7/16.
Sales, Albert Edward, e. Fulham (Wandsworth), 7081, Rfn., d. of w., Home, 27/10/16, formerly 2995, 25th London Regt.
Salter, Harry Francis, b. Liverpool, e. London (Chorley Wood), 1605, Sgt., k. in a., F. & F., 9/10/16.
Sanford, William, e. London (London), 3710, Rfn., k. in a., F. & F., 12/11/15.
Sanrey, August, b. Soho, e. London (London), 394074, Rfn., k. in a., F. & F., 25/3/18, formerly 8274, 9th London Regt.
Santler, Wilfred Francis, b. Bexley Heath, e. London (Watford), 1749, Rfn., k. in a., F. & F., 1/1/15.
Sapsted, Thomas, e. London (Islington), 391473, Rfn., d. of w., F. & F., 29/8/18, formerly 4326, 9th London Regt.
Sara, Harry, e. London (Lee), 2730, Rfn., d. of w., F. & F., 26/1/16.
Sargent, Horace, b. Barnsbury, e. London (Wood Green), 6070, Rfn., k. in a., F. & F., 25/9/16.

Sanger, Godfrey, b. Barry (Barry Dock), 393612, Sgt., d. of w., F. & F., 30/11/17, formerly 4316, 8th London Regt.
Saunders, Richard, b. Hackney, e. Hackney (Clapton Park), 6632, Rfn., d. of w., F. & F., 9/10/16, formerly 4904, 5th Essex Regt.
Scarfe, Frank Louis, e. London (Westminster), 393581, Rfn., k. in a., F. & F., 14/4/17, formerly 6068, 12th London Regt.
Schofield, Henry, e. Hackney, 892883, Rfn., k. in a., F. & F., 14/4/17.
Schonewald, Charles, b. Liverpool, e. London (London), 4525, Rfn., k. in a., F. & F., 1/10/16.
Scott, George, e. London (Hornsey), 391031, A/Sgt., k. in a., F. & F., 3/5/17, formerly 3658, 9th London Regt.
Scott, Sidney, b. Paddington, e. London (Willesden), 5503, Rfn., k. in a., F. & F., 22/12/16.
Scrider, John Benjamin, b. Ealing, e. London (Harlesden), 392121, L/Cpl., d. of w., F. & F., 20/9/17, formerly 5413, 9th London Regt.
Scrivener, Thomas Albert John, e. London (Brentwood), 2404, Rfn., d., Home, 16/2/17.
Seaborn, Allen James, b. Braxted, e. Little Totham (Little Totham), 393019, Rfn., k. in a., F. & F., 13/8/17, formerly 1766, Essex Regt.
Seabrook, Major Joseph, e. London (Elstree), 2963, Rfn., k. in a., F. & F., 9/9/16.
Sebright, Harrington, b. N. Cadbury, e. Castlecary (N. Cadbury), 7616, Rfn., d. of w., F. & F., 16/9/16, formerly 5596, 8th London Regt.
Seig, Thomas, b. Cardiff (Cardiff), 394388, Rfn., d. of w., F. & F., 9/8/18.
Servante, Walter Harold, e. London (Hornsey), 390521, Sgt., d. of w., F. & F., 16/4/17.
Sewell, Robert, b. Havre, e. Rouen (Rouen), 393078, Rfn., k. in a., F. & F., 3/4/18, formerly 7618, 28th London Regt.
Sewell, Williams, e. London (Maida Vale), 5028, Rfn., k. in a., F. & F., 1/7/16.
Seymour, Reginald Quicke, b. Exeter, e. Hounslow (Twickenham), 393894, Sgt., k. in a., F. & F., 14/4/17, formerly R/820, 8th Middx. Regt.
Sharp, James Gordon, b. Victoria, Australia, e. London (Workington, Cumb.), 392014, L/Cpl., k. in a., F. & F., 25/4/18, formerly 5251, 9th London Regt.
Sharp, Lionel Alfred, e. London (Acton), 390897, Rfn., k. in a., F. & F., 6/4/17, formerly 3421, 9th London Regt.
Sharp, Sidney, e. Dunmow (Dunmow), 392951, Rfn., k. in a., F. & F., 1/10/18, formerly 3464, 5th Essex Regt.
Sharpin, Frank Mason, b. Chelsea, e. London (Chelsea), 391892, Rfn., k. in a., F. & F., 2/9/18, formerly 5070, 9th London Regt.
Shaw, Alfred George, b. Camberwell, e. London (Peckham), 7541, Rfn., k. in a., F. & F., 9/10/16, formerly 5424, 8th London Regt.

APPENDIX I 631

Shears, Reginald, e. London (Westcliff-on-Sea), 2919, Rfn., k. in a., F. & F., 1/7/16.
Shearwood, William, b. Poplar, e. Poplar (Poplar), 415235, Rfn., d. of w., F. & F., 25/6/18, formerly 8175, 8th London Regt.
Sheppard, Stephen, e. Camberwell (Battersea), 393551, Rfn., k. in a., F. & F., 14/4/17, formerly 6215, 11th London Regt.
Sherlock, Leopold William, e. London (Hanwell), 391223, L/Cpl., k. in a., F. & F., 8/6/18, formerly 3962, 9th London Regt.
Sherman, Richard David, b. Ealing, e. Ealing (Hanwell), 393919, Rfn., k. in a., F. & F., 27/9/17, formerly 4708, 8th Middx. Regt.
Shillaker, John Marcham, e. London (Lincoln), 392359, Rfn., k. in a., F. & F., 26/5/17, formerly 5863, 9th London Regt.
Shilston, Christopher Thomas, b. Paddington, e. London (Paddington), 1427, Rfn., k. in a., F. & F., 1/7/16.
Side, Edwin Thomas, b. Camberwell, e. Camberwell (Nunhead), 394037, Rfn., k. in a., F. & F., 21/3/18, formerly 8103, 9th London Regt.
Simmonds, Archibald Llewellyn, b. Nash, Bucks, e. London (Fulham), 392640, Rfn., d. of w., Home, 13/11/18, formerly 6321, 9th London Regt.
Siret, Charles James, b. Woodland, Hants, e. London (London), 415036, Rfn., k. in a., F. & F., 8/9/17, formerly 5711, 11th London Regt.
Sizer, Thomas William, b. Walthamstow, e. Stratford (Walthamstow), 6053, Rfn., k. in a., F. & F., 9/10/16.
Skinner, Ronald Sweyn, b. Tibbenham, Norfolk, e. London (St. Paul's), 737, Sgt., d. of w., F. & F., 3/2/15.
Skinner, Sydney Archer Thompson, b. Burwash, Sussex, e. London (Stratford), 390242, Sgt., d., Nigeria, West Africa, 22/2/18, formerly 1961, 9th London Regt.
Skipper, George Alexander, b. St Pancras, e. London (Willesden), 390006, W.O., Class II, d. of w., F. & F., 27/9/17, formerly 1300, 9th London Regt.
Slade, Edward Fred, e. Kings Langley, 3604, Rfn., d., F. & F., 12/8/15.
Slade, Fred, b. Knutsford, Cheshire, e. Willesden (Harrow), 5872, Rfn., k. in a., F. & F., 9/9/16, formerly 2714, 9th Middx. Regt.
Slade, George William, b. Knutsford, Cheshire, e. London (Wealdstone), 5808, Rfn., k. in a., F. & F., 9/9/16.
Slater, Alfred, b. Bermondsey, e. Deptford, 393196, Rfn., k. in a., F. & F., 26/9/17, formerly 6972, 9th London Regt.
Smale, John, e. London (Streatham), 391405, Rfn., k. in a., F. & F., 27/9/17, formerly 4227, 9th London Regt.
Smart, Charles Frederick, b. Goole, Yorks, e. Goole (Goole), 7554, Rfn., k. in a., F. & F., 9/9/16, formerly 5466, 8th London Regt.
Smith, Albert Edward, b. Battersea, e. Battersea (Battersea), 393987, Rfn., d. of w., F. & F., 25/8/18, formerly 8051, 9th London Regt.

Smith, Alexander Douglas, e. London (Brockley), 3459, Rfn., k. in a., F. & F., 25/9/16.
Smith, Arthur Leonard, e. London (Marylebone), 2237, Rfn., d. of w., F. & F., 28/2/15.
Smith, Charles, b. Suffolk, e. London (Battersea), 390851, Rfn., d. of w., F. & F., 15/9/18, formerly 3337, 9th London Regt. M.M.
Smith, Cecil Winterton, e. London (Hendon), 3707, Rfn., k. in a., F. & F., 1/7/16.
Smith, Clarence James, b. Lambeth, e. Lambeth (Brixton), 395065, Rfn., k. in a., F. & F., 25/8/18.
Smith, Cyril Charles Bosworth, b. Swindon, e. London (Ealing), 418001, Rfn., d. of w., F. & F., 29/4/18, formerly 4107, 9th London Regt.
Smith, Edgar Whitehead, e. Chelsea (Hackney), 395043, Rfn., k. in a., F. & F., 25/8/18, formerly 1703, R.A.M.C.
Smith, Edward Charles, e. London (Finsbury Park), 393394, Rfn., d. of w., F. & F., 15/4/17, formerly 2737, 11th London Regt.
Smith, Eric Walter Martin, e. London (Streatham), 2563, Rfn., d. of w., Home, 12/6/15.
Smith, Frank John, b. Dalston, e. London (Kingsland), 391859, Rfn., k. in a., F. & F., 27/9/17, formerly 5020, 9th London Regt.
Smith, Harold, e. London (Stonebridge Park), 390340, Rfn., k. in a., F. & F., 25/12/17, formerly 2201, 9th London Regt.
Smith, Harold, b. Quenden, Essex, e. London (Fulham), 2479, Rfn., k. in a., F. & F., 9/10/16.
Smith, Harry, b. Plumstead, e. Greenwich (Charlton), 7703, Rfn., k. in a., F. & F., 9/9/16, formerly 5040, 20th London Regt.
Smith, Leonard Eaton, b. Camberwell, e. Camberwell (Camberwell), 393338, Rfn., d. of w., F. & F., 18/8/17, formerly 5327, 11th London Regt.
Smith, Norman Hattersley, b. Conisboro, Yorks, e. London (Wealdstone), 1376, L/Cpl., k. in a., F. & F., 21/4/15.
Smith, Owen, b. Greenwich, e. Camberwell (Lewisham), 394527, Rfn., k. in a., F. & F., 29/10/18.
Smith, Sidney George, e. London (Clapham), 5295, Rfn., k. in a., F. & F., 28/2/17.
Smith, Stanley Edward, e. Colchester (Colchester), 392409, Rfn., k. in a., F. & F., 14/4/17, formerly 5928, 9th London Regt.
Smith, Stephen, e. London (Hampstead), 392043, Rfn., k. in a., F. & F., 27/9/17, formerly 5286, 9th London Regt.
Smith, Sydney Harris, e. Hornsey (Muswell Hill), 393823, Rfn., k. in a., F. & F., 14/4/17, formerly 3104, 7th Middx. Regt.
Smith, Sydney William, b. Wembley, e. London (Harrow), 1874, Rfn., k. in a., F. & F., 24/4/15.
Smith, Thomas Walter, e. London (Shoreditch), 392736, Rfn., k. in a., F. & F., 14/4/17, formerly 6423, 9th London Regt.
Smith, Walter James, e. London (Romford), 4558, Rfn., k. in a., F. & F., 1/7/16.

APPENDIX I

Smith, Walter Leslie, b. Bexley, e. London (Bexley), 4373, Rfn., k. in a., F. & F., 1/7/16.
Smith, Walter Sidney, e. London (London), 4004, Rfn., k. in a., F. & F., 1/7/16.
Smith, William James, b. Bethnal Green, e. London (Bethnal Green), 394081, Rfn., k. in a., F. & F., 26/3/18, formerly 8281, 9th London Regt.
Smurthwaite, Thomas Arthur Frank, e. London (Kensal Rise), 394427, Rfn., d. of w., F. & F., 18/8/18.
Snelling, Harold Measday, e. London (Sandwich), 4746, Rfn., k. in a., F. & F., 1/7/16.
Snoswell, Arthur Cecil, b. Tulse Hill, e. London (Tulse Hill), 391332, Rfn., k. in a., F. & F., 11/3/17, formerly 4122, 9th London Regt.
Snoswell, Ernest Edgar, b. Herne Hill, e. London (Tulse Hill), 392540, Rfn., k. in a., F. & F., 25/4/18, formerly 585, R.A.M.C.
Softly, Clement Peter, e. London (Thriplow, Herts), 393689, Rfn., k. in a., F. & F., 14/4/17, formerly 5577, 8th London Regt.
Solly, John Algernon, e. London (Southend), 2441, Rfn., d. of w., F. & F., 29/4/15.
Soulby, Christopher, b. Kendal, Westmorland, e. Carlisle (Kendal), 393797, Rfn., k. in a., F. & F., 14/4/17, formerly 23529, Border Regt.
South, George Robert Stanley, e. London (Tufnell Park), 3473, Rfn., d. of w., F. & F., 11/7/16.
Southon, Herbert, b. Hammersmith, e. London (Fulham), 5721, Rfn., k. in a., F. & F., 25/9/16.
Sowerbutts, Frederick, b. Bethnal Green, e. London (Hackney), 7713, Rfn., k. in a., F. & F., 9/9/16, formerly 5170, 20th London Regt.
Sparrowhawk, Walter Ernest, b. Bloomsbury, e. Camberwell (Camberwell), 393130, Rfn., k. in a., F. & F., 14/4/17, formerly 6887, 9th London Regt.
Spashett, Reginald William, b. Ilford, e. London (Upton Park), 415186, Rfn., k. in a., F. & F., 15/4/18, formerly 6610, 10th London Regt.
Spencer, Reginald Stanley, b. Brentwood, e. London (Grove Park), 391085, Rfn., k. in a., F. & F., 14/4/17, formerly 3743, 9th London Regt.
Spikes, Thomas Richard, b. Peckham, e. London (E. Dulwich), 2074, L/Sgt., k. in a., F. & F., 9/10/16.
Spiller, Herbert Septimus, e. London (London), 392684, Rfn., k. in a., F. & F., 16/8/17, formerly 6368, 9th London Regt.
Spittle, Frank Thomas, e. London (Leyton), 2857, Rfn., k. in a., F. & F., 23/2/15.
Spong, Stephen Alfred George, b. Walworth, e. Camberwell (Camberwell), 393584, Rfn., k. in a., F. & F., 14/4/17, formerly 6182, 12th London Regt.

Spooner, Tom Clifford, e. London (Merton Park), 3214, Rfn., k. in a., F. & F., 1/7/16.
Springfield, Thomas, b. Holborn, e. London (London), 393491, Rfn., d. of w., F. & F., 23/8/17, formerly 5671, 11th London Regt.
Squire, Arthur, e. London (Crouch End), 393836, Cpl., k. in a., F. & F., 14/4/17, formerly 3386, 7th Middx. Regt.
Stacy, Samuel, e. Camberwell (Brixton), 415303, Rfn., d. of w., Home, 28/4/18, formerly 375602, 8th London Regt.
Stamp, Edwin Frederick, e. London (Hampstead), 3019, L/Cpl., d. of w., F. & F., 12/9/16.
Stamp, Sidney, b. Barnsbury, e. London (Finchley), 5739, Rfn., k. in a., F. & F., 9/9/16.
Standcumbe, John Frank, e. London (Walthamstow), 393314, Rfn., k. in a., F. & F., 10/4/17, formerly 5212, 11th London Regt.
Standley, Frederick, b. Birmingham, e. Birmingham (Birmingham), 7539, Rfn., k. in a., F. & F., 14/9/16, formerly 5422, 8th London Regt.
Staniforth, John Smallpage, b. Kentish Town, e. London (Hatch End), 393066, Rfn., k. in a., F. & F., 1/11/17, formerly 5291, 28th London Regt.
Stansfield, Harold, e. London (Finchley), 393741, Rfn., k. in a., F. & F., 14/4/17, formerly 2726, 2nd London Regt.
Stansfield, Harry, b. Manchester, e. London (Canonbury), 391902, Rfn., k. in a., F. & F., 8/7/17, formerly 5082, 9th London Regt.
Stanton, George Robert, e. London (Chelsea), 392084, L/Cpl., d. of w., F. & F., 2/7/18, formerly 5370, 9th London Regt.
Stanton, William Charles Fred, b. Hackney, e. London (Leigh-on-Sea), 390261, Sgt., k. in a., F. & F., 3/5/17, formerly 2011, 9th London Regt.
Staples, Grant Brown, b. Stoke Newington, e. Hornsey (Stoke Newington), 393806, Rfn., k. in a., F. & F., 13/8/17, formerly 2208, 7th Middx. Regt.
Starling, Ernest Herbert, b. West Ham, e. London (Kensington), 392092, Cpl., k. in a., F. & F., 27/9/17, formerly 5379, 9th London Regt.
Stebbings, George, e. Norwich (Bradenham), 6750, Rfn., k. in a., F. & F., 9/10/16, formerly 24493, Norfolk Regt.
Steer, James, b. Battersea, e. London (Battersea), 393552, Rfn., d., F. & F., 21/4/17, formerly 6184, 11th London Regt.
Stephens, Stanley Harry George, b. Newton Abbot, Devon, e. London (Wiltshire), 7623, Rfn., k. in a., F. & F., 9/10/16, formerly 5620, 8th London Regt.
Stephenson, Frank Holt, e. London (New Southgate), 391218, L/Cpl., k. in a., F. & F., 7/11/17, formerly 3956, 9th London Regt.
Stephenson, Harold Wilton, e. London (London), 4112, L/Sgt., k. in a., F. & F., 26/5/16.

Stephenson, John Alfred, e. London (Brentford), 3784, Rfn., k. in a., F. & F., 1/7/16.
Sterckx, John Lewis, b. Clerkenwell, e. London (Wood Green), 1753, Cpl., k. in a., F. & F., 9/10/16.
Stevens, Arthur Mayo, e. London (Palmer's Green), 3787, Rfn., k. in a., F. & F., 1/7/16.
Stevens, Douglas Charles Henman, e. London (Goodmayes), 3882, Rfn., k. in a., F. & F., 20/4/15.
Stilwell, Arthur James, e. London (New Barnet), 4380, Rfn., k. in a., F. & F., 1/7/16.
Stokes, Alfred, b. Shoreditch, e. Stratford (Dalston), 415223, Rfn., k. in a., F. & F., 16/8/17, formerly 7955, 7th London Regt.
Stokes, Arthur, b. Manchester, e. London (Sheffield), 391497, Rfn., d. of w., Home, 30/5/18, formerly 4365, 9th London Regt.
Stone, Frank Hubert, e. London (Camberwell), 2673, L/Sgt., k. in a., F. & F., 26/5/16.
Stone, Herbert, e. Stratford (Clapton), 393054, Rfn., d. of w., F. & F., 29/3/17, formerly 6795, 9th London Regt.
Storey, John, b. Arthurst, Cumberland, e. Carlisle (Cumberland), 7751, Rfn., d., Home, 22/12/16, formerly 23979, Border Regt.
Story, Goronwy, b. Henllam, Denbigh, e. London (Bowes Park), 392099, Rfn., k. in a., F. & F., 27/9/17, formerly 5388, 9th London Regt.
Strangward, Harold John, b. Marylebone, e. London (Cricklewood), 1768, Cpl., k. in a., F. & F., 30/5/16.
Stroud, Reginald Leslie, e. London, 2005, Rfn., d. of w., F. & F., 17/8/16.
Stubbs, Bernard Castle, e. London (Watford), 2655, Rfn., d. of w., F. & F., 23/6/15.
Suddes, Reginald, e. London (Kingsland), 390294, Rfn., k. in a., F. & F., 14/4/17, formerly 2105, 9th London Regt.
Summers, Herbert Frederick, b. Barnsbury, e. Stratford (Leytonstone), 415220, Rfn., k. in a., F. & F., 25/8/18, formerly 7951, 7th London Regt.
Summerton, George Henry, b. Stepney, e. London (Poplar), 7694, Rfn., k. in a., F. & F., 9/10/16, formerly 4969, 20th London Regt.
Sutherland, Albert Ronald, e. London (Brondesbury), 392000, Rfn., k. in a., F. & F., 24/5/17, formerly 5231, 9th London Regt.
Sutherland, Francis, e. Newcastle, 7522, Cpl., k. in a., F. & F., 24/1/17, formerly 5040, 8th London Regt.
Sutton, Harry, e. Wymondham, 6749, Rfn., k. in a., F. & F., 13/11/16, formerly 24510, Norfolk Regt.
Swan, Charles, e. London (Canonbury), 394206, Rfn., d., F. & F., 5/5/17, formerly 4141, 11th London Regt.
Swan, Larendon Haythorn, e. London (Melton Mowbray), 3597, Rfn., k. in a., F. & F., 4/9/15.

Swan, William Wilfred, e. London (Highgate), 393493, Rfn., k. in a., F. & F., 14/4/17, formerly 6133, 11th London Regt.
Sweeting, Gerald Talbot, e. London (Croydon), 2292, Rfn., k. in a., F. & F., 14/3/15.
Swinborn, John Dean, b. Bolton, Lancs, e. London (West Ham), 391686, Rfn., k. in a., F. & F., 25/4/18, formerly 4738, 9th London Regt.
Sykes, Hubert Charles, b. Deddington, e. Camberwell (Rotherhithe), 394010, Rfn., k. in a., F. & F., 27/9/17 to 3/10/17, formerly 8076, 9th London Regt.
Sylvester, William, b. Staines, e. Staines (Staines), 393886, Rfn., k. in a., F. & F., 14/4/17, formerly 3216, 8th Middx. Regt.
Syrett, Harold Charles, e. London (Finchley), 2943, Rfn., k. in a., F. & F., 1/7/16.

Tabbernor, William George, b. Ealing, e. London (Ealing), 390169 Sgt., d., Home, 22/8/17, formerly 1787, 9th London Regt.
Tait, Andrew Duncan, e. London (London), 4143, Rfn., k. in a., F. & F., 1/7/16.
Talby, Robert William, b. Islington, e. London (King's Cross), 5878, Rfn., k. in a., F. & F., 9/9/16.
Tapping, William George, e. London (London), 4379, Rfn., k. in a., F. & F., 1/7/16.
Tarling, Sydney Herbert, e. London (Fulham), 415067, Rfn., k. in a., F. & F., 14/4/17, formerly 4672, 12th London Regt.
Tarrant, George Frederick, e. London (Fulham), 3835, L/Cpl., k. in a., F. & F., 1/7/16.
Tasker, Stanley Thomas, e. Southall (Hounslow), 393912, Rfn., k. in a., F. & F., 14/4/17, formerly 4603, 8th Middx. Regt.
Taverner, Harry Alexander, b. Hersham, e. London (Hammersmith), 1880, L/Cpl., d. of w., F. & F., 26/4/15.
Taylor, Alfred, e. London (Willesden), 390691, Cpl., k. in a., F. & F., 27/9/17, formerly 3029, 9th London Regt.
Taylor, Alfred, b. Clifton-on-Teme, Worcs., e. London (Clifton), 391977, Rfn., k. in a., F. & F., 8/9/17, formerly 5189, 9th London Regt.
Taylor, Alfred Frank, e. London (Seven Kings), 2353, L/Cpl., k. in a., F. & F., 21/4/15.
Taylor, George, b. Camberwell, e. Camberwell (Camberwell), 392873, Rfn., d. of w., F. & F., 20/4/17, formerly 6588, 9th London Regt.
Taylor, Herbert Arthur, e. London (Willesden), 3504, Rfn., k. in a., F. & F., 1/7/16.
Taylor, Herbert John, e. London (Brondesbury), 4945, Rfn., d. of w., Home, 13/10/16.
Taylor, John Ernest, e. London (Richmond), 4772, Rfn., k. in a., F. & F., 1/7/16.

APPENDIX I 637

Taylor, Lionel William, e. London (Wimbledon), 2414, L/Cpl., k. in a., F. & F., 1/7/16.
Taylor, Oscar Albert, b. Lambeth, e. London (Stockwell), 391794, Rfn., k. in a., F. & F., 27/9/17, formerly 4923, 9th London Regt.
Taylor, Robert, b. Hackney, e. Hackney (Clapton), 393758, Rfn., k. in a., F. & F., 30/11/17, formerly 4987, 20th London Regt.
Taylor, William Adams, b. Dundee, e. Dundee (Dundee), 7557, Rfn., k. in a., F. & F., 9/9/16, formerly 5475, 8th London Regt.
Terry, Leslie Eaton, b. Clapham, e. London (Clapham Common), 1858, Rfn., k. in a., F. & F., 1/7/16.
Thirlwell, William Leonard, b. Hendon, e. London (Hendon), 7661, Rfn., k. in a., F. & F., 9/9/16, formerly 5734, 8th London Regt.
Thomas, Edmund Cleeton, b. Balham, e. London (Upper Tooting), 415119, Rfn., d. of w., F. & F., 14/8/17, formerly 5862, 12th London Regt.
Thomas, John, b. London, e. London, 390875, Rfn., k. in a., F. & F., 25/4/18, formerly 3391, 9th London Regt.
Thompson, Frank Lovell, b. Exeter e. London (London), 1907, L/Cpl., k. in a., F. & F., 1/7/16.
Thomson, Fritz Day, b. Shepherd's Bush, e. London (West Green), 392089, Rfn., k. in a., F. & F., 25/4/18, formerly 5376, 9th London Regt.
Thorn, Edward, b. London, e. London (London), 394309, Rfn., d. of w., F. & F., 17/8/17, formerly 3371, 11th London Regt.
Thornett, Albert Valentine, e. London (Hendon), 4116, Rfn., k. in a., F. & F., 1/7/16.
Thornton, William Ewart, b. E. Grinstead, e. London (Tooting), 5749, Rfn., k. in a., F. & F., 25/9/16.
Thorpe, George Frederick, e. London (Fulham), 390458, Sgt., k. in a., F. & F., 27/9/17, formerly 2480, 9th London Regt.
Tiffin, James Ernest, b. Islington, e. London (Islington), 393145, Rfn., k. in a., F. & F., 1/11/17, formerly 6903, 9th London Regt.
Tilbury, Joseph Henry, b. Lambeth, e. London (Vauxhall), 392806, Rfn., k. in a., F. & F., 31/8/18, formerly 6507, 9th London Regt.
Tingey, George Joseph, e. Deptford, 392868, Rfn., k. in a., F. & F., 14/4/17, formerly 6583, 9th London Regt.
Tinsley, Henry, e. London (Holloway), 415196, Rfn., k. in a., F. & F., 16/8/17, formerly 6573, 10th London Regt.
Todd, Charles, e. Fulham (Croydon), 415027, Rfn., d., Home, 5/11/17, formerly 2769, 25th London Regt.
Tolcher, Cecil Robert, e. London (Teignmouth), 5045, Rfn., d. of w., F. & F., 23/1/17.
Toll, George Henry, e. London (Palmer's Green), 2539, Rfn., d. of w., F. & F., 1/5/15.

Tomlinson, James Daniel, b. Leyton, e. London (Kilburn), 1630, Rfn., k. in a., F. & F., 26/10/15.
Tompson, Charles Robert, e. London (Watford), 4540, Rfn., k. in a., F. & F., 1/7/16.
Toms, Charles, b. Islington, e. London (Barnsbury), 393164, Sgt., k. in a., F. & F., 16/8/17, formerly 6930, 9th London Regt.
Townsend, George Charles, e. London (Battersea), 2946, Rfn., k. in a., F. & F., 9/9/16.
Tozer, Arthur William, b. London, e. London (Notting Hill), 1796, Rfn., d. of w., F. & F., 19/7/15.
Tozer, Edward Gidley, e. London (Highgate), 2527, Cpl., k. in a., F. & F., 1/7/16.
Trew, Walter Augustus, b. Kingston, e. London (St. Pancras), 390167, Rfn., k. in a., F. & F., 8/4/17, formerly 1785, 9th London Regt.
Trigg, Alfred Charles, e. London (Merton), 415231, Cpl., k. in a., F. & F., 4/11/18, formerly 4381, 8th London Regt.
Troy, Frederick William, b. Hanwell, e. London (Hanwell), 394362, Rfn., k. in a., F. & F., 18/9/18, formerly 8599, 9th London Regt.
Truscott, William Henry, b. Maidenhead, e. London (London), 1038, Rfn., k. in a., F. & F., 23/8/15.
Trussell, Alan Lionel, e. London (Colchester), 4462, Rfn., k. in a., F. & F., 1/7/16.
Tuck, Courtenay, e. London (Kensal Rise), 390324, Rfn., k. in a., F. & F., 26/3/18, formerly 2171, 9th London Regt.
Tulley, William, e. London (Highbury), 4865, Rfn., k. in a., F. & F., 1/7/16.
Tunbridge, Alexander, e. London (Harlesden), 392501, Rfn., k. in a., F. & F., 14/4/17, formerly 6045, 9th London Regt.
Tunnell, Richard Sidney, e. Lambeth (Streatham), 392872, Rfn., k. in a., F. & F., 14/4/17, formerly 6587, 9th London Regt.
Turner, Francis Henry, e. London (Wembley Hill), 2127, L/Cpl., k. in a., F. & F., 1/1/15.
Turner, Frederick, b. Kelvedon, e. Chelmsford (Coggershall), 393017, Rfn., k. in a., F. & F., 14/8/17, formerly 3263, 5th Essex Regt.
Turner, Gilbert, b. Southwark, e. Southwark (Bermondsey), 415307, Rfn., k. in a., F. & F., 28/3/18, formerly 375599, 8th London Regt.
Turvey, Harry Edward, b. Islington, e. London (Crouch End), 5922, Rfn., k. in a., F. & F., 2/10/16.
Turvey, Percy Charles, e. London (Holborn), 415083, Sgt., k. in a., F. & F., 15/8/17, formerly 3342, 12th London Regt.
Tye, George Harold, b. Retford, Notts, e. Sheffield (Sheffield), 394764, Rfn., k. in a., F. & F., 19/8/18.
Tymms, Christopher Henry Albert, e. London (Cobham), 5025, Rfn., k. in a., F. & F., 1/7/16.

APPENDIX I

Uglow, William Ernest Taylor, b. Cheshunt, e. London (Holborn), 1687, Rfn., k. in a., F. & F., 1/1/15.
Urie, Charles Edward, b. Hoxton, e. London (Bethnal Green), 7658, Rfn., k. in a., F. & F., 9/9/16, formerly 5717, 8th London Regt.

Vale, Alfred James, e. Halstead (Hednigham), 6696, Rfn., k. in a., F. & F., 9/10/16, formerly 3452, Essex Regt.
Vanryn, David, e. London (Willesden), 3448, Rfn., k. in a., F. & F., 24/4/15.
Venning, John Richard, b. St. Pancras, e. London (London), 372, Cpl., k. in a., F. & F., 5/5/15.
Vernon, Frank, e. London (Liverpool), 2512, Rfn., d. of w., F. & F., 7/2/15.
Vickers, Hedley Albert, e. Camberwell (Camberwell), 392817, Rfn., d. of w., F. & F., 17/5/17, formerly 6518, 9th London Regt.
Vining, Ernest George, b. Croydon, e. London (Croydon), 1928, Rfn., d. of w., F. & F., 9/6/15.
Vizard, Thomas, e. London (Paddington), 4442, Rfn., k. in a., F. & F., 1/7/16.
Vockins, John William, e. Lancaster (Carrforth), 419066, Rfn., d. of w., F. & F., 15/10/18, formerly 3837, Royal Lancs Regt.
Volke, Charles Richard, e. London (Forest Gate), 391126, Rfn., d. of w., Home, 12/6/17, formerly 3816, 9th London Regt.

Waddell, Percy Thomas, b. Ashford, Kent, e. London (Ashford), 7634, Rfn., k. in a., F. & F., 25/9/16, formerly 5654, 8th London Regt.
Wakeford, Sidney Thomas, e. London (Kilburn), 391410, Rfn., d. of w., F. & F., 3/5/17, formerly 4234, 9th London Regt.
Walden, George, e. London (Notting Hill), 4183, Rfn., k. in a., F. & F., 1/7/16.
Walder, Alfred Sydney Cornelius, e. Blackheath (Blackheath), 7681, Rfn., d. of w., F. & F., 26/1/17, formerly 4208, 20th London Regt.
Wales, Arthur Edward, b. London, e. London (London), 391408, Rfn., d. of w., F. & F., 24/4/18, formerly 4230, 9th London Regt.
Walford, Charles, e. Southall (Southall), 393883, Rfn., k. in a., F. & F., 16/8/17, formerly 3127, 8th Middx. Regt.
Walker, Arthur Alfred, b. Camberwell, e. London (Balham), 2080, Rfn., k. in a., F. & F., 1/7/16.
Walker, Herbert William, e. London (Lower Tooting), 4964, Rfn., k. in a., F. & F., 1/7/16.
Walker, Thomas, b. Sutton, e. London (Clerkenwell), 394273, Rfn., k. in a., F. & F., 21/9/18, formerly 3879, 11th London Regt.
Wallis, Charles Frederick, b. Croydon, e. London (Croydon), 393062, Rfn., k. in a., F. & F., 29/8/18, formerly 5456, 28th London Regt.

Walsh, John Joseph, b. Westminster, e. London (Fulham), 7535, Rfn., k. in a., F. & F., 25/9/16, formerly 5403, 8th London Regt.
Wandby, Alfred Robert, e. London (Stroud Green), 4033, Rfn., k. in a., F. & F., 1/7/16.
Ward, George, e. London (Battersea), 3615, Rfn., k. in a., F. & F., 9/9/16.
Ward, Percy Randall, b. Hammersmith, e. London (Shepherd's Bush), 390028, Rfn., k. in a., F. & F., 26/3/18, formerly 1403, 9th London Regt.
Ward, Ronald Derrick, e. Fulham (Wimbledon), 7084, Rfn., k. in a., F. & F., 8/10/16, formerly 3062, 25th London Regt.
Wardell, Robert Cyril, b. Wilmslow, Cheshire, e. London (Maidstone), 5730, Rfn., k. in a., F. & F., 9/9/16.
Warne, James, b. Camberwell, e. London (Camberwell), 1966, Rfn., k. in a., F. & F., 1/4/15.
Warner, Andrew, e. London (London), 3405, Rfn., d. of w., F. & F., 28/4/15.
Warr, Percy George, b. Dulwich, e. London (Brixton), 391399, Rfn., d. of w., F. & F., 10/8/18, formerly 4216, 9th London Regt.
Warwicker, William John, e. Camberwell (Peckham), 393588, Rfn., k. in a., F. & F., 14/4/17, formerly 6433, 12th London Regt.
Watkins, Albert George Richard, e. London (Hanwell), 390941, L/Cpl., k. in a., F. & F., 26/9/17, formerly 3508, 9th London Regt.
Watkins, John, b. Marylebone, e. London (St. John's Wood), 391626, Rfn., d. of w., F. & F., 24/8/18, formerly 4620, 9th London Regt.
Watson, Herbert Henry, b. Beverley, e. London (Hull), 7655, Rfn., k. in a., F. & F., 9/10/16, formerly 5710, 8th London Regt.
Watson, James, b. Isleworth, e. Twickenham (Twickenham), 393895, Rfn., k. in a., F. & F., 14/4/17, formerly 3424, 8th Middx. Regt.
Watson, William Francis, b. Bow, e. London (Walthamstow), 363, Sgt., d. of w., F. & F., 1/7/16.
Watton, Arthur, e. Clacton-on-Sea (Clacton), 393024, Rfn., k. in a., F. & F., 14/4/17, formerly 3233, Essex Regt.
Watts, Ernest, b. Warboys, e. London (Harrow-on-Hill), 5746, Rfn., k. in a., F. & F., 9/9/16.
Wayland, Henry George, e. Chelmsford (Colchester), 6759, Rfn., k. in a., F. & F., 9/10/16, formerly 2966, Essex Regt.
Weaver, George James, b. Peckham, e. London (Bermondsey), 394275, Rfn., d., F. & F., 14/4/18, formerly 6232, 11th London Regt.
Webb, Archie William, b. Holmwood, e. London (Dalston), 391421, Rfn., k. in a., F. & F., 27/9/17, formerly 4256, 9th London Regt.
Webb, George, b. Kensington, e. London (Kensington), 675, L/Cpl., d. of w., F. & F., 1/1/15.

APPENDIX I 641

Webb, Victor William, e. London (London), 391469, Rfn., k. in a., F. & F., 14/4/17, formerly 4322, 9th London Regt.
Weedon, William Otway, e. London (London), 2536, Rfn., k. in a., F. & F., 24/4/15.
Weight, Albert, b. Soho, e. London (Homerton), 4535, L/Cpl., d., Home, 6/3/16.
Weight, Frederick Charles, b. Soho, e. London, 394382, Rfn., k. in a., F. & F., 9/8/18.
Weil, Raphael Charles, b. Islington, e. London (Highbury), 6029, Rfn., k. in a., F. & F., 25/9/16.
Welch, Archibald Lawrence, e. London (Marylebone), 2427, Rfn., d. of w., F. & F., 7/1/15.
Welch, Harold Alfred, e. London (Highbury), 2626, Rfn., d. of w., F. & F., 28/4/15.
Wellman, George, b. Hoxton, e. London (Tooting), 390175, Cpl., d., Home, 4/9/17, formerly 1794, 9th London Regt.
Wells, Douglas Edward, e. London (Westminster), 2380, L/Cpl., k. in a., F. & F., 1/7/16.
Wesley, Charles, e. Gosport, 7521, Rfn., k. in a., F. & F., 25/9/16, formerly 5037, 8th London Regt.
Wesson, Alfred, b. St. Pancras, e. London (Tufnell Park), 391237, Rfn., k. in a., F. & F., 27/9/17, formerly 3988, 9th London Regt.
West, Henry, e. Clacton-on-Sea (Weeley, Essex), 392958, Rfn. k. in a., F. & F., 12/7/17, formerly 2922, Essex Regt.
West, Walter Harry, e. London (Hoddesdon), 4030, Rfn., k. in a., F. & F., 3/6/16.
West, William, e. Battersea, 393105, Rfn., k. in a., F. & F., 14/4/17, formerly 6858, 9th London Regt.
Weston, Thomas Charles, b. Holborn, e. London (Stepney), 394335, Rfn., k. in a., F. & F., 28/3/18, formerly 5255, 11th London Regt.
Westwood, William John, e. Battersea (Wandsworth), 394088, Rfn., k. in a., F. & F., 26/5/17, formerly 8291, 9th London Regt.
Wheatley, Claude James, e. Fulham (Chiswick), 7083, Rfn., k. in a., F. & F., 9/10/16, formerly 1986, 25th London Regt.
Wheatley, Robert William, e. London (Walworth), 394277, Rfn., d. of w., F. & F., 16/4/17, formerly 5349, 11th London Regt.
Wheeler, William David, e. London (London), 2915, Rfn., k. in a., F. & F., 26/11/16.
Whiffin, Bertie, b. Southwark, e. Camberwell (Bermondsey), 394020, Rfn., k. in a., F. & F., 25/4/18, formerly 8086, 9th London Regt.
Whitaker, George Joseph, b. Southwark, e. London (Newington), 415189, Rfn., k. in a., F. & F., 16/8/17, formerly 6586, 10th London Regt.
White, Albert, e. London (Charlton), 2544, Rfn., k. in a., F. & F., 1/6/16.

White, Alexander Clement, b. Stoke Newington, e. London (Palmer's Green), 390047, Sgt., k. in a., F. & F., 27/9/17, formerly 1467, 9th London Regt.
White, Charles Albert, e. London (Vauxhall), 4533, Rfn., k. in a., F. & F., 1/7/16.
White, Herbert Thornton, e. London (Herne Hill), 391574, Sgt., k. in a., F. & F., 14/4/17, formerly 4516, 9th London Regt.
White, Herbert William, e. London (Westminster), 4573, Rfn., k. in a., F. & F., 1/7/16.
White, Thomas, e. London (Hammersmith), 391288, Rfn., k. in a., F. & F., 28/3/17, formerly 4059, 9th London Regt.
Whitehouse, Sidney Charles, e. London (Paddington), 3116, Rfn., k. in a., F. & F., 1/7/16.
Whorwood, Reginald Henry, b. Chadwick End, e. London, 4481, Rfn., k. in a., F. & F., 9/10/16.
Wickens, George Edward, e. London (Uckfield), 2576, Rfn., k. in a., F. & F., 1/7/16.
Wickens, Thomas Martin, b. Crawley Down, e. London (Uckfield), 2574, Rfn., k. in a., F. & F., 9/9/16.
Wickens, Frederick James, e. London (London), 391333, Rfn., d. of w., F. & F., 8/6/17, formerly 4123, 9th London Regt.
Wiffen, Charlie, e. London (Queen's Park), 5750, Rfn., k. in a., F. & F., 20/7/16.
Wiffen, Frank, b. Romford, e. London (Twickenham), 5749, Rfn., k. in a., F. & F., 9/9/16.
Wigg, Richard Edward, b. Lewisham, e. London (Battersea), 1560, Cpl., k. in a., F. & F., 1/7/16.
Wiggins, Sidney Reginald, e. London (Highgate), 390666, Rfn., d., Home, 23/12/17, formerly 2976, 9th London Regt.
Wilcox, Henry John, b. Dulwich, e. Camberwell (Peckham), 394336, Rfn., k. in a., F. & F., 16/8/17, formerly 6204, 11th London Regt.
Wilde, George Richard, b. Brighton, e. London (Marylebone), 391972, Rfn., k. in a., F. & F., 29/11/17, formerly 5178, 9th London Regt.
Wilder, Herbert Edwin, e. London (Shepherd's Bush), 393638, Rfn., d. of w., F. & F., 17/8/17, formerly 5449, 8th London Regt.
Wilkins, George William, b. Kilburn, e. London (Holloway), 393328, Rfn., d. of w., F. & F., 14/4/18, formerly 5180, 11th London Regt.
Wilkinson, Leonard R., e. London (E. Dulwich), 2240, Rfn., k. in a., F. & F., 24/4/15,
Williams, Charles Cuthbert, e. London (East Ham), 393770, Rfn., k. in a., F. & F., 5/9/17, formerly 5148, 20th London Regt.
Williams, John, b. St. Pancras, e. London (London), 7571, Rfn., k. in a., F. & F., 2/10/16, formerly 5503, 8th London Regt.

APPENDIX I 643

Williams, John George, b. Fulham, e. London (Hammersmith), 392027, Rfn., k. in a., F. & F., 3/9/17, formerly 5266, 9th London Regt.
Williams, Leonard Hame, b. Lowestoft, e. Lowestoft, 392478, Rfn., k. in a., F. & F., 26/9/17, formerly 6016, 9th London Regt.
Williams, Stanley George, e. London (Wood Green), 2996, Rfn., k. in a., F. & F., 1/7/16.
Williams, Thomas Clifford, e. London (Bournemouth), 393057, Rfn., d. of w., F. & F., 28/4/18, formerly 4197, 28th London Regt.
Williams, Trevor, e. Stratford (West Ham), 393589, Rfn., d., F. & F., 18/5/17, formerly 5948, 12th London Regt.
Willis, Frederick Kenway, b. Stoke Newington, e. London (Stoke Newington), 7650, Rfn., d., F. & F., 10/10/16.
Willis, Stanley Frank, b. Clapham, e. Camberwell (Stockwell), 415208, Rfn., k. in a., F. & F., 13/8/17, formerly 7927, 7th London Regt.
Willmer, Alfred George, e. London (Highgate), 391551, Rfn., k. in a., F. & F., 14/4/17, formerly 4470, 9th London Regt.
Willows, William Peter, e. London (King's Cross), 3399, Rfn., k. in a., F. & F., 1/7/16.
Wilmot, Bernard, e. London (Streatham), 4320, Rfn., k. in a., F. & F., 25/9/16.
Wilmott, Arthur, e. Hornsey (Harringay), 393812, Rfn., k. in a., F. & F., 14/4/17, formerly 2584, 7th Middx. Regt.
Wilson, Allen William, e. London (London), 390883, L/Cpl., k. in a., F. & F., 27/9/17, formerly 3401, 9th London Regt.
Wilson, Edward Henry, e. London (Finchley), 2056, Rfn., k. in a., F. & F., 24/4/15.
Wilson, Edward Milton, b. Tooting, e. Kingston (Merton), 394515, Rfn., d. of w., F. & F., 24/10/18.
Wilson, Stanley, b. Leeds, e. London (Leeds), 391096, Rfn., k. in a., F. & F., 26/3/18, formerly 3767, 9th London Regt.
Wilson, William Charles, e. London (Shepherd's Bush), 391442, Rfn., k. in a., F. & F., 24/5/17, formerly 4287, 9th London Regt.
Winby, Gilbert Barnett, b. Edgbaston, Warwick, e. London (Hammersmith), 5954, Rfn., k. in a., F. & F., 25/9/16.
Wiseman, Harold Charles, e. Pinner, Herts (Pinner), 392528, Rfn., d. of w., F. & F., 19/5/17, formerly 6077, 9th London Regt.
Witts, Alfred, b. Alton, e. London (Royston), 7663, Rfn., k. in a., F. & F., 25/9/16, formerly 5740, 8th London Regt.
Wood, Charles Hunter, b. Frettenham, Norfolk, e. London (Norfolk), 5529, Rfn., k. in a., F. & F., 25/9/16.
Wood, George Gilbert Beaton, b. Hammersmith, e. London (Hampstead), 5887, Rfn., k. in a., F. & F., 9/10/16, formerly 4023, 28th London Regt.
Wood, William, b. Southwark, e. London, 7587, Rfn., k. in a., F. & F., 9/9/16, formerly 5538, 8th London Regt.

Woodcock, John Edward, b. Bethnal Green, e. London (Bethnal Green), 394300, Rfn., d. of w., F. & F., 19/4/17, formerly 5953, 12th London Regt.
Woods, Albert Shreeve, e. Great Yarmouth (Gorleston), 6731, Rfn., k. in a., F. & F., 9/10/16, formerly 24516, Norfolk Regt.
Woolcock, Charles, e. London (St. Levan), 393627, Rfn., k. in a., F. & F., 6/4/17, formerly 5050, 8th London Regt.
Worley, Reginald George, e. London (Brixton), 2408, Rfn., d. of w., F. & F., 4/4/15.
Wormall, William Arthur, e. London (Kensal Rise), 4153, Rfn., k. in a., F. & F., 1/7/16.
Worster, Sidney Herbert, b. Gravesend, e. London (Anerley), 392135, Rfn., k. in a., F. & F., 14/8/17, formerly 5452, 9th London Regt.
Wright, Arnold Henry, e. London (Salisbury), 2041, Rfn., k. in a., F. & F., 1/4/15.
Wright, Frederick Arthur, b. Balham, e. London (Crouch End), 3967, L/Cpl., k. in a., F. & F., 9/9/16.
Wright, John Edward, e. Stratford (Upton Manor), 393831, Rfn., d. of w., F. & F., 18/4/17, formerly 6538, 9th London Regt.
Wright, Sidney, e. London (Bromley), 2610, Rfn., k. in a., F. & F., 20/4/15.
Wright, William George, e. London (Acton Vale), 390306, Sgt., k. in a., F. & F., 8/9/17, formerly 2135, 9th London Regt.
Wyatt, George Edward, e. London (Kensington), 3202, Rfn., k. in a., F. & F., 29/4/15.
Wyatt, John Stevenson, e. London (Streatham Hill), 390414, Sgt., d. of w., F. & F., 6/7/18, formerly 2399, 9th London Regt.
Wyatt, Harry William George, b. Newington Butts, e. Kingston (Croydon), 394653, Rfn., d. of w., F. & F., 28/3/18.

Yetton, William Valentine, b. Bermondsey, e. Camberwell (Peckham), 394334, Rfn., k. in a., F. & F., 28/3/18, formerly 6195, 11th London Regt.
Young, Frederick George, e. London (Earl's Court), 390468, Rfn., k. in a., F. & F., 22/9/18, formerly 2503, 9th London Regt.
Young, John, b. Egremont, e. Carlisle (Cleator Moor), 7758, Rfn., k. in a., F. & F., 25/12/16, formerly 20903, Border Regt.
Young, Norman Stuart, e. London (Thornton Heath), 2497, Rfn., k. in a., F. & F., 21/4/15.
Young, Sidney John, b. Barnsbury, e. London (Holloway), 393398, Rfn., k. in a., F. & F., 28/3/18, formerly 2015, 11th London Regt.
Young, Victor H., b. Chiswick, e. London (Neasden), 1558, Rfn., k. in a., F. & F., 23/4/15.

APPENDIX II

DECORATIONS AND AWARDS GAINED BY 9TH BATTALION LONDON REGIMENT (QUEEN VICTORIA'S RIFLES)

OFFICERS

V.C.
Capt. Woolley, G. H. . . . 21.5.15

K.C.B.
Lieut.-Gen. Pitcairn Campbell, Sir W. . 23.6.15

C.M.G. 3rd CLASS
Lieut.-Col. Shipley, R. B. . . . 23.6.15

D.S.O.
Lieut.-Col. Dickins, V. W. F. . . . 13.1.16
Lieut.-Col. Roe, W. F. 13.1.16
Major O'Shea, T. 3.6.16
Lieut.-Col. Follett, F. B. 18.7.17
Lieut.-Col. Langworthy Parry, P. E. . 1.1.18
Capt. Baudains, G. La C. 26.7.18
Major Lindsey Renton, R. H. . . . 1.2.19

O.B.E.
Capt. Marten, L. H. 1.1.19
Lieut.-Col. Langworthy Parry, P. E. . 3.6.19
Major Cox, R. W. 3.6.19
Capt. Woodruff, N. F. 3.6.19
Capt. Burchell, J. M. 3.6.19
Capt. (Hon.-Major) Pixley, S. A. . . 3.6.19

M.B.E.
Capt. Parker, W. W. 3.6.19
Capt. Waghorn, H. C. 3.6.19
Capt. Langmead, H. F. 11.11.19
Capt. Leonard, G. S. 11.11.19

Military Cross

Capt. Sampson, S. J. M.	23.6.15
Lieut. Eccles, J. D.	3.6.16
Capt. Clarke, A. B. (R.A.M.C.)	13.10.16
Lieut. Stewart, H. R. (8th Middx. attd.)	13.10.16
Capt. Symes, E. D.	14.11.16
2nd Lieut. Mayer, G. D.	18.7.17
2nd Lieut. Bowditch, W. G.	18.7.17
Capt. Kinnison, C. H.	26.9.17
do. (Bar)	18.2.18
Capt. Prince, H. S.	26.9.17
Capt. Mackenzie, K. L.	18.10.17
Lieut. McAdam, W. A.	18.10.17
A/Capt. Ralls, F. H.	18.10.17
do. (Bar)	7.11.18
2nd Lieut. Jones, R. L.	18.10.17
Lieut. Wagstaff, B. G.	18.10.17
Capt. Baudains, G. La C.	18.10.17
Capt. Spencer Pryse	27.10.17
Capt. Eustace, G. (R.A.M.C.)	19.11.17
Lieut. Brown, S. S.	17.12.17
do. (Bar)	26.7.18
do. (2nd Bar)	16.9.18
Major Wilton, W. P.	1.1.18
Capt. Nichols, J.	1.1.18
Major Cowtan, A. L.	1.1.18
Capt. Andrews, J. C.	1.1.18
Lieut. Plunkett, H. J.	14.2.18
2nd Lieut. Mills, P. W.	7.8.18
A/Capt. Keeson, C. A. G. C.	16.9.18
Capt. Gray, W. (2nd Lon. R. Fus. attd.)	7.11.18
Capt. Clarke, P. S. (R.A.M.C.)	7.11.18
Lieut. Davies, W. A.	11.1.19
2nd Lieut. Powell, P. W.	11.1.19
Capt. Bowler, W. E. (17th Lon. attd.)	11.1.19
Capt. Smith, H. R.	1.2.19
A/Capt. Hodgson, T.	15.2.19
Lieut. Lacey, G. H.	15.2.19
Lieut. Hibbard, H. E.	15.2.19
A/Capt. Rayner, V. G.	2.4.19
Lieut. Tabberer, C. O.	2.4.19
A/Capt. Duncan, L.	3.6.19
Lieut. Forsyth, G.	3.6.19
Lieut. Holloway, S. J.	3.6.19
Capt. Woolley, G. H.	3.6.19

APPENDIX II

Mentions in Dispatches
Officers

Capt. Shea, S. V. (1st)	14.1.15
Lieut.-Col. Shipley, R. B.	31.5.15
Major O'Shea, T.	31.5.15
Capt. Culme-Seymour, G.	31.5.15
Capt. Sampson, S. J. M.	31.5.15
2nd Lieut. Cawston, E. P.	31.5.15
2nd Lieut. Woolley, G. H. (1st)	31.5.15
Lieut.-Col. Dickins, V. W. F. (1st)	1.1.16
Capt. Lindsey-Renton, R. H. (1st)	1.1.16
Capt. Andrews, J. C. (1st)	1.1.16
Capt. Roe, W. F.	1.1.16
Lieut. Murray, R. B.	1.1.16
Lieut.-Col. Dickins, V. W. F. (2nd)	15.6.16
Major O'Shea, T. (2nd)	15.6.16
Capt. Andrews, J. C. (2nd)	15.6.16
Lieut. Mackenzie, K. L. (1st)	15.6.16
Lieut.-Col. Dickins, V. W. F. (3rd)	4.1.17
Capt. Cowtan, A. L. (1st)	4.1.17
Lieut. Garside, F. G.	4.1.17
Lieut. Farmiloe, T. H.	4.1.17
Lieut. Brandram, A.	4.1.17
Lieut. Mackenzie, K. L. (2nd)	4.1.17
Major Lindsey-Renton, R. H. (2nd)	9.4.17
Capt. Brand, D. W. McL.	25.5.17
A/Lt.-Col. Follett, F. B. (2nd R. War. attd.)	18.12.17
Lieut.-Col. Langworthy Parry, P. E. (1st)	24.12.17
Lieut.-Col. Bradney, J. A.	24.12.17
Capt. Griffith, G. F.	24.12.17
Capt. Walker, H. S.	24.12.17
Lieut. Samuelson, H.	24.12.17
2nd Lieut. Worlledge, J. L.	24.12.17
Major Lindsey-Renton, R. H. (3rd)	25.5.18
Capt. Johnson, K. W.	25.5.18
A/Capt. Philbrick, A. N.	25.5.18
Major Cox, R. W. (1st)	25.5.18
Capt. Marten, L. H.	20.12.18
Capt. Woolley, G. H. (2nd)	20.12.18
Major Cox, R. W. (2nd)	30.12.18
Capt. Burchell, J. M. (1st)	30.12.18
Capt. Baudains, G. La C.	30.12.18
Lieut. Pickett, E. T.	5.3.19
Lieut. Hewitt, G. G.	25.3.19
Lieut.-Col. Dickins, V. W. F. (4th)	27.3.19
Lieut.-Col. Langworthy Parry, P. E. (2nd)	27.3.19
Lieut. Gordon, A.	5.6.19

QUEEN VICTORIA'S RIFLES

Capt. Burchell, J. M.	5.7.19
Major Cowtan, A. L. (2nd)	5.7.19
Capt. White, G. B.	5.7.19
A/Lieut.-Col. Powell, E. G. (Gren. Gds. attd.)	8.7.19
Major Lindsey-Renton, R. H. (4th)	10.7.19
Major Cox, R. W. (3rd)	10.7.19
Capt. Tolley, G.	10.7.19
Capt. McClure, G. B.	10.7.19
Lieut. Swift, H. W.	10.7.19
Lieut. Edgar, W. R.	10.7.19
2nd Lieut. Hall, S. C.	10.7.19
Capt. Oram, R. G.	28.8.19
Lieut. Palmer, F. N.	28.8.19
Capt. Franklin, S. S.	28.8.19
Major Shea, S. V. (2nd)	28.8.19
Major Warren, R. G.	3.2.20

FOREIGN ORDERS AND DECORATIONS
OFFICERS
Legion d'Honneur France

Lieut.-Col. Powell, E.G.H. (Gren. Gds. attd.)

Croix de Guerre, France

Lieut. Holloway, H. V.	7.1.19
Capt. Marten, L. H.	19.6.19

Croix de Guerre, Belgium

Capt. Prince, H. S.	11.3.18
Major Lindsey-Renton, R. H.	12.7.18
Capt. Johnson, K. W.	12.7.18
Major Cowtan, A. L.	12.7.18

Ordre de la Couronne, Belgium

Capt. Prince, H. S.	24.9.17

Ordre de l'Etoile Noire

Lieut. Gordon, A.	11.3.19

Order of the Wen Hu, 4th Class, China

Major Cox, R. W.	17.2.20

Order of St. Anne, Russia, " With Swords " 3rd Class

2nd Lieut. Langmead, H. F.
2nd Lieut. Leonard, G. S.

Order of St. Stanislas, Russia, " With Swords " 3rd Class

2nd Lieut. Langmead, H. F.

APPENDIX II

W.O.'s, N.C.O.'s, AND RFN.

Distinguished Conduct Medal

Lce.-Cpl. Peabody, H. D.	1.6.15
C.S.M. Pulleyn, E. H.	3.6.15
Sergt. Burgess, E. C.	23.6.15
C.S.M. Sheriff, A. (K.R.R.C. attd.)	14.1.16
C.S.M. Brawn, M.	1.1.16
Lce.-Cpl. Yates, A. J.	1.1.16
Lce.-Cpl. Eames, E. E.	2.6.16
Sergt. Brawn, W.	13.10.16
Sergt. Reeves, J.	1.1.17
C.S.M. Bowditch, W. G.	1.1.17
C.S.M. Mackenna, E. T.	4.6.17
do. (Bar)	5.12.18
Sergt. Madger, A. W.	20.10.17
C.S.M. Manktelow, T. W.	3.6.18
Lce.-Cpl. Stroud, S. O.	3.9.18
Sergt. Bull, P. C.	30.10.18
Sergt. Thomas, D. P.	31.12.18
Sergt. Savage, F. J.	14.2.19
Lce.-Sergt. Frost, A. W. G.	18.2.19

Military Medal

Sergt. Hickman, F. H. C.	2.6.16
Rfn. Darbey, W. H.	19.7.16
Sergt. Murch, C. E.	1.9.16
Sergt. Masters, W. T.	1.9.16
Sergt. Hutchings, E.	1.9.16
Sergt. Nathan, L.	1.9.16
Corpl. Packer, F. G.	1.9.16
Lce.-Cpl. Woodland, J. B.	1.9.16
Rfn. Armitage, P. M.	1.9.16
Rfn. Collins, L. G.	1.9.16
Sergt. Halfacre, W. R. B.	27.10.16
Sergt. Sim, C. K.	27.10.16
Sergt. Munnings, H. C.	27.10.16
Sergt. Telfer, G. F.	27.10.16
Sergt. Wilson, A. J.	27.10.16
Cpl. Riddle, R.	27.10.16
Cpl. Streather, W. A.	27.10.16
Lce.-Cpl. Dorrill, J. A.	27.10.16
Lce.-Cpl. Rose, F. J. R.	27.10.16
Rfn. Slaughter, A. W.	27.10.16
Rfn. Palmer, W. J.	27.10.16

Rfn. Squires, A. W.	27.10.16
Rfn. Mainwaring	27.10.16
do. (Bar)	30.10.17
Rfn. Hodgkinson, E. W. G.	27.10.16
Sergt. Arnold, G.	10.11.16
C.S.M. Brehaut, F. T. A.	11.11.16
Sergt. Barrett, W. V.	16.11.16
Sergt. Fitch, J. P.	8.12.16
Lce.-Cpl. Coventry, H.	8.12.16
Rfn. Wynter, H.	8.12.16
Rfn. Nugent, A. H.	8.12.16
Sergt. Roads, S.	19.12.16
Rfn. Smith, R.	6.1.17
Rfn. Bell, K. M.	9.2.17
Lce.-Cpl. Hooper, S. J.	11.2.17
Cpl. Rawson, F.	11.5.17
Rfn. Phillips, G. T.	15.6.17
Sergt. Spiller, H. J.	15.6.17
Sergt. Tuckley, H.	15.6.17
Sergt. Rowe, P. G.	15.6.17
Sergt. Pearson, W. H.	15.6.17
Rfn. Tolliday, A. L. W.	15.6.17
Rfn. Riddle, W. H.	15.6.17
Rfn. Reynolds, H.	18.7.17
Rfn. Seward, E. C.	18.7.17
Rfn. Hooper, W. A.	18.7.17
Rfn. Stroud, S. O.	18.7.17
Lce.-Cpl. Collier, S. C.	27.7.17
Lce.-Cpl. Seymour, G. T.	30.10.17
Sergt. Withers, C. J.	2.11.17
Sergt. Gander, A.	2.11.17
Sergt. Gessy, F. R.	2.11.17
Sergt. Hawkins, H. C. J.	2.11.17
Lce.-Sergt. Frost, A. W. G.	2.11.17
Lce.-Cpl. Haynes, W. B.	2.11.17
Lce.-Cpl. Cronin, A.	2.11.17
Lce.-Cpl. Moon, C. L.	2.11.17
Lce.-Cpl. Hornby, P. H.	2.11.17
Rfn. Borrie, W. A.	2.11.17
Rfn. Dutton, J. A.	**2.11.17**
Rfn. Wooller, A. H.	2.11.17
Rfn. Elkington, E. W.	2.11.17
Rfn. Thomas, C. F.	2.11.17
Rfn. Joyce, G. T.	2.11.17
Rfn. Howett, E. G.	2.11.17
Rfn. Pinner, J. W. G.	2.11.17
Cpl. Chapman, W. H.	19.11.17
Lce.-Cpl. Harrold, S. H.	19.11.17

APPENDIX II

Rfn. Weller, E.	19.11.17
Rfn. Thompson, E. H.	19.11.17
Rfn. Bryant, J.	19.11.17
do. (Bar)	13.5.19
Cpl. Sandys, E. T.	14.12.17
Lce.-Cpl. Matthey, H. E.	17.12.17
Rfn. Brushett, A. V.	17.12.17
Rfn. Saunders, H. S.	17.12.17
Rfn. Grate, W.	17.12.17
Rfn. Garrett, H. G.	17.12.17
Rfn. Sage, J. W.	17.12.17
Rfn. Eve, D. H.	17.12.17
Rfn. Gully, A. F.	17.12.17
Cpl. Savage, L. J.	17.12.17
Cpl. Lloyd, F. J.	17.12.17
Cpl. Hutchings, H. J.	28.1.18
Sergt. Tyler, A. J.	4.2.18
Rfn. Watson, W. H.	4.2.18
Sergt. Porter, A. T.	23.2.18
Rfn. Crocker, W. G.	13.3.18
Cpl. Neighbour, A. E.	15.3.18
Sergt. Lowis, F. J.	13.5.18
Rfn. Hutchings, J. W. C.	11.6.18
Sergt. Atkins, J. H.	11.6.18
Sergt. Marshall, A. E.	17.6.18
Cpl. Dyer, S. A.	26.6.18
Lce.-Cpl. Newman, C. T.	27.6.18
Rfn. Spratt, H. H.	16.7.18
Lce.-Cpl. Sherlock, F. S.	26.8.18
Sergt. Lyons, G. J.	26.8.18
Rfn. Finch, F.	26.8.18
Lce.-Cpl. Barnes, T. W.	29.8.18
Cpl. Irons, A.	29.8.18
Sergt. Wakefield, D. T.	21.1.19
A/Sergt. Alexander, S. J.	21.1.19
Rfn. Eves, A. W.	21.1.19
Rfn. Smith, C.	21.1.19
Rfn. Engleton, F. W. G.	21.1.19
Rfn. Gray, P. W.	21.1.19
Rfn. Cole, F. A.	21.1.19
Rfn. Curtis, R. H.	21.1.19
Lce.-Sergt. Cartmell, H. J.	21.1.19
Rfn. Green, R. C.	21.1.19
Sergt. Garrard, J.	24.1.19
Rfn. Porter, D.	24.1.19
Rfn. Combley, A.	24.1.19
Rfn. Hodson, H. W.	24.1.19
Sergt. Ridgley, J.	11.2.19

Rfn. Parker, L.	11.2.19
Sergt. Baxter, R.	7.2.19
Rfn. Twitchen, H. O.	7.2.19
Rfn. Lewington, C. J.	11.2.19
Rfn. Murphy, J.	11.2.19
Sergt. Kates, C.	11.3.19
Sergt. Dunn, S. E.	11.3.19
Cpl. Bunting, B. H.	11.3.19
Rfn. Silvey, C. H.	13.3.19
Rfn. Buchanan, C.	28.3.19
Sergt. Howell, J.	13.5.19
Rfn. Carrington, J. W.	13.5.19
Sergt. Shaw, C.	14.5.19
Rfn. Dove, B. (11th Lon., attd. 9th)	14.5.19
Sergt. Hart, A. G. (6th Lon., attd. 9th)	14.5.19
Lce.-Cpl. Addington, S.	14.5.19
Cpl. Lowe, T.	14.5.19
Rfn. Rossi, P.	14.5.19
Sergt. Law, W.	22.7.19
Sergt. Been, C. E.	22.7.19
Sergt. Butcher, C. E.	22.7.19
Rfn. Gosney, H.	23.7.19
Rfn. Trigwell, G. A.	19.8.19
Cpl. Bocking, H.	19.8.19
Rfn. Kramar, M.	20.8.19
Sergt. Mitchell, J.	20.8.19

Meritorious Service Medal

Sergt. Ure, D.	25.5.17
A/Sergt. Weatherley, W. H.	25.9.17
Sergt. Penny, H. T.	1.1.18
Sergt. Overall, V.	17.6.18
Sergt. Bull, P. L.	17.6.18
Sergt. Ashman, B. G.	17.6.18
Sergt. Marshall, A. E.	17.6.18
Sergt. Wells, E. J.	17.6.18
Rfn. Eddowes, F. E.	17.6.18
Rfn. Littleworth, T.	17.6.18
Rfn. Carrington, J. W.	17.6.18
Sergt. Fisher, F. C.	17.6.18
Sergt. Coleman, S. H.	17.1.19
Sergt. Lloyd, F. J.	17.1.19
Cpl. Jones, M. H. A.	17.1.19
Rfn. Bentley, A. F. J.	17.1.19
C.S.M. Keppel, G.	21.2.19
Lce.-Cpl. Peet, D. W.	5.5.19

APPENDIX II

C.S.M. Lott, G.	30.5.19
A/C.S.M. Jones, B. C.	30.5.19
Q.M.S. Andrew, W. J.	30.5.19
A/R.S.M. Budd, D. J. B.	30.5.19
A/Cpl. Lake, H. B.	30.5.19
Rfn. Sturgess, W. J.	30.5.19
Sergt. Riordan, J. R.	30.5.19
Sergt. Palmer, A. S.	3.6.19
C.Q.M.S. Perry, P.	3.6.19
Lce.-Cpl. Lea, F.	16.10.19

MENTIONS IN DISPATCHES

W.O.'s, N.C.O.'s AND RFN.

C.S.M. Sheriff, A.	14.1.15
Sergt. Brehaut, F. T. A.	31.5.15
Sergt. Halfacre, W. R. B.	31.5.15
C.S.M. Brawn, M.	31.5.15
C.S.M. How, H. J.	2.1.17
Sergt. Carr, G. R.	24.2.17
S.S.M. Mayor, P. E.	24.2.17
Sergt. Beavis, L.	25.5.17
Sergt. Scott, G.	25.5.17
Sergt. Bartlett, J.	25.5.17
Sergt. Ure, D.	25.5.17
Sergt. Coleman, S. H.	21.12.17
R.S.M. Tomlinson, H. G. R.	24.12.17
Sergt. Penny, H. T.	28.12.17
Cpl. Rawson, F.	9.1.18
Cpl. Lake, H. B.	7.4.18
Rfn. Catton	7.4.18
Rfn. Whalley, A. R.	7.4.18
Sergt. Haddon, E. D.	13.8.18
A/R.S.M. Munnings, H. C.	27.12.18
Sergt. Lingfield, E.	30.12.18
A/Sergt. Kent, F. W.	8.7.19
Lce.-Cpl. Walker, R. J.	8.7.19
A/Sergt. Weatherley, W. H.	8.7.19
Rfn. Morbey, S. A.	8.7.19
Rfn. Holden, R. B.	8.7.19
Sergt. Fisher, F. C.	8.7.19
Rfn. Price, R. S.	23.7.19
C.Q.M.S. Chapman, A. E.	28.8.19
C.S.M. Gibbs, B.	28.8.19
A/R.Q.M.S. Bartlett, J.	11.11.19

QUEEN VICTORIA'S RIFLES

FOREIGN ORDERS AND DECORATIONS
W.O.'s, N.C.O.'s AND RFN.

Cross of the Order of St. George, 4th Class, Russia

C.S.M. Sheriff, A. J. (K.R.R.C., attd. 9th) . 25.8.15

Medal of St. George, 4th Class, Russia

Rfn. Collins, L. G. 15.2.17

Croix de Guerre, France or Belgium

Rfn. Smith, R. 12.7.17
Rfn. Hawtin, R. J. 14.7.17
Sergt. Butcher, C. E. 9.7.18
A/C.S.M. Briggs, S. T. 9.7.18
Sergt. Smith, L. R. 9.7.18
Rfn. Wilding, A. P. 9.7.18
C.S.M. Mills, P. M. 9.7.18
Rfn. Bentley, A. T. G. 12.7.18

Medal for Military Valour, Italy

C.S.M. Mackenna, E. T. 24.5.17

Military Medal for Good Service, Portugal

A/Sergt. Robson 8.3.20

ADDENDA TO ROLL OF HONOUR
NAMES OMITTED FROM THE OFFICIAL WAR OFFICE LIST

OFFICERS

Lieut. Adamson, k. in a., 7/9/18. (See page 437.)
Lieut. Bartman, d. of w., 14/4/17. (See page 237.)
Lieut. Gibb, k. in a., 14/4/17. (See page 237.)
2nd Lieut. Arnold, A. L., k. in a., 15/8/17. (See page 251.)
2nd Lieut. Scott, R. B., k. in a., 8/9/16. (See page 184.)
2nd Lieut. Unwin, k. in a., 10/10/16. (See page 202.)

OTHER RANKS

Lce.-Cpl. Hull, k. in a., 18/5/18. (See page 418.)
Lce.-Cpl. Stiles, k. in a., 18/7/18. (See page 420.)
Rfn. Halls, k. in a., 25/4/18. (See page 416.)
Rfn. Hewlett, k. in a., 23/12/16. (See page 208.)
Rfn. Ireland, k. in a., 10/4/17. (See page 230.)
Rfn. Millington, Edward Anthony, k. in a., 23/1/17.
Rfn. Petherick, d. of w., 6/7/18. (See page 419.)

INDEX

Abeele, 250, 256
Ablainzeville, 303
Accident, Unfortunate, 133
Accidents, Chapter of, 224
Achicourt, 220, 222
Achiet le Petit, 295
Adamson, Lieut., 437
Addington, Lce.-Cpl. S., M.M., 652
Agny, 221, 295
Ailly-Le-Haut-Clocher, 133, 417
Alderton, 278
Alexander, A/Sergt. S. J., M.M., 651
Allason, Major (Beds.), 63, 70, 71, 73
Allen, Lieut. G. C., 279
Allenby, General, Lord, G.C.B., G.C.M.G., vii
Allied Offensive, The (August 8th, 1918), 421
Allsop, Rfn., 31
Alwin, Rfn., A. E., 33
Amalgamation of 1st and 2nd Battalions Q.V.R., 365, 368
Amalgamation of 1st and 6th Middlesex V.R.C., 536
Amalgamation of 1st and 19th Middlesex V.R.C., 571
Americans, The, 250, 409, 420, 423, 424, 443
Amiens, viii, 393, 394, 396, 418, 422, 426
Amigny-Rouy, 374, 376, 381, 387, 389
Amor, Lieut. E. H., 258, 259, 260
Anderson, Major D. F., 411
Andrew, Q.M.S. W. J., M.S.M., 653
Andrews, Capt. J. C., M.C., 11, 13, 46, 100, 102, 103, 107, 126, 138, 159, 177, 178, 188, 251, 262, 264, 265, 365, 646, 647
Andrews, A/C.S.M. E., 96
Angle Wood, 181
Annual Camp Training (1914), 1
Appleyard, Lce.-Cpl., 164
Argenvillers, 178, 179
Armistice, The, 452, 453
Armistice Day, xii, xiii
Armitage, Rfn. P. M., M.M., 164, 649
Arnold, Capt. H. W., 483
Arnold, 2nd Lieut. A. L., 251

Arnold, Sergt. G., M.M., 96, 650
Arques, 13
Arras, xii, 219-37, 238-47, 295, 380
Arthur, Rfn. C., 33, 35
Ashford, Rfn., 96
Ashman, Sergt. B. G., M.S.M., 652
Assault at Arms, Brigade, 316
Asser, Cpl. H. E., 67
Astill, 2nd Lieut. E. W. D., 367
Atkins, Sergt. J. H., M.M., 651
Attenborough, Lieut.-Col. Jas., C.M.G., 180, 186
Aubrey Camp, 271
Australian Troops, 298, 299, 396, 399, 407, 419, 427, 430
Auxi-le-Chateau, 281
Aviatik Operations, 335, 336, 338, 342, 348, 350
Avila, Rfn. L. F., xii, 18

Bailey, Capt. B. G., 279, 300
Baillemont, 288
Bailleul, xi, 14, 40, 41, 43, 47, 50
Baizieux, 417, 420
Bancourt, 303
Bapaume, 221, 256, 257, 316, 380
Barber Beaumont, Major J. T., 492, 493, 494, 495, 496, 498, 524
Barham, Col. A. S., C.M.G., V.D., 277, 348, 350, 353, 571
Barnes, Lce.-Cpl. T. A., M.M., 414, 651
Barnes, Cpl. H., 388
Barrett, Sergt. D. V., M.M., 650
Bartlett, Sergt. J., 653
Bartman, 2nd Lieut. C., 233
Bate, 2nd Lieut. M. C. T., 251
Bath, The First, 288
"Battle Surplus," 144, 158
Baxter, Sergt. R., M.M., 652
Bayencourt, 161, 165, 175
Bayliffe, Colonel, A. D., C.M.G., T.D., (12 London), 387
Beard, Cpl., 94
Beaumetz, 271
Beaudains, Capt. G. La C., D.S.O., M.C., 645, 646, 647
Beaudricourt, 178
Beaufoy, Col., 497
Beaumont, Capt. Spencer, 493, 497

655

Beaurains, 220, 222, 237, 250
Beavis, Sergt. L., 215
Bedford, Duke of, 569
Bedford Regt., 62, 64, 71, 72, 75, 434
Beecham, Rfn. Wm. Stanley, 344
Beeching, Major G. S., V.D., 531, 559
Been, Sergt. C. E., M.M., 652
Belcher, Sergt. D. W., V.C., 100, 101
Bell, 2nd Lieut. E., 397
Bell, Lce.-Cpl. N., 96, 97
Bell, Rfn. K. M., M.M., 650
Beloiel, 466
Bennett, 2nd Lieut. R., 163, 172
Bentley, Rfn. A. F. J., M.S.M., 652
Bercelaere, 81
Berenger, Charles Random de, 496, 497, 498, 499
Berguette, 204
Berles-au-Bois, 284
Bernafay Wood, 180, 202, 445, 446
Berneville, 248, 271
Berry, Lieut.-Col. A. R., T.D., x, 277, 279, 293, 294, 573, 574
Berry, Mrs., 574, 575
"Bertha" Post, 211, 212, 213, 214, 215, 216, 218
Bichancourt, xiii, 389, 418
Bienvillers, 177, 284, 287
Bihucourt, 300
Billon Farm, 180
Billon Wood, 120, 190, 430, 431
Bird, Col. Stanley George, C.B., 523, 526, 535, 537, 538, 555, 558, 559, 560
Bird, Col. Charles, 540, 541, 546, 547, 549, 550, 551, 553, 554, 555, 557, 559
Birles, 293, 459
Birtwistle, Lieut.-Col. A., 308
Bishop, Cpl., 45
Bixschoote, 81, 82
Blackburne, Lieut. Henry Devereux, 349, 352
"Black Buttons," 43, 131
Blackwood, Capt. H. S., 223, 237, 243, 279, 482
Blaireville, 288, 291, 292, 294
Blakeney, F.M. E., G.C.B., 535
Blangy, 396
Bloomsbury Rifles, xiv, 294, 560, 561, 568, 569
Booking, Cpl. H., M.M., 652
Bois Escardonneuse, 421, 424, 426
Bois des Bœufs, 249
Bois de Riez, 206
Boismason, Lce.-Cpl. J. W. P., 188
Bolton, Capt. D. W., 12, 46
Bonner, Rfn. G. E., 288
Borrie, Rfn. W. A., M.M., 254, 381, 420, 650
Borsberry, Sergt. Thomas Fredk., 289
Bouleaux Wood, 182, 183, 203
Bout de Ville, 204
Bourlon Wood, 263, 270, 271, 272
"Bow Bells, The," 178, 463
Boursies, 269
Boulden, Rfn. H., 463, 465, 467
Bowden, Rfn. C. R., 33
Bowditch, Capt. W., M.C., D.C.M., 222, 226, 227, 231, 237, 244, 646, 649
Bower, Sergt.-Major, 479
Bowes, Rfn., 406
Bowler, Capt. W. E., M.C., 263, 266, 267, 268, 270, 367, 385, 387, 388, 417, 423, 424, 426, 428, 433, 646
Bowran, Capt. (10th London), 348
Boyton, Sir J., M.P., 368, 369
Bradney, Col. J. A., C.B., T.D., 482, 483, 488, 647
Brake Camp, 317, 335
Brand, Capt. W. D. M., 213, 214, 215, 259, 260, 268, 647
Brand, Rfn. T. R., 33
Brandram, Lieut. T. C., 367
Bravery, Outstanding, 188
Brawn, Sergt. W., D.C.M., 185, 188, 649
Brawn, R.Q.M.S. Mark, D.C.M., 34, 63, 69, 96, 126, 434, 649, 653
Bray, 112, 114, 119, 120, 121, 124, 128, 179, 426
Brehaut, Capt. F. T. A., M.M., 96, 650, 653
Breul, Major F. A. du, 367
Brielen, 82, 85
Brigade—
13th Infantry, 12, 47, 52, 55, 56, 79, 82, 103, 104, 122, 131, 186
14th, 79
15th, 79
16th, 131
54th, 401
89th, 242
109th, 266, 267
140th, 435
167th, 132, 138, 182, 194, 222, 242, 249, 250, 263
168th, 132, 152, 199, 249, 250, 263, 272, 273
169th, xii, 132, 147, 152, 178, 179, 180, 182, 184, 196, 242, 243, 249, 250, 252, 253, 263, 267, 273, 365
173rd, 280, 303, 410, 411, 422, 431, 439, 446
174th, 280, 355, 410, 431, 437, 447
175th, 280, 309, 312, 334, 335, 348, 378, 410, 419, 423, 424, 426, 430, 432, 434, 435, 437, 439, 442, 446, 447

INDEX

Briggs, Sergt., S. T., 309, 310, 654
Brittain, Sergt., 215
Bronfay Farm, 114, 120, 180, 430
Brooker, Sergt. G. F., 548, 550
Brooker, Rfn. H. Brian, 76
Brookseinde, 81
Broome, Bugle-Major W. E., 480
Broomeswell Heath, 278
Browett, Lieut. A., 352
Browett, Lieut. Reginald, 96, 343, 344, 346, 349, 350, 352
Brown, Cpl., 34
Brown, Lieut. S. S., M.C., 129, 646
Brown, Cpl. Tom, 406
Browning, Rfn., 343
Brown's Farm, 318
Brushett, Rfn. A. V., M.M., 651
Bryant, Rfn. J., M.M., 329, 651
Buchanan, Capt. A. S., 482
Buchanan, Rfn. C., M.M., 652
Buck, Rfn., 170
Budd, A/R.S.M., D. J. B., M.S.M., 653
Bulfin, Major-Gen., 52, 79
Bulgaria, Surrender of, 442
Bull, Sergt. P., M.S.M., 652
Bull, Sergt. P. C., D.C.M., 649
Buller, Gen. Sir Redvers, V.C., 557, 558
Bull, Lieut. L. W., 459
Bullecourt, 223, 296-304, 305, 458, 459
Bullswater, 4
Bully Trench, 186
Bunting, Cpl. B. H., M.M., 406, 652
Burnell-Nugent, Brig.-Gen. F. H., 132, 140
Burchell, Capt. J. M., O.B.E., 43, 645, 647, 648
Burgess, Sergt. E. C., D.C.M., 107, 121, 649
Burrell, Rfn., 207, 208
Bushell, Rfn., 22
" Bus House," 106
Busk, Capt. Hans, 520
Butler, Cpl. Edmund Hearn, 301
Butler, Lieut.-Gen. R., 445
Butcher, Sergt. C. E., M.M., 652, 654
Buttes de Rouy, xiii, 374, 376, 377, 385, 386, 393

Cachy, 397, 398, 407
Caddy, Lce.-Cpl. D. J., 404
Cade, Rfn. Chas. Albert, 139
Caley, 2nd Lieut. P. R., 251
Calvert, Lieut. L., 400, 406
Cambigneul, 365
Cambrai, xiii, 258, 261 *et seq.*, 380, 442
Campbell, Major, 222
Campbell, Col. (2nd Cameron Highlanders), 78

Campbell, Lieut.-General Sir Wm. Pitcairn, K.C.B., 100, 537, 559, 574, 645
Campbell, Major Ronnie, 178
Canadians, The, 53, 81, 82, 83, 84, 85, 95
Canal du Nord, 265, 272, 316
Cantaing, 265
Cardonette, 130
Care Committees, Regimental, 574
Carnoy, 114, 116, 119, 120, 121, 124, 128
Carrington, Rfn., J. W., M.M., 651, 652
Carr, Sergt. G. R., 653
Carter, Capt. W. H., 12, 48, 53, 279
Cartmell, Lce.-Sergt. H. J., M.M., 651
Cary, 2nd Lieut. Richard Harry, 163, 171
Cator, Major-Gen. A. B. E., D.S.O., 354, 357, 410
Cattell, Rfn. Henry, 342
" Catterpillar, The," 71, 72
Catton, Rfn., 653
Cavalry Farm, 248
Cawston, Lieut.-Col. E. P., 12, 45, 53, 55, 279, 309, 647
Cemetery (St. Julien), 320, 321, 325, 326, 327, 328, 329, 331, 333
Centenary Celebrations, 554
Ceylon Wood, 429
Chalmers, Rfn., 92
Champ, Cpl., 401
Chapman, C.Q.M.S. A. E., 653
Chapman, Lce.-Cpl. Wm. Hy., M.M., 328, 346, 353, 650
Chateau Blanc, 104
Chateau Segard, 250, 256
Chauny, 374, 384, 385, 387, 389, 390
Cheap Ward Association, 561
Chedgey, Sergt. P. J., 215
Cherisy, 232, 233, 245, 248
Cheshire Regt., 44, 45, 47, 98, 99, 249
Cheshire Regt. Pioneers, 147, 182, 243
Cheylesmore, Major-General Lord, K.C.M.G., K.C.V.O., 560, 573, 574
" Chinese Attack, A," 419
Chipilly, 120, 121, 425
Chohole Gate, 484
Christmas—
 The First, 20, 25
 1915, 125
 1917, 360
 1918, 455
Chudley, 2nd Lieut., 325, 349
Citadel, The (Fricourt), 187, 189, 190, 194, 198, 199
C.I.V., The, v, xi, 540, 545, 555

2 U

Clark, Rfn. Guy, 97
Clark, Rfn., 416
Clarke, Lce.-Cpl. P. G., 95
Clarke, Rfn. J. R., 31
Clarke, Capt. A. Basil, M.C. (R.A.M.C.), 125, 137, 138, 167, 177, 185, 186, 187, 199, 246, 268, 646
Clarke, Capt. P. Selwyn, M.C. (R.A.M.C.), 419, 433, 646
Clayton, Sergt. W. J., 89
Clemenceau, vii
Cleverley, Rfn. R. H., 34
Cobham, Brig.-Gen. H. W., C.M.G., D.S.O., 443, 453, 466
Cochran, Gen., 422
Cockrane, Lord, 498
Codrington, Lieut.-Gen. Sir A., K.C.B., K.C.V.O., 573
Cohen, Cpl. C. B., 467
Cojeul Switch, 222
Cojeul River, 231, 242, 244
Cojeul Valley, 231
Coke, Brig.-Gen. E. S., C.M.G., 132, 178, 180
Cole, Rfn. F. A., M.M., 651
Cole, 2nd Lieut. A. P., 367
Coleman, Sergt. S. H., M.S.M., 652, 653
Coles, Sergt. C. F. C., 359, 376, 390, 399
Collier, Lce.-Cpl. S. C., M.M., 301, 302, 650
Collins, Rfn. L. G., M.M., 164, 169, 649, 654
Cologne, 472, 473
Colours, The Regimental, 524, 535
Combles, 180, 194, 203
Combley, Rfn. A., M.M., 651
Commanding Officers, Appointment of, 219
Communications, Difficulty of maintaining, 351, 381
Concerts, 125, 295, 316, 462-9, 471, 480, 484
Condren, 383
Conscientious Objector, The, 136
Contour Wood, 431
Corbett, Capt., M.C., 474,
Corbie, 112, 179, 373
"Corner, The Worst," 147
Corrie, Lieut.-Col. Malcolm, 569, 571
Coventry, Lce.-Cpl. H., M.M., 651
Cowtan, Major A. L., M.C., 12, 41, 44, 45, 70, 83, 84, 88, 89, 98, 100, 646, 647, 648,
Cox and Edwards, Messrs., 35
Cox, Capt. H. E. L., 12, 15, 45, 60, 88, 91, 96, 109, 110, 112, 121, 140, 158, 159, 163, 164, 167, 172
Cox, Lieut.-Col. Samuel Compton, 560, 561

Cox, E. W., Esq., 172
Cox, Major R. W., O.B.E., T.D., 11, 15, 32, 45, 63, 105, 117, 118, 172, 572, 645, 647, 648
Crater, The big (Achiet), 295
Crevecœur-sur-l'Escaut, 271
Cricket Matches, 486
Critchett, Capt. G. M., 482
Crocker, Rfn. W. G., M.M., 651
Croisilles, 380
Croix Barbée, 204, 219
Cronin, Lce.-Cpl. A., M.M., 650
Crook, Rfn. W. W., 218
Crosbie, 2nd Lieut. R. B., 279, 302, 435, 440
Crossthwaite, Sergt. W. W., 9, 16, 90, 91, 99, 102, 104, 108, 109, 113
Crowborough, 4, 7, 278, 458, 479
Culme-Seymour, Capt. G., x, xi, 3, 10, 11, 13, 14, 15, 24, 27, 40, 41, 44, 48, 52, 54, 57, 60, 69, 82, 84, 85, 88, 98-100, 647
Culme-Seymour, Mrs., 574, 575
Cunningham, Capt. K., 137, 158, 168, 170, 172
Curtis, Rfn. R. H., M.M., 651
Cuthbert, Sergt., 267

Dainville, 137, 316
Dallender, Rfn., 35
Damascus, Fall of, 444
Darby, Rfn. W. H., M.M., 255, 649
Darrell, Rfn. J., 96
Davies, Lieut. A. R., 546, 552, 553
Davies, Capt. R. fF. (G.M.), 178, 181, 184, 187, 548, 549, 550, 560, 572
Davies, Lieut. D. G., 248
Davies, Lieut. W. A., M.C., 646
Davies, Rfn. J. S., 90
Davies, Mrs. R. fF., 574
Davis, Lieut. C. V., 129, 171
Dawe, Sergt. 343
Day, Lieut.-Col. F. R., D.S.O. (Norfolk R.), 473
Day, 2nd Lieut. W. P., 325
Debenham, Messrs., Ltd., 35
"Decisive Battle of the War," 443
Deks, Lieut. G., 487
Delville Wood, 180
Demicourt Raid, 257
Demobilisation, 471
Densham, Cpl., 45
Devereux, Rfn., 62
Devon Rifles, 509, 515, 552
Devonshire Regt., 1st, 25, 62, 65, 72, 73, 117
De Winton, Brig.-Gen., 279
Diaries, Regimental, xi
Dickebusch, 105

INDEX 659

Dickins, Col. V. W. F., D.S.O., V.D.,
  x, xi, 1, 2, 4, 10, 11, 30, 33, 41,
  44, 45, 47, 60, 63, 82, 99, 104,
  107, 108, 114, 119, 121, 123, 125,
  126, 127, 132, 134, 135, 136, 137,
  138, 141, 159, 160, 161, 162, 175,
  176, 177, 178, 180, 181, 183, 185,
  193, 198, 199, 201, 207, 359,
  559, 572, 574, 645, 647
Dickins, Major Wyndham, 121, 527
Dickins, 2nd Lieut. E. F., 366, 418
Dickins, Lieut.-Col. H. F., V.D., 557
Dickins, Mrs. Vernon, 574, 575
Dinner, A memorable, 143
" Dirty Bucket Camp," 317
Division—
  2nd, 269, 272
  5th, 12, 37, 131
  8th, 407, 408
  12th, 425, 436, 438, 442
  14th, 222
  18th, 399, 407, 425, 438
  28th, 52
  30th, 222
  32nd, 444
  37th, 147
  46th, 147, 152, 444
  47th, viii, 269, 272, 424, 426, 427,
    428, 429, 432, 438
  51st, 357
  56th, viii, xii, 130, 131, 140, 147,
    152, 175, 182, 195, 203, 222, 243,
    249, 256, 263, 269, 272
  58th, viii, 280, 300, 356, 383, 389,
    409, 410, 412, 417, 418, 424, 425,
    436, 438, 443, 445, 450, 453, 454
  60th, viii
  74th, 435, 436, 437, 438
Dixon, Lce.-Cpl. Cecil, 170
Dixon, Rfn. G. S., 33
Dorrill, Lce.-Cpl., J.A., 649
Doullens, 133, 134
Douvre, River, 28, 32
Dove, Rfn. B., M.M., 652
Dowswell, 2nd Lieut. Chas. Victor, 202
Dranoutre, 23, 40, 47, 49, 50
Dublin Fusiliers, 51
Duck's Bill Crater, 206, 209
Duisans, 249
Duke of Cumberland, 491, 492, 501, 502
Duke of Cumberland's Sharpshooters,
  491, 492, 493, 494, 498, 499, 500,
  502, 504, 515
Duncan, Capt. L., M.C., 102, 367, 472,
  646
Dunlop, Lieut.-Col. Buchanan, D.S.O.,
  187
Dunn, Rfn. H. S., 33
Dunn, Sir William, 335
Dunn, Sergt. S. E., M.M., 428, 652

Duren, 472
Dutton, Rfn. T. A., M.M., 255, 650
Dyer, Cpl. S. A., M.M., 651

Eames, A/C.S.M. E. E., D.C.M., 124,
  143, 266, 649
Earl, Lce.-Cpl., 207
" Earwig, The," 521, 570
East Surrey Regt., 63, 64, 72, 75
East, Capt., 561
Easterbrook, Lieut. H. G., 366, 397
Ebers, Rfn. L. C., 23, 24
Ecacheries, 452, 454
Eccles, Capt. J. D., M.C., 116, 124,
  142, 179, 181, 183, 185, 187, 646
Ecoust St. Mein, 302, 303
Eddowes, Rfn. F. E., M.S.M., 652
Edgar, Lieut. W. R., 648
Edward VII, King, inspection, by 556,
  558, 559
Edwards, 2nd Lieut. H., 367
" Egg, The," 226, 227, 231, 237
Elkington, Rfn. E. W., M.M., 255, 650
Elliott, Lieut., 459
Elliott, Rfn., 463, 465, 467
Ellis, Major R., 509
Ellis, Rfn. F. E., 41
Ellis, Rfn. F. H., 330
Ellis, Rfn. M. G., 418
Elverdinghe, 82, 88, 94, 357, 365
Elzenwalle, 105
Embarkation Orders, 5, 280
Engleton, Rfn. F. W. G., M.M., 651
Epehy, 434, 436
Esher, Viscount, 55, 371
Etinhem, 121
Eustace, Capt. G., M.C. (R.A.M.C.),
  279, 293, 305, 306, 307, 312, 335,
  354, 358, 646
Eve, Rfn. D. H., M.M., 651
Eves, Rfn. A. W., M.M., 651
Experiences, First, 284

Fairall, C.S.M., 47, 117
Falfemont Farm, 180, 182, 184, 186,
  193, 194
Fargus, Lieut. F. B. A., 11, 13, 15, 32
Farley, Bandmaster W. A., 480
Farmer, Rfn., 330
Farmiloe, Lieut. T. H., 116, 647
Farquhar, Lord, 480
Farrar, A/Cpl. H. A., 90
Fate, Irony of, 133
Fauquissart sector, 218, 220
Fauset, Rfn., 443
Faviers Wood, 180
Favreuil, 297, 298, 299, 300
Fazakerley-Westby, 2nd Lieut., 11,
  69, 70, 73, 75
Fenton, Capt. H. A., 572

Feore, Sergt. Arnold, 484
Fergusson, Lieut.-Gen. Sir Charles, K.C.B., K.C.M.G., D.S.O., M.V.O., 12, 15, 39, 43, 79, 98, 99
Fernandez, Capt. John, 563
Fielding, 2nd Lieutenant Francis Willoughby, 171, 172, 482
Fienvillers, 133, 134
Fife-Cookson, 2nd Lieut., 485
Fildes, 2nd Lieut. G. P., 482
Finch, Rfn. Frank, M.M., 413, 651
Finigan, Capt. D. O'C., 572
Fippard, Lce.-Cpl. H. J., 96
Fires, 31, 133
Fisher, Lieut. F., 368
Fisher, Sergt. F. C., M.S.M., 462, 652
Fitch, Sergt. J. P., M.M., 650
" Flame " Post, 211, 214, 215, 216
Flammenwerfer demonstration, 134
Fleetwood, Lieut. C. P., 135, 171, 173
Flemming, Capt. H., 12, 83, 84, 86, 91, 575
Flemming, Lieut. L. D., 482
Flemming, R., Esq., 574, 575
Fletcher, Lieut. R. M., 279
Fletcher, 2nd Lieut. F. J., 367, 400
Foaden, Lieut. G., 201
Follett, Lieut.-Col. F. B., D.S.O., M.C., 218, 219, 223, 242, 243, 244, 645, 647
Fonquevillers, 152, 177, 178
Fontaine-les-Croisilles, 233
Football matches, 25, 52, 55, 133
Forbes, Archibald, 571
Forsyth, Capt. G., M.C., 125, 132, 462, 646
Fovant, 162, 484, 486, 487
Francvillers, 421
Franklin, Capt. S. S., 648
Franklin, Rfn., 45
Freeman, Sergt.-Instructor A., 548
Freeth, Brig.-Gen. G., C.B., C.M.G., D.S.O., 242
Fremantle, Col. T. F., 497
Fremicourt, 263, 271
French, F. M. Lord, K.P., O.M., K.C.M.G., G.C.B., G.C.V.O., vi, vii, xiv, 56, 77, 79, 84, 484
Fresnes, 131
Fricourt, 115, 121, 187, 198, 204, 446
Friend, Lieut. L. W., 368
Frost, Lce.-Sergt. A. W. G., M.M., 254, 649, 650
Fryer, Rfn. E. S., 24
Fusier, Rfn. V. C., 55

Galley, Rfn. R. G., 31
Gallop, Cpl. Harry, 397
Gander, C.S.M. A. E., M.M., 250, 254, 650
Garrard, Sergt. J., M.M., 651
Garrett, Rfn. H. G., M.M., 651
Garrett, Rfn. J. S., 448
Garside, Lieut. F. G., 129, 137, 171, 647
Gas, First use of, 81, 84
Gaudiempre, 178, 288
Gaward, Rfn., 207
Gellatley, Mr. Thomas, 526, 559
Gentelles, 396, 397, 398, 403
German Retreat, 1917, 220, 291, 421, 431
Gessy, Cpl. F. R., M.M., 254, 650
" G.G.B. " Magazine, 570
" G.G.B." Token, 570
Gibb, Lieut., 228
Gibbs, C.S.M., B., 653
Gibbs, Sir Phillip, 149, 238
Gillate, Rfn. G. W., 97
Ginchy, 199
Gittens, Lce.-Cpl. W. R., 18
Glencorse Wood, 250, 251, 252, 253
Glisy, 402, 417
Gloucester Regt., 120, 204
Goddard, Lieut. R. P., 129
Godley, Gen. Sir A. J., K.C.B., K.C.M.G., 418, 432, 434, 439
Goldie, Lce.-Cpl. C., 464
Gommecourt, 142, 146–76
Goodinge, Lieut. W., 171, 482
" Goods, The," 295, 316, 466
Gordon, Lieut. A., 647, 648
Gore, Lieut.-Col. E. J. M., T.D., 488
Gorrell, Rfn. T., 463, 465, 467
Gosney, Rfn. H., M.M., 652
Gough, Cpl. W., 31
Gough, Gen. Sir H., G.C.M.G., K.C.B., K.C.V.O., 373
Gould, Capt. (10th London), 411
Gourlay, Capt. W. B. (R.A.M.C.), 399
Gouy-en-Artois, 220, 250
Grafenstafel, 81, 351, 352
Graham, Lieut. W. H., 368
Grandcourt, 281
Grandeglise, 466
Grate, Rfn. W., M.M., 651
Gray, Rfn. S., 441
Gray, Rfn. W. J., 190
Gray, Rfn. P. W., M.M., 651
Grebaucourt Wood, 435
Green Grassier (Lens), 446
Green, Rfn., 207
Green, Rfn. R. C., M.M. (" Jumbo "), 416, 651
Greenhill, Major Barclay, 521
Grenas, 288
Grenfell, F.-M. Lord, G.C.B., G.C.M.G., 555
Griffith, Capt. G. F., 12, 19, 279, 320, 325, 326, 331, 333, 340, 343, 345, 346, 349, 352, 647

INDEX

Grosville, 291
Grubb, Lieut.-Col. H. W., C.M.G., D.S.O., 243
Gubbins, Rfn. S., 25
Guemappe, 248
Guillemont, 182, 184
Gully, Rfn. A. F., M.M., 651
Gum Boots, Issue of, 122
Gutteridge, 2nd Lieut. R. H., 198

H.A.C., The, vi, vii, 111, 498, 500, 502, 506
Hackney Riflemen, 498
"Hackney Villa," 320, 337, 340
Haddon, Capt. A. R., 223, 225, 367, 397, 399, 400, 414
Haddon, Sergt. E. D., 653
Haig, F.M. Lord, K.T., G.C.B., O.M., G.C.V.O., K.C.I.E., vii, 77, 166, 271, 305, 335, 395, 406, 424
Hale, Major, 570
Halfacre, Sergt. W. R. B., 649, 653
"Half-way House," 251
Halifax, Lieut. J. H., 216, 222
Hall, Lieut. S. C., 266, 267, 269, 270, 367, 401, 422, 475, 648
Hall, Lieut. H. G., 71
Hallett, Rfn. F. W. M., 106
Halloy, 137, 142, 143, 146
Halls, Rfn., 416
Hamilton, Capt. E. W., 11, 46, 223, 226, 227, 237, 487
Hangard Wood, 393-408, 410, 412, 417
Hannescamp, 177
Hanover Square Volunteers, 527-32
"Happy Valley, The," 179, 180, 426, 427, 428, 429, 430, 431
Hardcastle, Lieut.-Col. B. W., 571
Hardecourt, 180, 181, 184, 185
Harington, Capt. A. D. L., 279, 324, 325, 326, 340, 342, 349, 355, 358
Harper, Lieut, 301, 302
Harrison, Major J. E. W., 572
Harrison, 2nd Lieut. H. A., 367
Harrold, Rfn. S. H., M.M., 329, 650
Hart, Rfn. H. G., 33
Hart, Sergt. A. G., M.M., 651
Hart, Sergt., 441, 442
Havre, Arrival at, ix, xii, 9, 280
Havrincourt, 303, 305, 314, 316
Hawkes, 2nd Lieut. H. S., 367
Hawkings, Lieut. F., 434
Hawkins, 2nd Lieut. H. C., M.M., 253, 650
Hawtin, Rfn. R. J., 236, 246, 654
Haynes, 2nd Lieut. N., 251
Haynes, Lce.-Cpl. W. B., M.M., 255, 650
Hazebrouck, 13

Hebuterne, 137, 138, 141, 142, 147, 152, 160
"Hell Corner," 205
Helmet, new shrapnel, issued, 135
Henderson, Capt. R. W., 482, 572
Heninel-sur-Cojeul, 223, 231, 233, 237, 246
Herbert, Lieut. D., 279
Hewitt, Lieut. G. G., 647
Hewlett, Rfn., 207, 208
Hibbard, Lieut. H. E., 646
Hickman, Sergt. F. H. C., M.M., 143, 649
High Wood, viii
"Hill 60," x, 54, 56, 74, 77, 81, 82, 86, 95, 97, 103, 104, 127, 244, 483
"Hill 60," Q.V.R. Memorial, 80
"Hill 60," The graves at, 79
Hindenburg, xiii, 220, 241, 380, 394, 406
Hindenburg Line, viii, 221, 222, 224, 263, 265, 266, 267, 268, 269, 270, 271, 272, 443, 444
Histories, Regimental, ix
Hobbs, Major-Gen. Sir J. J. T., K.C.B., K.C.M.G., 407
Hockley, Cpl., 125
Hodgkinson, Lieut. E. W. G., M.M., 101, 279, 358, 367, 650
Hodgson, Capt. T., M.C., 134, 139, 164, 426, 435, 442, 646
Hodson, Rfn. H. W., M.M., 651
Hoellen, Lce.-Cpl. A. E., 31
Holden, Rfn. R. B., 653
Holland, Gen. Sir Arthur, K.C.B., K.C.M.G., D.S.O., M.V.O., 466
Hollebeke, 305
Holloway, 2nd Lieut. H. V., 367, 400, 412, 648
Holloway, Capt. S. J., M.C., 102, 160, 646
Holms, Capt. J. C., 45, 102, 107, 119
Hooper, Lce.-Cpl. S. J., M.M., 650
Hooper, Rfn., M.M., 301, 302
Hooper, Rfn. W. A., M.M., 650
Hooper, Sergt. H. F. A., 75, 95
Hornby, Lce.-Cpl. J. H., M.M., 254, 650
Horne, Gen. Lord, G.C.B., K.C.M.G., 454
Hoskins, Rfn. Wm., 49
Houghton, Lieut. P. S., 11, 70, 158, 159, 167, 172
Houghton, Lieut. R., 492, 493
Houtkerque, 365
Houvin-Houvigneul, 134, 137]
How, 2nd Lieut. H. J., 96, 237, 244, 653
Howard, Lieut. Hon. A. J. B., 481, 482
Howard, Rfn., 201
Howell, Sergt. T., M.M., 254
Howell, Capt. O. A., 572

Howes, Rfn. R., 468
Howett, Rfn. E. G., M.M., 650
Hull, Major-Gen. Sir C. P. A., K.C.B., 175, 195
Humbert, Gen., 390
Hunt, 2nd Lieut. L. G., 440, 442
Hunter, Capt. J. E. A., 12, 482
Hunter, Lieut.-Col. A. J., C.M.G., D.S.O., M.C. (K.R.R.C.), 103
Hunter, Lieut. J. S., 171
Hunter, 2nd Lieut. J. B., 11
Hurst, Lieut. R. C., 368
Husey, Lieut.-Col. R. R., M.C., 180, 182
Hussars, 19th, 48
Hutchings, Sergt. E. B., M.M., 649
Hutchings, Cpl. H. J., M.M., 260, 651
Hutchings, Rfn. J. W. C., M.M., 651
"Hyde Park Corner," 110

Imperial Representative Corps, 551
Imperial Yeomanry, 510, 551, 555
Incident, Notable, 349
Inglis, Lieut. G., 482
Ingram, Sergt., 281, 282, 284, 287, 289, 292, 297, 300, 302
Inns of Court Volunteers, 560, 561
Inspection, A threefold, 112
Inverness Copse, 250, 251, 253
Ipswich, 162, 278
Ireland, Rfn., 230
Irish Division, 266
Irish Fusiliers, Royal, 202
Irish Rifles, Royal, 267, 472
"Irma" Post, 211, 212, 214, 216, 217
Irons, Cpl. Albert, M.M., 413, 651
Irvine, John D., 147
Ivergny, 220
Ives, Lce.-Cpl., 343

Jackson, Brig.-Gen. H. C., C.B., C.M.G., D.S.O., 279, 293, 309, 353, 378, 379, 417
Jacob, Q.M.S., E. F., 280
Jacob, Lieut.-Gen. Sir Claud, K.C.B., K.C.M.G., 365
Jaeger, Rfn., 207
Janet Farm, 329, 331, 333, 339
Jarvis, 2nd Lieut. D., 367, 400, 401
Jeakes, Major J. W., 567, 568, 571
Jeffreys, Major-Gen. G. D., C.B., C.M.G., 472
Jeffreys, Sergt., 309
Jenkins, Lieut. F. N., 367
Jephson, Rev. W. V., 486
Jerome, Col. C.R.E., 79
Johnson, Capt. K. W., 45, 49, 279, 290, 301, 345, 354, 358, 647, 648
Johnson, Lieut. G. R., 366
Johnson, Lieut. R., 264, 366, 463, 465, 466, 467

Johnstone, Capt. R., 559
Johnstone, Lieut. D. F., 216, 230
Jolly, Lce.-Cpl. L., 18
Jones, A/C.S.M. B. C., M.S.M., 653
Jones, Brig.-Gen. L. O. W., 122
Jones, Cpl. M. H. A., M.S.M., 652
Jones, Lce.-Cpl. H., 28
Jones, Lieut. A. L., 367
Jones, Lieut. R. L., M.C., 253, 646
Jones, Rfn., 467
Joyce, Rfn. G. T., M.M., 255, 406, 650
Judge, Lieut. F., 279, 546
Jury Farm, 320, 321, 325, 327, 329, 330, 331, 332, 333

Kaiser's Birthday, 1915, 42
Kates, Sergt. C., M.M., 652
Kavanagh, Major-Gen. C. M., K.C.B., K.C.M.G., C.V.O., D.S.O., 132
Keats, Sergt., 428
Keeson, Capt. C. A. G. C., M.C., xiv, 301, 360, 367, 385, 397, 400, 412, 416, 419, 422, 423, 482, 646
Keeson, Major A. D., 502, 505, 523
Kempton Park, 355, 357, 359, 360
Kennedy, Lieut. (Beds), 71
Kent, A/Sergt. F. W., 459, 653
Keppel, C.S.M. G., M.S.M., 652
Kidby, Rfn. A., 49
Kildare Post, 434, 439, 440, 441
King's visit to the Army, 455
King's (The) Message to his army, The, 20
Kingswell, Cpl., 346
Kinnison, Lieut. C. H., M.C., 86, 646
Kit, Marching, 297
Kitchener, F.M. Lord, vii
Kneale, Rfn. W. C., 33
K.O.S.B., 12, 33, 40, 42, 52, 55, 56, 58, 59, 78, 79, 97, 98, 114, 121, 132, 473
K.O.Y.L.I., xii, 12, 14, 15, 16, 25, 26, 56, 59, 96, 97, 98, 109, 114
K.R.R.C., 142, 249, 256, 371, 472, 555
K.R.R.C., 1st Volunteer Battalion, 538
K.R.R.C. Service Company, 548, 549, 550
Kramar, Rfn. M., M.M., 652
Kruisstraat, 104, 105, 107

Lacey, Lieut. G. H., M.C., 440, 442, 646
La Fere, 380, 382
Lagnicourt, 263, 264, 297, 299
La Gorgue, 205, 207, 219, 220
Lake, A/Cpl. H. B., M.S.M., 653
La Houssoye, 130
La Margarita, s.s., 280
Lane, Lieut. E. A. J. A., 102, 114, 162, 171, 173, 487

INDEX

Langemarck, 82
Langley, Lieut., 216
Langmead, Capt. H. F., 645, 648
Langston, Rfn., 416
Larch Wood, 61, 63, 69, 73, 80, 98, 99
Laventie Posts, The, 210–19
Lavington, 2nd Lieut. D., 400
Law, Sergt. W., M.M., 652
Lea, Lce.-Cpl. F., M.S.M., 653
Leather, Rfn., 115
Lebucquiere, 257, 268
Le Cateau, 444
Lees, Major T. P., 11, 14, 41, 45, 47, 61, 63, 65, 67, 69, 70, 71, 73, 74, 75, 88, 572
Leith, 2nd Lieut. L. A., 367
Lens, 446, 447, 450
Leonard, Capt. G. S., 645, 648
Les Bœufs, 193, 196, 200, 202
Lestrem, 204
Le Transloy, 195, 199
Letters, Riflemen's, 20, 124
Leuze Wood, 179, 180, 181, 182, 183, 184, 186, 188, 203
Lewington, Rfn. C. J., M.M., 652
Lewis, Lce.-Cpl. Richard Frank, 168
Lewis, Rfn. H. H., 544
Lewthwaite, Rfn. Stanley Basil, 315
Licence to drill, 505
Liez Fort, 373, 374
Limieux, 204
Lindenhoek, 24
Lindsay, Col. Hon. Chas. Hugh, 534, 568
Lindsey-Renton, Major R. H., D.S.O., ix, xi, 1, 2, 12, 27, 45, 50, 88, 96, 105, 111, 112, 126, 133, 139, 158, 163, 177, 183, 186, 192, 193, 205, 207, 210, 212, 215, 217, 264, 265, 267, 268, 270, 366, 373, 374, 381, 382, 384, 386, 389, 393, 423, 425, 426, 427, 434, 435, 440, 442, 445, 446, 450, 456, 464, 645, 647, 648
Ling, Rfn. "Jock," 468
Lingfield, Sergt. E., 653
Lion Lane, 222, 223, 224, 225, 245
Littleworth, Rfn. T., M.S.M., 652
Lived, How they, 38, 40, 45, 282
Liverpool Scottish, 105
Lloyd, Capt. K., 83, 268
Lloyd, Gen. Sir Francis, G.C.V.O., K.C.B., D.S.O., 277, 278, 480, 483
Lloyd, Sergt. F., 399, 652
Lockley, Lieut. Norman C., 415, 435, 463, 465
Logeast Wood, 303
Londoners, Martial spirit of the, vi, vii

London Regiment—
1st (Royal Fusiliers), 132, 137, 176, 223, 224, 225, 238, 280, 360, 486
2nd ditto, xii, 132, 141, 147, 175, 180, 184, 186, 194, 197, 211, 216, 218, 220, 221, 232, 233, 238, 248, 249, 252, 263, 268, 269, 270, 273, 280, 336, 388, 410, 418, 422, 450, 472
3rd ditto, 132, 159, 176, 200, 211, 238, 270, 280, 396, 397, 400, 410, 431
4th ditto, 132, 176, 199, 200, 237, 238, 280
5th (L.R.B.), vi, xii, 132, 139, 142, 147, 149, 162, 171, 180, 182, 184, 185, 186, 194, 196, 197, 198, 200, 201, 233, 238, 243, 248, 251, 252, 263, 280, 486
6th (City Rifles), 238, 280, 419, 448, 472, 486
7th, 280, 486
8th (Post Office Rifles), vi, 176, 238, 300, 358, 398, 431, 437, 486
9th (Q.V.R.), v, viii, xiii, 55, 56, 60, 65, 69, 77, 92, 95, 98, 132, 147, 149, 150, 162, 175, 238, 242, 243, 277, 353, 366, 370, 378, 411, 426, 430, 432, 445, 472, 571
2nd Battalion, xiii, 95, 162, 277–361, 390
3rd ditto, xiii, 95, 163, 412, 479–88
9th (Reserve) Battalion, 488
10th (Hackney), xiii, 176, 280, 281, 302, 306, 320, 336, 347, 348, 350, 376, 377, 378, 383, 394, 398, 400, 401, 411, 426, 428, 429, 430, 431, 432, 435, 436, 439, 465, 472, 486
11th (Finsbury), 280, 281
12th (Rangers), vi, 2, 55, 147, 149, 168, 200, 210, 221, 238, 250, 269, 280, 336, 337, 348, 350, 356, 377, 378, 387, 401, 411, 419, 421, 422, 423, 424, 426, 427, 428, 429, 430, 431, 432, 435, 437, 439, 442, 447, 448, 455, 465, 472
13th (Kensington), vi, 55, 132, 150, 222, 238
14th (London Scottish), vi, vii, 132, 142, 147, 149, 150, 151, 176, 180, 181, 249, 273
15th (Civil Service), 427, 430
16th (Q.W.R.), vi, xii, 55, 132, 134, 147, 149, 150, 178, 180, 186, 204, 205, 209, 221, 233, 250, 252, 263, 267, 270, 273, 368
19th, 417
20th, 176
22nd (The Queen's), 424

London Regiment—
24th (The Queen's), 472
R.E., 147
"London Ridge," 351
London Riflemen, 498
London Territorials, vi, vii, 55, 147, 149, 174, 238, 335
Long, 2nd Lieut. A. G. H., 250
Longbridge Deverill, 279
Loos, Battle of, xii, 119, 120
Lott, C.S.M., G.H., M.S.M., 278, 281, 284, 292, 294, 300, 303, 316, 342, 355, 401, 405, 406, 653
Louverval, 257, 262, 271
Lowe, Cpl. T., M.M., 441, 463, 465, 652
Lowes, Rfn. A. R., 45
Lowis, Sergt. F. J., M.M., 651
"Loyal London Volunteers" (Rowlandson), 527, 528, 561
Loyal North Briton's Association, 498
Loyal Southwark Riflemen, 498
Luck, Instance of, 287
Ludlow, 2nd Lieut. Lionel, 202
Luscombe, Rfn., 35
Lyons, Sergt. George, M.M., 413, 418

McAdam, Lieut. W. A., M.C., 279, 327, 329, 331, 332, 334, 358, 367, 426, 459, 646
McBride, Lieut. W., 482
McClure, Capt. G. B., 648
MacDonagh, Lieut.-Gen., G.M.C., 371
McKenna, C.S.M. E. T., D.C.M., 124, 399, 400, 649, 654
MacKenzie, Capt. K. L., 125, 133, 135, 137, 255, 456, 457, 646, 647
MacKenzie, 2nd Lieut. D. A. Ord, 164, 194
Mackinnon, Col. H., 544, 545, 546, 547
McMoran, Sergt. C. A., 99
McTagart, Lce.-Cpl., 416
Machine Gun Section, 58
Maddock, 2nd Lieut. O.L., 202
Madge, Sergt. A. W., M.M., 254
Mainwaring, Lce.-Cpl. C. J., M.M., 254, 650
Maisey, Rfn., Frank Douglas, 61, 65
Malard Wood, 422, 461
Malcolm, 2nd Lieut. E. W. G., 269, 270, 368
Manicamp, 385
Manktelow, C.S.M. T. W., D.C.M., 649
Mansbridge, H., Esq., O.B.E., 369, 372
Marcoing, 265
Marest, 373
Markham, 2nd Lieut. W. H. E., 367

Marrieres Wood, 431
Marshall, 2nd Lieut. John, 343, 349, 353
Marshall, Sergt. A. E., M.M., 651
Marten, Capt. L. H., O.B.E., 277, 572, 645, 647, 648
Martin, Rfn. C., 31
Martyn's Farm, 31
Mary, Princess, Gift, 25
Masnieres, 272
Mason, 2nd Lieut Overton Trollope, 171
Masters, Sergt. W. T., 649
Matthews, Sergt. Jas. Victor, 319
Matthey, Lce.-Cpl. H. E., M.M., 651, 652
Maulde, Fort, 448, 451
Mauquissart Crater, 206, 207
Maxse, Gen. Sir Ivor, K.C.B., 293, 334, 336, 350, 353, 356, 573
Mayer, Capt. G. D., M.C., 214, 245, 367, 376, 397, 426, 429, 430, 646
Mayor, S.S.M. P. E., 653
Meaulte, 194, 195, 426, 446
Medals, Regimental, 496, 502, 507, 514
Meeking, 2nd Lieut. Norman Arthur, 163, 170, 172
Memorial Service, 123, 484
Merville, 219
Messines, Battle of, xii, 120
Messines Ridge, 17, 249
Methoer, Rfn. W. A., 33
"Michael Attack," The, 380
Middlesex Regiment—
228, 238
7th, 132, 176, 205, 249
8th, 132, 176, 272, 273
V.R.C., 1st, 519, 537
6th, 536
11th, 533
19th, 568, 569, 571
37th, 569
Middlesex Volunteer Corps (1859), 565
Mills, Lieut. A. E., 330, 433
Mills, C.S.M., P. W., 654
Mine, Adventure in a, 115
Miraumont, 256, 295
Mitchell, Sergt. J., M.M., 652
"Moated Grange," 106
Mobilisation Orders, 2, 6
Mœuvres, 266, 270, 271, 272
"Mogg's Hole," 206
Monchiet, 221
Monchy-au-Bois, 284, 294
Monker, Rfn., 94
Monmouth Regt., 1st, 49
Monro, Gen. Sir Chas., G.C.B., G.C.S.I., G.C.M.G., 112
Moon, Lce.-Cpl. C. L., M.M., 254, 650
Morbey, Rfn. S. A., 653

INDEX

Morgan, Lce.-Cpl. L., 31
Morlancourt, 179, 423
Morland, Lieut.-Gen., Sir T. L. N., K.C.B., K.C.M.G., D.S.O., 79
Morris, Rfn., 165
Mory, 303
"Mound of Death," 105, 109
Mounted Infantry, 502, 526
Mourant, Lce.-Cpl. R. W., 31
Mow Cop Raid, 305–15
Mud, Awful experiences of, 24, 123, 355, 360
Munnings, C.S.M. H. C., M.M., 140, 401, 649, 653
Murch, Sergt. C. E., 649
Murphy, Rfn. J., M.M., 652
Murray, 2nd Lieut. R. B., 12, 647

Nathan, Lieut. G., 129, 482
Nathan, Sergt. L., 649
National Rifle Association, 521, 534
"Neb, The," 205
Neighbour, Cpl. A. E., 651
Neuve Chapelle, 51, 204, 205, 206
Neuve Eglise, 14, 25, 33, 40, 42
Neuville Vitasse, viii, 222, 223, 224
Newbold, Rfn. Wm., 170
Newman, Lce.-Cpl. C. T., M.M., 651
Newman, Rfn. J. C., 207, 218, 381, 420
Newnham, Capt. L. A., 196, 198, 242
New Year's Day Incident (1915), 34
Nicholl, Lieut.-Col. Sir John, 562, 564
Nicholls, Rfn. H. B., 24
Nicholls, Rfn., 122
Nichols, Capt. J., M.C., 11, 21, 40, 41, 45, 47, 57, 88, 178, 179, 180, 181, 182, 183, 184, 188, 258, 366, 382, 405, 419, 426, 646
Nichols, Lce.-Cpl., 76
Niederaussem, 468, 472, 473, 474
Nightingale, Rfn., 169
Ninous, Gen., 112, 113
Nivelle, Gen., 241
Norfolk Regt. (9th), 53
Northey, Gen. Sir Edward, K.C.M.G., C.B., 79, 554, 556, 559
Northumberland Fusiliers, 62, 73
Northumberland Hussars, 398
Nortleulingham, 250
Nottingham Riflemen, 500
Noyon, 221
Nugent. See Burnell-Nugent
Nugent, Rfn. A. H., M.M., 650

Oakley, Rfn., 207, 208
Oberaussem, 472
Ococks, Lieut. Col. F. Page, V.D., 554, 555, 558, 559
Offensive, The Great German, 380
Ogilvie, 2nd Lieut. W. F., 139, 184

O'Gowan, Major-Gen. Sir R. Wanless, 45, 79, 103, 112
Oise, The, xiii, 374, 382, 383
Oliphant, Major-Gen., 556
"Onward, Queen Victorias," 5
Oram, Capt. R. G., 482, 486, 648
Ormrod, Capt. (R.W.F.), 100
O'Shea, Lieut.-Col.T.,D.S.O.("Tim") 1, 11, 15, 40, 88, 126, 142, 264, 366, 385, 417, 452, 645, 647
O'Shea Camp, 264, 271
O'Shea, Mrs., 574
Ouderdom, 52, 53, 84, 104, 250
"Our Club," 525
Overall, Sergt. V., M.S.M., 652
Oxford and Bucks L.I., 256
Oxonian, s.s., 8

Packer, Cpl. F. G., 168, 170, 649
Page, Capt. H. J., 480, 482
Page, Mrs., 480
Palmer, Lieut. F. N., 648
Palmer, Rfn. W. J., M.M., 649
Palmer, Sergt. A. S., M.S.M., 463, 465, 467, 653
Parker, Capt. W. W., 573, 645
Parker, Sergt., 47, 652
Parry, Lieut.-Col. P. E. Langworthy, D.S.O., O.B.E., T.D., x, 277, 278, 279, 280, 291, 294, 295, 300, 303, 312, 317, 320, 334, 335, 336, 345, 346, 347, 348, 352, 353, 356, 357, 358, 359, 363, 573, 574, 645, 647
Parry, Mrs. Langworthy, 574
Parslow, 2nd Lieut. Albert J., 202
Payne, Rfn. A., 96
Peabody, Cpl. H. D., D.C.M., 62, 63, 64, 65, 66, 96, 442, 649
Pearson, Rfn. Sidney John, 61
Pearson, Sergt. W. H., M.M., 245, 650
Peet, Lce.-Cpl. D. W., M.S.M., 652
Pemberthy, Rfn. F. A., 394, 416
Penny, Sergt. H. T., M.S.M., 652, 653
Peronne, 221, 380
Perry, C.Q.M.S. P., M.S.M., 653
Perry, Rfn. Horace Smith, 87
Peruwelz, 452, 466
Petherick, Rfn., 419
Philbrick, Capt. A. N., 279, 366, 385, 439, 459, 461, 647
Phillips, Lieut. T. E., 526
Phillips, Rfn. G. T., M.M., 247, 650
Pickett, Lieut. E. T., 198, 647
Picquigny, 131, 204, 446
Pierremande, 389
Pinner, Rfn. J. W., M.M., 255, 650
Pixley, Major S. A., 645
Pixley, Sergt. S., 521, 560
Platoon Commander, Importance of, 424

Ploegsteert, 50
Plumer, F. M. Lord, G.C.B., G.C.M.G., G.C.V.O., 102, 111
Plummer, 2nd Lieut. A., 367, 397
Plunkett, Lieut. H. J., M.C., 646
Plunkett, Lieut. J. R., 368
Poelcapelle, 81, 320, 355, 359
"Poison Gas," 487
Pole-Carew, Lieut.-Gen. Sir R., K.C.B., C.V.O., 483
Pollard, Capt. R. P., 485
Polygon Wood, 252
Pont Du Hem, 209, 219
Pont Remy, 204
Poperinghe, 52, 250, 329
Poplar Trench, 439, 440
Porter, Rfn. D., M.M., 651
Porter, Sergt. A. T., M.M., 651
Porter, C.S.M. W., 486
Potter, Rfn., 25
Powell, Col. E., D.S.O. (R.B.), 472
Powell, Lce.-Cpl., 463, 465, 467
Powell, Lieut.-Col. E. G. H., 365, 366, 373, 381, 386, 405, 422, 434, 446, 455, 464, 471, 472, 648
Powell, 2nd Lieut. P. W., M.C., D.C.M., 367, 428, 430, 433, 646
Precedence, How it was lost, 508-18
Price, Rfn. R. S., 653
Prince, Capt. H. S., M.C., 279, 305, 306, 309, 310, 312, 313, 354, 358, 367, 646, 648
Prince of Wales, H.R.H., The, 178, 455
Prince, 2nd Lieut. J. C. B., 368
Prince, 2nd Lieut. W. F. J., 367
Prisoners' Experiences, 175, 391, 575
Prisoners of War Committee, 574
Prisoners' Statements, German, 377
Pritchard, Rfn., 395
Probyn, Capt. S. S. C., 482
Pulleyn, Sergt. E. H., D.C.M., 47, 65, 66, 67, 75, 96, 649
Pym, The Rev., 131

Quaker's Protest, A, 566
Quarry Post, 305, 306, 307, 311
"QuaVeRs, The," 463
Queant, 297, 300
"Queen Victoria Street," 110
Quevaucamps, 452, 466
Quick, Lieut., 447
Q.V.R.—
Amalgamation, 365, 368
Badge, 121
Band, 359, 390
Casualties, xiii, 84, 104, 123, 125, 141, 143, 163, 171, 177, 193, 202, 217, 237, 249, 298, 300, 318, 415, 418, 419, 424, 431, 437, 450
Equipment Fund, 480

"G.O.M.," 142
Head-quarters, 536
Honours, xiii, 126, 426
Marching Song, 468
Memorial Service, 123, 484
O.C.A., 43, 45, 107, 125, 445
"Stunt," A, 48, 336
Queens (R.W.S.) Regt., 374, 417

Railway line, Guarding the, 4, 5
Ralls, Capt. F. H., M.C., 230, 250, 253, 417, 423, 430, 646
Rampling, 2nd Lieut., W. L., C.B., C.M.G., D.S.O., 376, 388
Ramsay, Major-Gen. F., 443, 466
Ramus, Sergt. S. L., 96
Randle, Rfn. G. C., 548
Rashleigh, Lieut. H. P., 103, 106, 116, 123, 482
Raven, Lieut. C. H., 368
Rawlinson, Lieut.-Gen. Lord, G.C.V.O., K.C.B., K.C.M.G., 203, 393, 396, 417, 425, 432, 442, 471
Rawson, Cpl. F., M.M., 650, 653
Rayner, Lieut. V. G., M.C., 368, 646
Read, Lieut., 52
Read, Rfn., 342
Recruiting, 481, 483
Recruiting marches, 480
Redgell, Rfn., 47
Redgell, Sergt. P. J., 138
"Red House, The," 210
Redman, 2nd Lieut., 440
Reed, Lieut., 459
Reeves, Sergt. J., 456, 457, 649
Regnauville, 220
Reigersberg, 335, 354
Reinforcing, 425
Reninghelst, 111
Reserves, Territorial, 481, 487
Revetsburg, 40
Reynolds, Rfn. H., 223, 650
Rhine, With the Army of the, 470-5
Riach, Rfn. J., 463, 465
Rice, Lieut. A. K., 279
Richards, Col. Smith, C. B., 567, 570, 571
Richards, 2nd Lieut. W. E., 269
Richardson, Brig.-Gen., M.E., D.S.O., 379, 411
Richardson, Sergt. G. F., 548
Richmond, Capt. P., 279, 320
Riddle, Rfn. R., M.M., 246, 650
Ridgeley, Sergt. J. M.M., 428, 651
Riez Bailleul, 205
Rifle Brigade, 472
Rifle, Book of the, 497
Rifle, New short, issued, 143
Riordan, Sergt. J. R., M.S.M., 653

INDEX

Riviere, 288, 291
Roads, Sergt. S., M.M., 650
Robermetz, 210
Roberts, Lord, Death of, 13
Roberts, Rfn., 94
Robertson, F.-M. Sir William, G.C.B., G.C.M.G., K.C.V.O., D.S.O., vi
Robson, A/Sergt., 654
Roclincourt, 271
Roe, Lieut.-Colonel F. W., D.S.O. (R.A.M.C.), 10, 41, 45, 84, 95, 99, 126, 645, 647
Rolason, 2nd Lieut. Leslie Norton, 349
Rollitt, Lieut. D., 185
Rongy, 448, 449, 451
Roper, Rfn. F., 301
Rose, Lce.-Cpl. F. J. R., 167, 649
Rose, Lieut. C. H., 96, 279
Rose, Rfn., 122
Rossi, Rfn. P., M.M., 442, 652
Rouez Camp, 373, 374
Rouge Croix, 209
Roundhay Camp, 271
Rowan, Rfn., 422
Rowe, Sergt. P. G., M.M., 245, 650
Royal Berkshire Regt., 424, 448
Royal Fusiliers, 398, 442
Royal Naval Division, 434
Royal Victoria Rifle Company, 504, 506, 507-17
Roye, 221
Rum, Value of, 28, 285, 349
Rumegies, 448, 463
Rumsey, Lieut. A. C., 137, 139, 194
Ruses, Hun, 144, 145
Russell, Rfn. W. D., 397
Russell-Jones, Capt. W. F., 43, 279, 331, 485
Rycroft, Major-Gen. Sir W.H., K.C.B., K.C.M.G., 37

Sachin, 220
Sage, Rfn. J. W., M.M., 651
Sailly Laurette, 128, 129, 130, 138, 167
Sailly-au-Bois, 137, 142
St. Amand, 137, 146, 147, 165, 173, 175, 177, 178
St. Catherine Camp, 271
St. Eloi, 51, 81, 105, 106, 111
St. Emilie, 435, 436, 437
St. Floris, 220
St. George's Rifles, xiv, 491, 527-36, 568
St. George's Vase, 534
St. Giles's and St. George's (Bloomsbury) R.V.C., 491, 560, 561, 563, 565, 569, 570
St. Gobain, 375, 387, 389
St. Jean Capelle, 50, 89, 92, 94
St. Julien, 317, 318, 320, 337, 349, 350, 460

St. Pancras, V.R.C., 567
St. Quentin, 377, 378, 380, 443, 444
St. Requier, 179
St. Venant, 204
St. Yves, 50
Salient, Life in the, 316, 317
Salisbury, Marquess of, 510, 513, 514
Sampson, Capt. R. H., 83, 107, 482
Sampson, Major S. J. M., M.C., x, 12, 16, 18, 27, 31, 39, 43, 45, 47, 49, 50, 51, 52, 53, 60, 75, 126, 127, 128, 129, 130, 131, 135, 136, 138, 141, 166, 167, 426, 430, 573, 646, 647
Sampson, S. A., Esq., 574, 575
Samuels, Major, 159
Samuelson, Capt. H., 279, 291, 305, 306, 307, 309, 312, 318, 343, 358, 367, 387, 397, 424, 435, 437, 448, 450, 451, 452, 647
Sanctuary, 2nd Lieut. C. R., 440
Sanctuary Wood, 252
Sandys, Cpl. E. T., M.M., 651
Santler, Rfn. W., 31
Saulcourt Wood, 435, 436
Saunders, Rfn. H. S., M.M., 651
Savage, Sergt. F. J., 649
Saxby, 2nd Lieut. Geo. Scrase, 237
Scherpenberg, 103, 104
Scloppetaria, 497
Scott, Major Claud, V.D., 573
Scott, Major S., 368, 369
Scott, 2nd Lieut. R. B., 184
Scott, Sergt. G., 653
Scottish Wood, 105, 106, 108
Seaman, Rfn., 422
Sedgeley, Lieut. H. F., 440
Selback, Rfn., 207, 208
Sellick, Cpl. C. B., 443, 456, 458
Sendall, Cpl. Harold, 65, 87
Sensee River, 232, 233, 443
Sentry, The smart, 114
Serques, 256
Servais, 375, 376
Seward, Rfn. E. C., M.M., 301, 302
Seymour, Rfn. Sidney, 65
Seymour, Lce.-Cpl. G. T., M.M., 254, 650
Shaw, Sergt. C., M.M., 652
Shea-Simonds, Major S. V., 11, 14, 15, 16, 42, 46, 485, 486, 572, 647, 648
Shell-fire, Effect of, 29
Shepherd, Capt. H., 10, 11, 15, 41, 48, 88, 456
Sherlock, Lce.-Cpl. Fredk., M.M., 414
Sherlock, Lce.-Cpl. F. S., M.M., 651
Sherriff, C.S.M. A. J., 96, 126, 649, 653, 654
Sherwood Foresters, 121, 196

Shipley, Lieut.-Col. R. B., C.M.G.,
T.D., x, 1, 2, 4, 10, 11, 33, 41, 43,
44, 45, 46, 47, 60, 74, 75, 94, 97,
99, 118, 161, 244, 480, 540, 541,
542, 546, 547, 560, 572, 573, 574,
645, 647
Shipley, Mrs., 574
Shoolbred, Col. R., C.M.G., 134, 180,
186
Shooting matches, 497, 498, 500, 507
Shore, C.Q.M.S., F., 33, 575
Short, Rfn. Frank, 211
Shute, Cpl., 463, 465, 467
Shuttleworth, Sergt., 52
Siegfried Line, 221
Silvey, Rfn. C. H., M.M., 652
Sim, Lieut. N. Y., 185, 188
Sim, Sergt. C. K., M.M., 41, 45, 49,
50, 135, 142, 143, 167, 203, 649
Simmonds, 2nd Lieut. Percy Graham,
168, 169, 170, 171
Sinclair, Rev. R. H., 123, 484
Skipper, C.S.M. G. A., 352
Slaughter, Rfn. A. W., M.M., 649
Smith-Dorrien, Gen. Sir H., G.C.B.,
G.C.M.G., D.S.O., 14, 36, 60, 69,
79, 82, 85
Smith, Lieut.-Gen. Sir Harry, 533
Smith, Lieut. H. R., 368, 646
Smith, 2nd Lieut. R. S., 215, 216, 230
Smith, 2nd Lieut. W. E., 463, 468
Smith, Rfn. C., M.M., 440, 651
Smith, Rfn. R., M.M., 650, 654
Smith, Rfn. Sidney George, 288
Smith, Sergt. L. R., 654
Sniping Squad, 55
Snoswell, Rfn. Arthur Cecil, 283, 285,
286, 289, 290
Snoswell, Rfn. E. E., x, 281, 282, 285,
288, 289, 294, 295, 298, 302, 313,
314, 316, 318, 354, 355, 356, 360,
366, 388, 415
Snow, Major E. Graham, 551, 554
Somme, Battles of the, viii, x, xii,
146 et seq., 446, 457
Souastre, 237
Soundy, Sergt. H. E., 25, 48, 96
South African War, 540, 571
South African War Memorial, 555
Southampton, 7, 280
Spaul, 2nd Lieut. E. A., 214, 228
Special Emergency Camp, 1900, 547
Spencer, Capt. (12th London), 387
Spenser-Pryse, Capt. M.C., G., 326,
327, 331, 332, 334, 345, 348, 354,
358, 367, 646
Spiller, Sergt. H. J., M.M., 245, 650
Spittle, Rfn. F. T., 47
Spooner, Rfn. C. A., 96
Sports, 129, 474, 485, 486

Spratt, Rfn. H. H., M.M., 651
Springfield, 320, 328, 331, 348
Squires, Rfn. A. W., M.M., 203, 650
Staffordshire Regt., 178, 283
Stambruges, 452, 455, 463, 464
Stancombe, Rfn. J. F., 230
Stanley, Brig.-Gen. H., 242
Steddall, Lieut.-Col. R., 567, 568,
569, 570, 571
Steenvoorde, 111, 112
Stephenson, Lce.-Sergt. H. W., 139
Stewart, Lieut. H. R. (8th Middlesex),
646
Stiles, Lce.-Cpl., 420
Stock Exchange hoax (1814), 498
Stone, Lce.-Sergt. F. H., 139
Stone, Rfn. H. V., 384
Stone, Lieut. Palmer, 492
Stranack, Lieut. W. S., 171, 482, 484,
485
Stranger, Rfn. G. N. H., 414
Strathcona, Lady, 480, 481
Streather, Cpl. W. A., 203, 649
Street, Lieut.-Col. H., D.S.O. (Devonshire Regt.), 103
Stronge, Capt. W. H., 279, 320, 458
Stroud, Lce.-Cpl. S. O., D.C.M., M.M.,
300, 302, 403, 413, 649, 650
Stubbs, Rfn. B. C., 86, 108
Sturgess, Rfn. W. J., M.S.M., 653
Suffolk Regt., 250, 383, 410, 431, 440
"Summer Time" adopted, 143
Summerhays, Lieut. D. L., 12, 48, 61,
62, 69, 70, 73, 75, 76
"Surbiton Villas," 252
Surrey Regts., vi
Surtees, Rfn., 188
Sussex Regt., 446
Sus-St. Leger, 250, 281, 282
Sutherland, Lieut.-Col. A. H., 562,
564
Sutherland, Rfn. A. R., 301
Swift, Capt. H. W., 345, 349, 648
Swoffer, Lce.-Cpl. F. A., 95
Symes, Capt. E. D., M.C., 181, 184,
185, 186, 251, 646
Symonds, Lieut.-Col. W. F. J.,
D.S.O. (11th London), 398, 411

Tabberer, Lieut. C. O., M.C., 112, 117,
124, 131, 137, 368, 646
Tadpole Copse, 263, 267, 268, 270,
272
Tadworth, 483
Tailes Wood, 426
Talmas, 130
Tank attack, 178, 190
Tanqueray, Col. W. M., V.D., 43, 45,
46, 107, 125, 294, 554, 556, 558,
560, 572, 573, 574

INDEX 669

Taylor, A/R.Q.M.S., 385, 418, 422, 448, 452
Taylor, Lce.-Cpl. Lionel Wm., 170
Taylor, Lieut. A. A., 185
"Teddy Bear Coat," 25
Telfer, Sergt. G. F., M.M., 96, 168, 203, 649
Tergnier, viii, 387
Territorial Army, The, vi, vii, 491, 571
Thesiger, Rfn. Ernest, 462
Thomas, Mr. Beach, 174
Thomas, Rfn. C. F., M.M., 650
Thomas, Sergt. D. P., D.C.M., 418, 649
Thomson, Rfn. C. T., M.M., 255
Thorpe, Sergt., 307, 309
Tilloy, 223, 249
Times, The, 271
Tolley, Capt. Geo., 573, 648
Tolliday, Rfn. A. W., M.M., 246, 650
Tomlinson, R.S.M., H. G. R., 280, 358, 653
Toop, Sergt., 485
Torpedo, Aerial, 110
Torpedo, Bangalore, 205, 258, 259, 260
Transport Section, 10, 57, 385, 386, 439, 443, 456-61
Treasurer, Lce.-Cpl. W., 301
Trench digging extraordinary, 140, 141
Trenches, State of, 17, 19, 23, 27, 39, 50, 122, 201, 205, 227, 268, 286, 292
Trescault, 303
Treux, 204
Trew, Capt. A., 523
Trew, Rfn. W. A., 222
Trigger Wood, 429
Trigwell, Rfn. G. A., M.M., 652
Trones Wood, 180, 442
Truce, Informal, 165, 166
Truscott, Rfn. W. H., 117
Tuckley, Sergt. H., M.M., 245, 650
Turner, Lce.-Cpl. F. H., 31
Turner, Major-Gen. Sir A. E., 556, 557, 558
Twitchen, Rfn. H. O., M.M., 652
Tyler, Sergt. A. J., M.M., 651

Uglow, Rfn. W., 31
" Ulick," 353
Upward, Lieut. W., 76, 114
Underhay, Capt. C. T., 337
Unwin, 2nd Lieut., 202
Ure, Sergt. D., M.S.M., 652, 653

Valley of Death, The, 180, 181, 184
Varney, C.S.M., 258

Vaux-Marquenneville, 131
Vendhuile, 271
Vernon, Rfn. F., 33
Victoria and St. George's Rifles (1st Middlesex), R.V.C., 491, 537
Victoria Cross, The First Territorial, xii, 78
Victoria, Queen, 504, 525, 541, 551, 554, 558
Victoria Rifles, xiv, 491, 496, 517, 518, 519, 524
Victoria Rifles' Lodge, 127, 187
Victoria Trench, 186
Vignacourt, 421
Village fighting, 130
Ville sur Ancre, 194
Villers Bretonneux, 365, 394, 397, 398, 403, 406, 407, 408, 410
Villers Cotterets, 393, 394
Villers-Faucon, 436, 442
Villers l'Hôpital, 178
Vincent, Col. Sir Howard, 556
Vlamertinge, 82
Volunteers, The, v
Volunteer Rifle Corps, The first, 491, 514
" Volunteer Sharpshooters, Instructions for," 495
Volunteer reviews, 499, 501, 529, 532, 560, 563, 568
Voormezele, 105, 106, 108

Waghorn, Capt. H. C., 214, 215, 216, 645
Wagstaff, 2nd Lieut. B. G., M.C., 253, 367, 646
Wailly, 288
Wainwright, Rfn., 330
Wakefield, Sergt. D. T., M.M., 651
Wald, 473
Walker, Capt. H. S., 279, 308, 320, 326, 328, 329, 330, 331, 332, 334, 358, 647
Walker, Lce.-Cpl. R. J., 653
Wallace, Lieut., 223, 231
Waller, Capt. A. E., 121, 122
Wancourt Line, 222, 223, 224, 226, 227, 229, 231, 244, 249
Wanquetin, 248
" War, Glory of," 288
War, Outbreak of, 1
Ward, Major C. H. Dudley, D.S.O., M.C., 140, 174
Ward, Major Robert, 562
Warren, Capt. R. G., 11, 46, 572
Warren, Major R. O., V.D., 560, 648
Warren, 2nd Lieut. Alan R., 202
Warrington, Sergt. G. R., 64, 95
Warwickshire Regt., Royal, 205, 249
Watson, Rfn. W. H., M.M., 651

Watson, 2nd Lieut. S. B., 266, 269, 270
Watten, 256
Weatherley, A/Sergt. W. H., M.S.M., 652, 653
Webb, Lce.-Cpl. W., 33
Webb, Rfn. W., 463
Wedge Wood Farm, 181, 182
Weekley, Lieut.-Col. G. M., V.D., 554, 556, 560, 572
Weller, Rfn. E., M.M., 651
Wellington, Arthur, Duke of, 518, 521, 522, 523, 568
Wells, Rfn. W., 446
Wells, Sergt. E. J., M.S.M., 652
West Kent Regiment (Q.O.R.), xii, 12, 14, 15, 55, 56, 58, 59, 79, 97, 187, 417
West Riding Regt. (D. of W.), 12, 56, 59, 115, 288
Whale Oil, Issue of, 284
Whalley, Rfn. A. R., 653
Wheaton, C.S.M., 391
Wheeler, Rfn., 344
Whigham, Major-Gen. Sir R. D., K.C.B., K.C.M.G., D.S.O., 472
Whitaker, Capt. Wm., 516
White, Capt. Graham B., 279, 292, 300, 358, 367, 648
"Whizzbangs," The, 132, 462
Wickens, Rfn., 62
Wieltje, 82, 88, 90, 96
Wightwick, Lieut. S., 279, 326, 327, 331, 332, 333, 334
Wilding, Rfn., A. P., 654
Wilkinson, Rfn. L. R., 90
Willeman, 220
Willoughby, Major R. M. P., T.D., 479, 482, 568, 573
Wilson, 2nd Lieut. F. R., 266, 368
Wilson, Sergt. A. J., M.M., 141, 168, 649
Wilton, Major W. P., M.C., T.D., 279, 291, 292, 305, 357, 358, 572, 646
Wilts Regt., 128
Winnipeg, 320, 326, 331, 348
Winter, Wettest on record, 23
Wippenhoek, 256
Wiring feat, 218

"With our Backs to the Wall," 395, 396
Withers, Sergt. C. J., M.M., 254, 650
Wizernes, 250, 256, 359
Woodland, C.Q.M.S. J. B., M.M., 649
Woodroff, Capt. N. F., 69, 75, 645
Woods, Capt. G., 181, 184, 188
Wooller, Rfn. A. H., M.M., 255, 650
Woolley, Capt. G. H., V.C., M.C., xii, xiii, 11, 15, 16, 61, 62, 64, 65, 68, 69, 70, 77, 78, 79, 83, 88, 95, 107, 122, 244, 483, 645, 646, 647
Worgan, Brig.-Gen. Rivers, D.S.O., 411
Worlledge, Lieut. J. L., 279, 290, 301, 305, 306, 307, 309, 310, 312, 313, 647
Wortley, Major Hon. E. J. M. Stewart, 549
Wright, Lieut. E., 482
Wright, Rfn. H. J., 34
Wulverghem, xii, 14, 18, 25, 26, 39, 41, 49
Wurst Farm, 334, 336, 340 351, 357
Wyatt, Sergt. J. S., 388, 419
Wyld, Capt. J. W. G., D.S.O., M.C., 312, 391
Wyndham, Lieut.-Col. W. G. Crole, 553, 554
Wynn, Major A., 8, 572
Wynter, Rfn. H., M.M., 650

Yates, Lce.-Cpl. A. J., D.C.M., 84, 126, 649
Y.M.C.A., The, 479
York and Lancashire Regt. (84th), 48
Yorkshire Regt., West, 220
Young, Rfn. S. J., 384
Ypres, 52, 84, 103, 303, 317, 351
Ypres, Second Battle of, xii, 81, 82–99, 127
Ypres, Third Battle of, 248 et seq., 320–53

Zeebrugge, 119
Zeppelin visits, 55
Zillebeke, 54, 63, 69, 102, 103, 250
Zonnebeke, viii, 81, 352
Zutkerque, 354

www.ingramcontent.com/pod-product-compliance
Lightning Source LLC
Chambersburg PA
CBHW061931220426
43662CB00012B/1871